IN THIS SERIES*

1 Daire Hogan and W.N. Osborough (eds), *Brehons, serjeants and attorneys: studies in the history of the Irish legal profession* (1990)
2 Colum Kenny, *King's Inns and the kingdom of Ireland: the Irish 'inn of court', 1541–1800* (1992)
3 Jon G. Crawford, *Anglicizing the government of Ireland: the Irish privy council and the expansion of Tudor rule, 1556–1578* (1993)
4 W.N. Osborough (ed.), *Explorations in law and history: Irish Legal History Society discourses, 1988–1994* (1995)
5 W.N. Osborough, *Law and the emergence of modern Dublin: a litigation topography for a capital city* (1996)
6 Colum Kenny, *Tristram Kennedy and the revival of Irish legal training, 1835–1885* (1996)
7 Brian Griffin, *The Bulkies: police and crime in Belfast, 1800–1865* (1997)
8 Éanna Hickey, *Irish law and lawyers in modern folk tradition* (1999)
9 A.R. Hart, *A history of the king's serjeants at law in Ireland: honour rather than advantage?* (2000)
10 D.S. Greer and N.M. Dawson (eds), *Mysteries and solutions in Irish legal history: Irish Legal History Society discourses and other papers, 1996–1999* (2000)
11 Colum Kenny, *King's Inns and the battle of the books, 1972: cultural controversy at a Dublin library* (2002)
12 Desmond Greer and James W. Nicolson, *The factory acts in Ireland, 1802–1914* (2003)
13 Mary Kotsonouris, *The winding-up of the Dáil courts, 1922–1925: an obvious duty* (2004)
14 Paul Brand, Kevin Costello and W.N. Osborough (eds), *Adventures of the law: proceedings of the 16th British Legal History Conference, Dublin 2003* (2005)
15 Jon G. Crawford, *A star chamber court in Ireland: the court of castle chamber, 1571–1641* (2005)
16 A.P. Quinn, *Wigs and guns: Irish barristers and the Great War* (2006)
17 N.M. Dawson (ed.), *Reflections on law and history: Irish Legal History Society discourses and other papers, 2000–2005* (2006)
18 James Kelly, *Poynings' Law and the making of law in Ireland, 1660–1800* (2007)
19 W.E. Vaughan, *Murder trials in Ireland, 1836–1914* (2009)
20 Kevin Costello, *The Court of Admiralty of Ireland, 1575–1893* (2011)
21 W.N. Osborough, *An island's law: a bibliographical guide to Ireland's legal past* (2013)
22 Felix M. Larkin and N.M. Dawson (eds), *Lawyers, the law and history: Irish Legal History Society discourses and other papers, 2005–2011* (2013)
23 Daire Hogan and Colum Kenny (eds), *Changes in practice and law: a selection of essays by members of the legal profession to mark twenty-five years of the Irish Legal History Society* (2013)
24 W.N. Osborough, *The Irish stage: a legal history* (2015)
25 Thomas Mohr, *Guardian of the Treaty: the Privy Council appeal and Irish sovereignty* (2016)
26 Joseph C. Sweeney, *The life and times of Arthur Browne in Ireland and America, 1756–1805* (2017)
27 Niamh Howlin, *Juries in Ireland: laypersons and law in the long nineteenth century* (2017)
28 Patrick Hyde Kelly (ed.), *The case of Ireland's being bound by acts of parliament in England, stated, Dublin 1698* (2018)
29 Mary Phelan, *Irish speakers, interpreters and the courts, 1754–1921* (2019)

ALSO AVAILABLE

The Irish Legal History Society (1989)

* Volumes 1–7 are published by Irish Academic Press

Irish Speakers, Interpreters and the Courts, 1754–1921

MARY PHELAN

FOUR COURTS PRESS
in association with
THE IRISH LEGAL HISTORY SOCIETY

Set in 10.5 pt on 12.5 pt Ehrhardt MT for
FOUR COURTS PRESS LTD
7 Malpas Street, Dublin 8, Ireland
www.fourcourtspress.ie
and in North America for
FOUR COURTS PRESS
c/o IPG, 814 N Franklin St, Chicago, IL 60622

A catalogue record for this title is available
from the British Library.

ISBN 978-1-84682-811-9

Printed in England by
CPI Antony Rowe, Chippenham, Wilts.

To Claire, Steve and Alex

Contents

Abbreviations

CSO	Central Statistics Office
DIB	*Dictionary of Irish biography*
DUP	Democratic Unionist Party
ER	east riding
HC	house of commons
ILHS	Irish Legal History Society
JP	justice of the peace
MS	manuscript
NAI	National Archives of Ireland
NLI	National Library of Ireland
NR	north riding
NUIG	National University of Ireland, Galway
ODNB	*Oxford dictionary of national biography*
OED	*Oxford English dictionary*
PRONI	Public Record Office of Northern Ireland
RIA	Royal Irish Academy
RIC	Royal Irish Constabulary
RM	resident magistrate
SDLP	Social Democratic and Labour Party
SR	south riding
UCD	University College Dublin
WR	west riding

Tables and illustrations

TABLES

FIGURES

PLATES

Plates appear between pages 146 and 147

Acknowledgments

I am grateful to the Faculty of Humanities and Social Sciences at Dublin City University for a sabbatical in 2015–16 that freed up time for more archival work to greatly expand on work previously carried out for my PhD thesis. I would like to thank my PhD supervisor, Prof. Dorothy Kenny, and examiners, Prof. Michael Cronin and Prof. Cormac Ó Cuilleanáin, and Dr Lesa Ní Mhunghaile for their suggestions and recommendations.

I would like to thank Dr Aidan Kane, NUI Galway, for sharing information with me about the house of commons Parliamentary Papers database; Gregory O'Connor, National Archives of Ireland, for sharing his in-depth knowledge of registered papers, country letter books and grand jury presentment books; Paddy Sarsfield, Ken Martin and other staff at the National Archives of Ireland and staff at the National Library of Ireland and the Royal Irish Academy.

I also owe thanks to the following for facilitating access to grand jury books of presentments: Peter Beirne, Clare Library Local Studies Centre, Ennis; Amanda Branigan, Louth Archives, Dundalk; Niamh Brennan, Archives Service, Donegal County Council, Letterkenny; Caitlin Brown and Mary Butler, Roscommon County Library; Dr Mary Clark, Dublin City Archives, Pearse Street; Gemma Eaton and staff at the Public Record Office of Northern Ireland; Treacy Flynn, Leitrim County Library, Ballinamore; Rene Franklin, Clare County Archives; Pat Gannon, Sligo County Library; Mary Guinan-Darmody, Tipperary Studies, Thurles; Ivor Hamrock, Local History Department, Castlebar Central Library, Mayo; Catríona Lennon, Monaghan County Library Services, Clones; Michael Lynch, Kerry Library, Tralee; Brian McGee, Cork City and County Archives; Colm McQuinn, Fingal County Council Archives, Swords; Patria McWalter and Mary Qualter, Galway County Library Headquarters; Martin Morris, Longford County Archives; Joanne Rothwell, Waterford County Archives, Dungarvan; Tony Storan, Limerick Studies; Catherine Wright, Wicklow County Archives; and staff at Kilkenny Local Studies and Cavan Archives.

I would also like to thank the following: Críostóir Mac Cárthaigh, National Folklore Collection, University College Dublin; Patricia Hassett, Office of Public Works, Swiss Cottage, Cahir, County Tipperary; Renate Ní Uigín, Honorable Society of King's Inns; Máire Nic Mhaoláin for her generous advice on Irish-language matters. Thanks also to Kitty Barry, Thurles, who kindly gave me a copy of the unpublished O'Carroll diaries. Others who were very helpful were Prof. Patrick Geoghegan, Trinity College Dublin; Dr Conor Hanly, NUI Galway; Prof. Margaret Kelleher of UCD; and Cormac Leonard, who was engaged in parallel work on deaf people and sign-language interpreters.

I was delighted to receive a detailed email, with carefully referenced research, from Paul Conway, Queensland, Australia, great-great-grandson of Mayo interpreter Simon Conway.

Finally, I am very pleased that this book is being published by the Irish Legal History Society and Four Courts Press. My thanks to Robert D. Marshall of the ILHS for liaising with me about publication of this book. I am grateful to Dr Regina Uí Chollatáin, head of UCD's School of Irish, Celtic Studies and Folklore, and Dr Kevin Costello, Sutherland School of Law, UCD, for their careful reviews of the manuscript, and I owe a particular debt of gratitude to Dr Niamh Howlin, also of Sutherland School of Law, for her detailed suggestions. Thanks also to Martin Fanning, Sam Tranum and their colleagues at Four Courts Press, and to Julitta Clancy for indexing this book.

DATA SET

For detailed information on grand jury payments to interpreters year by year in each county plus references to interpreters from the chief secretary's registered papers and country letter books held in the National Archives of Ireland, see:

> Mary Phelan, *Database of Irish language court interpreters, 1754–1921* (2019), http://doi.org/10.5281/zenodo.3345182.

For a corpus of transcriptions of newspaper articles compiled for this book, see:

> Mary Phelan, *Newspaper references to Irish language court interpreters, 1796–1922* (2019), http://doi.org/10.5281/zenodo.3347971.

CHAPTER ONE

Introduction

A GREAT DEAL of time, effort and determination are required to change the language of a country, and it took centuries to change the language of Ireland from predominantly Irish to predominantly English. A key aim of the British was for Irish people to use the English language. To this end, in each century from the fourteenth to the eighteenth, a law was passed aimed at increasing the use of English. In 1366 the Statute of Kilkenny provided that:

> if any English, or Irish living amongst the English, use the Irish language amongst themselves, contrary to the ordinance, and thereof be attainted, his lands and tenements, if he have any, shall be seized into the lands of his immediate lord.

While the statute was aimed mainly at English people who used Irish, it clearly signalled the official policy to all. In 1465, an act provided that Irishmen living in the counties of Dublin, Meath, Louth and Kildare 'shall go apparrelled like Englishmen and wear their beards after the English manner, swear allegiance, and take English surname'. Examples of suitable surnames provided in the act were towns such as Sutton, Chester, Trim, Skryne, Corke and Kinsale; colours such as white, blacke or browne; occupations such as smith or carpenter, cooke or butler.[1] This law signalled a lack of interest in existing Irish surnames and family genealogies. In 1537, the Act for the English Order, Habite and Language laid down that everyone 'shall use and speak commonly the English tongue and language' and that they should 'cause to procure his said childe and children to speak the English tongue and language' and that children should be brought up in places 'where they may have occasion to learn the English tongue, language, order and condition'. The act also provided that 'spiritual promotion' to posts such as vicar, parson, provost, dean and archdeacon could only be given to English speakers, 'unless, after four proclamations in the next market-town, such cannot be had'. Any man who took orders would have to 'learn and teach the English language'.[2] Anglicization was extended to place names, obliterating meaningful names in the Irish language. By the time of Petty's or Pender's census circa 1659, all names of people and places had been anglicized. This was confirmed by law in 1665 when

1 5 Edw. 4, c. 3.
2 28 Hen. 8, c. 15, ss 3, 7, 9.

an act provided that 'new and proper names more suitable to the English tongue may be inserted with an alias for all towns, land and places [...] which new names shall thenceforth be onely names to be used'.[3] In 1695, an act reinforced the 1537 act for the English order, habit and language, providing that a sufficient number of schools be established 'to instruct and inform the youth thereof in the English language'.

The Administration of Justice (Language) Act (Ireland) (1737) is key to understanding the manner in which interpreter provision developed. It followed similar legislation introduced in England in 1731,[4] and extended to Wales in 1733,[5] whereby the language of the courts and all documentation was to be English. The act provided that:

> all proceedings whatsoever in any courts of justice within this kingdom, and which concern the law and administration of justice, shall be in the English tongue and language, and not in Latin or French, or any other tongue or language whatsoever.[6]

Ostensibly, the primary purpose of the act was to put a stop to lawyers and the judiciary using Latin and French in court. However, its effect was much more extensive because in practice it meant that any Irish speaker, regardless of whether they were defendants, complainants, plaintiffs or witnesses, who spoke English, some English or even a little, would not be permitted to speak Irish through an interpreter, even if an interpreter was present in court. The same applied to Welsh speakers in courts in Wales where the situation was even worse than in Ireland because there was never any system of salaried interpreters there. It is worth keeping in mind that at the time of writing the 1737 act was still in force in Northern Ireland, where it continued to have the same effect – that is to say it prevented Irish speakers from using Irish in court on the grounds that they also spoke English.

The shift from Irish to English was a slow process with a gradual switch first to bilingualism and then eventually to English only. Bilingualism became an advantage for land agents, summons servers, law clerks and of course interpreters. English became the dominant language, the language of power and property, and it became more and more difficult for monolingual Irish speakers to sell at fairs, to obtain employment as shop assistants, servants or labourers, or even to become priests, Christian brothers and nuns. Those who did not acquire English were left behind as Irish became associated with being poor, uneducated, old and dispossessed.

3 17 & 18 Car. 2, c. 2, s. 234.

4 4 Geo. 2, c. 26, Courts of Justice Act 1730. This act covered England and the court of exchequer in Scotland.

5 6 Geo. 2, c. 14.

6 11 Geo 2, c. 6, Administration of Justice (Language) Act (Ireland) 1737.

There were dramatic changes in the population, which increased from an estimated 6.8 million in 1821 to just over 8 million in 1841.[7] The years of the Great Famine, between 1845 and 1849, resulted in large-scale death and emigration, and by 1851 the population had fallen to 6.5 million. There was considerable variation in the rates of excess mortality caused by the Famine, with Irish-speaking provinces the worst-affected; 'Connacht accounted for 40.4 per cent of the total, Munster for 30.3 per cent, Ulster for 20.7 per cent, and Leinster for 8.6 per cent.'[8] After the Famine, emigration continued, people started to get married later or not at all and the population continued to fall. By 1891 it had dropped to 4.7 million and in 1901 to 4.4 million. In addition to emigration, there was some migration from rural to urban areas. The population living in towns increased from 1.2 million in 1841 to 1.5 million in 1911. This was another factor in the rise of English because the language was more commonly spoken in the towns. However, the change in the rural population for the same period was much more dramatic, with a fall from 7 million to just under 3 million.[9] In 1800 half the population spoke Irish and just before the Famine some 4 million Irish people spoke the language, but by 1851 'less than a quarter of the population spoke the language and only five per cent were monolingual Irish-speakers'.[10] Although 5 per cent is a small proportion, it equates to a substantial number of 327,500 monolingual Irish speakers out of a total population of 6.55 million. There is agreement that these figures are an under estimate.

J.J. Lee has questioned why Irish people shifted from bilingualism to monolingual English. He examines and refutes a number of arguments about the reasons behind the change. It has been argued that English was necessary for economic reasons; Lee gives the examples of Denmark, Sweden, Norway, the Netherlands, Flanders and Finland, which kept their languages and performed well economically. Another argument is that the Irish language had not modernized sufficiently to keep up with progress. Here, Lee shows that other languages had to and did keep up with the changes in society. He acknowledges that emigration to English-speaking countries may have been a factor, but points out that many people from other non-English speaking countries had no knowledge of English prior to their arrival in the United States. According to Lee, 'the whole state apparatus was an agency of anglicization',[11] and of course the courts were an integral part of the state apparatus.

Tony Crowley emphasizes the frequent simplification of the history of the Irish language.[12] He details the various ebbs and flows of English and Irish over the centuries and analyses the effect of multiple factors such as schooling through

7 F.S.L. Lyons, *Ireland since the Famine* (London, 1985), p. 37.

8 J.S. Donnelly, 'Mortality and emigration' in W.E. Vaughan (ed.), *A new history of Ireland,* v: *Ireland under the union, 1801–1870* (Oxford, 2010), p. 351.

9 Lyons, *Ireland since the Famine*, p. 46.

10 G. Ó Tuathaigh, *Ireland before the Famine, 1798–1848* (Dublin, 1982), p. 57.

11 J.J. Lee, *Ireland 1912–1985: politics and society* (Cambridge, 1989), p. 666.

12 Tony Crowley, *Wars of words* (Oxford, 2005), p. 1.

English, the use of Irish by Protestants for proselytization, the use of English by the Catholic church, the use of English at Maynooth College, the use of Irish by Scottish settlers in Ulster, the interest of antiquarians in the Irish language, education through English after the establishment of the national school system in 1831, the link made by Young Irelanders between language and nationalism, the use of Irish as the language of instruction in some Protestant schools, the Great Famine with its double toll of death and emigration, the bata scóir and punishment for children who spoke Irish, an association of shame or of poverty and misery with the speaking of Irish, the use of English by politicians, the establishment of organizations such as the Society for the Preservation of the Irish Language in 1876, the Gaelic Union in 1880 and Conradh na Gaeilge or the Gaelic League in 1893.

JUDGES, LAWYERS AND THE IRISH LANGUAGE

There is evidence that some judges and lawyers spoke Irish. For example, in his reminiscences, journalist Maurice Lenihan recalled that on one occasion, Barry Yelverton, Lord Avonmore, was hearing a case of cow-stealing in Tralee where the defendant addressed him in Irish saying he had no defence as the judge had seen him driving the cows. Yelverton did not let on that he understood, but was sympathetic to the man's plight, did not allow him to plead guilty, found a mistake in the bill of indictment and allowed him to go.[13] Baron Smith learnt Irish 'in order not to be dependent on the fidelity of interpreters in cases where witnesses could not speak English, the interpreters sometimes not being very reliable for reasons best known to himself [*sic*]'.[14] In the introduction to his English-Irish dictionary, Edward O'Reilly lauded Smith for his study of the Irish language, 'in which he has made great progress, and set a praiseworthy example to other gentlemen of the bar'.[15] John Philpot Curran spoke Irish, which he had learnt as a child.[16] Edward Deane, Castlebar petty sessions magistrate, acted as interpreter on at least one occasion at Mayo assizes crown court when the court interpreter was absent.[17]

The custom of fostering children meant that many children of well-off families learnt Irish as their first language. Born in Kerry, Mr Justice Robert Day (1745–1841) was fostered by one of his father's tenants until he was 7 years of age and his first language was Irish.[18] Peter O'Brien, prosecution lawyer in the Maamtrasna case and later Lord O'Brien of Kilfenora, was not fluent in Irish but had some knowledge of the language:

13 *Limerick Reporter*, 1 Jan. 1867.
14 Ibid.
15 E. O'Reilly, *Sanas Gaoidhilge Sagsbeurla: an English-Irish dictionary* (Dublin, 1817), p. 2.
16 W.H. Curran, *The life of the Right Honourable John Philpot Curran, late master of the rolls in Ireland* (London, 1819), p. 87.
17 *Mayo Constitution*, 28 Mar. 1833.
18 E.B. Day, *Mr Justice Day, 1745–1841* (Exeter, 1938), pp 136–7.

> On one occasion he had to try a case the issue of which depended on the exact meaning of a word in the Irish language. The services of a professor of Irish, who had written several books in the Irish language, were enlisted, yet he did not speak or understand what the Irish peasant so aptly calls 'cradle' Irish – that is to say, he had not heard it spoken from the cradle, but had acquired it late in life. The professor, according to himself, was a very efficient Irish scholar.
>
> 'I believe you have written many books in the Irish language?' asked the Chief Justice, with a bland smile.
>
> 'Yes, my lord,' answered the professor.
>
> 'You have, I understand, a thorough knowledge of the language?'
>
> 'Yes, my lord.'
>
> My father, who, when a boy, had picked up a little Irish from the peasants in Clare, said: 'Now, Professor, can you tell me how to say this simple sentence in Irish – Have you seen a hare pass by here?'
>
> The expert admitted defeat. 'Well,' continued the Chief Justice, 'can you say, Are the hounds in sight?' The Professor had again to acknowledge himself defeated. 'And yet,' said his interrogator, 'you call yourself an Irish scholar. I fear your Irish is not of any practical use.' Turning to one of the Irish-speaking witnesses, my father said a few words to him in Irish. The man, who was overjoyed at being addressed in his own tongue, left the court probably under the impression that the Judge spoke Irish fluently.[19]

Daniel O'Connell, who was also fostered[20] and a fluent Irish speaker, claimed somewhat flippantly in a speech that the interpreters he used to meet on circuit had only two faults – 'that they knew neither English nor Irish'.[21] One record was found of O'Connell taking on the role of interpreter. In 1827 in an appeal taken by the parishioners of Timoleague, County Cork under the Tithe Composition Act, O'Connell began examining an Irish-speaking witness through an interpreter 'who endeavoured to convey the meaning of the witness in a most melodious jargon of Irish and bad English'. Counsel for the respondent asked O'Connell to take over as interpreter, which he did.[22] According to Seán Ó Faoláin's biography, O'Connell's knowledge of Irish came in useful on another occasion:

> Once a perjuring witness, in a will case, kept on swearing that the testator was alive when his hand signed the will; but O'Connell noticed that the witness used the same phrase every time: 'Bhí beatha ann'; literally, 'There was

19 G. O'Brien (ed.), *The reminiscences of Lord O'Brien (of Kilfenora), lord chief justice of Ireland* (London, 1916), p. 137.

20 G. Murphy, 'The Gaelic background' in M. Tierney (ed.), *Daniel O'Connell: nine centenary essays* (Dublin, 1948), p. 157.

21 *Southern Reporter & Cork Commercial Courier*, 11 July 1837.

22 *Irish Law Recorder*, 22 Dec. 1827, p. 103.

> life in him.' After battering at the man for about an hour O'Connell suddenly challenged him to deny, by his God who would judge him, that there was a live fly in the dead man's mouth when his hand was put to the will. In terror the witness admitted the conspiracy.[23]

While other judges may not have understood Irish, some listened attentively to what was being said by the interpreters. When three Downe brothers were on trial for the murder of Timothy Angling at Ennis assizes in 1827, a witness was asked if he belonged to the party of the Downes or the party of the Anglings. When the interpreter interpreted this question, he said 'party' in English, rather than using an Irish equivalent. Mr Justice Torrens noticed this and asked 'Interpreter, have you no Irish word for party?' whereupon the interpreter replied 'No, my Lord, there is none in the language', something the judge found 'very extraordinary indeed'.[24]

The use of Irish interspersed with English must have been a frequent cause of misunderstanding and miscommunication. According to a possibly apocryphal anecdote, Baron Forster presided over a case at Limerick assizes where a man was accused of an aggravated assault with a 'cleh alpeen' or 'cleith ailpín', a shillelagh or cudgel with a knob at the end.[25] The prosecutor said 'the prisoner, Mick Molony, gave him a wipe of a cleh alpeen, and laid him neatly on the ground'. The judge told the jury the case was clear: 'It is in evidence before you, from the very prosecutor himself that the prisoner at the bar gave him a wipe of a clean napkin, and, with truly humane tenderness, laid him gently on the earth. – Of course, gentlemen, you will acquit the prisoner.' This was met by laughter and one of the lawyers had to stand up and explain that the cleh alpeen 'would have felled an ox'.[26]

Negative attitudes to the Irish language were evident in 1907 when county court Judge John Walker Craig took issue with a witness' signature in Irish on an agreement and said that a legal document should be signed in English as no court in Ireland would recognize a signature in Irish. The witness was south Monaghan travelling Gaelic teacher Eudhmonn O'Toole. The judge said, 'You know the result of this sort of thing will be that there will have to be an interpreter appointed in every County Court.'[27] In 1910 at Enniskillen quarter sessions, the word 'meitheal', or 'mehel' as it was spelt in the newspaper report, caused Craig some irritation. Solicitor John F. Wray was cross-examining a witness and asked her if it was 'the custom for a "mehel" of men to come to the bog to cut turf'. The judge asked what he meant; Mr Wray said it was an Irish word and that the witness would soon explain what it meant. The Judge then asked, 'Couldn't you get an English word that would suit equally as well? We talk English in this Court, and we have no interpreter here except yourself. Call it something else.' Mr Wray then explained

23 Seán Ó Faoláin, *King of the Beggars* (Dublin, 1980), p. 116.
24 *Finn's Leinster Journal*, 21 Mar. 1827.
25 J.W.Hurley, *Shillelagh: the Irish fighting stick* (Pipersville, PA, 2007), p. 27.
26 *Kerry Examiner*, 26 Apr. 1842.
27 *Irish Independent*, 4 Jan. 1907.

that it was an Irish farming custom whereby farmers would contribute a day's work to help a neighbour cut the turf quickly. Later, Mr Wray asked the witness what the usual number of men in a mehel was, but the judge said, 'I do not want your mehel. Talk some English. I do not know Irish. It is a very interesting language, but I have not learned it.'[28] By the time of the 1901 census, of 499 magistrates, only 37 stated that they spoke Irish; of 348 justices of the peace, a mere 20 said they spoke the language.

THE ROLE OF THE INTERPRETER

Interpreters listen to what is said in one language and repeat it aloud in another language. By contrast, translators read something in one language and write it in another language. Interpreting is a complex process with a high cognitive load where interpreters draw on their short-term memory to carry out their work. Interpreting is never an easy task; there is no time to think about the best possible translation, to consult a dictionary (if one is available), or to consult with a colleague. Interpreters have to come up with solutions on the spot. The interpreters who are the subject of this book may not have had access to any dictionaries or other materials relating to the law. While some of the information they had to interpret consisted of straightforward narrative accounts of events, they also had to interpret evidence from expert witnesses and English legal language, something that must have presented great difficulty in the absence of exact Irish-language equivalents. In order to provide comprehensible interpreting, they needed to understand the meaning of English legal terms and to be able to translate, explain or paraphrase them in Irish.

Interpreters were provided so that the courts could understand what was being said by non-English-speaking complainants and witnesses, but the practice around interpreter provision for non-English-speaking defendants was 'not settled' as late as 1916.[29] While defendants who did not speak English were allocated an interpreter during magisterial investigations to ensure that they understood the evidence against them, if they were defended by counsel at trial, it was assumed that they only needed to have new evidence interpreted. These matters were discussed at the appeals, first to the court of king's bench and then to the court of criminal appeal, against the conviction of Chinese man Lee Kun in London for murder. The background to the case was that when Lee Kun was charged before a magistrate, an interpreter interpreted the evidence against him. At trial, he was defended by counsel, his evidence was interpreted into English and he was found guilty. Athough there was no major difference between the evidence given before the magistrate and the evidence given at the trial itself, the fact that evidence in English was not interpreted into Chinese for him at trial served as grounds for

28 *Freeman's Journal*, 3 Nov. 1910.
29 *The King v Lee Kun* (1916: 346) 1 K.B. 337.

appeal. While both appeals were unsuccessful, the judgments contain useful background information on interpreter provision at trials on indictment for criminal offences and case law on the issue for the future.

Defence lawyer Tristram Beresford stated that it was not necessary to interpret 'the speeches of counsel for the prosecution or the defence or the summing-up of the judge … for the speeches form no essential part of a trial, and the real purpose of the summing-up is to direct the jury as to the law'.[30] Chief Justice Lord Reading noted that practice varied from court to court, with some judges insisting on interpreting being provided in all cases, while others allowed defence counsel or defendants to waive access to an interpreter. In addition, a distinction was made between cases where defendants had access to legal counsel and cases where they did not. For example, if a defendant had legal counsel, 'the practice has been for the Court not to require the translation of the evidence unless the accused or his counsel applied for it'.[31] At the final appeal, Lord Reading gave three reasons why evidence should be interpreted: first, because 'the prisoner has the right to make a statement to the jury', something that he could not do if he did not know the evidence against him; second, under the Criminal Evidence Act 1898 defendants were entitled to go into the witness-box and give evidence; third, defendants needed to understand the evidence against them in order to help their counsel with the cross-examination. Lord Reading also found that 'If the right to challenge [jurors] was not interpreted to the prisoner, this would be such a grave irregularity as to vitiate the trial.'[32] He went on to explain that:

> The reason why the accused should be present at the trial is that he may hear the case made against him, and have the opportunity, having heard it, of answering it. The presence of the accused means not merely that he must be physically in attendance, but also that he must be capable of understanding the nature of the proceedings.[33]

The ruling in *Lee Kun* (1916) was:

> When a defendant ignorant of or insufficiently acquainted with the English language is represented on his trial by counsel, the general rule is that the evidence must be interpreted to him, unless he personally or by his counsel dispenses with a translation. Such dispensation is in every case at the discretion of the judge, who must always be satisfied (including the case of deaf and dumb defendants fit to plead) that [the] defendant substantially understands the evidence and the case against him.[34]

30 *The King v Lee Kun* (1916: 342) 1 K.B. 337.
31 *The King v Lee Kun* (1916: 343) 1 K.B. 337.
32 *Lee Kun* (1916: 295) 11 Cr. App. R. 293.
33 *Lee Kun* (1916: 300) 11 Cr. App. R. 293.
34 *Lee Kun* (1916: 293) 11 Cr. App. R. 293.

THE GRAND JURIES

The grand juries played a pivotal role in interpreter provision. The date of their establishment is unclear but Hancock dates their involvement in fiscal administration back to the reign of James I, 1603–25.[35] The grand juries were 'the foremost institutions of local government in eighteenth-century Ireland',[36] and continued to play an important role in the nineteenth century. There were forty grand juries: one for each of the thirty-two counties, and one each for the counties of the cities of Cork, Dublin, Kilkenny, Limerick and Waterford, and for the towns of Carrickfergus, Drogheda and Galway. The high sheriff, who was appointed by the lord lieutenant, selected between twelve and twenty-three members of the landed gentry to sit on the grand jury, which met twice a year at the county courthouse before the spring and summer assizes. According to Neal Garnham, 'The inevitable result was a system in which ties of patronage, kin, and mutual interest were vitally important in jury selection.'[37] The grand jury officers were the treasurer, secretary, county surveyor and the high constables or baronial collectors.[38] Catholics were not allowed become members until 1793. The main remit of the grand juries was to pay for work done locally to improve and repair local infrastructure such as roads and bridges.

The other function of the grand juries related to the legal process. Judge Robert A. Day, in an address to the County Dublin grand jury in 1795, explained that the grand jury was 'an intermediate body between accusation and trial'. The grand jury could take into account the evidence of their own senses, viva voce evidence of witnesses and written depositions of witnesses for the prosecution, which were sworn before a magistrate, and sent to the grand jury with the bill of indictment – a practice in Ireland that he disagreed with. Day recommended personal examination of witnesses by the grand juries.[39] The grand juries went through all indictments to decide if they should go to trial; surviving lists of indictments indicate if there was a 'true bill' or 'no bill'. If there was a true bill, a prosecution was taken. Judge Day, in 1798, explained that the task involved examining:

> with perfect attention the evidence for the Crown, the nature of the charge, the credit and consistency of the Witnesses, the character of the Party accused; and to satisfy yourselves of his guilt, as far as *ex parte* evidence can satisfy, before you involve a fellow-subject in all the inconveniences of a public Trial.[40]

35 W.N. Hancock, 'Local government and taxation in Ireland' in J.W. Probyn (ed.), *Local government and taxation* (London, 1875), p. 194.
36 Neal Garnham, *The courts, crime and the criminal law in Ireland, 1692–1760* (Dublin, 1996), p. 630.
37 Ibid., p. 631.
38 R.B. O'Brien, *Dublin Castle and the Irish people* (London, 1909), p. 209.
39 R.A. Day, *A charge delivered to the grand jury of the County of Dublin at the quarter sessions of the peace held at Kilmainham* (Dublin, 1795).
40 Day, *A charge delivered,* p. 18.

The grand juries needed interpreters when taking oral evidence from Irish-speaking witnesses. In 1816, Baron Smith was hearing a robbery case at Mullingar summer assizes where complainant John Cooke 'could not speak a word of English'. When Smith went through the bill of indictment compiled by the grand jury, he could find no mention of an interpreter and fined Magistrate Henry £100 for neglecting his duty. This caused consternation and the following day the high sheriff explained that Cooke understood English but could not speak it and that John Fetherston, a member of the grand jury, who understood Irish but could not speak it, was able to act as interpreter between Cooke and the grand jury. The fine was not enforced due to the particular circumstances of the case.[41]

Over time the grand juries became responsible for courthouses, prisons, minor marine works, 'lunatic' asylums and 'fever' hospitals. They paid some court officials, including clerks, gaolers, interpreters for Irish and local constables. Accounts were published twice a year and included expenditure on both infrastructure and salaries. The 1815 *Report from the select committee on grand jury presentments*[42] *of Ireland* found that 'the law appears to be neglected' and stated that 'the title of the Act under which Grand Juries derive their authority to make the Presentments required, should appear upon the face of such Presentments'. This was a move to ensure that there was a legal basis to all presentments, thus blocking the grand juries from introducing new types of payments at their own discretion. Payments should be 'imperative presentments', provided for by law. In the county of Galway presentments, starting from 1808, there is no mention of any acts, and the practice of including a reference to the act commences only in spring 1832 and is applied somewhat haphazardly thereafter. However, there was considerable variation from county to county and some grand juries, such as Tyrone's, were meticulous about citing the acts. Many early books of presentments are in the form of manuscripts. To tackle this issue, another recommendation of the select committee was that the copies of presentments submitted to parliament should be printed, not handwritten, as 'the specifications, are, in many instances, so indistinct, that it is impossible to form an accurate opinion on them'.[43]

The presentments had to be paid by occupiers of land and the total bill for the county was divided up by barony so that a cess or tax could be collected by the sub-constable. There were allegations of 'jobbing' in relation to the grand juries. As they were comprised primarily of the wealthy, they could make local arrangements such as: 'You suffer the road to be brought through my park, and I will have the bridge constructed in a situation where it will make a beautiful object to your house. You do my job, and I will do yours.'[44] The grand juries were largely replaced

41 J.C. Lyons, *The grand juries of the County Westmeath* (Ledestown, 1853), pp 41–4.

42 Grand juries could make 'presentments' to allow for payments for road works and bridges and could sanction payments of certain salaries. Interpreters had to apply for presentments. All presentments had to be 'fiated' or passed by a judge.

43 *Report from the select committee on grand jury presentments of Ireland, 1814–15*, HC 1815 (283), vi, 4.

44 Sidney Smith, cited in O'Brien, *Dublin Castle*, p. 204.

by county councils in 1898 with the passing of the Local Government (Ireland) Act, which allowed for elections for county councillors, urban district councillors and town commissioners.[45] The act does not mention interpreters specifically, but from that point onwards the county councils became responsible for paying court interpreters, who were 'existing officers'.

The grand jury books of presentments are essential to a study of interpreting in the nineteenth century because they include payments to assizes and quarter sessions interpreters, who were usually named in the accounts, thus enabling the establishment of facts about where and when interpreters were provided, whether they were also paid by grand juries to serve in additional posts such as court crier or bridewell keeper, how much they were paid and how payments changed over time – in some cases being reduced and ultimately ceasing.

NEWSPAPERS

Newspaper reports that mention interpreters are a significant source of information in this volume. The earliest newspaper record found of interpreting between Irish and English dates back to 1797 when the oath of allegiance was administered, 'at the request of the inhabitants' of Glenahiry, Co. Waterford, to a large number of people with the help of Catholic priests who 'interpreted into the Irish language for those for whom this was necessary, and its import and tendency commented upon very forcibly.'[46] *Finn's Leinster Journal* and the *Freeman's Journal* date back to the 1760s. A number of local and national newspapers were founded in the nineteenth century; for example, the *Tuam Herald* (1837), *Nenagh Guardian* (1838), *Nation* (1842), *Irish Times* (1859) and *Westmeath Examiner* (1882). The turn of the century saw the launch of more newspapers, such as the *Meath Chronicle* (1897), *Connaught Telegraph* (1900), *Irish Independent* (1905), *Munster Express* (1908) and *Connacht Tribune* (1909). The overall number of newspapers increased from 109 in 1853 to 230 in 1913.[47]

The nineteenth century saw great changes in the newspaper industry. In the first half of the century, newspapers were largely dependent on news from London; the *Freeman's Journal*, for example, regularly used articles from the *London Gazette*, the official journal of record. Access to the express editions of the London papers was controlled by Dublin Castle.[48] Newspapers were expensive as they had to be printed on stamped paper. There was a tax of 1*s.* 6*d.* on advertisements. The *Freeman's Journal* cost 3½*d.* in 1779 and 4*d.* by 1800, was published three times a week and consisted of four pages. According to journalist Andrew Dunlop, tax on advertisements was abolished in 1853, and the requirement to use stamped paper

45 J.J. Clancy, *A handbook of local government in Ireland* (Dublin, 1899), p. 85.
46 *Freeman's Journal*, 28 Dec. 1797.
47 J. Lee, *The modernization of Irish society, 1848–1918* (Dublin, 1973), p. 13.
48 Mark O'Brien, 'Evolution of a discipline' in Kevin Rafter (ed.), *Irish journalism before independence* (Manchester, 2011), p. 12.

for news in 1855. This brought about a 'great revolution in the newspaper world' and when the *Irish Times* commenced publication in 1859, it was the 'first penny daily morning newspaper' and was soon matched by the *Daily Express* and the *Freeman's Journal*. Meanwhile, the price of evening papers was reduced to a half-penny.[49] These significant price reductions over the course of sixty years meant that more people could afford to buy newspapers.

Changes in transport and the introduction of the telegraph also had an impact on newspapers. Mail coaches were introduced in Ireland in 1790 and the British Mail Office was set up in the early 1800s to manage mail between England and Ireland.[50] In 1779, articles from the *London Gazette* appeared five days later in the *Freeman's Journal*. The time lag was reduced to four days by 1800. The growth of the railway network facilitated the development of the post office. New towns were built along the railways and this facilitated the development of the provincial press.[51] Steamships began to operate between Ireland and Britain around 1824.[52] The advent of the telegraph and in particular the laying of the transatlantic cable from Valentia to Newfoundland meant that news reports could be transmitted far more speedily. Reports for the morning papers were sent after 6 p.m., when a reduced rate applied.[53] The cost of sending telegraphs increased to such an extent that for a three-year period, journalists could only send condensed reports of important events; the cost went down to less than a tenth when the government took over the Magnetic Telegraph Company in 1870.[54]

Journalist Andrew Dunlop described shorthand as the 'open sesame' to journalism and essential for court reporting. This was probably Pitman shorthand, based on a phonetic approach and invented in 1837. Gregg shorthand, a form of stenography, followed in 1888. Dunlop wrote of the 'strain of taking down the exact words of a rapid speaker' in proceedings that could last as long as five or six hours. He complained about the acoustics in the Four Courts building, where, according to him, it was impossible to hear in two of the thirteen courts. Similarly, it was impossible for reporters to hear anything said by the judges in the No. 1 Nisi Prius Court. According to Dunlop:

> The judge on the bench, if he misses a word, or thinks he mis-interprets the answer of a witness, and all know how frequently that occurs, can have the answer repeated. The reporter would run the risk of being committed for contempt of court if he claimed the same privilege.[55]

49 Andrew Dunlop, *Fifty years of Irish journalism* (Dublin, 1911), p. 280.
50 R.B. O'Brien, *Dublin Castle*, p. 332.
51 M. O'Brien, 'Evolution of a discipline', p. 16.
52 Lyons, *Ireland since the Famine*, p. 57.
53 F. Higginbottom, *The vivid life: a journalist's career* (London, 1934), p. 107.
54 Dunlop, *Fifty years of Irish journalism*, p. 42.
55 Ibid., p. 71.

According to Dunlop, a staff of five or six reporters from the *Freeman's Journal* attended the Phoenix Park murder trials at Green Street courthouse in April–May 1883 to take down verbatim reports which were published in the evening papers each day, one hour after the court had risen.[56] Frederick J. Higginbottom was working for the Press Association and his reports were 'carried by messengers on outside cars from the court to the telegraph office'.[57]

In the nineteenth century and well into the twentieth, reporters were anonymous and there was no byline with the reporter's name. The identities of newspaper editors were generally known, but those of court reporters were not. Dunlop worked as a 'murder correspondent' from 1880 to 1886. He made the point that anonymity meant that 'the editor or it may be the proprietor of the newspaper is the person responsible to the public for what appears in its columns', but that when reporting on cases in small towns, it was inevitable that his identity would become known and he would be seen as the 'responsible individual' for the publication of reports on local cases.[58]

There was interesting crossover between lawyers and journalists. William O'Brien was originally a reporter on the *Cork Examiner* before joining the bar and eventually becoming a judge of the queen's bench division.[59] Barry Yelverton, who was called to the Irish bar in 1764, also wrote for the press in London.[60] George Lawrence, Timothy Healy and Richard Adams were all journalists before being called to the bar.[61] David Plunket was called to the bar in 1862 and also wrote for the *Daily Express*.[62] John Adye Curran also combined his early career as a barrister from 1860 with reporting for three newspapers: the *Irish Times*, the *Freeman's Journal* and *Saunders's News-Letter*. According to Curran, 'Circuit-reporting was done by members of the Bar, payment being at the rate of 10s 6d per day's report.'[63] Curran was appointed Dublin police magistrate in 1881 and another barrister, Richard Gamble, who later was appointed judge, wrote for the *Daily Express* and 'sometimes when busy asked me [Curran] to report for him'.[64] Dunlop mentions that his *Daily Express* colleagues included 'one who is now a judge of the High Court of Justice in Ireland, one who became a County Court Judge, three who became Queen's Counsel, one who is a Bishop of the Church of Ireland – all leader

56 Ibid., p. 106.
57 Higginbottom, *The vivid life*, p. 48. An 'outside car' was a two-wheeled, single-horse-drawn open car on which passengers sat on each side. Colin Divall, *Cultural histories of sociabilities, spaces and mobilities* (Abingdon, 2015), p. 158.
58 Dunlop, *Fifty years of Irish journalism*, p. 180.
59 T.M. Healy, *The old Munster circuit* (Dublin, 1939), pp 14–15.
60 Roderick O'Flanagan, *The Irish bar: comprising anecdotes, bon-mots, and biographical sketches of the bench and bar of Ireland* (London, 1879), p. 53.
61 Healy, *The old Munster circuit*, pp 14–15.
62 Daire Hogan, *The legal profession in Ireland, 1789–1922* (Dublin, 1986), p. 76.
63 J. Curran, *Reminiscences of John Adye Curran K.C.* (London, 1915), p. 40.
64 Ibid., p. 41.

writers'.[65] Some practising lawyers provided newspapers with accounts of court cases. Matthias Mc Donnell Bodkin's knowledge of Pitman shorthand helped him secure a place 'as an unpaid probationer' with the *Freeman's Journal*. He explains that the 'length or brevity' of descriptions is dependent on 'the amount of available space' and that 'the Irish reporter is a Jack of all trades', unlike in England where 'press work is specialized'. Bodkin combined his work as a barrister and later as a county court judge for County Clare from 1907–24 with ongoing involvement in newspapers. A barrister called Breakey no longer practised as such but wore the wig and gown 'as a sure means of getting admission to any Court that might be crowded' and reported for the *Freeman's Journal*.[66] There was also a crossover between politicians and journalists; Felix M. Larkin has found that thirty-eight members of parliament had careers in journalism.[67]

The potential newspaper readership increased with national school education through English. The national school system was established in 1831 and although the standard of teaching was not always exemplary and attendance was not made compulsory until 1892, access to education did lead to increasing levels of literacy in English. In 1841, only 47 per cent of the population could read, a proportion that increased to 67 per cent by 1871.[68] Between 1848 and 1914, the number of schools doubled from about 4,500 to 9,000 and the number of pupils from half a million to 1 million.[69]

The place of the Irish language in newspapers is relevant. Regina Uí Chollatáin has found that from the 1860s, provincial newspapers such as the *Tuam News*, the *Celt*, and the *Cashel Gazette* included columns in Irish. The Gaelic League published *Irisleabhar na Gaedhilge,* a monthly magazine, from 1882 to 1909, and the best-known weekly newspaper in Irish, *An Claidheamh Soluis,* amalgamated with *Fáinne an Lae*, from 1899 to 1931. These publications mainly focused on 'the creation of a modern Irish literature' and 'As the revival progressed, Irish language newspapers and journals assumed more of a role in language maintenance and revival, instead of public discourse and news.'[70] While *An Claidheamh Soluis* did cover cases taken by the Royal Irish Constabulary in relation to the use of names in Irish on carts, including the best-known case, that of Niall Mac Giolla Bhrighde in Donegal, it did not provide regular coverage of court cases involving interpreters. A frequent criticism

65 Dunlop, *Fifty years of Irish journalism*, p. 45.

66 McDonnell M. Bodkin, *Recollections of an Irish judge: press, bar and parliament* (London, 1914), p. 26.

67 Felix M. Larkin, 'Double helix: two elites in politics and journalism in Ireland, 1870–1918' in Ciaran O'Neill (ed.), *Irish elites in the nineteenth century* (Dublin, 2013), p. 129.

68 E.G. Ravenstein, 'On the Celtic languages in the British Isles: a statistical survey', *Journal of the Statistical Society of London*, 42:3 (1879), p. 587.

69 Lee, *The modernization of Irish society*, p. 27.

70 R. Uí Chollatáin, 'Newspapers, journals and the Irish revival' in Rafter (ed.), *Irish journalism before independence*, p. 168.

of research relating to the Irish language is lack of consultation of and reference to Irish-language source texts. However, no Irish-language sources on the topic of interpreters were located.

While acknowledging that newspapers are very useful potential sources of historical information and 'crime presented good journalistic copy' and as a result was reported widely, Garnham cautions that 'Reports tend to cover the unusual and exceptional, rather than the commonplace' and recommends questioning the veracity of reports.[71] A 1999 handbook on newspaper journalism advises court reporters to 'Watch for courtroom drama, with a witness breaking down, an outburst from the dock or a disturbance in the public gallery' and suggested that 'Quotes add liveliness and corroboration to your report.'[72] A 2001 handbook recommends that 'A court report should try to answer in its first few sentences these five questions: Who was accused? Where does he or she live? What was he or she accused of? How did he or she plead? What was the court's decision and sentence?'[73] Nineteenth- and early twentieth-century reporters applied these principles consistently. Court reports begin by outlining the place and the actors, with names of justices, lawyers for the prosecution and the defence, and all the parties (prisoners or defendants, plaintiffs and witnesses). Names of jurors were provided as well and any situation that included an interesting or unusual reaction was more likely to be reported. Some accounts read like court transcripts, with long columns of dialogue taken down verbatim. Many newspaper reports include the name of the interpreter.

RESEARCH ON INTERPRETERS

Existing research on the topic of Irish-language court interpreters provides a fragmented picture and it is difficult to establish how much interpreting was happening, how the system was organized and when, where or indeed if, interpreter provision ceased. For example, Louis M. Cullen correctly states that 'there were salaried court interpreters in Meath, Westmeath, Wicklow in 1807 but not in Dublin or Laois'.[74] Similarly, Gerard O'Brien mentions that 'By 1814 interpreters were needed only in 'very few cases' in Louth and Armagh although they 'continued to be a standard feature of the courtroom in Clare'.[75] The difficulty is that such items of information have no context and as a result tell us very little. The lack of research on the topic has been acknowledged by Niall Ó Ciosáin,

71 Garnham, *The courts, crime and the criminal law*, pp 4–5.

72 H. Clother, 'Law and disorders – covering the courts' in R. Keeble, *The newspapers handbook* (1999), pp 209, 210.

73 G. Harris and D. Spark, *Practical newspaper reporting* (Oxford, 2001), p. 109.

74 L.M. Cullen, *The emergence of modern Ireland, 1600–1900* (London, 1981), p. 89.

75 G. O'Brien, 'The strange death of the Irish language, 1780–1800' in G. O'Brien (ed.), *Parliament, politics and people: essays in eighteenth century Irish history* (1989), p. 169.

according to whom, 'one central issue which has not been explored in detail is the use of Irish in law courts, particularly after the 1820s'.[76] While scholars accept that Irish-language court interpreters were made available, the general consensus, most likely based primarily on assumptions around the decline of the Irish language, is that court interpreter provision ended much earlier than was in fact the case. For example, Diarmait Mac Giolla Chríost writes of the 'falling use of interpreters in the expanding judicial system following the 1787 Act for paid magistracy',[77] while Neal Garnham suggests that interpreters 'were continually employed until the mid-nineteenth century'.[78]

This book builds on work by three researchers. Máire Ní Dhonnchadha's dissertation on court interpreters for Irish from 1850 to 2000 combines historical cases such as *R. v. Burke* and *R. v. Myles Joyce* with folk and fictional accounts of interpreters. She found that prior to 1900, court interpreters 'were clerks of the court, barristers, solicitors and policemen' and worked 'at least in Counties Meath, Galway, Mayo and Dublin'. Her recommendation that grand jury presentments 'should be accessed and studied in detail'[79] has been followed here. Lesa Ní Mhunghaile devoted a substantial proportion of a chapter on the place of the Irish language in the legal system from 1700 to 1843 to the use of Irish in the courts. Drawing on a wide range of sources, she found that Irish and English coexisted in the lower courts until at least the 1830s and that some manor courts operated entirely through Irish. Based on the information available to her, she concluded that 'the employment of interpreters at the assizes courts was common in some counties up to at least the 1830s'.[80] This volume has revisited her sources. Nicholas Wolf devoted a chapter of *An Irish-speaking island* to the topic of interpreter provision to the courts and at elections and provided evidence of court interpreters still being employed in a number of counties in 1866.[81] However, there are issues with Wolf's work, in particular his finding (in line with some previous research) that subsequent to *R v. Burke* (1858), anyone who was bilingual could freely opt to use either English or Irish as they preferred in court. Other more minor matters are the conflation of witness expenses with payments to interpreters,[82] the absence of distinction between crown and private prosecutions,[83] as well as the blanket finding

76 N. Ó Ciosáin, 'Gaelic culture and language shift' in Laurence M. Geary and Margaret Kelleher (eds), *Nineteenth-century Ireland: a guide to recent research* (Dublin, 2005), p. 151.
77 Diarmait Mac Giolla Chríost, *The Irish language in Ireland from Goidel to globalization* (Abingdon, 2005), p. 97.
78 Garnham, *The courts, crime and the criminal law*, pp 112, 193.
79 Máire Ní Dhonnchadha, 'Irish language interpreting in the courts since the 1850s' (MA, DCU, 2000), p. 65.
80 Lesa Ní Mhunghaile, 'The legal system in Ireland and the Irish language, 1700–*c.*1843' in M. Brown and S.P. Donlan, *The laws and other legalities in Ireland, 1689–1850* (Surrey, 2011), p. 331.
81 Nicholas Wolf, *An Irish-speaking island* (Madison, 2014), p. 157.
82 Ibid., p. 157.
83 Ibid., pp 158–9.

that 'statements by witnesses as to their language proficiency were delivered prior to entering the dock under oath'.[84]

The timespan of this book is, broadly speaking, from the date of the earliest record of a salaried interpreter, in 1754, until the establishment of the Irish Free State in January 1922. However, while some grand jury presentment records from the earlier period have survived, there is a dearth of background information about the situation in the eighteenth century as newspaper reports of court proceedings involving Irish-language court interpreters commence after the Act of Union (1801). Consequently, the main focus is on what is often referred to as 'the long nineteenth century' ending with the establishment of the Irish Free State and the subsequent recognition of the Irish language in the 1922 and 1937 constitutions.

Everyone in Ireland knows that the British took measures to eliminate the Irish language, particularly in the public sphere. But if that was the case, why were salaried Irish-language interpreters provided in court? It seems contradictory. Also, why did the system in Ireland develop differently from that in Wales, where despite a similar law providing that all court proceedings had to be in English, there were never any salaried interpreters? The answer to these questions lies with timing and the role of the grand juries. The kingdom of England and Wales had been created in the first half of the sixteenth century. The Act of Union was much later, in 1801, which meant that in Ireland there was slightly more autonomy, something that allowed the grand juries to introduce salaries for court interpreters and the Irish parliament to pass legislation to that effect.

From the point of view of legal history, this book sheds light on the role of the grand juries and on measures taken to ensure that the courts understood the evidence of Irish-speaking witnesses. The grand juries were very aware of the need for interpreters because they dealt with Irish speakers constantly when deciding if cases should go to trial or not. They pioneered the introduction of salaries for interpreters, first at assizes and later at quarter sessions courts and decades later the legislators caught up. However, the grand juries lost their discretion to introduce new payments that did not have a statutory basis and as a result were unable to provide for salaried interpreters at new courts such as the petty sessions and the insolvent debtors' court.

It would be a mistake to view interpreter provision with rose-tinted lenses as access to interpreters' services in all courts was restricted to monolingual Irish speakers. The backdrop to interpreter provision throughout the period is the Administration of Justice (Language) Act (Ireland) (1737), which provided that all proceedings had to be in English, something that would have a negative effect on the experience of Irish speakers in the courts. A great deal of time and energy was expended on bullying and browbeating Irish speakers about their alleged knowledge of English. If it was found that parties were lying under oath about their knowledge of English, there were repercussions – the case could be dismissed or

84 Ibid., p. 162.

they could be found in contempt of court or put on trial for perjury. If witnesses 'refused' to speak English, they could be denied their expenses at assizes. A further concern was the widespread use of summons servers, process servers and civil bill officers as interpreters. In any situation where an interpreter is needed, trust is essential and it is highly unlikely that Irish speakers who were reliant on interpreters trusted this particular group of people to behave impartially and provide accurate interpreting. The courts system was far from inclusive and, in effect, and perhaps counterintuitively, despite the presence of interpreters, was an instrument of linguistic imperialism. Recruitment was based on a system of patronage, with few attempts to test applicants to establish their competency. A major drawback was the fact that a distinction was made between criminal and civil cases with salaried court interpreters employed to work in criminal cases only and not in civil cases where plaintiffs and defendants were expected to either cover the cost of interpreters for themselves and for Irish-speaking witnesses or rely on volunteers. There were so many negative aspects attached to interpreter provision – no standards, summons servers and process servers being used as interpreters, pressure to speak English – that the very provision was an incentive to learn English so as not to be ridiculed in court and not to be reliant on others.

Interpreting is a notoriously difficult area on which to carry out research because once an interpreter has spoken, there is rarely a record of what was said in the source language and only occasionally of what was said in the target language. These problems are even more pronounced in the case of historical research. However, interpreting does leave traces and it has proved possible to uncover a wealth of information from a variety of sources: digitized newspaper archives and parliamentary debates, hard-copy grand jury presentment books, and correspondence with the chief secretary's office in Dublin Castle. This book is unique in its approach to the issue of interpreter provision and its extensive and comprehensive use of these sources. Its contribution is to separate out the situation in the different courts in order to provide a clear and definitive understanding of the workings of the system of interpreter provision, but it is broader than this because it also sheds new light on attitudes of and to Irish speakers. The Maamtrasna case, a total aberration because a police constable acted as interpreter at the trials, is considered, as is the topic of policemen as interpreters. This book contributes to both legal history and the history of the Irish language and in particular to an understanding of the plight of Irish speakers who appeared in court as defendants, complainants and witnesses. It also sheds light on the appointment, remuneration and identity of a large number of interpreters, who of course were Irish speakers who had found a way to turn their bilingualism into an income stream. Appendix B contains biographical information on over 90 interpreters, allowing us a glimpse at the men who took on this role.

CHAPTER TWO

Statutory provision for interpreters

THE ADMINISTRATION OF Justice (Language) Act (Ireland) (1737), titled 'An Act that all proceedings in courts of justice within this kingdom shall be in the English language', created a problem for the courts because it put an end to any accommodation through Irish of those who were not entirely fluent in English. This meant that those judges and lawyers who spoke Irish could no longer communicate directly through the language with Irish-speaking parties appearing in court. There was also an additional problem: the penal laws excluded Catholics, who were more likely to understand Irish, from working as law officers and judges. Consequently, interpreters were widely needed in the eighteenth century and may originally have been whoever was available – practising barristers, lawyers, court staff or indeed volunteers who happened to be in court. The absence of a reliable system meant that the situation was no doubt all too frequently chaotic. This led to the grand juries pioneering the introduction of salaried interpreters, first at assizes and later at quarter sessions. Eventually, parliament introduced legislation to provide a statutory basis for these payments. However, in civil cases, plaintiffs and defendants were not entitled to avail of salaried court interpreters and had to find alternative solutions.

INTERPRETERS AT ASSIZES

John McCavitt dates the introduction of the assizes courts back to the late 1500s when, over time, a network of circuits was established.[1] In 1613, according to the State Papers, it was 'very inconvenient that the judges are unacquainted with the Irish language, and cannot understand the witnesses that speak no English, whereby they cannot so well judge the case'.[2] There were assizes courts in Carrickfergus, Cork, Drogheda, Galway, Kilkenny, Limerick and Waterford. In addition, there were five assize circuits where judges moved from town to town to hear cases around the country. Serious cases such as murder were heard at the assizes, where the grand jury brought in an indictment, and the trial was presided over by one or two senior judges in the presence of a petty jury.[3] According to Terence Dooley, a plaintiff who prosecuted a case at assizes would incur prohibitive costs of between

1 John McCavitt, 'Good planets in their several spheares', *Irish Jurist*, 24:2 (1989), p. 247.
2 Calendar of the State Papers relating to Ireland cited in Crowley, *Wars of words*, p. 41.
3 W.E. Vaughan, *Murder trials in Ireland, 1836–1914* (Oxford, 2009), p. 4.

£10 and £20, including payments to witnesses and to court officials such as clerks, bailiffs, doorkeepers and criers.[4]

In theory, grand jury presentments could only be made for items that were covered by legislation. In practice, however, grand juries passed presentments for items that were not covered by legislation and this is what happened in the case of interpreters. The earliest surviving record of an interpreter being paid a salary is for Donegal in April 1754, twenty years before the introduction of legislation providing for such a post: 'We present two pounds to be levied and paid to the Treasr. And by him paid to Owen McConigall for his years wages as Interpreter 2 0 0.' It is unlikely that the Donegal grand jury was the only one in the country to pay an interpreter a salary. Unfortunately, there are few surviving records for this early period and those that have survived shed little light on this issue; in the case of grand jury books of presentments for Louth (1711–31)[5] and Antrim (1727–67)[6], there are no payments to interpreters, and in the case of Meath (1761–76)[7] the first record of a payment to an interpreter is for 1775. The Meath manuscript records cannot be considered complete; they go backwards and forwards in time in a rather confusing fashion, with some entries made retrospectively, and the fact that there are no recorded salaries for interpreters before 1775 does not necessarily mean that this was in fact the case. It is possible that other grand juries, like Donegal, faced with the problem of dealing with large numbers of Irish speakers in the eighteenth century, conscious of the need to understand what was being said by witnesses, and keen to ensure successful prosecutions, introduced the post of interpreter and the law caught up with this provision some years later.

Three laws were passed providing for salaried interpreters at assizes in 1773, 1796 and 1836, an indication that the authorities accepted, and continued to accept, that there were sufficient numbers of monolingual Irish speakers to justify such posts. A curious feature of the laws passed on interpreter provision is the refusal to explicitly acknowledge the existence of the Irish language. Rather than refer to 'Irish interpreter' or 'interpreter for the Irish language' they merely refer to 'an interpreter', it being understood that the interpreter would be for the Irish language. Such failure to acknowledge the existence of the language is described by Patricia Palmer as 'an ideologically-motivated strategy'.[8] There are no Court Interpreter Acts; rather, interpreter provision appears as an afterthought towards the ends of acts relating mainly to other topics. The earliest law that mentions payments to court interpreters relates to public roads, part of the remit of the grand juries, was passed in 1773–4 and made it lawful for them to pay 'any sum

4 T. Dooley, *The murders at Wildgoose Lodge: agrarian crime and punishment in pre-Famine Ireland* (Dublin, 2007), p. 110.

5 Grand jury presentments for County Louth, 1713–32, MS 11,949, NLI.

6 Grand jury presentment books, County Antrim, ANT/4/1, PRONI.

7 National Archives of Ireland. The volume for Meath 1785–90 could not be found.

8 Patricia Palmer, *Language and conquest in early modern Ireland* (Cambridge, 2009), p. 46.

of money not exceeding five pounds for an interpreter at such assizes'.[9] The capping of the salary at £5 per half-year may have reflected a belief that the need for interpreters was unlikely to increase. This law was introduced, debated and passed in the Irish parliament, then submitted to the lord lieutenant and council for approval and finally submitted to the king and council in England. If bills were not approved, that was the end of them; if changes were made, the Irish parliament could either accept or reject the bill in its entirety but could not make any further changes.[10] A similar law relating to public roads passed in 1796, under Grattan's parliament, contained the same provision,[11] as did the 1836 Grand Jury (Ireland) Act.[12]

The rate of pay for interpreters at assizes remained fixed by law at a sum not exceeding £5 per half-year from 1773–4 through the nineteenth century and even into the twentieth century. The wording of the laws allowed the grand juries to reduce the rate of pay in line with any reduction in the amount of work carried out and made it difficult to increase pay if more work was being carried out – in new courts, for example. The norm was for the assizes to be held twice a year in Lent and summer but from 1877 a winter assize was added in certain counties,[13] leading eventually to successful requests to the chief secretary's office at Dublin Castle for payment for extra interpreting.

Assizes interpreters received extra payments for their work at special commissions that were held when 'exemplary hangings or at least exemplary trials were deemed necessary for the public peace'.[14] For example, James Clerk was paid an extra £5 for interpreting at a special commission in Mayo in 1807.[15] Similarly, in County Limerick, James Kennedy received a number of extra payments in spring 1816 and again at each assize between spring 1822 and spring 1825.[16] In Clare, two extra payments of £5, to be levied off the baronies of Bunratty and Tulla, were made by the grand jury to Pat Curtin, who was employed at special sessions under the Insurrection Act in summer 1824 and spring 1825.[17]

The County Dublin Grand Jury Act 1844 set the rate for interpreters at quarter sessions in the county at £10 per half-year, but there is no evidence that this

9 13 & 14 Geo. 3, c. 32, s. 22, An act for the amendment of public roads, for directing the power of grand juries respecting presentments, and for repealing several laws heretofore made for these purposes.
10 J.C. Beckett, *A short history of Ireland* (London, 1958).
11 36 Geo. 3, vol. 9, c. 55, s. 34. For the amendment of the public roads, for directing the power of grand juries respecting presentments, and for repealing several laws heretofore made for those purposes.
12 Grand Jury (Ireland) Act 1836, 6 & 7 Will. 4, c. 116, s. 79.
13 Vaughan, *Murder trials in Ireland*, p. 86.
14 Dooley, *The murders at Wildgoose Lodge*, p. 219.
15 *Accounts presented to the house of commons, of the presentments passed by the grand juries of Ireland, at the spring and summer assizes, in the year 1807*, HC 1808.
16 Presentments made on the county of Limerick, 1816, 1822, 1825, Limerick Studies Archives.
17 Clare grand jury presentment books, 1824–5, 1D-4–90, NAI.

provision ever resulted in the employment of salaried court interpreters in Dublin (see chapter 12).

INTERPRETERS AT QUARTER SESSIONS

There were quarter sessions courts in Carrickfergus, Cork, Galway, Kinsale, Limerick, Londonderry, Kilkenny, Waterford and Youghal,[18] presided over by justices of the peace, who were 'unpaid amateurs'.[19] There was no great enthusiasm to become a justice of the peace in the early nineteenth century and, as a result, some were not entirely suited to the role. In part of County Cork, they were reputedly 'brewsters, malsters, distillers and rackrent landlords'.[20] At quarter sessions, the grand jury brought in an indictment, and a petty jury was involved. From 1851, the court consisted of an assistant barrister and a number of magistrates.[21] The assistant barristers, retitled county court judges in 1877,[22] were paid professionals and were the sole judges in cases involving civil bills. The criminal business heard at quarter sessions was 'a very small fraction' of the total work of the court, with one day designated for criminal cases, appeals and licensing. Cases could be appealed at the next assizes, where all the evidence would be reheard.[23] The quarter sessions were held, as the name indicates, four times a year. The division between assizes and quarter sessions with more serious cases being heard at the former and less serious cases at the latter was not absolute, and if the assizes were due to sit before the quarter sessions, they could hear less serious cases that would normally have been heard at quarter sessions.[24]

Once again, just as the grand juries had been proactive regarding employing interpreters at assizes, so also were they proactive some years later regarding employing interpreters at quarter sessions. Despite the absence of statutory provision and a failed attempt to introduce legislation in 1817,[25] surviving books of presentments indicate that the grand juries introduced salaries for interpreters at quarter sessions in 1797 in Donegal, in 1802 in Tyrone, in 1811 in Sligo, in 1813 in Galway, in 1814 in the county of Kilkenny and by 1819 in Roscommon. The salary at quarter sessions in these places at this time was £5 per half-year, the same rate as at assizes, despite the fact that quarter sessions work involved a greater

18 R.B. McDowell, 'The Irish courts of law, 1801–1914', *Irish Historical Studies*, 10:40 (1957), pp 375–6.
19 Ibid., p. 371.
20 Ibid., pp 363–91.
21 Vaughan, *Murder trials in Ireland*, p. 86.
22 Lyons, *Ireland since the Famine*, p. 75.
23 Healy, *The old Munster circuit*, pp 63–4.
24 Vaughan, *Murder trials in Ireland*, p. 4.
25 A bill to regulate the presenting, levying, and applying of money, required for the making and repairing of public roads and buildings, and for other public purposes, under the direction of grand juries in Ireland.

time commitment. The county of Galway was more generous: in spring 1824, John Kirwan (also a solicitor) was paid a total of £20 for a half-year – £5 each for interpreting at assizes, the record court, the insolvent court and at quarter sessions even though strictly speaking, by law he was only entitled to one payment of £5.

However, there was some tightening up of unauthorized spending by the grand juries. In 1822, Mayo court interpreter Simon Conway wrote to the lord lieutenant to complain that the grand jury had decided to cut his pay from £60 to £10 per year, the amount they were authorized to pay. Conway made the point that when the act was passed in 1773–4, the civil bill court and the insolvent court did not exist. His work as an interpreter took up 'sixty or seventy days' a year, 'there being eight sessions, two assizes, and two, or perhaps more Insolvent Courts every year', and he suggested that £70 per annum would be appropriate recompense. Conway enclosed certificates supporting his case from the high sheriff, the clerk of the peace, the assistant barrister, three attorneys and the chief justice of the king's bench. An annotation on the reverse of his memorial describes him as 'a very deserving public officer'.[26]

Similar concerns about remuneration were voiced by a number of people towards the end of the decade. In 1828, a group of seven quarter sessions magistrates and twelve attorneys sent a joint letter to the lord lieutenant to the effect that each year in Kerry there were over 10,000 civil bills plus crown business and that many witnesses spoke only Irish. They explained that the grand jury had been paying an interpreter, but that the judges:

> did not consider themselves warranted in fiating a Presentment for an interpreter at quarter sessions though they concurred in the absolute necessity of such an Officer and expressed regret that there was no law to sanction them in fiating a Presentment for him.

They requested that an act of parliament be passed to provide for a salaried interpreter at quarter sessions.[27] The following year, Assistant Barrister John Macan made a similar plea for a salaried interpreter at quarter sessions in County Cork; an annotation on the correspondence by Chief Secretary Francis Leveson Gower reads: 'I trust that the evil complained of is daily becoming less pressing, but nevertheless I think it ought to be remedied if a measure could be invited.'[28] Despite his request for an interpreter, Macan wrote that he was convinced from his experience that:

> the Irish language is, in all those courts, the great instrument of perjury – that its continuance seriously obstructs the investigation of truth, and

26 CSO/RP/1822/68, NAI.
27 CSO/RP/1828/520, NAI.
28 CSO/RP/1829/137/3, NAI.

> therefore the due administration of justice, and interferes with the improvement of the peasantry and the good order and peace of the entire county.[29]

In March 1837, the *Sligo Champion* reported that interpreter Owen McGoolrick, who worked at both assizes and quarters sessions, sought payment of £5 from the Sligo grand jury for his work at quarter sessions. He informed the grand jury that it cost him £10 a year to attend the quarter sessions and if he was not paid, he could not continue. The foreman of the grand jury said he had no power as 'the sum already allowed him was specified on the act'. The reporter commented that 'We think this a case of great hardship, the poor man is very attentive to his business and civial [*sic*] having a great deal to do; but those who do most are the worst paid.'[30] The preamble to the Grand Jury (Ireland) Act 1836 had made it unlawful for grand juries to make presentments for raising any money 'unless under the authority and by virtue of the provisions of this Act'.[31]

Finally, in 1837, the Small Debts Recovery (Ireland) Act became law.[32] This act allowed for a payment not exceeding £15 for each half-year and also allowed for either 'one interpreter for the whole of such County or separate interpreters for each District' to work at quarter sessions. This provision must have resulted from a realization that it was difficult for one interpreter to travel to a number of different courts, particularly in the larger counties. The act also provided that the assistant barrister, rather than the grand jury, would have the power to appoint and remove interpreters. The reasons for this change are unclear although it may have been an attempt to take some power away from the grand juries. An important negative consequence was that for many assistant barristers the default option was to appoint a process server as interpreter. While this made sense for them because they knew the process servers (for whom interpreting would be a supplementary income), it was quite a cynical approach, since most people hated process servers. Similar provisions for interpreters appear fourteen years later in the Civil Bill Courts (Ireland) Act 1851[33] which included a provision to employ separate quarter sessions interpreters for each district and to 'direct the Salary to be presented as aforesaid to be paid among such interpreters'. This option was implemented at different times over the course of the nineteenth century. For example, a second interpreter was employed from 1839 in Sligo,[34] at an unknown time prior to 1845 in County Cork, from 1867 in Kerry,[35] from at least 1868 in county Galway[36] and

29 CSO/RP/1829/137/3, NAI.
30 *Sligo Champion*, 18 Mar. 1837.
31 6 & 7 Will. 4, c. 116.
32 7 Will. 4 & 1 Vict., cc 43, 44.
33 14 & 15 Vict., c. 57, s. 20.
34 County of Sligo, county at-large presentments, spring 1839, Sligo County Library, LGOV780.
35 *Tralee Chronicle & Killarney Echo*, 1 Mar. 1867.
36 County of Galway, schedule of presentments, summer 1868, County Library Headquarters, Galway. The three divisions were Galway, Loughrea and Clifden.

from 1876 in Donegal.[37] A footnote in an annual report on local government in 1883 states that:

> Whenever an Interpreter is employed the Court may order him such compensation as may be reasonable, in cases where such interpreters are not paid by salary for the discharge of each duty.[38]

This proviso acknowledged an ongoing need for interpreters in those counties where the post of interpreter had been abolished.

NON-PROVISION OF INTERPRETERS IN CIVIL CASES

While salaried interpreters were employed in criminal cases, they were not made available in civil cases such as tithe, libel and insurance cases; parties were expected to recruit and pay their own interpreters. The practice in most civil cases in common law countries through the centuries is that plaintiffs and defendants are expected to cover the cost of interpreters for themselves and for witnesses who do not speak the language of the court. The cost of interpreter provision would then be covered in a settlement, if applicable. The question of payment was dealt with at the Rolls in the 1843 case *Plunkett v. Williams and others*, in which the decision was that 'a party examining by means of an interpreter, a witness ignorant of the English language, must bear the expense of the interpreter's services on the cross, as well as the direct examination'.[39]

Lack of provision of interpreters in civil cases led to a great deal of confusion in the courts. Ad hoc solutions had to be found in two tithes cases heard at the *nisi prius* court in Cork.[40] In the first, in 1836, one of the two defendants could not speak English and 'his fellow-prisoner was his interpreter' and told the court that the man was in a state of great destitution.[41] In the second, in 1838, when Baron Pennefather could not understand the Irish-speaking defendant, the tithe rebellion commissioner – probably not the most desirable person for this task – volunteered to interpret for his prisoner.[42] In other cases, witnesses and court attendees were asked to act as interpreters. In 1839, in an insurance case, a witness called Honor Burke was called and it took three attempts to locate someone in court who could act as interpreter for her. The first volunteer, 'an old man … on crutches', was sworn in but was unable to interpret what she said. Then it was proposed that Honor

37 County of Donegal, schedule of presentments, spring 1876, Donegal County Archives, Lifford.

38 Annual report of local government board for Ireland, being the 11th report under the Local Government Board (Ireland) Act, 35 & 36 Vict., c. 69 (1883), p. 214.

39 *Irish equity reports argued and determined in the high court of chancery, the rolls court, and the equity exchequer during the years 1843 and 1844* (1844), vi, pp 80–2.

40 The court of king's bench was divided in two – a criminal side and a civil side, the *nisi prius* court.

41 *Saunders's News-Letter*, 7 Nov. 1836.

42 *Freeman's Journal*, 29 May 1838.

Burke could in fact speak English and that she be asked 'on her oath can she speak English'. A man called William Ormsby was produced and sworn and declared that he knew Honor Burke and heard her speak English. Then, an attorney named Egan made an attempt, but said 'that the Irish he [*sic*] spoke was so difficult to understand that he would not undertake the task of examining her'. Finally, Mr Henderson, 'a Galway gentleman', was sworn in and 'she answered all his questions not only with fluency but with apparent eloquence.'[43] In 1839 in *Hennon v. Lynch*, a damages case heard at the court of common pleas, an interpreter was brought from Galway to interpret for an Irish-speaking witness who refused to give evidence unless he was paid 12 shillings a day plus travel expenses as had been promised by the plaintiff. He was threatened with imprisonment and then withdrawn.[44]

In 1859, at the court of probate, in a case about the validity of a will, an interpreter was needed to examine an Irish-speaking witness and a Mr Brown, also a witness, who had already been examined, was proposed. The court at first declined this proposal, but then decided to allow it 'upon the understanding that the defendant's solicitor, who likewise could speak Irish, would check the evidence'.[45] In 1869 Dr McEvilly, bishop of Galway, was subpoenaed as a witness at the court of common pleas and then recruited as interpreter for the plaintiff's mother.[46]

In 1877 the Galtee Boy libel case at the court of queen's bench involved two Irish-speaking witnesses.[47] Isaac Butt, acting for defendant John Sarsfield Casey, 'asked was there no one in court who could interpret the evidence?' and, when nobody volunteered, complained that 'such a fact was a disgrace to the country'. The registrar 'appealed to Mr Butt', perhaps expecting him to interpret, but 'Mr Butt said in a jocular way that he thought it was the duty of the Clerk of the Crown to interpret the evidence.' An interpreter, a Mr Dwyer, was found but 'Considerable laughter was caused by the witness frequently answering in English to questions put by counsel before the interpreter had translated them.'[48] A second witness, John Shaughnessy, managed to answer some questions about rent and his family in English but ran into difficulty when it came to reclamation, and even more problems when the judge asked him 'whether it was the March gale [rent] he was paying'. Another witness, Mr Riordan, was sworn in as interpreter, despite objections from Mr Heron for the prosecution. The defendant was about to go looking for an interpreter, but Mr Butt, 'thinking he was about to interpret, said – "It would be still worse with Mr Casey."' Mr Butt most likely meant that it would be worse because Casey was the defendant. In the end, Revd John Walsh, 'who was present, proffered himself as an interpreter, and was sworn'.[49]

43 *Tuam Herald*, 1 June 1839.
44 *Freeman's Journal*, 15 June 1839.
45 *Irish Times*, 5 Dec. 1859.
46 *Freeman's Journal*, 13 May 1869.
47 *Weekly Irish Times*, 8 Dec. 1877.
48 *Freeman's Journal*, 3 Dec. 1877.
49 *Freeman's Journal*, 4 Dec. 1877.

CONCLUSION

The initiative to provide salaried interpreters came originally from the grand juries, who were dealing with Irish speakers on a daily basis. Interestingly, there was also pressure from lawyers and judges, who were concerned that justice could not be served otherwise. Interpreters like Simon Conway and Owen McGoolrick also played their parts. Nicholas Wolf has suggested that Irish speakers 'helped drive these changes by seeking redress in the courts, by insisting on using Irish when giving testimony',[50] but monolingual Irish speakers had no choice – if they were to appear in court, they could only speak Irish. Nor did they have a voice – they could only communicate with officialdom through an interpreter. Parliament did not appreciate the urgency of the need for interpreter provision and was extremely tardy about introducing legislation. While the solution of providing salaried court interpreters was unique to Ireland – there was no such system in Wales or Scotland, for example – and, it could be argued, very innovative for its time, it has to be seen in a particular context. The system was restricted to criminal cases at assizes and quarter sessions and did not encompass the petty sessions courts. Significantly, interpreters were made available to monolingual Irish speakers only and, as will become evident throughout this book, there was constant pressure to speak English.

50 Wolf, *An Irish-speaking island*, p. 149.

CHAPTER THREE

The extent of interpreter provision

THIS CHAPTER EXAMINES interpreter provision at three key points: 1807, 1841–3 and 1898–1901, in order to establish which grand juries employed interpreters and for how long. These dates correspond to government reports detailing interpreter provision. The data for 1807, focusing mainly on the assizes, is taken from a report detailing interpreter payments by eighteen grand juries.[1] The data for 1841–3 is taken from an appendix to the *Minutes of evidence taken before Her Majesty's commissioners of inquiry into the state of the law and practice in relation to the occupation of land in Ireland*, which contains a 'statement of county cess' (1845). This statement contains invaluable information on the overall spend on interpreters at assizes and quarter sessions by eighteen grand juries, not all of which were included in the earlier data set. This information was used to estimate retrospectively how many grand juries employed interpreters at the earlier date of 1807. The information relating to the end of the century is drawn from two government reports: *Grand jury officers (Ireland) return* (1898) and *Local government (Ireland) officials* (1901), supplemented by grand jury books of presentments. These sources show that the actual extent of interpreter provision, in terms of both geography and time, is far greater than previously believed.

INTERPRETER PROVISION IN 1807

Accounts presented to the house of commons, of the presentments passed by the grand juries of Ireland, at the spring and summer assizes, in the year 1807 provides the information on interpreters contained in table 1. The report lists the salaries of interpreters and of other officers of the court before the introduction of salaries for interpreters at quarter sessions. The information on interpreters has been extracted from more detailed information for each county.

According to these accounts, in 1807, of the forty grand juries, eighteen employed court interpreters. Most interpreters were paid a half-year's salary of £5 as laid down by law, although in the city of Limerick the rate had dropped to £3 8*s.* 3*d.* and the assizes interpreter in Donegal was only paid £6 for the year. Despite the absence of legislation providing for salaried interpreters at quarter sessions, there are two instances of payments to interpreters for their work at quarter

1 *Accounts presented to the house of commons, of the presentments passed by the grand juries of Ireland, at the spring and summer assizes, in the year 1807*, HC 1808.

Table 1 Interpreter presentments, 1807

Cavan	Summer • To sheriff for providing criers and interpreters, £22 15*s.* 0*d.* • To an interpreter this assizes, £5
Clare	Spring • To Michael Canny, deputy clerk of the crown, for his attendance at this assizes, £20 • To same, as interpreter in the crown court, £10 • To same, as interpreter in the record court, £10 • To Daniel Mangan, for acting as interpreter, £5 Summer • To Michael Canny, deputy clerk of the crown, for his attendance at this assizes, £20 • To same, as interpreter in the crown court, £10 • To same, for supplying an interpreter in the record court, £10
City of Cork	Spring • Thomas Neale, interpreter of the Irish language, £3 8*s.* 3*d.* Summer • Robert Stunnell, interpreter of the Irish language, £3 8*s.* 3*d.*
County of Cork	Spring • To the interpreter, the like (i.e. half-year's salary), £5 Summer • To the interpreter, half-year's salary, £5
Donegal assizes	Lent • To the Irish interpreter, £2 • John Farrel, for interpreting at sessions, £5 • To the interpreter, £2 Summer • To the Irish interpreter, £2 • John Farrel, for interpreting at sessions, £5
Fermanagh assizes	Summer • To Robert Petty, for interpreting Irish, £5
County of Kilkenny	Lent • To the clerk of the crown, for providing an interpreter, £5
City of Limerick assizes	Spring • To Thomas Egan, for having attended the court this assizes as interpreter, £2 10*s.* 0*d.* Summer • To Thomas Egan, for having attended the court this assizes as interpreter, £5
County of Mayo	Spring • To James Clerk, interpreter, salary at special commission and this assizes, £10 Summer • To James Clerk, interpreter, £5

County of Meath	Lent • To George Ladley, as interpreter, half a year's salary, £5
County of Roscommon	Spring • To Edward Henderson, interpreter to the crown court, this assizes, £5
County of Tipperary	Summer • W. Bakerville, interpreter at this assizes, £5; same at last Nenagh sessions, £4 • To William Rigney, acting as interpreter in crown court, £5 • Timothy McDermot, cryer and interpreter, 'was nil'd'
County of Tyrone	Lent • To Hugh O'Friel, for interpreting, £5
County of Waterford	Spring • Interpreter, £5 Summer • J. Hearne, interpreter, £5
City of Waterford	Spring • Interpreter, £5
County of Westmeath	Lent • High sheriff, for providing cryers and interpreters, £11 7*s.* 6*d.* Summer • High sheriff, for providing cryers and interpreters, £11 7*s.* 6*d.*
County of Wexford	Lent • To John Bourne, deputy clerk of the crown, for having provided an interpreter this assizes, £5 Summer • To the clerk of the crown, for providing an interpreter, £5
County of Wicklow	Spring • To the clerk of the crown, for providing an interpreter, £5 Summer • To John Bourne, deputy clerk of the crown, for providing an interpreter pursuant to the statute, £5

sessions, in Donegal and Tipperary. The county of Clare is an anomaly: Michael Canny was paid £40 a year as clerk of the crown, plus £20 for interpreting in the crown court and £10 for interpreting in the record court. He was also paid £10 for supplying an interpreter in the record court, while the named interpreter, Daniel Mangan, was paid half this amount. The presence of Wicklow is surprising because of its proximity to Dublin and because it was 'the only county in which the figures [for Irish speakers] in none of these three censuses [1851, 1861 and 1881] passed 2.5% in any barony'.[2]

2 G. FitzGerald, 'Estimates for baronies of minimum level of Irish-speaking amongst successive decennial cohorts: 1771–1781 to 1861–1871', *Proceedings of the Royal Irish Academy*, 84:3 (1984), pp 117–55 at p. 138.

There are some problems with the accounts for 1807. They do not include any presentments for the towns of Carrickfergus and Galway, or for the counties of Monaghan and Sligo. In addition, while the presentments for counties Galway and Kerry are included, they are very brief and do not include a breakdown of salaries. Similar problems arise for Armagh, Down, the town of Drogheda, Leitrim, Limerick and Longford. This posed a problem: apart from the eighteen grand juries listed in table 1, where else were interpreters provided in 1807?

An answer to this question was found in the appendix to the *Minutes of evidence taken before Her Majesty's commissioners of inquiry into the state of the law and practice in relation to the occupation of land in Ireland*, which contains a statement of county cess (1845) for thirty-eight grand juries (all except the city of Limerick and the town of Drogheda) and includes twice-yearly payments to court interpreters at assizes and quarter sessions in 1841, 1842 and 1843. This information consists of the amount paid each year by the grand juries and does not include names of interpreters or courts. Interpreters' salaries appeared as a separate item which had to be completed by the grand juries and the accuracy of this set of data has been confirmed by comparisons with books of presentments for various counties. The heading 'Salary for interpreter' is provided for all counties except the city of Dublin, where there was no such post. Over this three-year period, the amount paid in each county is static, an indicator that the need for interpreters was steady throughout this time. This source shows that salaried county interpreters were still employed by eighteen grand juries in 1841–3,[3] as outlined in table 2.

These figures are significant because they include payments to interpreters by seven grand juries that were not included in the 1807 figures: namely the county and the town of Galway, Kerry, Leitrim, county of Limerick, Monaghan and Sligo. If interpreters were provided between 1841 and 1843, then the likelihood is that they were also provided in 1807. Therefore, the figure for interpreter provision by grand juries in 1807 in the preceding section can be raised from eighteen to twenty-five. Armagh can also be added because the last payment to an interpreter in that county was in spring 1807.[4] That makes twenty-six.

The situation regarding Louth is problematic. The earliest surviving nineteenth-century book of presentments for County Louth is for 1810, and includes a payment of £2 5*s.* 6*d.* to Charles Connor, cryer, for acting as an interpreter. This may have been a one-off payment or one of a series. In 1820 there was a payment of £5 to the clerk of the peace for providing an interpreter. However, there were no

3 According to the statement of county cess, in 1841–3, no interpreter salaries were paid in the counties of Antrim, Armagh, Carlow, Down, Dublin, Fermanagh, Kildare, Londonderry, Longford, Louth, Meath, Westmeath, Wexford, Wicklow, King's County, Queen's County, cities of Kilkenny and Waterford and the town of Carrickfergus.

4 Interpreter salaries appear in the Armagh books of presentments for 1797–1801 and 1805–7, PRONI.

Table 2 Interpreter presentments, 1841–3

County of	Lent 1841	Summer 1841	Lent 1842	Summer 1842	Lent 1843	Summer 1843
Cavan	£7 10*s.*	£7 10*s.*	£7 10*s.*	£7 10*s.*	£7 10*s.*	£7 10*s.*
Clare	£5	£5	£5	£5	£5	£5
Cork	£40	£35	£35	£35	£35	£35
City of Cork	£3	£3	£3	£3	£3	£3
Donegal	£20	£5	£20	£20	£20	£20
Galway	£20	£20	£20	£20	£20	£20
Galway town	£5	£5	£5	£5	£5	£5
Kerry	£20	£20	£20	£20	£20	£20
Kilkenny	£5	£5	£5	£5	£5	£5
Leitrim	£10	£10	£10	£10	£10	£10
Limerick	£20	£17 10*s.*	£20	£20	£20	£20
Mayo	£30	£30	£30	£30	£30	£30
Monaghan	£1 10*s.*	–	£1 10*s.*	£1 10*s.*	£1 10*s.*	£1 10*s.*
Roscommon	£7 10*s.*	£7 10*s.*	£7 10*s.*	£7 10*s.*	£7 10*s.*	£7 10*s.*
Sligo	£20	£20	£20	£20	£20	£20
Tipperary	£20	£20	£20	£20	£20	£20
Tyrone	£5	£5	£5	£5	£5	£5
Waterford	£7 2*s.* 4*d.*	–	£7 2*s.* 4*d.*	£7 2*s.* 4*d.*	£7 2*s.* 4*d.*	£7 2*s.* 4*d.*

payments to interpreters in 1815, or 1823–40.[5] According to the 1851 census, 18.7 per cent of the population of Louth spoke Irish and English, and the percentage of monolingual Irish speakers was very low, at 0.06 per cent. Still, it is possible that in 1807 salaried interpreters were provided in Louth, which would give us a total of twenty-seven.

The situation in Longford is not altogether clear as Longford County Archives do not have printed abstracts of presentments for the years between 1778 and 1816. Their manuscript records indicate that interpreters were not provided between 1759 and 1777, when one was provided. The problem with manuscript records is that there may be more than one version. For example, in Cavan County Library, there are two sets of manuscript books of presentments for summer 1812, Lent 1813

5 IE LHA G5, Louth County Archives Service, Dundalk.

and spring and summer 1815, with payments to interpreters included in one set of books but not in the other. It is possible that interpreters were provided in Longford in 1807 because: (1) there is a precedent in 1777; (2) interpreters were provided in the surrounding counties of Cavan, Leitrim, Roscommon and Westmeath; and (3) decades later, in 1851, 'there were probably still small Irish-speaking communities in the Baronies of Granard and Longford in the north, and Rathcline in the west'.[6] That makes a tentative twenty-eight (70 per cent) of the forty grand juries. This is a sizeable proportion, and higher than would generally be expected.[7]

If we map out the information contained in the presentment records for eighteen grand juries in 1807 plus the Armagh grand jury presentments for the same year, and information on seven additional grand juries from 1841–3, plus Longford and Louth, we obtain the picture of salaried court interpreter provision in 1807 depicted in figure 1.

The map in figure 1 is broadly similar to Reg Hindley's more detailed reconstruction of the Irish language in 1800 based on literary sources and the censuses for 1851, 1881 and 1911. In this context, the words of Edward O'Reilly in the preface to *Sanas Gaoidhilge Sagsbeurla: An Irish English dictionary*, published in 1817, make sense:

> The great utility of this language to the lawyer, is proved frequently in the year. In every county, at every sessions, trials occur in which prisoners or witnesses can be heard only through the medium of an interpreter, probably but ill qualified for such an office, and who, by the mistake of a single word in the evidence, may cause the acquittal of a murderer, or the murder of an innocent.

INTERPRETER PROVISION IN 1841–3

By 1841, salaried court interpreters were no longer employed in Armagh, Fermanagh, Longford, Louth, Meath, Westmeath, Wexford, the city of Waterford or Wicklow, but provision was unchanged for the remainder of the country. The situation in towns and cities is of interest. Interpreters continued to be provided in the city of Cork and the town of Galway in 1843, but not in the city of Waterford (although the post was later reintroduced there). The city of Limerick was not included in the statement of county cess, but according to newspaper reports an

6 B. Ó Cuív, *Irish dialects and Irish-speaking districts* (Dublin, 1980), p. 24.

7 In the case of Carlow, books of presentments date back to 1800 and there are records of payments of £11 7*s.* 6*d.* to the sub-sheriff for providing two interpreters, in both 1812 and 1814. In Queen's County (Laois), where records commence in 1805, there is one record of a payment of £5 to the sheriff for providing interpreters in 1816. Interestingly, an interpreter was in attendance at the 1818 elections, suggesting the presence of some Irish speakers. In King's County (Offaly), where records start in 1830, no payments were found. The Kildare records start quite early, in 1791, but no payments to interpreters were located.

Figure 1 Interpreter provision in 1807

Figure 2 Interpreter provision in 1841–3

interpreter was employed there until 1854.[8] Consequently, the city of Limerick can be added to the other eighteen grand juries which paid salaries to interpreters in 1841–3, thus making a total of nineteen.

If we consider interpreter provision on the basis of the four provinces, the map in figure 2 above shows that interpreter provision in the province of Leinster is confined to the county of Kilkenny. The situation in the province of Ulster had also changed; interpreters were still provided in Cavan, Monaghan, and of course Donegal but provision had ceased in Fermanagh,[9] which is somewhat surprising given that it was surrounded by counties that did employ interpreters. In Tyrone, Stephen Nealus or Nealis worked as an interpreter from 1826 until his death in 1859,[10] after which he was not replaced. Provision ceased in Armagh in 1807. By contrast, in Connaught and Munster, interpreter provision continued unchanged in 1843 with all grand juries employing interpreters.

INTERPRETER PROVISION IN 1898

At the turn of the century there were substantial changes compared to 1843, with salaried interpreters no longer provided in the counties of Cavan, Kilkenny, Limerick, Monaghan, Roscommon and Tyrone and the cities of Limerick and Waterford. Searches of books of presentments reveal that in 1898, salaried interpreters were still employed by ten grand juries – Clare, county of Cork, Donegal, town of Galway,[11] county of Galway, Kerry, Mayo, Sligo, Tipperary's south riding, and county of Waterford, – or by a quarter of the grand juries. While most grand juries employed one interpreter, there were two in Cork, Donegal and Sligo and three in Galway. Although it is not at all surprising to find that salaried interpreters were still active in Clare, Cork, Donegal, Galway, Kerry, Mayo and Waterford, it is surprising that interpreters continued to be employed in Sligo and Tipperary at the end of the nineteenth century. There was a charitable reason for continued provision in Tipperary's south riding; the situation of interpreter Michael Nugent was discussed at a north Tipperary council meeting in 1899 where a Mr Trench was in favour of abolishing the position. However, solicitor Mr Power, who seemed to know Nugent, suggested that the interpreter should continue to be paid, as he was about 85 years of age, not entitled to superannuation, and this was 'his only means of sustenance'. The council agreed to this proposal.[12] Figure 3 shows the

8 *Limerick & Clare Examiner*, 8 Feb. 1854.

9 A search of the Fermanagh books of presentments in PRONI proved fruitless as salaries were not recorded in the years 1792–1819; the book of presentments for 1822–33 also did not include salaries. There was no record of payment to an interpreter in the presentments laid on the county of Fermanagh at summer assizes 1838, NLI.

10 Tyrone books of presentments, PRONI.

11 The post of interpreter for the town of Galway disappeared with the passing of the Local Government Act 1898 and the decision to no longer have separate assizes there.

12 *Nenagh News*, 5 Aug. 1899.

Figure 3 Map of interpreter provision in 1898

nine counties (plus the town of Galway) where interpreters were provided in 1898.

The 1901 and 1911 censuses list very few interpreters and give an erroneous impression of the situation at that stage. Although only a minority of interpreters listed their occupation as such, this is probably because by this stage interpreting was an ancillary rather than a main source of income. In 1913 the insurance commissioners issued a special order to the effect that work as 'occasional interpreter at County Courts in Ireland and Wales' would be considered 'as subsidiary employment only, and not as the principal means of livelihood'.[13] Still, there were at least seventeen salaried interpreters in 1901 and fourteen in 1911 (see appendix A for details). County councils continued to pay court interpreters in seven counties – Clare, Cork, Donegal, Galway, Kerry, Mayo and Waterford – and possibly also in Sligo, until at least the 1920s.

Why did interpreter provision continue for so long? One important reason is because the grand juries and later the county councils were in control. Appointments and payments were made at local level. If interpreter provision had been centrally controlled by the chief secretary's office, perhaps it would have ended far earlier. Another possible reason is that the cost (a topic dealt with in the next chapter) was very low in comparison to the possible consequences of not providing interpreters. For example, in 1849 at Tipperary spring assizes, Mr Gason questioned the need for an interpreter but Mr Sadlier responded that 'if the interpreter were removed, you would find very many unable to speak anything but Irish'.[14] Such a situation could result in undesirable delays and adjournments and consequent inconvenience and expense for all concerned. It was more convenient to provide an interpreter just in case. A third reason emerged at the end of the nineteenth century with the Gaelic League playing an active role in highlighting Irish language issues and access to interpreters at their meetings and in letters to newspapers. Fear of negative coverage and bad publicity may well have become a factor at that stage. A fourth linked reason, from 1898 onwards, when elected councils replaced the grand juries, may have been the reluctance of councillors who were dependent on votes to eliminate the post of interpreter in Irish-speaking areas. A fifth reason was suggested at a case heard at Dingle quarter sessions in 1913 where Dr O'Connell for the plaintiff advised new county court judge Dromgoole to allow 'a number of Irish witnesses who will not speak English' to speak Irish through the interpreter because otherwise 'if one makes a mistake it will be a cant in the district for years'.[15] The implication here is that the witnesses are bilingual but their preference is to speak their first language, which is Irish. Dromgoole agreed but perhaps O'Connell took advantage of the fact that he was newly appointed and unfamiliar with how interpreter provision normally worked.

13 *Ballymena Observer*, 10 Jan. 1913.
14 *Tipperary Vindicator*, 24 Mar. 1849.
15 *Kerryman*, 26 Apr. 1913.

CONCLUSION

Interpreter provision at assizes and quarter sessions was far more widespread and longer-lasting than previously believed. The extent of interpreter provision in 1807, with definitely twenty-six and probably at least twenty-eight out of forty grand juries paying salaries, is greater than many would expect. Moreover, even more grand juries may have provided interpreters previous to 1807; this is certainly the case for Londonderry, where interpreters were provided until 1801 and may possibly be the case for Carlow, King's County and Queen's County. In 1843, court interpreters were provided by nineteen grand juries, a figure that was further reduced to ten in 1898 and eight in 1921. For information on when interpreter provision ended in each county, see chapter 12.

CHAPTER FOUR

Remuneration of salaried interpreters

EACH HALF-YEAR, THE grand juries could pay court interpreters a maximum of £5 at assizes and, from 1837, £15 at quarter sessions. These were good salaries for seasonal work, good enough in the first half of the nineteenth century for professionals and men of property to consider it worth their while to take on this role. However, court interpreters were treated differently from other court officials in two important ways. The first was that they were not entitled to fees.[1] For example, in 1848, a total of £16,201 18*s.* 10*d.* in fees was paid to 555 clerks at petty sessions, an average of £29 each over and above their salary.[2] Court criers were also paid fees. The second was that, unlike other officials, interpreters were not entitled to superannuation paid by the grand jury, which explains why so many of them continued to work for as long as they were able. In 1884, an unnamed partially deaf interpreter at Cork assizes was described by Mr Justice O'Brien as someone who 'possessed no intelligence whatever'. The context was a trial on a count of felonious killing where the defendant could not speak or understand English, and the interpreter could not be found. The judge commented that 'that was always the way in that court', and after some time the interpreter appeared. The judge described the situation as a 'public scandal' and a Constable Dowling was sworn as interpreter.[3] Deafness was not an obstacle to some judges, who continued working; a Tipperary judge reportedly thought an action for the price of a Singer sewing machine concerned a dispute between singers over a harmonium.[4]

How did interpreters' salaries compare to other salaries? The salaries of teachers provide a useful point of comparison. John Leslie Foster, commissioner of education, wrote in 1811 that 'the whole reward of the annual labour of a [hedgeschool] master appears to be on average from 30*l* (pounds) to 40*l* per annum, who for this sum is to find a school-house, and maintain his family'.[5] Foster suggested that the potential income was not sufficient to encourage qualified, educated people to become school teachers. In 1851, Hugh Dorian's starting salary as a national school teacher was £15. In addition, the pupils each paid a fee of one shilling, which

1 Of course, from the point of view of Irish speakers it was advantageous not to be expected to pay fees to interpreters.
2 *Petty sessions clerks (Ireland): a return, showing the number of petty sessions, the number of clerks, and the amount of fees received by them in each county of Ireland in the year 1848*, HC 1850 (304) li, 527.
3 *Freeman's Journal*, 19 Mar. 1884.
4 J. McArdle, *Irish legal anecdotes* (Dublin, 1995), p. 111.
5 *Reports from the commissioners of the board of education in Ireland, 1809–12*, HC 1812 (342), 47, i, p. 342.

equated to another £8 per annum, making his total pay £23.[6] Those interpreters who worked at both assizes and quarter sessions could potentially earn £40 for the year. However, this was not always possible and assizes interpreters' salaries were capped at £10 a year, not a huge amount given the responsibility of interpreting at serious trials. Furthermore, as some grand juries reduced the pay in line with the reduction in demand, the job, although part-time, probably became less attractive. Interpreters needed to combine their work as interpreters with other sources of income in order to cover travel expenses and make a living (see appendix B). In 1807 the full rate of £5 per half-year was paid to interpreters at assizes, with just one exception, the city of Cork, where the amount had been reduced to £3 8*s*. 3*d*. By the 1840s, however, according to surviving books of presentments, nine grand juries had reduced their rates considerably.

Table 3 Reduced rates for interpreters

County of	Year	Half-year's salary	Payments to interpreters
Cavan	1843	£7 10*s*.	• Terence Dolan, £1 10*s*., Ballyconnell sessions • Patt Smith, quarter sessions and assizes, £6[7]
Clare	1843	£5	• Pat Blake, assizes, £5[8]
City of Cork	1845	£3	• Bartholomew Neenan, £3[9]
Kilkenny	1843	£5	• Richard Hickey, assizes, £3 • John Ryan, sessions, £2[10]
Leitrim	1843	£10	• Book of presentment not found
Monaghan	1838	£1 10*s*.	• Michael Monaghan, assizes, £1 10*s*.[11]
Roscommon	1844	£7 10*s*.	• Interpreters, £7 10*s*.[12]
Tyrone	1843	£5	• Stephen Nealus, assizes and quarter sessions, £5[13]
Waterford	1841	£7 2*s*. 4*d*.	• Assizes, £4 12*s*. 4*d*. • Quarter sessions, £2 10*s*.[14]

6 Dorian, Hugh, *The outer edge of Ulster: a memoir of social life in the nineteenth century*, ed. B. Mac Suibhne and D. Dickson (Dublin, 2000).
7 County of Cavan, abstract of presentments granted spring assizes 1843, NAI.
8 County of Clare, undischarged quaeres and abstract of presentments granted at spring assizes held in Ennis, on 25 February 1843, NAI.
9 *Cork Examiner*, 2 July 1845.
10 County of Kilkenny spring assizes 1843, Kilkenny County Library.
11 County of Monaghan, a schedule of applications for presentments, spring 1838, NLI and Monaghan Local Studies, Clones.
12 County of Roscommon, schedule of applications for presentments applied for and taken from the applications, lodged with the secretary of the grand jury, summer 1844, Roscommon County Library.
13 County Tyrone books of presentments, TYR 14/1/62, PRONI.
14 Statement of the accounts of the treasurer of the county of Waterford spring assizes 1841, NLI.

While the majority of reductions in salaries were most likely due to a reduction in demand for interpreters, it is surprising that there was no payment for interpreting at quarter sessions in Clare. However, this was remedied by 1854 when full payments were made to the two interpreters at assizes and quarter sessions. In Tyrone, Stephen Nealus' salary was increased to £15 per half-year in 1848. However, in the county of Waterford, the salary at quarter sessions increased to £5 in 1854 but never reached the full amount of £15.

The mechanism for a reduction in salary lay in challenges by members of the grand juries. Some challenges were overruled but others were successful. For example, in 1840, at the county of Kilkenny assizes, Captain Bryan objected to the quarter sessions crier being paid an additional salary for acting as interpreter because 'he had no notion of voting away the public money to the servant of a gentleman who was paid £3500 a year by the country'. As a result of this intervention, the interpreter's salary was reduced to £2.[15] In 1850, in Cavan, the interpreter's presentment was passed by the grand jury despite some opposition. However, this may have been the last occasion on which an interpreter was paid there.[16] Similarly, in 1856 at county of Limerick assizes, the foreman of the grand jury queried why interpreter Roger Green was to be paid a double salary, one at assizes and one at quarter sessions and was supported by Sir D. Roche, who stated that 'There is no reason why he should get more at the quarter sessions than at the Assizes.' Mr C. Powell commented that 'His services are but seldom in requisition.' Despite the discussion, the presentments were passed.[17] Likewise, in 1860, at Tipperary's north riding spring assizes, Mr Lanigan 'asked if the situation was necessary, as he hadn't known an instance for several years of the interpreter's services being required'. Once again, the presentment was passed.[18]

In 1898, ten grand juries still employed interpreters. All interpreters working at assizes were paid £5 per half-year and most interpreters at quarter sessions were paid £15. However, there were discrepancies. In the county of Galway, all interpreters, whether at assizes or quarter sessions, were paid £5. In Sligo, one interpreter at quarter sessions was paid £5 while the other was paid half that amount. In the county of Waterford, the Dungarvan quarter sessions interpreter, who also interpreted at Waterford assizes, was paid £3. In Donegal, Daniel Boyce was paid £5 for interpreting at assizes and £10 for interpreting at division of Lifford quarter sessions while Condy Boyle was paid £5 for his work at me division of Donegal quarter sessions. However, two government reports shed further light on the situation in Donegal. According to the 1898 *Grand Jury Officers (Ireland) Return*, Condy Boyle was paid the large amount of £80 in salary plus fees. The

15 *Kilkenny Journal*, 14 Mar. 1840.
16 *Anglo-Celt*, 5 July 1850.
17 *Limerick Reporter*, 26 Feb. 1856.
18 *Nenagh Guardian*, 17 Mar. 1860.

1901 report *Local government (Ireland) officials* breaks this figure down into a salary of £16 plus emoluments (extra payments) of £64, while Daniel Boyce was paid £43 plus emoluments of £60. No further information was found on the date of introduction of the lucrative system of emoluments in Donegal or their existence elsewhere.

The Local Government (Ireland) Act 1898 led to changes and amalgamations that affected interpreters. Questions were raised in the house of commons about some interpreters' pay, questions answered by the chief secretaries of the day. Patrick O'Sullivan, of Killorglin, County Kerry, had been working as a court interpreter on a salary of £30 per year and was doing work previously carried out by two interpreters.[19] Almost a decade earlier, in 1889, the County Kerry grand jury had expressed support for his application for an increase in pay. It seems that O'Sullivan had to pay his own train and hotel expenses, resulting in expenditure of £140 per year when his daily rate was 4*s.* 3*d.* per day. However, Gerald Balfour, chief secretary for Ireland, maintained that the lord chancellor of Ireland had no power in this matter and that a case had not been made to justify an increase in salary.[20]

Under the 1898 act, Galway town and county were merged and as a result 'the interpreter of Irish has lost the emoluments he received from the town grand jury, and is obliged to do for nothing work for which £25 a year was previously paid'. In the house of commons, Mr Wyndham explained that the amalgamation took place in January 1900 and the interpreter was appointed in March 1901, which meant that he was not an existing officer under section 109 of the act and had no grounds for claiming compensation.[21]

In October 1906, the position of interpreter in the Loughrea division of County Galway became vacant. The work involved attending quarter sessions in four towns, but on a salary of £10 with no allowance for expenses under the Local Government Act. The matter was raised in the house of commons and the reply from Mr Augustine Birrell, another chief secretary for Ireland, indicates that the maximum annual amount the county council could pay was £30, which was divided by the three different divisions in the county, Galway, Clifden and Loughrea. He accepted that recruiting an interpreter in Loughrea had been difficult and said the matter could be considered at a later date if amendments were made to the Local Government Act,[22] which was unlikely. Further questions were raised in 1911 on behalf of 'Antony McDonnell',[23] with Mr Birrell providing a similar answer, but

19 O'Sullivan had begun as a quarter sessions interpreter in the spring of 1873, work he shared with assizes interpreter Michael Collins. O'Sullivan was paid £7 per half-year until the death of Collins in 1887, when he became interpeter at both assizes and quarters sessions, on a combined salary of £40 per annum.

20 HC Debates, 4 Mar. 1898, vol. 54, cc 603–4.

21 HC Debates, 22 July 1902, vol. 111, cc 88–9.

22 HC Debates, 27 Mar. 1907, vol. 171, cc 1776–7.

23 Anthony O'Donnell is referred to as Anthony McDonell in HC Debates.

with an additional explanation that the Local Government Act had put an end to an allowance for acting as interpreter in city cases at the recorder's court.[24] In 1920, Galway county council agreed to pay Anthony O'Donnell a war bonus of £25 in addition to his salary of £30. The *Connacht Tribune* reported that 'his predecessor was getting a salary of £55',[25] but this seems unlikely unless this figure included additional emoluments. In August 1920, Cork county council decided that they did not recognize county court judges and therefore did not recognize any court officials, including interpreters, and refused to sanction any payments.[26] Some interpreters (Michael McNamara in Clare, Edward Collins in Cork) later successfully challenged such decisions in court.

Nicholas Wolf has suggested that interpreter provision was 'a relatively significant cost',[27] but was that really the case? In 1807, the total cost of interpreter provision for twenty-seven grand juries was around £300; in 1841–3, with fewer grand juries paying county interpreters at assizes, but greater expenses in the form of twice-yearly payments of a maximum of £15 at quarter sessions, the total cost was around £500. To provide some context, in 1840 a total of £99,272 was spent by all the grand juries on salaries of county officers out of a total expenditure of £1,269,879.[28] A mere 0.5 per cent of county officers' salaries or 0.04 per cent of total expenditure was being spent on interpreters. In 1898, by which time ten grand juries provided interpreters, the cost was approximately £400, including emoluments paid to interpreters in Donegal. No central funding was needed to pay interpreters; instead, the salaries were raised locally, on a county-by-county basis and only those counties that employed interpreters had to pay their salaries.

CONCLUSION

Salaried court interpreters were treated differently from other officials employed by the grand juries. They were not entitled to fees or superannuation, possibly because it was felt that their work would not be required in the long term. However, this was also a way of undervaluing the work of interpreters, who were subject to the whims and vagaries of particular members of the grand jury who objected to their salaries being paid or who felt they should be reduced. While there was local sympathy for the plight of Patrick O'Sullivan in Kerry, no mechanism was found to increase his pay above the amount permissible by law. However, Donegal grand jury managed to find a way to pay emoluments to Condy Boyle and Daniel Boyce.

24 HC Debates, 31 July 1911, vol. 29, c. 160.
25 *Connacht Tribune*, 7 Feb. 1920.
26 *Cork Examiner*, 6 Aug. 1920.
27 Wolf, *An Irish-speaking island*, p. 156.
28 *Commissioners to revise laws by which monies are raised by grand jury presentments in Ireland: reports, minutes and appendix* (1842), p. ix.

CHAPTER FIVE

Appointment of interpreters

PRIOR TO 1922, Irish-language court interpreters were exclusively male and were literate; some manuscript versions of early grand jury books of presentments include the interpreters' signatures when they collected their pay. Also, some wrote to the chief secretary's office at Dublin Castle requesting salary increases or payments for extra work. Therefore, Irish interpreters or their families had enough economic capital to ensure that they could obtain a basic education; rather than being expected to work on the family farm, or in a shop or as a servant or a labourer, they were able to attend school. They were also in an environment where they were exposed to both Irish and English. Perhaps, however, in a system that relied heavily on patronage, their most important asset was social capital, the network of contacts that ensured they could request letters of recommendation from influential members of the community in order to obtain employment.

However, the largest single group of interpreters was made up of summons servers, process servers and civil bill officers who all did similar work, but were attached to different courts. All had to travel considerable distances and keep records of when and where summonses were served and attend their respective courts. Summons servers were attached to the lowest courts, the petty sessions, and had to be able to read and write. They served summonses in all cases except those prosecuted by the constabulary. Process servers, who were appointed by assistant barristers, were attached to the quarter sessions courts and paid £10 a year plus a fee of six pence for every process under £10 actually served, and one shilling for sums over that amount. If they could not serve a process, they were not entitled to any payment. A letter to the *Irish Times* in 1881 described the life of a process server: 'Starting at break of day and before it, plodding away, receiving curses at every step, shunned and feared or hated by every one, the process-server arrives back late at night, hungry, weary, and footsore, after his journey of forty miles, by which he is fortunate if he has made perhaps three or four shillings.'[1] According to Mr Ussher, a solicitor from Lurgan, between salary and payments less car hire, civil bill[2] officers earned approximately £22 a year, which,

1 *Irish Times*, 28 Sept. 1881.

2 A civil bill 'was a short document containing the names of plaintiff and defendant, a short statement of the plaintiff's cause of action, and the date and place on and at which the defendant was to appear to answer the plainitff's claim. The document was to be served personally on the defendant at least six days before the commencement of assizes'. D.S. Greer, 'The development of civil bill procedure in Ireland' in J. McEldowney and P. O'Higgins (eds), *The common law tradition* (Dublin, 1990), p. 28.

according to him, was 'manifestly insufficient remuneration for the services he renders, especially when it is taken into account that the nature of his duties prevents him from engaging in any settled occupation at which he might earn a livelihood'. Furthermore, if he were to fall ill or have an accident, he would have no earnings at all and there was no possibility of a pension, and 'he has nothing to look forward to in the evening of his days but the workhouse.'[3] Summons servers, process servers and civil bill officers were all bearers of bad news and their work was dangerous and subject to a great deal of intimidation, including physical attacks on them and their property. They cannot have been a popular choice as interpreters among Irish speakers.

The assizes salary of £10 a year was sufficient to induce James Wherland, insurance agent, conservator[4] and parish constable, to apply to the city of Cork grand jury for the post of Irish interpreter in 1833 even though he did not actually speak Irish and intended to pay a deputy to carry out the work. Presumably Wherland had calculated that he could make a profit on such an arrangement. However, Baron Foster refused to sanction the application.[5]

It was highly unusual for an interpreter to be dismissed but this is what happened in 1853 when Baron Pigott dismissed the Donegal assizes interpreter.[6] Unfortunately, the newspaper report did not include the reasons for dismissal.[7] Instead, notices were given that all persons qualified for the post should attend the first day of the Letterkenny sessions at midday 'to be examined as to their fitness for acting as Irish interpreter'.[8] No further information was found on the recruitment process in this instance.

From 1837 onwards interpreters at quarter sessions could be paid a salary of £30 a year, a tempting prospect that led to reported instances of bribery in Kerry, and there may well have been unreported instances elsewhere. As we have seen, the assistant barrister had the power to appoint and remove interpreters; it may have been unwise to concentrate this power in just one person. In June 1858 questions were raised in the house of lords about William McDermott, assistant barrister for County Kerry. Apparently, McDermott had financial problems and when the post of interpreter became vacant in 1850, he promised it to a man called Galavan in exchange for £37. This was a substantial sum of money to secure a post that would ensure an annual salary of £30. However, McDermott did not keep his word and

3 W.H. Dodd, 'Prize essay on the differences in the organization of local courts in Ireland, Scotland and England ...', *Journal of the Statistical and Social Inquiry Society of Ireland*, 7:52 (1877/8), pp 189–201 at p. 196.

4 A conservator was a person appointed to prevent nuisances. *Southern Reporter*, 19 Oct. 1833.

5 *Southern Reporter & Cork Commercial Courier*, 24 Aug. 1830.

6 Possibly James Kerrigan of Rathglass, who was interpreter at assizes and quarter sessions from at least 1840 to at least 1849.

7 Archivist Niamh Brennan very kindly checked the Donegal grand jury minutes book for 1853 and reported that proceedings were to be initiated against a long list of contractors for non-performance of contracts but found no mention of an interpreter.

8 *Ballyshannon Herald*, 23 Sept. 1853.

instead allocated the job to Michael Collins in exchange for a payment of £30. These facts emerged in court when Galavan became insolvent. Further charges were made against McDermott – that he had previously received £20 from Tralee shopkeeper Morto Hurley[9] on his appointment to the post; and that he had received £40 from another man, Thomas Griffin, but this amount had been refunded.[10] The earl of Donoughmore raised the matter in the house of lords and preparations were made for a committee to enquire into the matter, but McDermott resigned and the matter was dropped.[11]

Lawyers became involved in arguing that their clients should be appointed as interpreters, suggesting that candidates considered this expenditure as a worthwhile investment. In 1862, a barrister and a solicitor spoke at the spring assizes on behalf of recently appointed quarter sessions interpreter Henry Roach, who hoped to be appointed at assizes as well. Another applicant, Owen Dunne, represented by a solicitor only, was also interested in the post of assizes interpreter. An argument was made for Roach that for the post at quarter sessions to be worth his while, he would need to be paid £40 a year for working at both assizes and quarter sessions. Dunne's solicitor presciently suggested that Roach's other role as relieving officer would prevent him from properly filling the duties of interpreter, but this objection was overruled and Roach was unanimously appointed to both courts.[12]

In 1865, an advertisement for an interpreter at Cork's west riding quarter sessions appeared in the *Cork Examiner* (fig. 4).[13]

The procedure is not entirely clear from the advertisement and very little notice is provided to allow time for applicants to garner support and letters of recommendation. No newspaper coverage of the appointment process was located, but it seems likely that interested parties were expected to attend the sessions at the appointed time.[14] The appointee was most likely Humphrey Kelleher, also a process server.

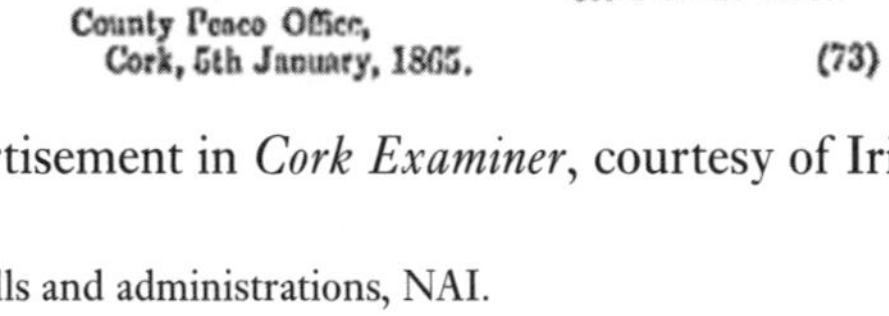
INTERPRETER WANTED.

CORK COUNTY—WEST RIDING.

I HEREBY give NOTICE that the CHAIRMAN will, at MACROOM SESSIONS, on WEDNESDAY Next, at 10 o'Clock a.m., select and appoint a fit and proper person to the Office of Interpeter for the West Riding, at a Salary of £30 a year.

NOBLE JOHNSON,
Clerk of the Peace.

County Peace Office,
Cork, 5th January, 1865. (73)

Figure 4 Advertisement in *Cork Examiner*, courtesy of Irish Newspaper Archive

9 Calendar of wills and administrations, NAI.
10 *Kerry Evening Post*, 19 June 1858.
11 A. Todd, *On parliamentary government in England* (London, 1869), ii, pp 744–5.
12 *Connaught Telegraph*, 12 Mar. 1862,
13 *Cork Examiner*, 9 Jan. 1865.
14 The county of Cork grand jury books of presentments do not name the interpreters employed between spring 1865 and spring 1899.

In 1871, Mr Rush of Ballinrobe was appointed interpreter at Mayo quarter sessions. According to the *Mayo Examiner*, the chairman 'was guided in his selection by proficiency and high character'.[15] However, Rush died a couple of months later and John H. Richards, chairman of the county and county court judge, reported at Claremorris quarter sessions that he had received fourteen applications for the post of interpreter. He said they all had 'good testimonials', 'but of all he considered Peter Rippingham of Ballinrobe, who was very highly recommended, the most eligible, he would therefore appoint him interpreter'.[16]

On the death of Rippingham in 1893, thirteen men of all ages and backgrounds applied for the post of interpreter at Mayo quarter sessions, an appointment once again at the discretion of Richards. The surviving file of letters provides very interesting insights into the applicants and their referees. Some applicants were in straitened circumstances. Thomas Hession, a 64-year-old clock maker with a 'young, long family' applied and a priest wrote a letter suggesting that it would be 'a good act of charity' to employ him. Patrick Hennelly, who worked intermittently as a steward, submitted two testimonials and suggested that the post of interpreter 'would leave me 9 months of the year at home very much to the benefit of my family consisting of my mother and three sisters who, indeed, requires help and care'.

Some emphasized their knowledge of the Irish language: retired teacher Patrick Hughes explained that he had been examined by the Board of National Education and held a certificate to show his 'completed knowledge of Irish'. John Hynes' referee wrote that 'He gave Colonel O'Hara a little law once' and 'if his flow of Irish is anything like his English he should be very valuable'. Luke Loftus stated that he spoke Irish since the age of 14. Others submitted testimonials from people in positions of authority. James Murphy was supported by a parish priest, a curate and three justices of the peace 'as he is fully acquainted with the Irish language'. Edward Maguire, son of a doctor, and an 'admirable Irish scholar', had the support of Justice of the Peace Charles Lynch.

Meanwhile, Ballinrobe rector James Treanor testified to the sobriety and good conduct of Peter Morris. Two applicants had some experience in the field: Patrick Deasy had acted as substitute interpreter at assizes for eighteen years and at October sessions for several years, 'without ever a fault having been found', while Michael Sords, also a publican, wrote that he had experience as interpreter at Ballinrobe petty sessions, in magisterial enquiries and under the Crimes Act, 'all of which being convicted with Murder and Manslaughter'. Both submitted short letters of recommendation from various justices of the peace.

In the end, the successful candidate was 26-year-old John Kane, son of a tenant of landlord Thomas Ruttledge, who provided three letters on his behalf, stating that he would be 'much obliged' if Kane got the job and offering to introduce him to Richards. Ruttledge was not just a landlord; he had been appointed magistrate

15 *Mayo Examiner*, 17 Apr. 1871.
16 *Ballinrobe Chronicle*, 24 June 1871.

in 1855[17] and sheriff in 1865, meaning he was an influential member of the grand jury.[18] Kane also submitted a short letter from Martin May, national school teacher, who certified that he could speak Irish fluently 'and also interpret it from a witness to the satisfaction of the County Court Judge'.[19] The combination of patronage and knowledge of Irish was enough to counteract youth and inexperience. However, Kane ran into difficulties in 1899 when he became embroiled in a controversial case heard by Judge Dane.

There is some evidence of local efforts to examine applicants to assess their competency for the post of interpreter. In 1881 a letter writer to the *Sligo Champion* complained that despite four candidates for the post of interpreter having been examined by Dr Cox and Mr Peter O'Connor, county court Judge Mr Hamil, QC, had appointed an unnamed person who was an outsider and who 'declined to undergo the test of examination'.[20] However, in 1895, a competitive examination was held before Dean Townsend, and John Downs of Riverstown was appointed to Sligo assizes and Ballymote quarter sessions.[21]

In June 1895, an advertisement for a new assizes interpreter appeared in the *Waterford Standard* (fig. 5). The successful candidate was civil bill officer Edward Walsh.[22] However, Walsh's experience at assizes was not sufficient to ensure his appointment to the post of interpreter at Dungarvan quarter sessions in 1902, after the changeover from grand juries to county councils. Thomas Veale (Tomás de Bhial), the successful applicant, who was only 18 years of age, was recommended by Councillor Mr Hayes, the Augustinian Fathers, several citizens of Dungarvan,

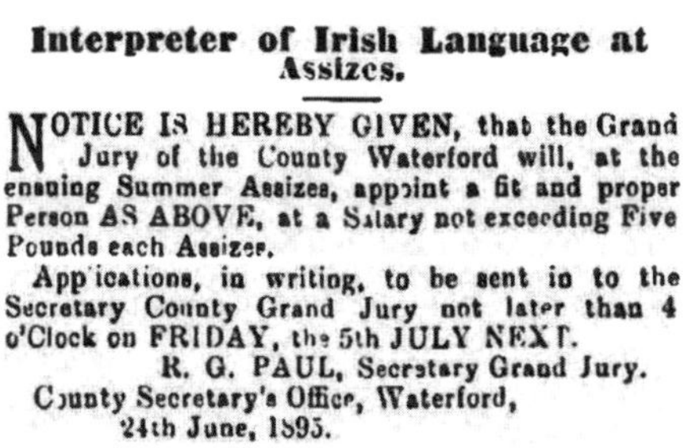

Interpreter of Irish Language at Assizes.

NOTICE IS HEREBY GIVEN, that the Grand Jury of the County Waterford will, at the ensuing Summer Assizes, appoint a fit and proper Person AS ABOVE, at a Salary not exceeding Five Pounds each Assizes.

Applications, in writing, to be sent in to the Secretary County Grand Jury not later than 4 o'Clock on FRIDAY, the 5th JULY NEXT.

R. G. PAUL, Secretary Grand Jury.

County Secretary's Office, Waterford,
24th June, 1895.

Figure 5 Advertisement in *Waterford Standard*, courtesy of British Newspaper Archive.

17 *Connaught Telegraph*, 14 Mar. 1855.
18 Ibid., 1 Mar. 1865.
19 Crown and peace records, 1C-78-51, NAI.
20 *Sligo Champion*, 9 July 1881. The interpreters are not named in the 1881 Sligo grand jury book of presentments, but in spring 1883 James Eakins was the interpreter at the quarter sessions court for Ballymote division and Thomas Ray was the interpreter at quarter sessions in Sligo division. There was also an unnamed interpreter at assizes (Sligo County Library).
21 *Sligo Champion*, 15 June 1895.
22 County of Waterford grand jury book of presentments, spring 1895, Waterford County Archives, Dungarvan.

and in a sign of changing times, in a letter in Irish from the local branch of the Irish League, and by telegram from the general secretary of the Gaelic League. Fifteen councillors voted in favour of Veale and two in favour of Walsh. A majority voted for a salary of £10 a year. Veale thanked the councillors in Irish,[23] something that previously would have been unthinkable.

In 1901 in Tralee, Mr Broderick, a local solicitor, reminded Judge Shaw, KC, that the civil bill officer, John Jones, had sent a petition 'praying that he may be appointed interpreter for Tralee instead of the existing interpreter, who, Jones says, is incompetent for the office'. Jones' application seems to have been based on his being 'a distinguished Biblical Irish scholar' and his ability to translate the Bible into Irish. The judge suggested that 'He ought to be a missionary of the Irish Church Missions' and said that there was no vacancy, 'and he must wait until Dowd, the present man, goes out'.[24] Michael Dowd was interpreter at quarter sessions.

In 1902 at Skibbereen quarter sessions, a solicitor called Mr Wolfe asked the judge about the appointment of a process server and interpreter at Bantry. The context was that Humphrey Kelleher, who had been fulfilling these two functions, had taken his own life a month previously; his son was willing to take his place as process server, but not as interpreter, as he did not speak Irish. The son had the support of all the solicitors in Bantry bar one, a Mr Flynn, who favoured a man called Power from 'Glengariffe [*sic*]' who 'could speak Irish well'. Flynn argued that there were already two process servers in Bantry but none in Glengariffe where it was difficult to have processes served. The judge's preference was for someone who could fulfil both functions, but his main concern was the need for 'a good sober man', because 'He had remarked people coming into Court under the influence of drink frequently, and he would not tolerate it in future.' However, he was persuaded by the advice of various solicitors, one of whom suggested that it would be preferable to separate the jobs of interpreter and process server as 'the interpreter must be away in Macroom at the time of the services of the processes', while another confirmed 'that is the reason the deceased used rarely serve any processes'. After some discussion, young Kelleher was appointed process server 'particularly for the Glengariffe District' and the judge said he would accept applications for court interpreter.[25] The new appointee was Irish scholar Pádraig Stúndún.

CONCLUSION

Testimonials were important; prospective interpreters had to show that they were trustworthy, reliable and well-perceived by important members of the community.

23 *Cork Examiner*, 26 Nov. 1902.
24 *New Irish Jurist and Local Government Review*, 2 (1901), p. 70.
25 *Southern Star*, 25 Oct. 1902.

The role of lawyers is also interesting, with barristers and solicitors representing applicants in some cases and in other cases solicitors getting involved in making a case in favour of particular applicants. While there were some local attempts to examine applicants for the post of interpreter, there was no centralized, nationwide system, yet another feature of the authorities' lack of interest in the matter.

CHAPTER SIX

Interpreting at petty sessions

THE PETTY SESSIONS were non-jury courts established in the 1820s to regularize and rationalize how magistrates dealt with minor cases: it was the task of the unpaid justices of the peace, and later the paid stipendiary magistrates, to hear evidence and decide on guilt or innocence. The lowest courts are always the busiest and as petty sessions covered both criminal and civil cases, meeting at least once a fortnight, they inevitably dealt with far more Irish speakers than any other type of court. Civil cases relating to trespass, assaults and abusive language were common and were often private prosecutions taken by complainants against defendants. If the court found for the complainant, the defendant could be ordered to pay a fine, sometimes with a percentage to be paid to the complainant, and costs of one or two shillings payable to the complainant. Defendants could be ordered to pay damages or compensation and if they did not comply, they could receive a short prison sentence in default. Crown cases were taken by the police. If found guilty, defendants could be given a fine or a prison sentence and would have to pay costs. The new courts proved popular and, according to C.P. Crane:

> The law was so cheap in Ireland, and the people naturally so litigious, that the number of cases at far away sessions was sometimes enormous. Often, however, I have travelled many miles to hear a few cases of trespass of a goat, or a few hens in a neighbour's haggard.[1]

Most cases started at petty sessions level, where there were two magistrates, and if sufficiently serious, were referred on to either the quarter sessions or the assizes although magistrates acting alone could also do this.[2] Unlike the higher courts however, and despite a number of missed legislative opportunities, no statutory provision was ever introduced for salaried interpreters at petty sessions. Moreover, there may have been local reluctance to provide salaried interpreters at the new lower courts due to the potential costs given that a large number of these courts met frequently. In the absence of a policy, there is evidence that some courts devised their own local solutions. For example, in 1835 interpreters at Dungarvan petty sessions were paid out of petty cash:

1 C.P. Crane, *Memoirs of a resident magistrate, 1880–1920* (Edinburgh, 1938), p. 96.
2 Vaughan, *Murder trials in Ireland*, p. 4.

> The costs and charges received, within the year ending the 31st December 1835, on all summonses, informations, warrants and convictions, received by clerk of petty sessions, out of which sum he has to pay for stationery, interpreter &c, £45 14s 8d.[3]

However, by 1849 the system in Dungarvan had shifted to employing a summons server to act as interpreter.[4] Indeed, there was an unsuccessful attempt in 1849 to introduce a law whereby summons servers would act as interpreters for no extra payment.[5] This suggests that there was some concern about the absence of a system of interpreter provision at petty sessions and may have been an attempt to legislate for what had become the practice on the ground.

The most valuable item of official information on the topic is from 1894 when John Morley, chief secretary for Ireland, gave a carefully worded statement to the house of commons. According to him, in 497 of the 606 petty sessions districts, 'no Irish-speaking persons have been charged with offences in the memory of the present clerks'. It is worth nothing that his reply does not include Irish-speaking witnesses and plaintiffs. That left 109 districts where Irish *was* used in 1894, and there 'provision is made for an interpreter, when the services of one are required, by the employment of a person duly sworn so to act'. Morley elaborated on the situation as follows:

> There is no statutory provision applicable to Petty Sessions, but where necessary, and on application, I have been informed the Crown provides an interpreter in criminal cases. Paid interpreters are rarely required, at Petty Sessions, as there are usually present in Court persons who volunteer to interpret upon the occasion arising.[6]

This statement would suggest that the system relied on volunteer interpreters in the first instance. However, the statement is unclear, probably deliberately so, and does not explain who exactly the paid interpreters were. In fact, correspondence with the chief secretary's office shows that the paid interpreters at petty sessions were summons servers who originally were not entitled to any extra payment for their interpreting work. For example, in 1888 T. Moran of Achill Sound was told that he was not entitled to any payment for interpreting at petty sessions because 'it appears that it is part of your duty as Summons Server to attend the petty sessions'.[7] However, the office agreed to pay five shillings, on submission of a certificate from the clerk of petty sessions, to summons servers who acted

3 *A return of the courts of petty sessions in the several counties of Ireland ... for the year ending 31 December 1835*, HC 1836 (415) xlii, 219.
4 *Cork Examiner*, 20 June 1849.
5 Bill for the more speedy trial and punishment of offences in Ireland (1849).
6 'The Irish language in Irish law courts', 10 Apr. 1894, *Hansard*, 4th ser., vol. 32, c. 112.
7 CSO/LB/50, p. 419, NAI.

as interpreters,[8] and summons servers in five counties – Clare, Donegal, Galway, Kerry and Mayo – wrote to Dublin Castle requesting payment for interpreting at petty sessions. The reasons behind the introduction of payment by Dublin Castle have not been ascertained; just as there was pressure from magistrates and lawyers for interpreter provision at quarter sessions, there may have been similar pressure from those summons servers who acted as interpreters for remuneration for extra work. Morley also stated that the crown provided interpreters in criminal cases only, thus making a distinction between criminal and civil cases. This is corroborated by correspondence from February 1888 from the chief secretary's office stating that interpreters were provided in crown cases only,[9] as 'public funds cannot be used to pay fees in private prosecutions.'[10]

In order to find out more, 188 newspaper reports that mention interpreters at petty sessions in nine counties in the years 1831–1920 were examined and broken down into categories (see figure 6). Of the 188 cases, 40 were crown cases while the remaining 148 were civil cases. However, all possible solutions regarding interpreter provision were applied to both types of cases. The table shows that a number of solutions were available. There are 40 mentions of 'the interpreter' and 43 of 'an interpreter', but no further information is provided on the identity of these interpreters, who could be a summons server, a quarter sessions interpreter, someone else who was a regular interpreter or indeed a volunteer. In addition, there are five references by name or function to quarter sessions interpreters. For example, in 1861 Father Lavelle was accused of violently assaulting Ellen Walsh, who was quoted as saying 'she would rather cut her head off than prosecute her priest'.[11] The case was adjourned because, despite repeated requests, Walsh maintained she could not give evidence in English and Colonel Knox stated, 'We have no funds to pay an interpreter',[12] suggesting implicitly that if they had funds they would pay an interpreter. The problem was solved a fortnight later when quarter sessions interpreter Patrick Flynn was sworn in.[13] It is probable that funds had been located to pay Flynn for his work, possibly due to concern about Father Lavelle's high profile, his advocacy for Irish speakers, his frequent court appearances, media interest in the case and the fact that it was a crown case taken by Sub-Inspector Abbott.[14]

Another solution was for summons servers to act as interpreters, with fourteen instances reported in the newspapers. Some petty sessions courts paid summons servers the modest sum of one shilling for acting as interpreters.[15] For

8 CSO/LB/50, p. 419 and CSO/LB/52, p. 442, NAI.
9 CSO/LB/52, p. 214, NAI.
10 CSO/LB/52, p. 449, NAI.
11 *Morning Post*, 17 Sept. 1861.
12 *Dublin Evening Packet & Correspondent*, 12 Sept. 1861.
13 *Ballyshannon Herald*, 27 Sept. 1861.
14 *Abbott v. Lavelle*.
15 *Western People*, 10 July 1915.

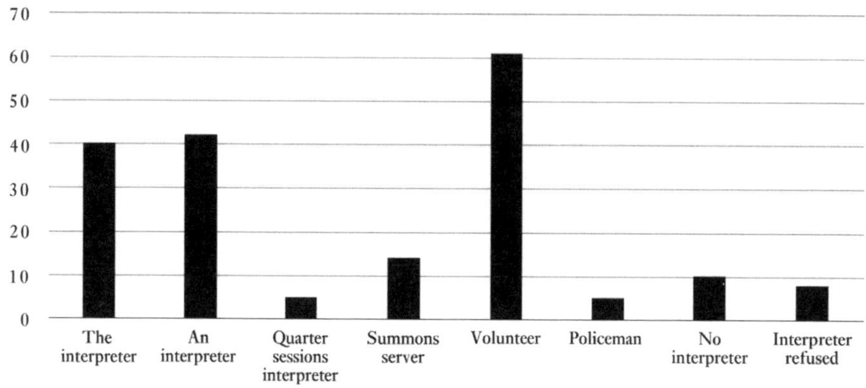

Figure 6 Interpreter provision at petty sessions

example, in 1885, at Dungarvan petty sessions, a substitute interpreter replaced Patrick Keane,[16] who was elsewhere serving processes. The chairman asked the clerk to

> tell Keane when he goes about serving processes, to send a proper person in his place as interpreter, or else I won't sit here seeing the court convulsed with laughter listening to this interpreter. I cannot help laughing myself. I won't sit here all day listening to this interpreter's burlesque. If Keane goes to serve processes he must have a proper man to interpret after him.[17]

Very often, there were no interpreters available and volunteers had to be found. For example, in 1878 at Milltown petty sessions in Kerry, it became apparent that an interpreter was required and the following conversation ensued:

> Sir John Godfrey – Who will we get to interpret?
> The name of John Quirk was mentioned.
> Mr Quirk – Oh, your worships, I understand it very well, but I could not interpret (laughter).
> Sir John Godfrey said he thought a man named Michael Corcoran, who was in court, could interpret?
> Corcoran – Oh, I beg your pardon, Sir John, I couldn't do it (renewed laughter).
> Mr Eagar – Come here, Corcoran. I hear you are looking out for an interpretership (laughter), so you are [*sic*] better show us now that you are capable to fulfil the position.

16 Patrick Keane, also a civil bill officer, was Waterford quarter sessions interpreter from 1885–1902.
17 *Waterford Standard*, 22 Apr. 1885

> Corcoran – Very well, sir. He then proceeded to administer the oath in Irish, and examine the witness.[18]

Fifty-three instances involving named volunteer interpreters were located. They included court attendees, defendants from other cases, a doctor, a valuer, a land agent, the son of a defendant, the daughter of a defendant, a water bailiff, a poor law guardian, a relieving officer, an army pensioner and a bridewell keeper. Court staff regularly volunteered to act as interpreters – an attorney, magistrates, a court bailiff, solicitors, petty sessions clerks, court keepers and registrars. At the turn of the twentieth century, members of the Gaelic League and national school teachers also took on the role. Some volunteers managed to negotiate payment for their efforts. For example, in 1869, at Ballinrobe petty sessions, Michael Rush[19] agreed to act as interpreter for an Irish-speaking witness in a trespass case 'upon the understanding that he would receive half a sovereign[20] for his services'.[21]

Policemen, and in one case, a retired policeman, agreed to act as interpreters in five instances and there are indications that this may have been a frequent occurrence in some petty sessions courts, a solution which must have been even more unpopular than that of summons servers taking on the role. There is an early example from 1832 of constable Mannix acting as interpreter at Ballylongford petty sessions in Kerry,[22] while the remaining examples relate to the early twentieth century. In 1901, constable Leahy acted as interpreter in an assault case heard at Youghal petty sessions. According to the chairman of Youghal board of guardians, the constable 'appeared to have a perfect knowledge of the language', and he was complimented by the judge 'on his quickness and smartness in translation'.[23] Also in 1901, at Belmullet petty sessions it was suggested that constable Patrick Brennan could act as interpreter. However, District Inspector Wallace informed the court that while policemen could act as interpreters in trespass cases, 'It is against our instructions to allow a constable to act as interpreter' in crown cases.[24] This would suggest that policemen were permitted to interpret in civil cases. The following year in the same court, there was no official interpreter and 'Constable Patrick Brennan, who interpreted on such occasions was temporarily transferred that day.'[25] In 1912 at Ring petty sessions, Constable Walsh swore in a witness, described as 'an old Irish speaker' and interpreted his evidence.[26] In 1889, retired

18 *Kerry Sentinel*, 6 Dec. 1878.
19 Michael Rush was appointed interpreter two years later in 1871. *Ballinrobe Chronicle*, 24 June 1871.
20 A sovereign was worth £1.
21 *Mayo Constitution*, 20 Apr. 1869.
22 *Kerry Evening Post*, 22 Sept. 1832.
23 *Cork Examiner*, 18 Oct. 1901.
24 *Western People*, 25 May 1901.
25 *Mayo News*, 27 Sept. 1902.
26 *Munster Express*, 27 July 1912.

policeman Michael Keane was described as the 'Irish interpreter at court of petty sessions at Corofin',[27] suggesting that he was regularly employed there.

On ten occasions, according to the newspapers, no interpreter was available and all but two cases were adjourned. For example, in 1862, no interpreter was available on at least two occasions at Galway town petty sessions, and Magistrate E.C. Burke commented somewhat enigmatically that 'if the public business was to be adjourned for want of an interpreter, it was time to have a remedy'.[28] The first unadjourned case took place in 1879 at Killorglin petty sessions where a 9-year-old boy was prosecuted for breaking the telegraph wire. The defendant told the court in Irish that he could not speak English. Despite this, rather alarmingly, the case went ahead and the boy was fined ten shillings or in default fourteen days' imprisonment.[29] The second unadjourned case involved a serious miscarriage of justice and took place in 1893 at Falcarragh petty sessions when an innocent man was sent to prison. The background to the case was that a summons for malicious injury that should have been served on Daniel Curran was mistakenly served on his Irish-speaking brother Edward, who attended court to try and explain that a mistake had been made. Despite the fact that he spoke only Irish and in the absence of an interpreter, the magistrates decided to proceed with the case and he was sentenced to a month with hard labour in Londonderry jail.[30] Two weeks later in *Curran v. the Justices of the County of Donegal*, despite some initial resistance from Mr Justice O'Brien, who suggested that 'Although he was not Daniel he may have been the right man', a writ of habeas corpus for the immediate release of Edward Curran was granted by the three judges at the queen's bench division.[31] This case highlights the danger of not making an interpreter available for Irish speakers.

On eight occasions, access to interpreters was refused on the grounds that it was believed that the person spoke English. Four of these occurred at Castlebar petty sessions, where Sir Samuel O'Malley seems to have had a particular antipathy to Irish speakers. For example, in 1833, a complainant was ordered off the table because he would not speak English and the case was not heard.[32] In 1837, in a burglary case, Sir Samuel O'Malley refused to listen to a witness' evidence because he could not speak English.[33] In 1839, in a case about an attack on a house, a number of witnesses for the defence 'refused' to speak English. On being questioned about his schooling, one man admitted that he had attended school for nearly a year and when handed a book 'he made out letter P'. Despite his preference for speaking Irish, 'Sir Samuel got him to tell it in pretty good English'. O'Malley then decided to take informations

27 *Cork Examiner*, 16 Sept. 1889.
28 *Galway Vindicator & Connaught Advertiser*, 11 June 1862.
29 *Kerry Sentinel*, 19 Aug. 1879.
30 The petty sessions order book, CSPS/1/4503, 30 May 1893, records the error: 'Daniel Curran otherwise Ned Curran', NAI.
31 *Freeman's Journal*, 15 June 1893.
32 *Connaught Telegraph*, 20 Nov. 1833.
33 Ibid., 15 Nov. 1837.

or statements against the witnesses who refused to speak English, presumably with a view to prosecuting them for perjury.[34] Also in 1839, in a case of assault and robbery, the magistrates refused to hear the evidence of the complainant's brother because he 'refused to speak English'.[35] There was constant pressure on Irish speakers to speak English, as stated by Timothy Healy MP in the house of commons in 1883:

> If a man came up in a Court of Petty Sessions, as was very frequently the case, and took the book in his hand, and happened to know enough English to be able to say 'thank you,' he would not be allowed to give his evidence in any other language than English.[36]

Some magistrates took a milder approach and made attempts at persuasion. For example, in 1870 Mr Stritch RM, Ballinrobe petty sessions, asked plaintiff Mary Malone, 'Do you know English? For if you can speak bad English it will do us.'[37]

Most prosecutions at petty sessions were private and Irish speakers who took private prosecutions faced a significant barrier to justice: they had to either recruit and pay their own interpreter and hopefully get enough in costs to cover this expense or accept whatever volunteer happened to be in court. Similarly, defendants who did not speak English had to recruit their own interpreters. If either side wished to call an Irish-speaking witness, they would need to cover the cost of an interpreter. Court reporters were not necessarily privy to private arrangements to pay interpreters but there are some mentions of the issue dating from the 1880s onwards. For example, in 1884 at Cong petty sessions in an assault case, the complainant protested that he could not tell his story in English but, having been told that he would have to pay an interpreter, agreed to use English.[38] Unusually, in 1892 a complainant 'brought an interpreter to the table with him' at Killorglin petty sessions,[39] suggesting that this was a private arrangement. In 1893 an Irish-speaking defendant in an assault case heard at Dingle petty sessions was instructed to pay four shillings to the interpreter.[40] In 1896 at Ballinrobe petty sessions, summons server Michael Connor sued a man for five shillings for interpreting,[41] and in 1898, he sent a claim to Dublin Castle for payment for interpreting but according to the reply, '[I]t has been reported that you have already been paid for your services by the parties by whom you were employed on those occasions.'[42] In 1900 Honor Malley sued Honor Casey for abusive language and the resident magistrate ordered that the latter pay

34 *Mayo Constitution*, 16 July 1839.
35 *Connaught Telegraph*, 25 Dec. 1839.
36 HC Debates, 17 Aug. 1883, vol. 283, cc 1022–81.
37 *Mayo Examiner*, 12 Dec. 1870.
38 *Ballinrobe Chronicle*, 25 Oct. 1884.
39 *Kerry Sentinel*, 27 Feb. 1892.
40 Ibid., 18 Mar. 1893.
41 *Ballinrobe Chronicle*, 7 Nov. 1896.
42 CSO/LB/79, p. 732, NAI.

one shilling to the man who interpreted Malley's evidence.[43] In 1901, then former county interpreter Humphrey Kelleher was present at Bantry petty sessions when an interpreter was required but refused to take on the role unless he was paid five shillings. The defendant's husband offered two and six, which Kelleher 'indignantly refused', and the bench said they would not allow Kelleher to accept payment from him and instead said they would send a certificate to the crown solicitor and 'he should be satisfied with what he would get'. Apparently, Kelleher had previously been paid one shilling for similar work, so he then said he would accept two and six. The bench again refused permission and Kelleher eventually agreed to await payment from the crown solicitor.[44] County interpreter Peter Rippingham appears to have been a regular interpreter at Ballinrobe petty sessions in the early 1880s,[45] where he was presumably paid by litigants for his services. In 1893 when publican Michael Sords applied for the post of Mayo interpreter, a letter of recommendation stated that he 'had been in the habit of acting constantly as Irish interpreter' at Ballinrobe petty sessions.[46] Again, it is highly unlikely that Sords would have undertaken this work for no payment. However, in 1917, summons server John Ward claimed that he had been interpreting free of charge at Dungloe petty sessions, for the previous twenty-two years.[47] So it is possible that other summons servers similiarly acted as interpreters without applying for payment.

CONCLUSION

Desmond McCabe in his study of petty sessions courts during the time period 1820–45 found that people in Mayo used the courts in 'enormous numbers', while those in Galway accessed the courts in high numbers.[48] Despite their popularity, the fact that there was no statutory provision of interpreters at petty sessions was highly problematic and discriminatory for Irish speakers. It also increased pressure on magistrates, who were impatient with and disbelieving of Irish speakers. To solve the problem, summons servers, when available, acted as interpreters. Alternatively, volunteers who happened to be in court took on the role of interpreters. Policemen, both serving and retired, were regular interpreters in some petty sessions courts. While cases were usually adjourned if no interpreter could be found, some cases did go ahead despite the fact that defendants did not understand the proceedings. In private prosecutions, Irish speakers were severely discriminated against because they faced additional inconvenience and costs as they had to recruit and pay their own interpreters.

43 *Ballinrobe Chronicle*, 21 June 1900.
44 *Southern Star*, 24 Aug. 1901.
45 *Ballinrobe Chronicle*, 29 Jan. 1881, 9 July 1881 and 7 Jan. 1882.
46 Letter from John L. Hearne, 15 Sept. 1893, 1C-78-51, NAI.
47 CSO/RP/1917/187, NAI.
48 D. McCabe, 'Law, conflict and social order: County Mayo, 1820–45' (PhD, UCD, 1991) cited in Richard McMahon, 'The court of petty sessions and society in pre-Famine Galway' in Raymond Gillespie (ed.), *The remaking of modern Ireland, 1750–1950* (Dublin, 2004), p. 102.

CHAPTER SEVEN

Interpreter ethics

IN THE 1500s and 1600s the Spanish crown had a number of laws relating to the recruitment, duties and behaviour of interpreters in the New World.[1] However, in the case of Ireland, there is no evidence of a historical code of ethics for court interpreters. It is possible that circulars were sent from the chief secretary's office to or about interpreters, but again there is no evidence of this. Nevertheless, it would be a mistake to assume that interpreter ethics were unknown or considered unimportant in the nineteenth century. Ethical issues were discussed in trials in England in the late eighteenth and early nineteenth century and reported in detail in Irish newspapers. For example, *Finn's Leinster Journal* reported in 1791 on the trial of Jean-Baptiste Levett, charged with robbing diamonds from the Countess du Barry. Mr Rimonde had accompanied Levett's attorney to Newgate prison and acted as interpreter. On appearing in court as a witness, he was about to reveal what Levett had said, when he was interrupted and instructed not to do so, 'because it would tend to disclose the instructions of a client to his attorney, which would be illegal, Rimonde going to Levett, not as a friend, but solely in the capacity of an interpreter.'[2]

In 1813, the select committee of the house of commons on the affairs of the East India Company heard evidence from Lieutenant Colonel Sir John Malcolm, who contrasted the abilities of native and European interpreters as follows:

> The defect of native interpretation arises from their want of correct knowledge of the idiom of the English language; that of Europeans from their want of correct knowledge of the different and local idioms of the native languages. It must be almost the study of an European's life, to render himself fully competent for such an office; and I conceive, nothing but the prospect of a large salary could induce any European, of respectable talents, to devote his whole time to the accomplishment of that object.[3]

1 C. Giambruno, 'The role of the interpreter of sixteenth- and seventeenth-century Spanish colonies in the "New World"' in Carmen Valero Garcés and Anne Martin (eds), *Crossing borders in community interpreting* (Amsterdam, 2008), pp 27–49.

2 *Finn's Leinster Journal*, 6 Aug. 1791.

3 *Parliamentary Debates from the year 1803 to the Present Time* (1813), 11 Mar.–10 May 1813, *Hansard*, vol. xxv, p. 974.

When asked what salary 'would be necessary to an European gentleman so qualified, to undertake the important office of interpreter', Malcolm replied, 'I think the salary of a person employed as such interpreter should be inferior to none but that of the judges themselves who preside in the court.' Malcolm displays an excellent understanding of the issues around who should act as interpreter and the difficulty of finding a competent interpreter. There is no mention of what would be an appropriate salary for native interpreters.

A high level of awareness of ethical issues was also demonstrated during the eleven-week trial of Queen Caroline of Brunswick at the house of lords in 1820, which received extensive coverage in the *Freeman's Journal*. King George IV wished to divorce Caroline, and as she would not agree to this, he introduced a bill of pains and penalties, which was debated in parliament where she was effectively put on trial. Interpreters were required for a number of German- and Italian-speaking witnesses. The queen's interpreter was instructed 'to interfere if he found any difference between the German and English meanings of the questions and answer' rendered by the other interpreter. The lord chancellor 'directed the interpreter to use the same form of words, as to number and person, as the witness in translating her replies'. Earl Morton requested that counsel address the witness rather than the interpreter, and use 'did you' instead of 'did she' and use the first person singular when giving the answers. On one occasion, an interpreter risked losing face when he admitted that he did not understand an expression.[4] Two days later, the same newspaper reported that 'the Interpreter begged to be allowed to tell the witness to hold his tongue while he was speaking'.[5] When a peer complained about the incoherence and incorrectness of a translation (some understood Italian), the interpreter explained that 'the witness would persist in talking while he was translating, and he could not hear and speak too'.[6]

THE INTERPRETER'S OATH

An important means of emphasizing the need for accuracy was the interpreter's oath. The tradition of swearing in interpreters has been in existence for centuries. Official records such as those of select committees always mention that the interpreter was sworn, as do many newspaper reports. It seems that there was a high level of awareness of the requirement for the interpreter to take an oath in eighteenth- and nineteenth-century Ireland, far more than in twenty-first century Ireland, where court interpreters are not always sworn.

The main sources of information on interpreter oaths are books directed at justices of the peace and constables. Nun and Walsh mention interpreters being sworn in the case of jurats, statements that were included at the end of affidavits to record all the details of the oath or affirmation:

4 *Freeman's Journal*, 29 Aug. 1820.
5 Ibid., 31 Aug. 1820.
6 Ibid., 11 Sept. 1820.

> If an interpreter be employed, add, Sworn at &c, by the above-mentioned A.B., the same having been first read over and explained to him in the [Irish] language, by M.N. of _______, who was first duly sworn to interpret the same to the said A.B., before me J.P. &c. (Appendix cclviii)

In addition, in the context of issuing a warrant, information is provided on 'where interpreter is used':

> If it be necessary to use the intervention of an interpreter, he should also be sworn to interpret well and faithfully, and the jurat to the information modified accordingly.[7]

Levinge explained that:

> Also, when the defendant, or the party charged, does not understand the English language, the evidence should be interpreted to him. The interpreter's oath may be in the following form: 'You shall truly and faithfully interpret the evidence about to be given, and all other matters and things touching the present charge, and the [French, or as the case may be] language into the English language, and the English language into the [French &c] language, according to best of your skill and ability; so help you God.'[8]

Levinge went on to detail the processes. When the prosecution had examined the witnesses, it was the remit of the justice to read the depositions to the accused and then take down his statement if he wished to make one. The magistrate had to caution the accused 'that he is not obliged to say anything unless he desires to do so, but that whatever he does say will be taken down in writing, and may be given in evidence against him on his trial'.[9] If a statement was given, it had to be read over to the prisoner and signed by the magistrate. If the justice asked a question without first administering the caution, then that evidence could not be used if the case went to trial.

Humphreys, also in a book directed at justices of the peace, has a slightly different version of the interpreter's oath:

> You shall well and truly interpret and explain to the Court (and Jury) the evidence given in this case (trial or inquiry) according to the best of your skill and understanding. So help you God. [The interpreter is to be first

7 R. Nun and J.E. Walsh, *The powers and duties of the justices of the peace in Ireland, and of constables* (Dublin, 1841), p. 176.
8 E.P. Levinge, *The justice of the peace in Ireland* (Dublin, 1862), p. 81.
9 Ibid., p. 86.

> sworn, and he is then to administer the oath to the witness]. And in the *jurat* add: – Sworn before me, &c, &c, the same having been first read over and explained to him in the ___ language by C.D., who was first duly sworn to interpret and explain the same.[10]

Humphreys' version, with its focus on interpreting evidence to the court and jury rather than to the defendant who may not understand evidence given in English, shows what the priority was at the time. However, in his memoirs, Resident Magistrate Crane records an abbreviated version of the oath that includes both Irish-English and English-Irish:

> You shall well and truly interpret the Irish language into the English language, and the English language into the Irish language, to the best of your skill and ability. So help you God.[11]

The interpreter's oath was a serious matter and was administered to both staff and volunteer interpreters. For example, Mr Cullinane, a lawyer, was 'sworn in as an Irish interpreter',[12] and 'an old man was brought in on crutches and sworn to interpret'.[13] In 1853, in *Constable Bourke v. Revd O'Connor*, reference was made to information obtained through an interpreter who had not been sworn; the information was held to be informal.[14] Interpreters were permitted to explain the nature of the oath to children to establish if they understood and could be sworn in.[15] In 1861 Patrick Flynn, county interpreter for Mayo, requested that Ballinrobe petty sessions swear him as he did not usually interpret there. Lack of knowledge of the oath in Irish was on occasion a barrier to volunteers acting as interpreters. For example, an interpreter was required at Skibbereen petty sessions in 1901, but there were no volunteers 'owing to the fact that none of them had the legal wording of the oath in Irish'.[16]

The question of whether barristers who acted as interpreters needed to be sworn came up in Shrewsbury, Oxford, in 1848, during a case involving two Irishmen, both charged with stealing potatoes. One of the defendants spoke English but the other, Maloney, did not. Barrister McMahon offered to be sworn in as interpreter but Woolrych, described as *amicus curiae*, informed the court that he had been allowed to interpret in a murder case without being sworn. He did not specify the language, but given his surname, it was probably not Irish. The judge (Patteson J.) decided that 'Counsel are not privileged from taking an oath

10 H. Humphreys, *The justice of the peace for Ireland* (Dublin, 1867), p. 376.
11 Crane, *Memoirs of a resident magistrate*, p. 195.
12 *Freeman's Journal*, 20 June 1829.
13 Ibid., 29 May 1838.
14 *Kerry Evening Post*, 30 Nov. 1853.
15 *Waterford News*, 11 Jan. 1856.
16 *Mayo Constitution*, 24 Sept. 1861; *Southern Star*, 15 June 1901.

on giving evidence', but an alternative solution was found; Maloney's co-accused acted as interpreter.[17]

ACCURACY

Did interpreters interpret well and faithfully as they were sworn to do? Accounts of trials and newspaper reports indicate that the answer is not always. For example, in 1701 at the trial of Patrick Hurly at the court of king's bench in Dublin, John Crips gave evidence through an interpreter:

> And my Lord, he is telling a long story of this Holloway being a troublesome man.
> At this the Fellow spluttered and made a terrible noise in Irish.
> Interp. My Lord, he will not answer to the direct question.[18]

Instead of interpreting what was being said by Crips, the interpreter has summarized the information as 'a long story' and takes over from the lawyers by telling the court that the man 'will not answer to the direct question'.

However, there was an important safeguard: many people in court were aware of the importance of accuracy. For example, in 1811, at a Caravets and Shanavests trial,[19] two men were charged with robbing a guard of two blunderbusses and two pistols on the Cork mail coach. An interpreter was sworn for a witness called Margaret Sauce. Solicitor Mr Mac Nally asked the judges to direct the interpreter 'to give a literal translation of the answers of the witness' because he recalled a case in Waterford, 'where three innocent men were nearly convicted, on the false translation of the witness' answers'. However, the interpreter for Margaret Sauce unintentionally gave 'a much fuller answer to a question than was given by the witness'.[20] Similarly, in a book printed in 1843, James Hardiman recalled:

> The writer remembers the trial of a man charged with a capital offence, whose life was saved, by a bystander in court detecting the *interpreter* ignorantly translating an important part of the evidence of an Irish witness. On this evidence the man's life depended, and when correctly explained to the judge and jury, it led to his acquittal.[21]

17 E.W. Cox, *Reports of cases in criminal law argued and determined in all the courts in England and Ireland* (London, 1859), iii.

18 T.B. Howell, *A complete collection of state trials*, xiv: *1700–1708* (London, 1812), p. 421.

19 Caravets and Shanavests were rival groups whose feuding caused considerable violence, particularly in counties Tipperary, Waterford, Kilkenny, Limerick and Cork, 1806–11. The Caravets were a movement of agrarian protest while the Shanavests were prosperous farmers banded together to resist this challenge from the rural poor. S.J. Connolly (ed.), *Oxford companion to Irish history* (Oxford, 2002).

20 *A report of the trials of the Caravets and Shanavests* (Dublin, 1811), p. 21.

21 J. Hardiman, *Tracts relating to Ireland* (Dublin, 1843), p. 65.

There is occasional evidence of attempts at quality control. For example, in 1840 at Cork county criminal court, in an assault case, a witness was examined through the interpreter and the court checked with one of the jurors, who confirmed that 'she made the answers as delivered by the interpreter'.[22] In 1846 at Dingle petty sessions, a summons server acted as interpreter. However, the chairman realized that the man was 'interpreting fast and loose; which was a most iniquitous and nefarious proceeding; he might in that manner swear away a man's life'. The chairman took immediate action and ordered the police to turn the man out of court and to tell the clerk not to give him any more summonses to serve.[23]

As mentioned above, at the trial of Queen Caroline in 1820, counsel was asked to use 'Did you' rather than 'Did she' when questioning a witness and the interpreter was requested to use the same person as the witness when interpreting her reply. This is good practice when interpreting, particularly in a legal context, as information is much clearer and there is less likelihood of confusion regarding who did what. However, no instances of judges requesting counsel and interpreters to follow these instructions were found. Instead, interpreters tended to take their cue from counsels' way of questioning. If counsel used 'Ask him' then the interpreter would say 'He says that …' Margaret Kelleher suggests that during his examination of witness John Collins at the first Maamtrasna trial of Patrick Joyce, prosecuting lawyer Peter O'Brien deliberately switched to third person as an 'effective distancing tactic'.[24] Another possibility is that he wanted to slow down questioning to gain time to think about his next question.

Legal language must have presented enormous problems for interpreters. In 1863 a legal terminology issue arose at the court of exchequer where a plaintiff was asked if he knew what a libel was and the interpreter told the court, perhaps because he was not in a position to interpret the question, that he himself did not know what a libel was. A lawyer responded, to laughter, that 'they have no word in Irish for such things'.[25] According to another newspaper that reported on the same case, the interpreter told the court 'he could only interpret to the best of his skill', and Mr Carey, an additional interpreter, was sworn.[26]

Some witnesses spoke in a roundabout or confusing manner, possibly using incomplete sentences. This could create a difficulty for the interpreter, who might not wish the court to think that he was at fault. In 1845 in a murder case heard at Mayo crown court, Baron Richards stated that he could not understand the answers given by a witness through interpreter Simon Conway, who immediately appealed to Mr Buchanan, 'an excellent Irish scholar'. Buchanan confirmed Conway's accuracy and the judge agreed, saying:

22 *Southern Reporter & Cork Commercial Courier*, 11 Aug. 1840.
23 *Kerry Evening Post*, 7 Mar. 1846.
24 Kelleher, *The Maamtrasna murders*, p. 107.
25 *Dublin Evening Mail*, 16 May 1863.
26 *Saunders's News-Letter*, 18 May 1863.

> I have no doubt of that. It is not of the interpreter I complain but of the confused manner in which the witness answers. I know that Mr Conway is an excellent Irish scholar, and that there can possibly be no better interpreter. I have said so frequently elsewhere, and I have very often got valuable assistance from him in this court. So that it is not him I blame, but the wretched and confused way in which the witnesses give the answers.[27]

Interpreters are expected to be faithful to what was said and not omit or add information, but this can be very difficult in practice, particularly when information is being read aloud from a document. In 1833 at Donegal assizes, the clerk read out the indictment in English about a riotous assembly and the interpreter Mr Mulherran was told to translate it. However, according to the *Enniskillen Chronicle*,

> as the inventors of that dialect had not made due provision for the pleonasms and tautologies of courts of law, Mr Mulherran felt no small difficulty in executing this task. Having repeatedly paused in the course of the process, as if at a great loss, the crown solicitor proposed that another interpreter should be obtained; on which Mr Mulherran assumed an air of offended dignity, and seemed as if about to throw up his commission; but on second thoughts, he resumed his office, and went through the translation with astonishing volubility.

It is interesting that the crown solicitor noted that Mulherran was having difficulty interpreting the indictment into Irish and was prepared to find a replacement interpreter. Unusually, the prosecutor spoke in both English and Irish. When the defendant was given an opportunity to plead, he 'made a long and apparently energetic defence in Irish', which the interpreter, 'with a becoming horror of circumlocution', translated with the words 'not guilty'.[28] Mulherran was an experienced interpreter at this stage, having worked at assizes and quarter sessions for at least eight years. He may have developed this summarizing strategy because it was preferable to be brief and to the point to avoid judges getting impatient with convoluted answers. Even so, it is the interpreter who is making decisions about the information to be included or excluded and this is undesirable.

In other cases, omissions occurred accidentally. For example, in 1841 at Newport petty sessions in Mayo, clerk Mr Gillespie was sworn as interpreter for an Irish-speaking boy from Achill, who gave a description of events concerning damage to a new Catholic church. However, it was suggested that Gillespie omitted to mention that the boy said he heard a whistle. All agreed that this error was unintentional and a man called O'Boyle replaced him.[29] In 1864 at Skibbereen petty sessions,

27 *Mayo Constitution*, 18 Mar. 1845.
28 *Enniskillen Chronicle & Erne Packet*, 8 Aug. 1833.
29 *Mayo Constitution*, 23 Feb. 1841.

a newspaper reporter noted that the interpreter did not interpret the sentence 'I did strike him,' possibly a crucial piece of information from a witness in an assault case.[30]

While Mulherran and others abridged testimony, other interpreters made additions, often in an effort to be obsequious, often excessively so, to judges. In 1832, a dispute arose between two lawyers, Denis Leonard and Edward Stokes, in relation to interpreting provided by a policeman called Mannix at Ballylongford petty sessions court in Kerry. A response to a question from the bench was translated by Mannix as 'he acknowledges, your worship, that the prisoner told him he took the shovel'. Leonard objected to the manner in which the answer was interpreted – the Irish speaker had probably simply said 'he told me he took the shovel' – but Mannix insisted he had interpreted correctly, as did Stokes. Leonard asked the magistrates to pose the question again, and this time the answer was rendered correctly. The following day Mannix asked Leonard why he had misrepresented him to the court and Leonard explained the difference of effect of his first and second renderings, upon which the policeman told him he was ungentlemanly and 'like a blackguard'. Leonard lodged a complaint with the chief constable. The case went back to court where Stokes again stated that the interpretation was correct the first time. Mannix, however, was sworn and admitted that he did not interpret *verbum verbo* in the first instance, but he did interpret accurately the second time.[31]

Similar obsequiousness passed unnoticed in 1848 at Clonmel assizes. An interpreter was provided to father and son William and Laurence Cull, who were accused of murder.[32] They were not entitled to counsel because the government had discontinued the practice of providing such in capital cases. Therefore, as they did not speak English, they had to have an interpreter. Baron Richards found this situation 'very painful' and read through his notes aloud so the interpreter could translate them into Irish. One of the prisoners was allowed to ask questions of the witnesses and the interpreter translated in a rather obsequious way, saying, for example: 'He desires me ask my lord was there a way of fastening the door? He desired me the question my lord, how the beds were settled?'[33] The judge also examined the witnesses and investigated everything, basically acting as counsel, before finding the two men guilty and sentencing them to be hanged by the neck until they were dead.[34]

Lack of awareness of the role of the interpreter was a problem, in particular with summons servers who acted as interpreters in petty sessions courts. A summons server called Staunton, who regularly interpreted at Castlebar petty sessions, tended to start interpreting before speakers had finished speaking and even to

30 *Southern Reporter & Cork Commercial Courier*, 7 May 1864.
31 *Kerry Evening Post*, 22 Sept. 1832.
32 The official interpreter at the time of the trial was Thomas Heffernan.
33 *Tipperary Free Press*, 29 July 1848.
34 *Nenagh Guardian*, 2 Aug. 1848.

speak out and admonish the magistrate for not listening to his interpretation into English. In 1833, a prosecutor alleged that he had been beaten and robbed of fifty-five hanks of yarn. Staunton started to interpret a question before Mr O'Donel had completed it only to be told, '[Y]ou are the stupidest interpreter in Ireland, and the most forward.' When magistrate Charles O'Malley asked the prosecutor 'was he beaten or robbed when he was met by another man', Staunton intervened 'very angrily' to say, 'No, sir, don't you hear what he says?' Mr O'Donel responded that Staunton was 'one of the worst interpreters in Europe'.[35] Another interpreter, Martin Churchill, a summons server and police pensioner, displayed even less awareness of how to behave appropriately as interpreter. Churchill had acted as interpreter at Belmullet petty sessions in 1839 and, at the week-long constabulary court of inquiry that followed one year later, according to Doctor Lyons, 'It was impossible to get him to interpret honestly'. He was 'proving the service of his summonses, interpreting the testimony of Irish witnesses, and putting them questions, speaking to the magistrates, suggesting to the clerk, and busily interfering with every one within his reach'.[36]

(IM)PARTIALITY

The fact that interpreters were appointed on a county basis, to work at the assizes or at quarter sessions, meant that their loyalty lay with the court. They were probably reluctant to challenge anything said by other participants and would most likely do whatever they were asked to do. It is unlikely that interpreters felt they were there to help the Irish speaker present his case in the best possible way. There were requirements for constables, who could not be 'a gamekeeper, wood ranger, tithe proctor, viewer of tithes, bailiff, parish clerk, hired servant or tavern keeper'.[37] In contrast, many interpreters also worked as summons servers, process servers, civil bill officers, bailiffs, relieving officers, sanitary officers, gamekeepers and bridewell keepers. It is likely that these roles affected interpreters' impartiality and made it difficult for them to build up a relationship of trust with the Irish speakers who needed to access the courts or who appeared as witnesses. The most extreme example found was James Beatty, interpreter at Sligo assizes in 1816, who was also the governor of Sligo gaol and of the house of correction and submitted three presentments to the grand jury for having people whipped; two were rejected and one, for £3, granted. He was also paid £7 for providing an executioner to execute two people and whip one person.[38] It is difficult to imagine Beatty as an impartial interpreter.

As interpreters were aligned with the legal system and had absorbed its rationale regarding access to their services, some had no difficulty intervening to inform

35 *Mayo Constitution*, 7 Mar. 1833.
36 *Connaught Telegraph*, 4 Nov. 1840.
37 G. Broeker, *Rural disorder and police reform in Ireland, 1812–1836* (London, 1970), p. 147.
38 Sligo grand jury presentments, spring 1816, Sligo County Library.

the courts that the people they were interpreting for spoke English. For example, in 1829 at Cork assizes, when a complainant in a rape case did not respond to questions in English the court interpreter informed the court, 'My Lord, I have heard her speak English well.'[39] In 1841, although Simon Conway claimed that he 'discharged his duty efficiently and impartially',[40] that duty included swearing that certain people could speak English, which on at least one occasion meant that a witness was sent to jail.[41] In 1858, at Castlebar petty sessions, while the lawyers were talking among themselves, summons server and interpreter Mr Phillips had 'an animated conversation in Irish with the plaintiff'.[42] The inappropriateness of this was clear to the court reporter. In 1899, in a case discussed in more detail in appendix B, the interpreter, John Keane,[43] informed Judge Dane at Ballinrobe Sessions that he had spoken to the defendant in English on the day of the trial and the previous day. According to the judge:

> A litigant came up before me, and noisily insisted upon the interpreter of the court swearing him in in Irish, and the interpreter, who is a paid official of the court, a paid sworn official, proved to my satisfaction that not only was this man not ignorant of English, but that he thoroughly understood English, and that he spoke it, and had been speaking it to him on that very day and the day before.[44]

The precise way in which the information was provided is unclear, but it would appear that the interpreter volunteered the information, perhaps in an effort to ingratiate himself with the judge, or perhaps because he genuinely felt that a litigant who spoke English should not be allowed avail of his services.

There are also examples of interpreters expressing negative opinions about Irish speakers and criticizing what they said. In 1831 an interpreter at Castlebar petty sessions 'expressed a good deal of honest indignation at the stupidity' of two brothers who took a case and cross-case about a dispute over a ditch. Other interpreters sided with the authority of the court. William Makepeace Thackeray visited Ireland in 1842, and described a scene at the city of Waterford assizes:

> The witness is here placed on a table instead of a witness-box; nor was there much farther peculiarity to remark, except in the dirt of the court, the absence of the barristerial wig and gown, and the great coolness with which a fellow who seemed a sort of clerk, usher, and Irish interpreter to the court, recommended a prisoner, who was making rather a long defence,

39 *Dublin Evening Post*, 23 Apr. 1829.
40 *Mayo Constitution*, 24 July 1834.
41 Ibid., 3 Aug. 1841.
42 *Connaught Telegraph*, 19 May 1858.
43 John Keane was John Kane, the successful applicant for the post of Mayo interpreter in 1893.
44 *Irish Times*, 27 Oct. 1899.

> to be quiet. I asked him why the man might not have his say. 'Sure,' says he, 'he's said all he has to say, and there's no use in any more.' But there was no use in attempting to convince Mr Usher that the prisoner was best judge on this point; in fact the poor devil shut his mouth at the admonition, and was found guilty with perfect justice.[45]

Thackeray's ironic comment that the prisoner was 'found guilty with perfect justice' implies that the defendant was not heard in full. It is likely that the same happened at assizes and quarter sessions if the interpreter was ill or unavailable or in counties where provision of salaried interpreters had ceased. In 1881, 'Starro' wrote to the *Cork Examiner* about special sessions relating to malicious burnings heard by three magistrates in Cahirciveen. A 'rustic youth' required an interpreter and:

> A famous bailiff, commonly known by the name of 'Buck Dawley' and a very Uriah Heep in appearance, offered to act as interpreter. The evidence had not proceeded far when Canon Brosnan interposed, saying that 'Buck' was giving a misleading rendering of witness' testimony. Many others in court expressed themselves in a similar manner, and there was a general murmur of disapproval (in which even the police joined) through the entire body of the court. It was evident to every one conversant with the Celtic tongue that 'Dawley' not only mistranslated the evidence, but, what was worse, suppressed the most material points. Yet, notwithstanding all this, the magistrates, prompted by a packed and partisan jury of ratepayers, gave compensation in each case! Still further, 'Dawley', whose interpreting was objected to on the sworn testimony of the most respectable gentlemen in court, was allowed to act in other cases![46]

In contrast, some interpreters took the side of defendants. In 1848, during the Great Famine, an interpreter intervened in a very sad case heard at the record court in Galway where John Hernan pleaded guilty to stealing two pieces of rope. His wife and two children had died of hunger and he was hoping to return home and cut corn, and hopefully 'get some potatoes to eat'. In this case, the interpreter, most likely Thomas J. Reid,[47] intervened to say that he had known the prisoner for a long time and could vouch for him. He also supported his story and said that 'he himself had contributed to his support'. Despite this, Hernan was sentenced to a month in prison from the date of his arrest.[48] In 1885 a special court was held in

45 W.M. Thackeray, *The Irish sketch book: and notes on a journey from Cornhill to grand Cairo* (London, 1845), p. 52.
46 *Cork Examiner*, 23 May 1881.
47 *Thom's Irish Almanac: Galway Borough Directory* (Dublin, 1848).
48 *Tuam Herald*, 12 Aug. 1848. Hernan was released on 17 August (Galway prison general register, 1839–51, book 1/21/2 (town gaol of Galway), NAI.

Dingle under the Crimes Act to charge evicted tenants with retaking possession of farms on Lord Ventry's estate. The Irish-speaking tenants were not represented in court. The usual interpreter was asked to interpret but declined to do so. District Inspector Grey, who was in charge of the prosecution, then asked if anyone else in court would act as interpreter but nobody volunteered.[49] No reasons are provided for the interpreter's refusal but it is probable that he sympathized with the tenants' plight and was unwilling to participate in the legal process.

Interpreters acted as expert witnesses on occasion, particularly in relation to Irish surnames. For example, in 1841 at Tralee quarter sessions, a claimant told the court that his old name in Irish was Guyer, which in English was Dwyer. The court then referred to the interpreter, who 'showed that the one name was not a translation of the other'.[50] In 1888, a question arose at Ballyshannon quarter sessions as to whether a defendant's name was Moss or Mulmous leading to a very confusing discussion, with the plaintiff's solicitor suggesting that Mulmous was Irish for Moss while the interpreter stated that Mulmous meant 'a heap of turf'. The judge said that he would accept the interpreter's contribution and that moss was something that grew on a stone while Mulmous was 'equivalent to a heap of turf'. After some discussion, the process server swore that the defendant was known by both names and the case went ahead.[51]

For the uninitiated, the experience of speaking through an interpreter in court could be confusing. For example, in 1872, at Hollymount petty sessions in Mayo, in an assault case, the complainant had great difficulty understanding the role of the interpreter:

> He being an Irish witness, and the questions put through an interpreter, there was a regular passage of arms, or words, between them: the witness considered it was highly impertinent for the man who acted as interpreter to be 'putting him such questions as he had no right to be enquiring into his family affairs so inquisitively, it was no affair of his, that he was trying to make game of him, and putting cross-questions to make him slip a word for the attorney and damn himself, so he would not answer him anymore, but he would answer the gentleman himself.'[52]

BRIBERY

Modern-day codes of ethics specify that interpreters should not accept gifts from clients. While there is no evidence of Irish interpreters accepting bribes, there are anecdotes suggesting that some did so and altered their interpreting to ensure that

49 *Cork Examiner*, 5 May 1885.
50 *Kerry Examiner*, 12 Jan. 1841.
51 *Donegal Independent*, 16 June 1888.
52 *Ballinrobe Chronicle*, 13 Apr. 1872.

the desired result was achieved. The earl of Mayo reportedly said that the interpreters used to interpret as they chose and gave an example of two Irish-speaking litigants who needed an interpreter:

> After the case, one said 'What did you give the interpreter?' 'I gave him £5' was the reply. The other man said 'I gave him £10.' 'That pretty well settled the matter' observed the Earl.[53]

McArdle recounts a story about an old man who waylaid Daniel O'Connell and offered him ten guineas to act for his son who was 'on trial for his life'. O'Connell could not take the case but recommended another lawyer.

> When the court rose and O'Connell left the building, he saw across the road a delighted crowd around a handsome youth. Most prominent in the crowd was the old man he had met that morning. The great advocate strode up and held out his hand.
>
> 'The boy is free?'
>
> 'He is, thank God.'
>
> 'Well, you took my advice then and gave your ten guineas to James Lyons.'
>
> 'Begor no! I didn't waste it – I gave it to the interpreter.'[54]

Ten guineas would have been more than a year's salary for an interpreter at assizes at that time, and if this was indeed the amount, it would certainly be extremely tempting. It is also possible that the amount has been exaggerated over time to make for an even better story.

Michael Cronin moots two possible reasons for the identification of court interpreters as interventionist or manipulative: language and power, and a conflict between literacy and orality. Interpreters could 'tilt the balance in favour of those who were disadvantaged' and were 'potentially power brokers for the powerless'.[55] A similar story, about an interpreter in the west of Ireland, told by Lord Morris of Killanin, rings true:

> O'Gorman, for such was the litigant's name, had not the 'wan-wan' (£1 1s) essential to fee junior counsel in those parts, nor the six-and-eightpence necessary to secure the services of a 'mountainy attorney'; but he had half-a-crown and a small bottle of potheen, and with both he invested in an interpreter. The 'interpreter' is a very important functionary in parts of

53 *Irish Independent*, 7 Feb. 1924.

54 McArdle, *Irish legal anecdotes*, pp 94–5.

55 M. Cronin, 'Interpreting Ireland: literary and historical perspectives on the role of interpreters in Ireland' in M. Tymoczko and C. Ireland (eds), *Language and tradition in Ireland* (Amherst, 2003), p. 133.

rural Ireland, and on the occasion of the anecdote he succeeded so well in confusing the issues that the plaintiff lost his case, and the defendant, his client O'Gorman, won what is popularly known as a D.O.M. [dismissed on its merits] with costs against the plaintiff.[56]

CONCLUSION

It is not particularly surprising that despite being sworn to interpret well and faithfully, some interpreters did not meet this standard. Given that they had no training and that for the majority there was no test to establish whether or not they were competent, it is predictable that some would find it difficult or impossible to interpret accurately all the time, particularly when it came to legal terminology. However, there was a safeguard in that very often, people in court understood what was being said in Irish and English. Many interpreters may have done their best and endeavoured, in difficult circumstances, to provide a good service.

It appears that there was no written code of ethics although there was a level of awareness among judges, lawyers and indeed court reporters of what was acceptable and what was unacceptable. It does seem that many interpreters aligned themselves with the courts; this is not particularly surprising because they were appointed either by the grand jury or by the assistant barrister and were dependent on the grand jury to sanction payment. Some interpreters may have proved susceptible to bribes as suggested by anecdotes, but it is impossible to know to what extent.

56 J. O'M, 'Irish interpreters', *New Irish Jurist and Local Government Review*, 2 (1902), p. 69.

CHAPTER EIGHT

R v. Burke (1858)

THE ISSUE OF Irish-speaking witnesses supposedly feigning ignorance of the English language came to the fore in *R v. Burke*, an interesting case where a number of judges expressed their views on both sides of the argument. It is surprising that despite extensive provision of interpreters over a long period of time, this is one of only two examples of Irish case law located on interpreting.[1] Unfortunately, in recent years the case has been misunderstood as giving speakers of Irish the *right* to use that language in court. For example, according to Niall Ó Ciosáin, 'plaintiffs, defendants and witnesses were allowed give evidence in Irish through an interpreter, even when they were not strictly monoglot, a right confirmed by the Queen's Bench in 1856 [*sic*]'.[2] W.E. Vaughan states that the majority of the court decided that 'the witness had a right to give his evidence in Irish, even if he knew English'.[3] Similarly, Nicholas Wolf refers to 'the settling of the question in favor of Irish speakers in the *R v. Burke* decision in 1858'[4] and, more explicitly, 'Irish speakers could provide testimony in any language they preferred.'[5] Margaret Kelleher follows suit, suggesting that 'the legal system conceded the need to accommodate Irish in the courts, per the 1858 judgment.'[6] This widely shared view seems to be based on (a) the very reasonable words of Judge Christian concerning possible motives of bilingual persons for the use of Irish and (b) the agreement of seven judges with Judge Christian that it was not acceptable to hear evidence relating to a witness' knowledge of English at cross-examination.

The original Mayo assizes case heard in Castlebar before Justice O'Brien revolved around an attempt to discredit the witness, to show that he was lying about his knowledge of English, the implication being that if he could lie about that, then his testimony in favour of the defendant, testimony that could allow the defendant to be found not guilty, was probably also a lie. The background to

1 The other was *Plunkett v Williams & Others. Irish Equity Reports Argued and Determined in the High Court of Chancery, the Rolls Court, and the Equity Exchequer during the years 1843 and 1844*, vol. 6 (1844:80–2).

2 Ó Ciosáin, 'Gaelic culture and language shift' in Geary and Kelleher (eds), *Nineteenth-century Ireland* (Dublin, 2005), p. 150.

3 Vaughan, *Murder trials in Ireland*, p. 38.

4 Wolf, *An Irish-speaking island*, p. 272.

5 N. Wolf, 'When the Irish language was still the greatest language in the world', *Irish Times*, 29 Jan. 2015.

6 Kelleher, *The Maamtrasna murders*, p. 88.

the case is as follows. According to the *Connaught Telegraph*, Thomas Burke was accused of 'felonious assault', in reality rape, by Margaret Sheridan (at the time, complainants, including children, were named in the newspapers). She testified in Irish, as did her aunt Judy Syze.[7] A witness called Martin Thornton, aged about 17, who told the court that he 'never was more than a week or a fortnight at school', was called for the defence and also spoke in Irish through the interpreter. Crucially, before being sworn in, he 'professed an inability to speak English'[8] and, unusually, was not questioned about his knowledge of English directly after being sworn in. Instead, he was asked about his knowledge of English while under cross-examination. Thornton stated that he could 'only speak some words of English', 'a word here and there' and did not sing the 'Heights of Alma' in the presence of Bridget Reilly or Mary Anne Gorman. The song begins with:

> Ye loyal Britons, pray give ear
> Unto the news I bring you here
> While joy each Briton's heart doth cheer
> For the vict'ry gained at Alma
> 'Twas on September the eighteenth day
> In spite of dashing salt seaspray,
> We landed safe in the Crimea
> Upon our route for Alma[9]

Thornton also stated that he had not spent time with the prisoner during the assizes.

The prosecution had prepared for the trial by collecting information suggesting that Thornton did in fact speak some English and had met with the prisoner; two witnesses were called to challenge his claims. Mary Anne Gorman, described as daughter of an inspector of national schools, was sworn in and said that she had heard Thornton singing the 'Heights of Alma' and that he had spoken English; she heard him say 'room'. The judge instructed the interpreter to ask Thornton if he understood what Gorman had said and he swore that he did not. Miss Gorman then said she saw Burke in Thornton's company in the lodging house, and Thornton admitted he had been in the kitchen with Burke. The judge then asked the interpreter to ask Thornton if he knew what he was about to say, and said 'Heights of Alma' but Thornton said he did not and swore he could not repeat the words. Bridget Reilly, a servant from the lodging house, described as 'an intelligent little girl', was examined and said she heard Thornton singing 'Heights of Alma', and speaking to himself in English. She also had seen Burke and Thornton talking. Thornton had asked her in English to 'Take down the candle, Biddy.' However,

7 Judy Syze is referred to as Judith Lize in Cox, *Reports of cases* (London, 1861), vii, p. 45.
8 Cox, *Reports of cases*, viii, p. 44.
9 Traditionalmusic.co.uk. Donovan and others have recorded the song.

Thornton swore that he did not say these words. At this stage, the judge ordered Thornton to be detained for a decision on whether there were grounds for a prosecution against him for perjury.[10] Despite Thornton's evidence for the defence, Burke was found guilty and sentenced to three years' penal servitude.[11] Clearly the prosecution strategy of suggesting that the witness was untrustworthy had served its purpose.

R v. Burke went to appeal on the grounds that the issue of whether or not Thornton spoke English was a collateral matter, and was not the issue at trial.[12] The court of criminal appeal heard the case but decided that it should be re-argued before the twelve judges of the three law courts.[13] All the judges agreed that it was an important issue but opinions were divided; three judges (including Justice O'Brien from the original trial) felt it was admissible to hear the evidence on whether Thornton spoke English, while eight considered it inadmissible.[14] Mr Justice O'Brien, who had of course agreed to hear the evidence, felt that the presence of an interpreter meant that the witness 'gained the opportunity of preparing his answers and thereby evaded the ordeal of a cross-examination' and that this 'would give him an advantage that he was not entitled to' and that in this particular case, 'the whole evidence of the witness was a fraud upon the court'. For him, the manner in which the witness gave his evidence was not just a collateral matter. He was supported by Baron Pennefather, who said that in the interest of justice, it was correct to accept the evidence. Chief Baron Pigot also agreed, on three grounds: one, to contradict the witness; two, to show his bias; and three, to frustrate a deliberate fraud of the witness in favour of the prisoner.

The other judges disagreed. Mr Justice Jonathan Christian[15] acknowledged that 'mischief could follow' in some cases where witnesses who spoke English were allowed give evidence in Irish through an interpreter. However, for him, the question of whether or not Thornton had spoken English 'had no connection with the issue, which was the guilt or innocence of the witness at the bar'. He suggested that the desire to give evidence in Irish was not necessarily a desire to deceive the court or a fraud and that it was the language the witness 'knew best, and in which he could give his evidence in the most satisfactory manner'. He drew a comparison with a member of the court who found himself in a foreign country being examined in his own language, but discredited because 'he had been heard to speak a few words in Italian or French', and with a lady who could sing an Italian song being obliged to give evidence in an Italian court in that language. According to

10 *Connaught Telegraph*, 17 Mar. 1858.
11 *Freeman's Journal*, 13 Mar. 1858.
12 Ibid., 24 May 1858.
13 Ibid., 31 May 1858.
14 Judge Crampton was not present but had considered the case fully and concurred with the majority view. Cox, *Reports of cases*, vii, p. 65.
15 John Fleming suggested Jonathan Christian's father 'spoke Irish well'. 'Correspondence', *Gaelic Journal*, 6:1 (Apr. 1883), p. 186.

Christian, an objection could have been made to Thornton giving his evidence in Irish, and the judge could have heard evidence in order to decide which language should be used – an approach that, according to newspaper reports, was normal practice at all levels of the court system. Seven judges agreed with Christian and Burke's conviction was quashed.[16]

The law was that English was the language of all court proceedings and this remained the case after 1858. After all, judges do not have the power to overthrow laws and under the doctrine of precedent, lower courts are expected to follow case law. In the common law system, case law based on rulings or decisions by higher courts is a source of law. Such judgments create precedent, meaning that if a similar situation with similar circumstances arose after *R v. Burke*, i.e. a witness being cross-examined on a collateral issue, lawyers could refer to the ruling in that case. In *R v. Burke* the ruling is not that Irish speakers with a knowledge of English may opt to use Irish if they wish. As Justice Christian put it:

> The question whether the witness did or did not speak English was as much beside the issue at trial as whether he spoke Greek or Latin.[17]

The original case was really about whether or not Martin Thornton was a reliable witness – could he be believed? It could just as well have been based on evidence introduced to show that he had lied about another matter. The issue at hand was evidence, and specifically, contradiction on collateral matters that were not directly linked to the trial, and the ruling was that such evidence was not admissible. Cox's case summary is a useful reminder of the issues raised at appeal:

> A witness was called on behalf of a prisoner; before the witness was sworn he professed an inability to speak English. No question was then raised on the fact by the counsel for the Crown, and accordingly the witness was sworn in Irish, and gave his evidence in that language through an interpreter. On cross-examination he was asked whether, on a recent occasion, he had not spoken in English to two persons who were present in court, and shown to witness. He denied the fact, and those two persons were called by the Crown to contradict the statement to the jury as evidence:
>
> Held, that such evidence was inadmissible to show that the witness had made such a statement.[18]

R v. Burke continues to be cited as a case that made a ruling on what is acceptable evidence. For example, according to Routledge Evidence Lawcards:

16 *Freeman's Journal*, 3 June 1858.
17 Ibid., 9 June 1858.
18 Cox, *Reports of cases*, viii, p. xxxix

> The court held this to be a collateral matter, since his ability to speak English was not a fact in issue in the case, merely a way to question the credibility of the witness in suggesting that he had lied to the court. Had the case concerned whether the witness had made a specific statement which was in English his ability to speak English would have likely been a fact in issue, rather than merely a collateral matter, and the answer then could have been rebutted.[19]

Doak et al. also focus on the issue of rebuttal:

> the difficulty here was that the court refused to allow counsel to adduce any evidence in rebuttal, since this was deemed to be a collateral matter. While neither counsel nor the jury is required to believe the answer to a collateral question, counsel is prevented from calling further evidence to demonstrate that the evidence is not true.[20]

The following month, on 21 July 1858, witness Martin Thornton was arraigned for perjury at the crown court but the indictment against him was deemed 'informal' and after some deliberation, a *nolle prosequi* was entered.[21] Given the finding in *R v. Burke* that the disputed evidence relating to his knowledge of English was inadmissible, it would have been extremely difficult to sustain a prosecution.

While Justice Christian's comments on the language the witness 'knew best, and in which he could give his evidence in the most satisfactory manner' were very enlightened, he did not always take such a kindly approach and conformed more to his reputation for irascibility and unpredictable temper when,[22] the following year, in a trial for manslaughter at Mayo crown court, he informed a witness in the case, the Irish-speaking mother of the deceased, that he 'wished it to be understood generally, and conveyed to this witness in particular that he would not allow expenses to any witness as did not give their evidence in English'.[23] This was described by the *Mayo Constitution* as 'rather an extreme measure',[24] while the *Connaught Telegraph* wrote of Christian's 'petty, illiberal and illegal crusade against the Irish language'.[25] Denis Holland, owner and editor of the *Irishman*, using the pseudonym 'Allua', and without referring to the judge by name, responded with an article about what he termed the 'degradation of Ireland and Irishmen', namely 'that judges and lawyers on the Connaught circuit have been persecuting

19 *Routledge Evidence Lawcards* (7th ed., Abingdon, 2012–13), p. 90.
20 J. Doak, C. McGourlay and M. Thomas, *Evidence in context* (Abingdon, 2012), unpaginated.
21 *Connaught Telegraph*, 21 July 1858.
22 David Murphy, *Dictionary of Irish biography*, online.
23 *Mayo Constitution*, 15 Mar. 1859. In cases heard at assizes, witness expenses could be paid on a sliding scale (see ch. 10 in this volume).
24 *Mayo Constitution*, 15 Mar. 1859.
25 *Connaught Telegraph*, 13 Apr. 1859.

the unfortunate witnesses who could not give evidence in English – scoffing at them, and insulting them with revolting insolence'. According to Holland, 700,000 people spoke English only, while 1.8 million spoke English and Irish, but many of the latter spoke English 'imperfectly', and had to think in Irish 'and then translate their thoughts into indifferent English'. He went on to give an example:

> Who has not often seen a peasant witness pothered by some question thundered at him from Bench or bar, look stupid and almost idiotic, in his bewilderment, but brighten immediately with the clear light of keen intelligence when the query was put by the interpreter in his own native language?[26]

R v. Burke did not change anything for Irish speakers. It simply meant that they could not be challenged on their alleged knowledge of English during cross-examination and witnesses testifying to their use of the language could not be introduced at that late stage. The system of first swearing in Irish speakers and then asking them under oath if they spoke or had ever spoken English, and hearing witnesses who maintained that they had spoken English, continued. The courts simply had to ensure that questions relating to knowledge of English were asked before the case proper got underway.[27]

CONCLUSION

The Administration of Justice (Language) Act (Ireland) (1737), whereby Irish speakers who spoke English were obliged to speak English in court was still very much in force. The ruling in *R v. Burke* conferred absolutely no rights on Irish speakers. It did not allow them to choose if they wanted to speak Irish or English. There is no evidence that the kind words of Judge Christian altered attitudes to Irish speakers in any way. On the contrary, as we will see in chapter 10, newspaper reports demonstrate that there was ongoing distrust and suspicion of Irish speakers for many decades.

26 *Irishman,* 13 Aug. 1859, p. 75.

27 If the *R v. Burke* ruling had given a right to choose to use Irish or English in court, speakers of Welsh and English could have used the doctrine of precedent to argue for a similar right to use the Welsh language in courts in Wales.

CHAPTER NINE

The Maamtrasna case and policemen as interpreters

A NUMBER OF cases were heard at the Dublin special commission in Green Street in Dublin under the Prevention of Crime (Ireland) Act 1882,[1] legislation passed after the Phoenix Park murders of newly appointed Chief Secretary Lord Frederick Cavendish and Undersecretary T.H. Burke. The law allowed for trials to be held in a different county, with 'special juries'. Four cases involved Irish speakers – the Letterfrack trials of Patrick Walsh in August, and of his brother Michael Walsh in September, the Maamtrasna trials in November and the Lough Mask trials in December. As there was no salaried court interpreter in Dublin, a solution had to be found, and, most unusually for murder trials, RIC Constable Thomas Evans acted as interpreter at all of these trials. It is possible that Evans regularly acted as interpreter in a policing context; in 1877, he was based at Killanteene station, and despite being sick, had gone into the mountains with a magistrate to interpret a deposition from an injured man.[2]

The background to the first Letterfrack case was that a number of men broke into a house at night in April 1881 and dragged out John Lydon and his son Martin. Both were shot; John Lydon died immediately and Martin four days later. At the first trial of Patrick Walsh in August 1882, Margaret Lydon told the court that she had spoken in English to a magistrate and at the inquest but claimed that she did not have 'a good understanding' of the language. Constable Evans was allocated as interpreter but when she responded to a question 'in capital English', the judge instructed him to stand aside. However, the cross-examination was discontinued as she 'would not' answer the cross-examination questions in English.[3] As the jury could not agree on a verdict, a second trial was held and on this occasion Margaret Lydon gave evidence 'in tolerably good English' and Evans interpreted for witness James Faherty.[4] In September, at the linked trial of Michael Walsh for the murder of Constable Kavanagh, Evans took on a dual role as interpreter for witness Bridget English and very briefly as a witness for the prosecution, to testify that he had thoroughly searched the prisoner's house for a revolver or a hat.[5] This was

1 45 & 46 Vict., c. 25, Prevention of Crime (Ireland) Act 1882.
2 *Ballinrobe Chronicle*, 10 Nov. 1877.
3 *Irish Times*, 17 Aug. 1882.
4 *Freeman's Journal*, 22 Aug. 1882.
5 *Irish Times*, 29 Sept. 1882.

highly unusual but attracted no comment at the time, perhaps because of the unusual circumstance of the trials being held in Dublin.

The Maamtrasna murders continue to attract attention.[6] The facts of the case were shocking: John Joyce, his wife, his mother and his daughter were killed in their home in Joyce's country, Galway, where nearly 40 per cent of the population did not know English in 1871.[7] Two of his sons were seriously injured; one died shortly afterwards. Two days after the killings, three men, Anthony, John and Patrick Joyce – all monolingual Irish speakers – approached the police and gave statements alleging that they had seen a group of ten men go to the house. All three would later give evidence in Irish in court for the prosecution and be paid substantial rewards after the trials.[8] Information about the murders was communicated to Sub-Constable Patrick Kelly, who spoke Irish well and who acted as sworn interpreter during the taking of depositions by Mr Gardiner RM. Statements were written in English and then read and interpreted for Irish-speaking witnesses.[9]

As there was no system of interpreter provision at inquests, problems arose at the inquest which was held over a number of days in Maamtrasna. On the first day, a juror informed the coroner that a number of his colleagues could not understand the testimony of two doctors concerning the post mortems and suggested that Dr Ingham act as interpreter. Ingham proved unwilling and it was agreed that Dr Hegarty would 'state briefly the nature of the wounds' and one of the jurors would act as interpreter. Sub-Constable Lerhinan[10] told the inquest that he had acted as interpreter for Constable John Johnston when he spoke to Michael Joyce, the young boy who later died from his injuries.[11] A few days later, the interpreter for witness John Collins was an unnamed police constable. The coroner queried whether the witness had said 'dead' or 'killed' and he and 'another gentleman who happened to be present' agreed that the Irish word 'maro' meant 'killed' rather than 'merely dead'.[12]

Normal practice was for magisterial investigations to take place in public, but a magisterial investigation was held in private in Cong barracks before resident

6 See: T. Harrington, *The Maamtrasna massacre: impeachment of the trials* (Dublin, 1884); N. McAree, *Murderous justice* (Limerick, 1990); J. Waldron, *Maamtrasna: the murders and the mystery* (Dublin, 2004); M. Dungan, *Conspiracy: Irish political trials* (Dublin, 2009); S. Ní Chonaill, *Maum*, a play performed at An Taidhbhearc Theatre, Galway (2015); S. Ó Cuirreáin, *Éagóir* (Dublin, 2016); A. Hardiman, *Joyce in court* (London, 2017); C. Bairéad, *Murdair Mhám Trasna*, TG4 (2018); Kelleher, *The Maamtrasna murders*; C. Hanly, 'The Maamtrasna murders: the trial of Myles Joyce' in David Nash and Anne-Marie Kilday (eds), *Fair and unfair trials in the British Isles, 1800–1940* (London, 2019).

7 Ravenstein, 'On the Celtic languages of the British Isles', p. 590.

8 *Irish Times*, 11 Dec. 1882. Anthony Joyce and his brother John each received £500 while John's son Patrick received £250.

9 Brief on behalf of the crown, Oct. 1882, CSO/RP/3/045/23, NAI.

10 Lerhinan's surname is misspelt as Lenihan and Lenehan in various accounts.

11 *Freeman's Journal*, 24 Aug. 1882.

12 Ibid., 21 Aug. 1882.

magistrates Mr Brady and Mr Gardiner, in the presence of the prisoners, over a number of hours.[13] The prisoners were remanded and sent to Galway jail, where a second magisterial investigation took place, also in private.[14] Interpretation was most likely provided by a member of the Royal Irish Constabulary.

Sub-Constable Kelly was in charge of the witnesses during their stay in the crown witness house in Ballybough in Dublin. A colleague of his called Duffy, who was also in Ballybough, wrote to Dublin Castle suggesting that Sub-Constable Bryan Collins would be a more suitable person as he had been 'active in getting information' from the Irish-speaking witnesses.[15] However, a response from Richard Cooke rejected this suggestion, stating that Kelly 'was specially chosen for the duty', 'speaks Irish well' and 'no better man could be chosen for this duty'.[16] Two defendants, Anthony Philbin and Thomas Casey, turned approver[17] and gave queen's evidence against their eight co-defendants. A key problem throughout the trials was that defence solicitor Henry Concannon, who was from Tuam, County Galway, did not speak Irish and could not communicate directly with six of the eight defendants.[18]

There were thirty-one witnesses altogether – two resident magistrates, two doctors, a civil engineer, three RIC sub-inspectors and twenty-three Irish-speaking people from Galway. Separate trials were to be held for each defendant and the same personnel – judge, defence and prosecution teams – were involved in all the trials. The *Irish Times* reported that when the eight prisoners were arraigned, counsel for the defence told the court that some of them did not know English. Justice Charles R. Barry said, 'There ought to be an interpreter', and an interpreter called Kelly was sworn – this was most likely Sub-Constable Kelly.[19] A special correspondent for the *Morning News* commented that:

> There is something pathetic in the thought of the unlettered Connaughtman while evidence is being given in English, and remarks passed upon it in a similar tongue, straining eye and ear to endeavour to catch the meaning of what may mean to him life or death, before the interpreter can slowly puzzle out the phrases to him.[20]

At the first trial, of Patrick Joyce, who spoke English, approver Anthony Joyce was asked by Mr George Orme Malley QC for the defence, 'Don't you speak English?',

13 Ibid., 22 Aug. 1882.
14 *Belfast News-Letter*, 28 Aug. 1882.
15 CRF/1902/J13/25/38, NAI.
16 CRF/1902/J13/25/36, NAI.
17 An approver was an accomplice to a felony who admitted his guilt and gave evidence against his accomplices.
18 Waldron, *Maamtrasna*, p. 57.
19 *Irish Times*, 2 Nov. 1882.
20 *Morning News*, 2 Nov. 1882.

but did not respond. Malley then said, 'You know very well what I'm saying – can't you speak English?', but once again there was no reply. The attorney general suggested that he rephrase the question in a manner he felt would be more easily understood by an Irish speaker: 'Have you any English?' (An bhfuil Gaeilge agat?). Malley commented, 'Oh, he understands very well, can't you speak English?', but once again there was no response and Malley started to ask questions through interpreter Thomas Evans.[21] Similarly, the attorney general told the interpreter, 'Ask him if he has any English', and got the response 'No.' The attorney general then queried, 'None at all?', to which the answer through the interpreter was, 'None at all.'[22]

Mr Malley, instead of questioning the witness in detail about what he had told the court under oath, opted for a different strategy, that of drawing on prejudice against Irish speakers whom he branded liars. He commented on evidence given by Irish-speaking witnesses, saying:

> An Irish speaking witness upon a table may as well be allowed to go down when he gives his direct examination, as for endeavouring to make him contradict himself when he has an opportunity of hearing that which every Irish speaking witness understanding the English language, though he may not speak it. When he has an opportunity of hearing the question, and then having it interpreted by the interpreter, and listening to each word as it is delivered, he has an easy opportunity of making up his mind, and we know the mind of the Irish peasant is not so obtuse as not to be able to suggest the safeguard to be adopted by a witness when giving his evidence. Gentlemen, I might as well allow these witnesses to go down as to attempt to contradict them out of their own mouths, or to shake their evidence by proving out of their own lips that they are telling falsehoods.[23]

Given that many witnesses and defendants at the trial were Irish speakers, this was a risky strategy. Patrick Joyce was found guilty and sentenced to death.

At the second trial, that of Patrick Casey, who also spoke English, Irish-speaking witness Mary Casey was asked, through the interpreter, 'Ask her has she any English at all?', and the reply was 'No.'[24] There was one incident when Mr Stritch for the defence commented on what the interpreter said. He had just asked witness John Joyce this confusing question: 'If your uncle had made much noise would he be telling the truth?' The reply came back: 'He did not make much noise.' Mr Stritch responded: 'That is no answer, interpreter.' At that point Judge Barry intervened, saying, 'I must say that I have never heard better interpretation

21 Dublin October Commission, NAI, CRF/1902/J13/29, p. 15.
22 Ibid., p. 21.
23 Ibid., p. 55.
24 Ibid., p. 124.

in my life,' and Mr Stritch responded, 'I do not say anything to the contrary, my lord,' and continued his questioning but on a different tack.[25] It is impossible to know if the unsatisfactory reply came from the witness or from the interpreter or indeed if Mr Stritch understood Irish and was not happy with the interpretation. Nor do we know if the judge understood Irish or how he assessed the interpreter's performance. Barry was from Limerick, and had worked on the Munster circuit from 1848 until 1859.[26] He may have understood some Irish.[27] At the very least, he must have had experience of working with interpreters. On one occasion, Mr Murphy QC (for the prosecution) checked the translation of what witness Julia Casey had said:

> Mr Murphy – I thought she said he went out before breakfast time.
> The Interpreter – She says now it was after breakfast.
> Mr Murphy (to Interpreter) – Did you interpret her evidence correctly when you said she first stated he went out to work and came back to breakfast?
> Interpreter – I did.[28]

According to the *Freeman's Journal*, when the clerk of the crown told Patrick Casey the verdict of guilty, he 'looked around the court as if for the interpreter' and the clerk continued, asking him in English to say why a sentence of death and execution should not be awarded against him. Casey told the court in English, 'I have to say that I had nothing at all to do with it', but the court instructed the interpreter to respond, upon which the interpreter went to the dock 'and commenced to make the communication in English, but the prisoner asked him to speak in Irish', and the interpreter did so. The judge then donned the black cap and said that Casey would be hung at Galway jail on 15 December. Again, according to the *Freeman's Journal*:

> The condemned man stood motionless in the dock for a little while, then took his cap from the seat beside him and beckoned the interpreter to come near. He whispered to the interpreter, who informed the court that the prisoner had asked 'What day?' The unfortunate man was informed the 15th December, and he, looking upwards with a most reverent and touching aspect, exclaimed in the Irish language 'I have expectations of heaven.'[29]

25 *Irish Times*, 15 Nov. 1882.
26 Gerry McElroy, *DIB* online.
27 Kelleher suggests that Judge Barry 'had some knowledge of Irish' because he intervened to suggest an alternative translation when Evans was interpreting for witness Mary Joyce. *The Maamtrasna murders*, p. 113.
28 *Freeman's Journal*, 17 Nov. 1882.
29 Ibid., 18 Nov. 1882.

Casey, unable to assimilate the information about the date in English, had to request the interpreter's help.[30]

The third trial, that of Myles Joyce (Maolra Seoighe in Irish), was controversial because he had no English and none of the testimony in that language was interpreted for him. This was the first occasion on which Thomas Evans acted as interpreter for a defendant at the Dublin special commission. Mr Malley QC read out an affidavit from defence solicitor Concannon requesting a postponement and stating that Myles Joyce was illiterate and 'incapable of instructing us',[31] but the trial went ahead. The question of whether the defendant spoke English arose:

> The Attorney General asked the learned counsel for the defence if the prisoner spoke English.
>
> Mr Concannon replied that he thought he did not, and that it might be better to have the evidence of the witnesses who speak English interpreted to the prisoner in Irish.

Mr Concannon's response of 'I don't think so' would suggest that he had not communicated or attempted to communicate directly with Myles Joyce. Evans then stepped in and: 'The interpreter asked the prisoner in Irish if he understood the evidence that was being given in English, and informed the Court that the prisoner answered in the affirmative.'[32] This exchange is the crux of the matter. We can only guess that perhaps the defendant did not catch the question, or misunderstood it, or that the interpreter misunderstood his reply. Or perhaps, as Seán Ó Cuirreáin has suggested, Evans asked, 'An dtuigeann tú?' (Do you understand?), and Myles Joyce replied 'Tuigim' (I understand), meaning that he understood the interpreter's question.[33]

The result of this exchange was that Evans did not interpret the evidence given in English by civil engineer Ryan, approvers Anthony Philbin and Thomas Casey, Constable John Johnston, Dr Hegarty, Mr Gardiner RM and Sub-Inspector Phillips. Myles Joyce's lack of understanding was obvious to onlookers, with one reporter commenting that he 'did not appear to have the slightest knowledge of the language in which his trial is being conducted'.[34] When Myles Joyce was found guilty, 'the Clerk of the Crown informed the prisoner in the usual language of the result', but, according to reporters, the defendant 'seemed like a man who had only the vaguest notion of what was going on'.[35] So much so, that the judge belatedly called on the interpreter to interpret the verdict to the defendant. Evans then went on to interpret the defendant's response into English for the court but, according

30 *Nation*, 25 Nov. 1882.
31 *Belfast News-Letter*, 20 Nov. 1882.
32 *Freeman's Journal*, 20 Nov. 1882.
33 Ó Cuirreáin, *Éagóir*, p. 120.
34 *Freeman's Journal*, 18 Nov. 1882.
35 *Nation*, 25 Nov. 1882.

to the *Freeman's Journal*, 'It merely conveys the tenor, not the full words of the condemned man, who, in making the protestation frequently invoked the Son of God.'[36]

The fourth trial was that of Michael Casey, who, like Myles Joyce, had no English. In a letter dated 6 December 1882, crown counsel Murphy wrote to the lord lieutenant that defence barrister Malley had informed the prosecution after the convictions of the first three defendants that he had sent for a Mr Quin, 'as he had no person in Dublin sufficiently conversant with Irish to communicate with the prisoners', and requesting that the trial of Michael Casey be postponed until Quin arrived. However, this proposal was rejected.[37] The first day of Michael Casey's trial provides more information on interpreting. His solicitor, Mr Concannon, told the court that Casey did not understand any English and the judge directed that 'Then all the evidence must be interpreted to him.' The interpreter was instructed to tell the prisoner that he had the right to challenge the members of the jury, but Casey replied that 'he had no skill in such matters'.

The interpreter was then instructed to translate to the defendant 'the evidence of English speaking witnesses'. While listening to the interpretation, Casey 'interjected some remarks' at first, but then 'merely nodded his head in acknowledgment of the interpreter's services each time a sentence was translated'. While a civil engineer was giving evidence, Casey made some comments that led to some discussion. Mr Murphy QC (for the prosecution) suggested that, to avoid interruptions, an Irish speaker could sit beside Casey and interpret his comments to Mr Concannon. The judge was willing to put up with the interruptions and Mr Murphy 'thought it would be better if the interpreter communicated to the prisoner that his counsel and solicitor were watching the case for him', presumably so that he would not feel the need to speak. Then the judge suggested that Mr Evans could stand near Casey and 'communicate to Mr Concannon anything of importance that the prisoner said. Mr Evans is a man of sufficient intelligence to distinguish what was important.'[38] The interpreter then stood beside Mr Concannon but the prisoner 'made no further remark'.[39] This raises the question of where exactly Evans had been standing. If he had been interpreting what the civil engineer said in English, one would expect him to have been positioned near Casey. Also of note here is the judge's unusual suggestion that the interpreter, who was a policeman, and presumably keen on a conviction, would decide what the defence counsel needed to know.

The following day, Michael Casey and the four remaining defendants decided to plead guilty rather than risk being found guilty and condemned to death. Evans was 'called and directed by the Attorney-General to communicate to the prisoner, Michael Casey, that his counsel was about to plead guilty for him'. Mr Murphy,

36 *Freeman's Journal*, 20 Nov. 1882.
37 CRF/1902/J13/10/9, NAI.
38 *Freeman's Journal*, 21 Nov. 1882.
39 *Belfast News-Letter*, 21 Nov. 1882.

QC, then said that the interpreter must communicate the information that the counsel had withdrawn the plea of not guilty to the charge of murdering John Joyce, but Mr Justice Barry held that they must plead guilty themselves. All five did so in Irish through the interpreter. When it was time to pronounce the sentence, the interpreter was once again directed, this time by the judge, to tell the men that they had been sentenced to death. The sentences on these five men were subsequently commuted to life imprisonment. The first three defendants Patrick Joyce, Patrick Casey and Myles Joyce were hanged.[40]

The newspapers of the day contain no evidence of a problem with interpreting during the Maamtrasna trials. On the contrary, the *Freeman's Journal* reported that 'The Irish speaking witnesses gave their evidence through the interpreter with surprising clearness',[41] and described Evans as 'the accomplished police interpreter'. The reporter commented that 'This was so satisfactorily accomplished by the interpreter [....] that the proceedings were in no way delayed.'[42] Justice Barry also commented: 'I think I ought to say a word for the intelligent interpreter, who discharged his duties, which were very difficult, in a most admirable manner.'[43]

Immediately after the trials, in December 1882, with approval from Lord Lieutenant Earl Spencer, twenty-nine RIC men involved in the Maamtrasna investigation were promoted, given a 'first class favourable record' or paid a gratuity. Thomas Evans was paid a gratuity of £10, while Bryan Collins and William Lerhinan were awarded £5 each. Sub-Constable Patrick Kelly, clearly seen as pivotal to the prosecutions, was promoted to constable and received a first-class favourable record.[44]

Myles Joyce's trial was the ultimate Kafkaesque experience – an innocent man on trial for his life who cannot understand a word of the evidence against him given in English even though an interpreter is present in court. At the time, as explained in the introduction, the fact that he had legal counsel was sufficient, he was not automatically entitled to an interpreter. However, his solicitor did request an interpreter, a request that was granted by the court but, due to some confusion or misunderstanding, was not realized. Concannon did not pursue the issue when the interpreter informed the court that the prisoner understood. However, the ultimate responsibility lay with Judge Barry.

40 After the trials, Irish-speaking policemen were selected to protect approvers Anthony Philbin and Thomas Casey. In 1884 Constable Daniel Gallivan, Cappaduff, who was charged with protecting Anthony Philbin from the end of the trials until January 1884, made a statement in which he wrote, 'I understand Irish,' and described how he overheard Philbin and his cousin Watt Henihan conversing in Irish and, 'They had no means of knowing that I understood.' Similarly, Constable Daniel Leahy stated that Casey had spoken in Irish to Higgins (one of those charged with the Huddy murders at Lough Mask). Leahy heard a sentence in Irish but the two men continued their conversation in a whisper. CRF/1902/J13/20/25, NAI.

41 *Freeman's Journal*, 15 Nov. 1882.

42 Ibid., 21 Nov. 1882.

43 *Irish Times*, 22 Nov. 1882.

44 *Flag of Ireland*, 16 Aug. 1884.

Over time, people came to appreciate that there had been a number of problems with the trials and that Myles Joyce was most likely innocent. In August 1883, Timothy Harrington spoke about the case in the house of commons and, referring to Myles Joyce, said:

> He was conveyed more than 200 miles from his home, and put upon his trial in Dublin. Not a single word of English was he able to speak; not a single word of his own language were the jury who tried him able to comprehend. The Judge, who tried him, was to him as much a foreigner as if he were a Turk trying the case in Constantinople. The very crier of the Court, and the counsel who represented him, were foreigners to him; and the whole trial, as far as he was concerned, was an empty show and a farce. As if to make the farce still more ludicrous, the very interpreter employed by the Crown to interpret the language of the Court to this unfortunate man was a policeman.[45]

The response of Mr Porter, the attorney general for Ireland, included the following:

> He could remind the hon. Member who had called attention to this matter that the policeman who interpreted was not one of those engaged in the investigation of the case. The officer was under the immediate control of the prisoner's attorney; and he had, no doubt, done his work faithfully and well, notwithstanding that differences of opinion had arisen as to the proper interpretation to be put upon certain words.[46]

Porter's response contains some interesting information; the fact that Evans had not been involved in the investigation was seen as an important factor. It certainly was an important factor, but one that, as we have seen, did not apply at the September Letterfrack trial, where Evans was both interpreter and a policeman involved in the investigation. Also, Evans 'was under the immediate control of the prisoner's attorney', which may refer to the Casey trial where he was instructed to stand next to Concannon. However, there is no evidence of Concannon controlling the interpreter in any way. In any case, the norm would be for interpreters to be under the control of the judge rather than defence lawyers.

In 1884, Thomas Casey's public confession that he had committed perjury and that Myles Joyce and the four men sentenced to penal servitude were not involved[47] refocused interest on the case. Harrington went on to write a book about the Maamtrasna case and,[48] along with fellow members of parliament Charles

45 HC Debates, 13 Aug. 1883, vol. 283, cc 294–390.
46 Ibid.
47 *Freeman's Journal*, 16 Aug. 1884.
48 Harrington, *The Maamtrasna massacre*.

Stewart Parnell and Maurice Healy, requested an inquiry into the Maamtrasna trials on numerous occasions – but this was not granted. They were concerned about many issues around the trial, including depositions that were not shared with the defence; interpretation provided by a policeman; the fact that the trials were held in Dublin, which meant that the Maamtrasna defendants were not tried by their peers; and that the surviving Joyce boy was not permitted to give evidence because he did not understand the implications of taking an oath in court.

Attention continued to focus on the very idea of a policeman acting as interpreter in court. For example, an editorial in the *Irishman* in 1884 made the rather convoluted point that the defendants could not understand how evidence given in Irish was interpreted to the court and described the use of policemen as interpreters as 'shocking', asking, 'What guarantee had the public that the policemen who interpreted the evidence against Myles Joyce and others were competent to discharge so serious and solemn a duty? They had none whatever.'[49] There has been some misinformation about Evans, purporting to show that he was not an appropriate interpreter because he did not understand Connaught Irish. A member of the council of the Gaelic Union suggested in 1886 that he was from the south of Ireland.[50] According to Jarlath Waldron, he was from Donegal, spoke Ulster Irish, and was unfamiliar with Connaught Irish.[51] RIC records give Evans' place of birth as Mayo-Galway.[52] However, Evans stated in the 1901 census that he was born in County Galway.[53] He may have grown up in Oughterard. RIC officers were usually stationed in a different district from where they were born and reared.[54] The authorities were aware that some defendants and witnesses did not speak English, that there was no salaried interpreter in Dublin and that they needed to recruit a suitable person. Evans may have been carefully selected. From the point of view of Dublin Castle, he was the ideal candidate to act as interpreter at the Dublin special commission: he had some interpreting experience, he was a policeman, he spoke Connaught Irish and in addition he was a Protestant, which ensured that he had the trust of the authorities.

The controversy over Constable Evans acting as court interpreter led to steps being taken to prevent similar situations arising at future trials. In 1887, MP Maurice Healy suggested an amendment to the criminal law and procedure (Ireland) bill. His wording was, 'in case any witness examined under this section shall not speak English, the interpreter employed shall not be a policeman or other person in the service of the Crown otherwise than as an interpreter', but Chief

49 *Irishman*, 20 Sept. 1884.

50 *Freeman's Journal*, 2 Jan. 1886.

51 Waldron, *Maamtrasna*, p. 58.

52 RIC service records 1816–1922, NAI.

53 In 1901 Thomas Evans was living at 4 Glanmire Terrace, Upper Annaville Road, Rathmines and Rathgar East in Dublin. At the time of writing, the census forms for a number of streets in this area had not been digitized.

54 J.M. Sullivan, 'Irish police gleanings', *Am. Inst. Crim. L. & Criminology*, 4 (1913–14), p. 877.

Secretary Arthur Balfour responded that while the first part of the amendment, stopping at the word policeman, was acceptable, 'Inconvenience would arise from the adoption of the remaining part of the Amendment.'[55] Presumably, the official position would be not to use policemen as interpreters in court but to retain the option of using other court officials in the service of the crown such as court clerks but in particular summons servers, who regularly acted as interpreters in crown prosecutions at petty sessions. The new provision was included in the Criminal Law and Procedure (Ireland) Act 1887. This was very innovative but, unfortunately, the provision was not retained in later laws, possibly because the act proved to be extremely unpopular; Timothy Harrington MP published a damning collection of newspaper reports of cases taken under the act detailing severe sentences handed down for fairly minor misdemeanours.[56]

A quarter of a century after the Maamtrasna trials, James Joyce described the 'comic and at times tragic' questioning of Myles Joyce about his alleged involvement in the crimes. The interpreter is described as 'excessively ceremonious', while Myles Joyce is 'the patriarch of a miserable tribe unused to civilized customs, who seemed stupefied by all the judicial ceremony'. According to Joyce:

> The magistrate said: 'Ask the accused if he saw the lady that night.' The question was referred to him in Irish, and the old man broke out into an involved explanation, gesticulating, appealing to the others accused and to heaven. Then he quieted down, worn out by his effort, and the interpreter turned to the magistrate and said:
>
> 'He says no, "your worship".'
>
> 'Ask him if he was in that neighbourhood at that hour.' The old man again began to talk, to protest, to shout, almost beside himself with the anguish of being unable to understand or to make himself understood, weeping in anger and terror. And the interpreter, again, dryly:
>
> 'He says no, "your worship".'[57]

Joyce's description is an amalgam of what may well have transpired in many cases, but it is more fiction than fact; prior to the passing of the Criminal Evidence Act in 1898, defendants were not allowed to give evidence.[58] Myles Joyce was not questioned in court and the only time he spoke was when he was condemned to death.

55 HC Debates, 13 May 1887, vol. 314, cc 819–940.

56 T. Harrington, *Diary of coercion, part III, being a list of the cases tried under the Criminal Law and Procedure Act from September 1888 to 1st January 1890* (Dublin, 1890).

57 J. Joyce, 'Ireland at the bar' in Ellsworth Mason and Richard Ellmann (eds), *The critical writings of James Joyce* (Ithaca, NY, 1989), pp 197–8.

58 C. Jackson, 'Irish political opposition to the passage of criminal evidence reform at Westminster, 1883–98' in John McEldowney and Paul O'Higgins (eds), *The common law tradition* (Dublin, 1990), p. 185.

In 2012, two members of the house of lords, David Alton and Eric Lubbock, unsuccessfully sought a review of Myles Joyce's conviction in the hope that he would be declared a victim of a miscarriage of justice.[59] In 2015, then Taoiseach Enda Kenny commissioned a review of the case, which was carried out by Dr Niamh Howlin.[60] In April 2018, Myles Joyce was granted a posthumous pardon by President Michael D. Higgins.

THE LOUGH MASK TRIALS AND THE PARNELL COMMISSION

The Lough Mask case was a trial for the murder of bailiff John Huddy and his grandson, who had set out to serve some processes; their bodies were dumped in Lough Mask. These murders took place in January 1882, before the Maamtrasna murders, and some believe the cases were linked.[61] However, the Lough Mask trials followed the Maamtrasna trials. Many witnesses and one defendant, Patrick Higgins, were monolingual Irish speakers. Sub-Constable Fitzgerald and Constable Bryan Collins acted as interpreters during the investigation and the latter was the interpreter at indictment before the grand jury,[62] while constable Thomas Evans was once again the interpreter at the trials. However, for reasons unknown, neither Collins nor Evans was in uniform at the Dublin special commission, something that caused some confusion for Justice William O'Brien. 'Bryan Collins, interpreter', appeared in court to corroborate the taking of a deposition from Kate Higgins, daughter of defendant Patrick Higgins.

When the trial proper began, Constable Evans, 'who acted so skillfully as interpreter in the Maamtrasna trials', was sworn in and 'was requested to explain to Patrick Higgins his right to challenge the jury'.[63] This would suggest that the court did not provide the explanation, but rather it was up to Constable Evans to do so. According to the *Daily Express*, Mr Murphy QC (for the prosecution) asked Evans, 'You were not the interpreter for him at Galway?' and he replied, 'No, sir.'[64] According to the *Irish Times*, when English-speaking Catherine Moran was questioned about being sworn in, defence lawyer Mr Adams commented that the exchange was not being interpreted to the prisoner, whereupon Evans 'informed the prisoner of the examination'. It seems, therefore, that the court instructed the interpreter to interpret the evidence for the defendant. Shortly afterwards, Irish-speaking witness James Flynn was being examined by the second lawyer for the

59 David Alton, 'Speeches, articles and books from Lord David Alton', davidalton.net/2011/06/03/the-west-of-ireland-the-maamtrasna-murders-3.

60 N. Howlin, 'Report on the Trial of Myles Joyce, November 1882' (Dublin, 2017), http://www.justice.ie/en/JELR/Report_by_Dr_Niamh_Howlin_Maamtrasna_Murders.pdf/Files/Report_by_Dr_Niamh_Howlin_Maamtrasna_Murders.pdf.

61 *Cork Examiner*, 21 Aug. 1882; *Ballinrobe Chronicle*, 26 Aug. 1882; Waldron, *Maamtrasna*, p. 20.

62 *Irish Times*, 9 Dec. 1882.

63 Ibid., 8 Dec. 1882.

64 *Daily Express*, 8 Dec. 1882, MS19748, NAI.

defence, Mr Teeling, who said that 'the witness' evidence should be interpreted to the prisoner', whereupon 'The Interpreter said he was speaking in Irish, which the witness understood' and Mr Teeling had to apologise to the court. The solicitor general commented disapprovingly, '[I]f this were done for the purpose of wasting time it should be discontinued.'[65] Approver Matthias Kerrigan was then examined through Evans as interpreter. Judge O'Brien told the jury that the fact that Higgins did not understand English 'formed an additional and strong ground for the exercise of great vigilance and circumspection in arriving at a conclusion so deeply momentous'.[66] However, the jury failed to agree on a verdict and a new trial was held immediately.

At Patrick Higgins' second trial, the solicitor general asked Evans to depose that he had 'truly interpreted' the evidence of Kate Higgins the previous Friday (during the first trial) and he did so. A juror gave the judge a list of questions and witness Bridget Kerrigan was recalled and asked why she had removed some blood off the barn. She replied 'For fear you (the interpreter) should come, or the like of you, and take myself and all in my house'. The judge then addressed Evans, saying, 'You are a constable?' and he replied, 'I am my Lord, and she knows it.' It is strange that this fact was not made clear from the beginning of the trial. It is surprising that the judge was not aware of this given that as we have just seen, the reporter from the *Irish Times* knew and so did Mr Murphy for the prosecution. Judge O'Brien's two-hour charge to the jury was not interpreted at all to Patrick Higgins, and according to the *Irish Times*, 'the prisoner maintaining a demeanour of listless indifference, which, however, in some measure at least, may probably have been due to the fact of his not understanding English'.[67] Nevertheless, in his summing-up for the jury, the judge mentions 'the intelligent interpreter, who was a police officer'.[68] At the end of the trials the judge suggested that Constable Evans 'was entitled to the highest approbation and the greatest mark of service that the Constabulary authorities can render to him by promotion and otherwise'.[69]

When the second defendant, Thomas Higgins, appeared in court, Mr Murphy QC (for the prosecution) asked, 'Can he speak English?' and he replied, 'A little.'[70] However, there was no discussion because 'a little' was clearly considered sufficient and as the defendant understood the question and replied in English, he was not allocated an interpreter. During this case, the judge commented that he found it 'a strange thing' that John Halloran Snr gave his evidence in English while his son did so in Irish.[71] A question arose about the word 'boreen', an unfamiliar concept to

65 *Irish Times*, 8 Dec. 1882.
66 *Daily Express*, 11 Dec. 1882, MS19748, NAI.
67 *Irish Times*, 11 Dec. 1882.
68 *Freeman's Journal*, 14 Dec. 1882.
69 Ibid., 21 Dec. 1882
70 Ibid., 15 Dec. 1882.
71 Ibid.

the Dublin jurors. A juror queried the difference between a boreen and a street. Mr Justice O'Brien said, 'I was about asking the same question', and Evans explained, not at all satisfactorily, that it was 'a little place in front of a country house'.[72]

The question of language ability was briefly raised once again at the trial of the third defendant, Michael Flynn, who was asked if he understood English or not. He replied, 'I understand a few words of it, but not very well',[73] and was not allocated an interpreter. All three defendants were found guilty and sentenced to death.

Thomas Evans was based in Galway until 1884, when he was promoted to head constable[74] and transferred to Longford; he retired from the force the following year. Despite his retirement and the negative publicity subsequent to his work at the Maamtrasna trials, he was recruited again to interpret for two witnesses from the Lough Mask case, Matthias Kerrigan and his wife Bridget Kerrigan, at the Parnell commission in London in November 1888.[75] However, there were differing assessments of his work. According to the *Evening Telegraph*, as reported in the *Ballinrobe Chronicle*, 'the evidence was interpreted by an Irish policeman with great facility',[76] while in Macdonald's *Diary of the Parnell commission* his efforts are described as follows:

> The interpreter, speaking in a hard, rapid, clattering voice, was almost as unintelligible as the Erse-speaking witness.[77] The Bench could not hear him. Counsel could not hear him. To make himself heard the interpreter moved off to the extremity of the solicitor's bench. Then it was found that he was too far away from his witness. They craned their necks, each in the other's direction, the interpreter turning his hand into an ear-trumpet, the witness doing likewise, as they bawled in their diverse tongues.[78]

At the Parnell commission, Kerrigan was questioned about a payment of sixpence that he had made to a man called Flynn; he was asked what the payment was for and 'after a short colloquy with the witness' the interpreter said he was collecting money for the Land League. At this point Timothy Harrington MP intervened as follows:

72 *Irish Times*, 16 Dec. 1882.

73 *Belfast News-Letter*, 19 Dec. 1882.

74 A number of the newspaper reports from 1882 refer incorrectly to Thomas Evans as head constable.

75 *Freeman's Journal*, 9 Nov. 1888.

76 *Ballinrobe Chronicle*, 10 Nov. 1888.

77 'Erse' originally referred to Scots Gaelic and later to Irish and Manx, *OED*.

78 The Parnell commission was a judicial inquiry established to investigate letters published by the *Times* purportedly signed by Parnell but in fact forged by Richard Pigott. A number of articles in the *Times* alleged that Parnell and others condoned the Phoenix Park murders and agrarian crime. The commission also examined the land war and the Plan of Campaign. J. Macdonald, *Diary of the Parnell commission revised from the Daily News* (London, 1890), p. 22.

Mr T. Harrington – I think the interpreter should put the question he is asked to put, and not add any of his own. He deliberately suggested the League to the witness.

The Interpreter – I did not.

Mr Harrington – You did, I happen to know Irish myself.

The President – Pardon me. You must put this in regular form. If you throw doubt upon the correctness of the interpreter we will have to have another here.

Was Harrington cognizant of the link between Thomas Evans and the Maamtrasna trials? It is most surprising that none of the newspapers commented on the connection.

POLICEMEN AS INTERPRETERS

We have seen that Thomas Evans and his colleagues Bryan Collins and Patrick Kelly spoke Irish fluently, but were they exceptions? In the nineteenth century policing was new and the role of the police was very different from today. At the start of the nineteenth century the grand juries appointed constables, who, according to Galen Broeker, were so poorly paid that they also held other jobs.[79] A county constabulary system was set up in 1822. The focus was on crime prevention rather than the investigation of crime and, according to Levinge, in the absence of evidence, 'the practice of questioning prisoners by police officers is entirely opposed to the spirit of our law'.[80]

The Royal Irish Constabulary (RIC) was established in 1836. In 1852, Francis Head listed the duties of the RIC men: keeping the peace; distributing and collecting voting papers for the poor law guardians; taking the census; escorting prisoners and convicts; collecting fines and penalties greater than sixpence; acting as billet-masters and as auctioneers for the distress sales; enforcing fishery laws; assisting the board of health; acting as masters of weights and measures; preserving order in sessional and assize courts; collecting statistics on crops and stock. According to their standing rules and regulations, 'the constabulary are not to converse with prisoners or question them respecting the offences with which they may be charged'.[81] However, Vaughan describes a loophole where if a conversation developed, the policeman could pursue it.[82] Only from 1864 was evidence from police questioning accepted.

Although there was no requirement at the time for the police to have a knowledge of Irish, in itself an indicator of the prejudice against the language, it was clearly an asset for those who did speak it. For example, Major George Warburton

79 Broeker, *Rural disorder and police reform*, p. 29.
80 Levinge, *The justice of the peace in Ireland*, p. 63.
81 F. Head, *A fortnight in Ireland* (London, 1852), p. 176.
82 Vaughan, *Murder trials in Ireland*, p. 63.

was moved from Wicklow to Clare in 1816 and 'it was his knowledge of Gaelic that must have assured his selection for western Clare'.[83] Similarly, Thomas Vokes was appointed chief magistrate of police in Limerick and used his knowledge of Irish to his advantage.[84]

There is some evidence of Irish-speaking policemen assisting magistrates in their enquiries. For example, in 1830, at Clonmel assizes, a policeman called John Ryan testified in a murder case that he questioned the victim in hospital before his death and one of his comrades 'interpreted truly and fairly'.[85] A similar death-bed case in 1833 in Slievegrine, Waterford, led to a court case where questions were raised about Sergeant Glynn's proficiency in Irish; he was examined by the interpreter in Irish but failed to understand him or the interventions of a judge and a member of the jury in Irish. However, a second policeman stated that he understood Irish and had been present while another man took down the declaration.[86] Some policemen picked up Irish; in 1848, Head Constable John Mullarkey told Judge Ball at Ennis crown court that he had been in County Clare for 15 years and understood Irish well.[87] In 1859, according to Inspector-General Brownrigg, constabulary detectives, known as 'disposables', were 'always ready [...] to converse – many of them – in the Irish language.'[88]

Knowledge of Irish could be important to prosecute some cases. In 1832 at Kerry assizes, Sergeant Giles Sullivan appeared as a witness in a case where Jeremiah O'Connor was one of four defendants accused of conspiracy and defended by Daniel O'Connell. O'Connor had made an anti-tithe speech in a mixture of English and Irish to a huge crowd. When Sullivan told the court that he understood Irish, O'Connell insisted on his conveying what had been said in Irish and proceeded to translate the information into English as: 'My brothers, do you know what the varnish of your tyrants' carriage is made of? It is made of the marrow of your shins.'[89] Tony Crowley has suggested that this was 'a tactic in order to embarrass the legal and political authorities', but this is improbable as it was important for evidential purposes to establish in court if the sergeant did in fact speak Irish and if he could repeat what was said in that language. If the sergeant had been unable to say the words in Irish, he would not have been a credible witness.[90] In any case, there would have been nothing unusual about a policeman in Kerry speaking Irish in 1832.

83 S.H. Palmer, *Police and protest in England and Ireland, 1750–1850* (Cambridge, 1988), p. 212.
84 R.H. Addison, *Recollections of an Irish police magistrate* (London, 1862), p. 37.
85 *Pilot*, 5 Apr. 1830.
86 *Waterford Chronicle*, 9 Mar. 1833.
87 *Clare Journal*, 28 Feb. 1848.
88 B. Griffin, 'Prevention and detection of crime in nineteenth-century Ireland' in N. Dawson (ed.), *Reflections on law and history* (Dublin, 2006), p. 112.
89 *Mayo Constitution*, 29 Oct. 1832
90 See, for example, *Freeman's Journal*, 4 Apr. 1872. See also the section on select committees and commissions in ch. 9 in this volume.

We have seen that policemen acted as interpreters at petty sessions, something that occurred in other courts occasionally. For example, in 1847 as part of the magisterial investigation of the murder of two children in Cork, Philip Somerville JP questioned a boy through interpreter Constable Jordan.[91] In 1864, Constable Murphy acted as interpreter for a man from Galway at Kilkenny quarter sessions,[92] probably because there was no longer a salaried court interpreter there. However, in 1884 the presence of a policeman as interpreter at Connaught winter assizes in Sligo was depicted as an unusual event. Acting Sergeant Reddington took on the role of interpreter for 'an aged man', who was accused of attempting to maim and wound his son-in-law's cattle. According to the newspaper report, the police officer's position 'was as novel as it was ludicrous', and the situation was seen as unique. No explanation is provided as to why a police officer acted as interpreter in this case rather than the assizes interpreter. In any case, the defendant claimed that he could not understand the interpreter and the judge commented, 'Better get some other man who understands Connemara Irish.' The replacement found was Keane, a process server.[93] In 1901, Constable Leahy acted as interpreter in an assault case taken by an Irish-speaking 'respectable elderly farmer' against 'a man apparently of the tramp class'. According to the chairman of Youghal board of guardians, thc constablc 'appeared to have a perfect knowledge of the language' and was complimented by the judge 'on his quickness and smartness in translation'.[94] RIC constables continued to use their language skills to gather information on crimes. In 1907, in Ballinrobe, an Irish speaker complained that he had been robbed of £6. However, the police 'were unable to know the old man's complaint until they procured an Irish-speaking constable, who acted as interpreter.'[95]

In 1916, an unusual case was that of an Irish-speaking Englishman with a French name, Claude Chavasse,[96] who was charged under the Defence of the Realm Regulations with refusing to answer questions put to him by a sergeant in Ballingeary, Cork. At Macroom petty sessions he was fined £4 with £1 costs or one month's imprisonment. At appeal, the sergeant explained that neither he nor the other policemen in the village spoke Irish but most people in Ballingeary did, including the parish priest, schoolmaster and schoolmistress. A constable in Macroom communicated in Irish with Chavasse as the sergeant did not trust anyone in Ballingeary to undertake this task.[97] Also in 1916, Pádraic Ó Conaire,[98] author and member of the Gaelic League executive, visited Donegal to collect data about the speakers of Irish and was arrested under the Defence of the Realm Act

91 *Southern Reporter & Cork Commercial Courier*, 6 Apr. 1848
92 *Kilkenny Journal*, 19 Oct. 1864.
93 *Sligo Champion*, 26 Dec. 1884
94 *Cork Examiner*, 18 Oct. 1901
95 *Connaught Telegraph*, 23 Mar. 1907.
96 The incident is mentioned on Chavasse's bio on ainm.ie.
97 *Cork Examiner*, 31 Mar. 1916. Chavasse's surname was spelt as Chevasse in newspaper reports.
98 See short biography in Irish at ainm.ie.

for supposedly making unlawful sketches of naval and military works. He spent a week in custody before appearing at a special court where the police said they had decided not to proceed with the case. Ó Conaire spoke in Irish at all stages, with Sergeant Connolly from Milford acting as interpreter in court. Resident Magistrate Mr Sparrow said that if Ó Conaire 'had not persisted in the farce of speaking Irish, he would not have been in his present predicament'. However, Justice of the Peace Mr Deeny spoke to Ó Conaire in Irish.[99] If the case had actually proceeded, presumably Ó Conaire would not have been allocated an interpreter.

In the 1901 census, a total of 139 then current or retired members of the RIC stated that they spoke Irish and English whereas in the 1911 census the figure had reduced considerably to 49.

CONCLUSION

It would have been impossible, particularly in the first half of the nineteenth century, and very difficult subsequently, for the police in Irish-speaking areas to manage without the input of Irish-speaking policemen. The Maamtrasna and Lough Mask cases demonstrate the value and importance of Irish-speaking policemen to understand what was said by Irish witnesses as late as 1882. No doubt in some places volunteers had to be found among the community, although there may have been some reluctance among Irish speakers to take on this role. While it was not unusual for police constables to act as interpreters in trespass cases at petty sessions (see chapter 6), it was highly unusual for them to appear at assizes and quarter sessions. The Letterfrack, Maamtrasna and Lough Mask cases were completely anomalous. Had the trials been held in Galway the local assizes interpreter would have carried out the work.

99 *Donegal News*, 8 Apr. 1916.

CHAPTER TEN

Interpreter provision in other settings

GIVEN THE HISTORY of land ownership in Ireland it is interesting to note that the earliest law located that mentions interpreters dates back to 1765–6 and provided for interpreters to be present when process servers served notices of ejectments:[1]

> If the tenant be unable to speak English, the process server may employ an interpreter to explain the nature and object of the ejectment (k); and it is not requisite that the interpreter should be sworn, or join in the affidavit of service, provided the process server depose that he saw the person employed, as he believed, interpreting the explanation.[2]

The provision is rather lightweight because it says the process server 'may' employ an interpreter rather than 'shall' employ an interpreter. It is unlikely that a process server would have paid an interpreter for his services – a volunteer would have sufficed. Furthermore, the phrase 'as he believed' is a loophole. While it is difficult to know if process servers did employ interpreters in these situations, and it is the case that many process servers were bilingual, it is worth noting that the law is quoted in a book on the law of landlord and tenant published in 1869.[3]

INQUESTS

Interpreters were regularly needed for Irish-speaking witnesses at inquests, but there was no official system for their provision, something that was very problematic, as we have seen in the Maamtrasna murders case. Other examples are available. In 1833 in Castlebar, Mayo, the foreman of the jury, the brother of a policeman, acted as interpreter for a member of the South Mayo Militia, who claimed he could not speak English.[4] In 1836 also in Castlebar, after a long discussion about whether or not witness Nancy Corley spoke English, coroner Joseph Bourke and some members of the jury took on the role of interpreter.[5] Similarly, in 1836, in

1 An ejectment is the act or process of ejecting a person from his holding.
2 1 & 2 Will. 4, c. 31, s. 12.
3 J.S. Furlong and D. La Touche, *The law of landlord and tenant, as administered in Ireland* (Dublin, 1869), ii, p. 983.
4 *Connaught Telegraph*, 16 Jan. 1833.
5 *Mayo Constitution*, 19 Feb. 1836.

Waterford, a member of the jury interpreted for the deceased's younger brother.[6] In 1842 in Bracaragh, Kerry, land agent Eugene O'Sullivan acted as interpreter at an inquest; he explained that he had cautioned the prisoner 'that he was to know that his making a declaration was no mitigation of any punishment, and that he was to expect nothing by making a voluntary declaration'.[7] In 1843 in Rahoon, Galway, the interpreter at an inquest was a Mr Val Browne.[8] In 1844, Edward Deane, justice of the peace, appeared as a witness in a murder case at Mayo assizes and told the court that he had acted as interpreter at an inquest.[9] In 1847, an interpreter was provided at the inquest into forty deaths from starvation in Bantry.[10] In 1862 in Castletown, Cork, the Revd Mr O'Reilly, PP, acted as an interpreter for two witnesses.[11] In 1867 in Macroom, Mr Michael Brosnan acted as interpreter, but confusion arose as to who had knocked down the witness' father. One of the jurors commented that the witness gave her evidence clearly, but there was a 'difference in the interpretation'.[12] In 1868 in Kilbrittain, Cork, an interpreter was provided for the mother of the deceased.[13] Two inquests in Belmullet in 1881 required an interpreter; in the first the interpreter was Father McManus[14] and in the second the interpreter was Mr J.L. Murphy, hotel proprietor.[15]

Only one instance of an interpreter being paid for work at an inquest was located. In 1915 Kerry interpreter Michael Dowd wrote to the chief secretary's office to request payment. As he had been called in by the Royal Irish Constabulary and not at the request of the coroner, payment was authorized in this case.[16]

ELECTIONS

While it made sense to provide interpreters to Irish speakers at elections, the exact reasons why this occurred have not been ascertained. No information was located on any such provision for speakers of Welsh in Wales. However, Irish speakers did not necessarily have a straightforward experience when it came to exercising their franchise.

In 1795, an act provided that there should be one place for every 100 electors to vote; electors had to register twelve months in advance; and there were various

6 *Waterford Chronicle*, 10 Dec. 1836.
7 *Kerry Evening Post*, 12 Mar. 1842.
8 *Galway Vindicator & Connaught Advertiser*, 19 Aug. 1843.
9 *Connaught Telegraph*, 31 July 1844.
10 *Cork Examiner*, 8 Jan. 1847.
11 *Skibbereen and Castletown board of guardians: copies or extracts of correspondence with the Skibbereen and Castletown boards of guardians and the poor law inspectors, with the poor law board, since November 1861* HC 1862 (424), p. 24.
12 *Southern Reporter & Cork Commercial Courier*, 19 Apr. 1867.
13 *Cork Examiner*, 2 Dec. 1868.
14 *Irish Times*, 10 Nov. 1881.
15 *Connaught Telegraph*, 10 Dec. 1881.
16 CSO/RP/482/15 and 1280/15, NAI.

oaths for the sub-sheriff, and also for voters.[17] Some of the oaths were very long – containing details of where people lived and about their property. Deputy sheriffs were required to ascertain people's right to vote and could reject voters.[18] The voters' oath, basically one very long sentence of at least 240 words, with one clause after another, must have been a serious obstacle to monolingual Irish speakers who at this stage were not provided with an interpreter. It is important to note that there was no secret ballot at the time.[19] In 1796 there was opposition in the Irish house of commons to the non-provision of interpreters at elections. During a discussion on amendments made in the house of lords to an election bill, F. Hutchinson stated that the requirement to take the oath in English would result in the disenfranchisement of many freeholders in Ulster and three-quarters of freeholders in Connaught to whom the franchise had been extended under the Roman Catholic bill. Henry Grattan, according to the *Northern Star*:

> reprobated in the strongest degree such an attempt to violate the faith of parliament to the people of Ireland, by the grossest insult on the Irish name, fame, and nation. It was an attempt to revive that obnoxious and tyrannical principle under which Ireland had for centuries groaned; it was an attempt to turn the venerated antiquity of the country into an instrument of slavery and disenfranchisement; it was an attempt to filch from the Catholics of Ireland, by a side wind, all that the legislature had conferred upon their loyalty. He trusted, therefore gentlemen would consider, before they ventured to urge such a principle – and if it was calmly withdrawn it was not his wish to go into discussion upon the subject. But if members on the other side of the house should persist in this breach of faith with gentlemen on this side, and with the grand body of Catholics in Ireland, he pledged himself for those friends of Ireland with whom he had the honour to act, that not only now, but after the bill should pass, so long as such a principle should continue to disgrace the statute books, and insult the nation, would he and his friends continue to reprobate and decry it session after session, in eternal deprecation, until it should be repealed.[20]

The chancellor of the exchequer on the same occasion expressed the view that for a man to benefit from a statute 'he should be obliged to take such oaths as should be required of him by the act in an intelligible language' – Irish clearly not qualifying as an intelligible language – and was challenged by Grattan, who asked:

17 An Act for regulating the election of members to serve in parliament, 35 Geo. 3, c. 29 (an act of the Irish parliament).
18 W. Finnelly, *The law and practice of elections in England, Scotland, and Ireland and of the trial of controverted elections* (London, 1830), p. clxxxix.
19 The secret ballot was introduced in 1872.
20 *Northern Star*, 21 Mar. 1796.

> What did the right honourable baronet mean by intelligible language? Did he mean that Welsh-English was the intelligible language? Or did he mean that Irish-English was that intelligible language? There were a great many worthy Irish gentlemen whom, the right honble baronet might be very intimately acquainted with, who, when they went to England were considered to speak but very bad English. The Scotch regiments which were here at this moment, he doubted not were brave soldiers and very worthy men – would it not be very hard if any of these gentlemen should be deprived of valuable rights because it happens that they may not speak English?[21]

Over two decades later, the Parliamentary Elections (Ireland) Act 1817 provided for interpreters and included an interpreter's oath:

> I A.B. do swear, That I will faithfully interpret such Oaths, Declarations, Affirmations, Questions and Answers as I shall be directed to interpret by the Returning Officer or Officers, his or their Deputies, and the Persons appointed to administer Oaths, Declarations and Affirmations at this Election.[22]

The *Account of sums paid to sheriffs at elections of 1818 and 1820 for writs and precepts, fees and expenses* (1820) shows that at the 1818 election in County Limerick, fourteen interpreters were employed for seven days, at half a guinea per diem. Two years later, also in Limerick, Michael Crowe was paid £7 for fourteen days' attendance in booth number one, at ten shillings per day, 'pursuant to 1 Geo. 4, section 9' and Thomas Egan was paid for thirteen days' attendance in booth number two. In County Galway, interpreters were provided at thirty booths or houses during an election at a cost of £293 15*s*. There were three interpreters in the town of Galway. Interpreters were also provided in the city of Cork for the 1820 election, but their pay was included with that of peace officers and a total figure given.[23] In the *Report from the select committee appointed to enquire into the expenses of sheriffs and other returning officers* (1820), Sir Henry Parnell stated that the expenses of sub-sheriffs had increased dramatically and in the 1818 general election in Queen's County the sub-sheriff's bill came to a handsome sum of £1,162 for five days' work.[24] Some elections lasted an inordinate length of time. For example, according to Dominick Browne, fifty-seven polling days were required for 10,000 voters to exercise their franchise in the 1813–14 election in Mayo.[25] As everyone involved, including the interpreters, was on a per diem rate, this clearly was a useful income supplement.

21 Ibid.

22 57 Geo. 3, c. 131, s. 15.

23 Sheriffs' charges and expenses at elections, 1818 and 1820, pp 6, 8, 12, 16, 19.

24 *Report from the select committee appointed to enquire into the expenses of sheriffs*, p. 8.

25 Ibid., p. 12.

The Parliamentary Elections (Ireland) Act, 1820 limited polls to fifteen days.[26] In places where there were 800 voters, two or more venues would be required for voting with one interpreter at each place of polling. The act set a rate of ten shillings a day for interpreters.[27] It also shortened the voter's oath considerably to a more manageable version:

> I A.B. do swear [or being a Quaker or Moravian, do solemnly affirm] that I will true answer make to all such questions as the sheriff's or other returning officer's deputy [as the case may be] presiding in this booth shall demand of me; and I do also swear [or being one of the people called Quakers or Moravians, do solemnly affirm] that I have not polled before at this election: and that I am as I believe twenty-one years of age. So help me God.

In 1826, an interpreter was provided at elections in County Armagh where, the reporter commented, 'the agents seem to take especial care that no man's conscience shall prevent him from voting for Mr Brownlow'.[28] A letter from Richard Westenra in 1834 illustrates the distrust around interpreter provision in County Monaghan at election time:

> To show you what rascals we have to deal with: the Farney [a barony in County Monaghan] men could all speak English on the late election, and in '32 they were obliged to have interpreters. This was all a trick to allow the interpreter to instruct them in Irish for whom they were to vote. Do you twig?[29]

The Irish Freeholder's Disenfranchisement Act 1829 provided that the right to vote was dependent on having a freehold estate of at least £10 a year.[30] This meant that men with such a freehold had to apply in writing thirty days before the cases would be heard and appear before the assistant barrister, who would sign a certificate if the property qualification was proven. If the assistant barrister turned down the application, the freeholder could appeal to a judge at assizes. For Irish speakers, the first hurdle was the letter in English and the second was an appearance in court. Under the act, anyone who refused to give evidence could be fined up to £10 or sent to prison for up to two months. In 1829, in Kilrush, Clare, prejudice against Irish speakers was evident when a man called Cunnedy who wished to register as a freeholder swore he could not speak English but when it was found on cross-examination that this was not the case he was committed to prison for fourteen

26 1 Geo. 4, c. 11.

27 J. Raithby, *The statutes of the United Kingdom of Great Britain and Ireland* (London, 1822), viii, p. 24.

28 *Belfast News-Letter*, 27 June 1826.

29 T2929/8/6, PRONI.

30 10 Geo. 4, c. 8. T.W. Williams, *An accurate abstract of the public general statutes passed in X Geo IV Anno 1829* (London, 1829).

days for 'prevarication'. He was followed by Matthew Coghlan, the next person to register, who also stated that he could not speak English. Revd Mr Martin, rector of Kilmurry, was sworn in and cross-examined by Mr O'Gorman about Coghlan's English-language proficiency:

> Do you, Mr Martin, recollect ever having a conversation with Coghlan, on any subject but that of tithes?
> Revd Mr Martin – I do.
> Mr O'Gorman – Can you now tell me on what subject it was?
> Revd Mr Martin – No, I do not know what it was about, but the conversation was in English.
> Mr O'Gorman – For what time was he speaking to you?
> Revd Mr Martin – For three minutes.
> Mr O'Gorman – It is of importance in this investigation to know, what these conversations were about; perhaps you may recollect any one subject on which he conversed in English with you. Can you tell, on what he was speaking to you?
> Revd Mr Martin – I cannot; these conversations made no impression on my mind at the time.
> Mr O'Gorman – Was there one of them that was not about tithes?
> Revd Mr Martin – I recollect that one which lasted for three minutes, was not about tithes.

Mr Cullinane, who acted as interpreter on occasion,[31] and who was clearly familiar with arguments around alleged bilingualism, then proceeded to ask some pertinent questions:

> Mr Cullinane – I now ask Mr Martin, if he can tell in the three minutes conversation he had with this man, how much of the time was occupied by his own observations.
> Revd Mr Martin – I cannot tell that.
> Mr Cullinane – I also ask Mr Martin if he will take upon himself to say that in any one of the conversations that he has had with Coghlan, there was one of them in which Coghlan attempted a sentence in English, that he was not obliged to finish in Irish?
> Revd Mr Martin – I cannot say that there was.
> Mr Cullinane – This was a point of the utmost importance, and it is one which Mr Martin should have had the candour to disclose on his direct examination. The reverend gentleman should have recollected that he was sworn to tell the truth, the whole truth, and nothing but the truth.

31 *Freeman's Journal*, 20 June 1829. A Michael Cullinan, possibly the same person, was paid £5 for interpreting at crown court in Clare in 1825.

> Barrister – I will not allow either side to throw out imputations of this kind.

Mr Cullinane was about to produce the parish priest and some of Coghlan's neighbours who were willing to swear that he did not speak English when the barrister announced that he accepted that this was the case.[32]

The amount of time taken up by the issue of language in what should be straightforward cases of whether or not men could register as freeholders is quite extraordinary. O'Gorman suggested that those claiming their franchise – and not only Irish speakers – were 'treated more like felons and criminals'.[33] In contrast, in 1830 at Waterford county court, an interpreter was provided for a man called James McGrath who wished to register to vote at the next elections. He told the court that he and his father held 40 acres of land worth £10 a year after rent and taxes and had thirty cows. According to the newspaper, the court jokingly asked: 'Who will you vote for at the next election, if we give you your vote?'[34] In 1833 at Westport quarter sessions, during registration as £10 freeholders, a lawyer complained, 'We ask but fair play; this day I have seen the very interpreter of the Court, sneering and casting imputations upon the complainants.'[35]

A letter to the editor of the *Times*, entitled 'Mocklawdry [mock law dry] Sessions', giving a fictional account, in fact a skit, of an Irish speaker who 'wanted to die a freeholder', appeared in 1840 and illustrates many of the prejudices prevalent at the time against Irish speakers:

> After sundry other questions to the same point, his worship interposed. 'Why, Mr Hobson, pursue this further. The witness has sworn repeatedly he understands not one word of English, and only recollects that he was called repeatedly by his own name in English, and the moment he was called in Irish he immediately answered to the call. Again, observe the unconscious vacancy of his countenance, while I am now speaking of him, and while the question is putting to the interpreter in English, and contrast it with its intelligence the moment the same interpreter speaks to him in his native language.' (Sensation). Here the witness addressed the interpreter in Irish, in a low tone. Hobson insisted upon knowing what he said; the interpreter answered at once, 'He asked me, was his freehold safe? and then added, 'the Judge looks like a fair man, but I fear he is against me' (Applause) 'I thought so' said his worship, somewhat elated, 'the man understands English, as much as he does Chinese'. Mr Hobson proceeds – 'Do you know Neal Fahy?' – What a fool's question, and he my own half-brother.' 'Neal was an honest

32 Ibid., 23 June 1829.
33 Ibid., 24 June 1829.
34 *Waterford Chronicle*, 20 Mar. 1830.
35 *Connaught Telegraph*, 10 Apr. 1833.

sort of a boy?' – 'The biggest rogue from this to himself and that was a long way off.' 'Where is he now?' – 'Where he ought to have been long ago.' – 'Where is that?' – 'To be sure you don't know.' 'Name the place where Neal Fahy is now.' – 'I must be a witch to tell you that.' (A laugh). 'Neal Fahy was transported?' – 'It was yourself seen him aboard ship?' – 'But mercy was extended to him?' – 'How could that be when you were the prosecutor?' (Laughter). Mr Hobson here appealed to the Bench and complained that he could not get a single direct answer from the witness. His worship then said, 'Interpreter, tell the witness that he is not to give argumentative answers to any questions proposed to him, however absurd he and others may think them to be'. The interpreter hesitated and then said 'Please, your Lordship, I have no ready Irish for 'argumentative'. 'Then tell him' said his worship somewhat hastily 'to answer yes or no in the first instance, and explain either answer afterwards.' Cross-examination resumed. 'Is Neal Fahy now in Ireland? – It is not so easy to get a return chaise from Botany Bay. (Laughter). Neal Fahy is now in Botany Bay? – Those who ride can find, and it was you who sent him there. 'Upon your oath don't you know that Neal Fahy was in Ireland within the last month?' 'How can he be in Ireland and in Botany Bay at the same time?' His worship, quasi in furore, here suddenly interposed – 'Interpreter, ask the witness if he was in Botany Bay a month ago could he now be in Ireland.' 'I never was in Botany Bay, my Lord' 'But, supposing you had been a month ago, could you be here now?' 'I am here now sure enough, and steam does wonders they say' His worship then addressed Mr Hobson – 'Well, Mr Hobson, will you proceed after this?' – 'But one or two questions more, your worship.' Did Neal Fahy ever break gaol? – Only twice. Did he ever run a race with the horse police? They were galloping after him across the country one day, but somehow or other he got away from them all. 'You are all done now' said Sleveeny 'your two questions are over.' 'We shall try a third' said Hobson 'You have sworn that you are Thady Muckabawn. Upon your oath, did he not die last night; and are not the neighbours now waking him?' – 'I am very glad to hear of my own death, but weak as I am, I am not dead yet'. Here the witness fell into a fit of coughing. 'You are a dying man'. 'We are all that, God help us' [Sleveeny here called upon the Court to protect the witness. 'It was cruel thus to sport with the infirmities of a paralytic old man trembling on the brink of the grave.'] 'One question more' said Hobson 'and it shall be the last. Are you not Neal Fahy himself?' Here the witness got a violent fit of coughing, but contrived to get out, 'I am but a poor subject for a joke'. 'Oh, Mr Hobson' said his worship, 'I must put a stop to this; I shall register this man forthwith.' 'Not yet, your worship. Come forth now, Thady Muckabawn, and give the lie face to face to Neal Fahy, who swears that he is you. Come forth, dead or alive, ghostly or bodily, and meet Neal Fahy, and again convict him of perjury! 'The ghost came out of a nook where he had

> been conveniently concealed, and was lifted up upon the table in the same identical costume as the witness. The instant he appeared upon the table Neal Fahy forgot all his self-possession, and abruptly exclaimed in English 'Oh! by the holy St Bridget, I am caught again; there he is himself. Boys, make way for another martyr' and with a bound of elastic vigour, which all the Bolognas who have ever been imported from the continent to play harlequin in the London theatres might have envied, this paralytic old patient cleared the dock, and found a ready passage through the mob, who were cheering him as he flew by them with cries of 'God speed you Neal Fahy; you have done the best you could for your religion and your country. Let us see the man who would harm you.' The police were in immediate pursuit, but the people, in order to confound the scent, were running in different directions. Sleveeny was seen blessing himself and lifting up the whites of his eyes in mute astonishment, while his worship was left to meditate upon that 'unconscious vacancy' of countenance which expressed so admirably a total ignorance of the English language. I am, Sir, &c, B.[36]

The description stereotypes the Irish speaker as duplicitous, willing to perjure himself by swearing that he does not understand one word of English, unable to give a direct answer to any question, taking advantage of the presence of the interpreter to confuse matters, deliberately misunderstanding questions, and making fun of Mr Hobson, the lawyer. The surname Muckabawn sounds like 'muc bán' or 'white pig' in Irish while the first name Thady, from Tadhg in Irish, was commonly used in a disparaging way to refer to a generic Irishman.[37] The judge is gullible, sympathetic to the witness and easily fooled that he understands English 'as much as he does Chinese'. The witness' lawyer is called Sleveeny, based on the Irish word slíbhín or sleeveen in English, a sly or untrustworthy person. The interpreter is possibly in cahoots with the witness but Hobson is suspicious of him – what is he saying to the witness? The interpreter quickly comes up with a plausible excuse and later does not know how to say 'argumentative' in Irish, the subliminal message here being that Irish speakers are argumentative but don't even have a word in their language to describe this characteristic. The court attendees are clearly on the side of the witness, and collude to foil the efforts of the police.

The *Account of expenses incurred by the returning officer at every election for a county, or city, or borough, in Ireland, during the months of June and July 1841* (1843) included information on the amount spent on interpreters. Some seats were uncontested and no elections held. In the county of Cork there were seven polling booths, 1,680 voters and seven interpreters employed for five days each at ten Irish shillings each or a total figure of £9 13*s.* 10*d.* In Kinsale, for the borough of

36 *Times*, 25 Aug. 1840.

37 Tadhg is also the origin of Teague, the Northern Ireland nickname for Catholics. I am grateful to Máire Nic Mhaoláin for her insight on Thady Muckabawn's name.

Kinsale, there was one polling booth and one interpreter was paid £2 6*s.* 1*d.* for five days' work. No interpreter was provided in the city of Dublin. In the county of Kerry there were four booths, with four interpreters, paid a total of £10. In County Tipperary there were twelve booths, seven used as polling booths, four as qualifying booths and one as sheriff's booth. There was one interpreter who was paid £2 for four days' work.[38] In 1844 M.J. O'Connell MP suggested that it was impossible to poll a hundred voters in an hour because of the time involved in having an interpreter repeat the oath.[39]

John Mitchel described the five-day election in Galway in 1847 during the Famine, where he acted as agent for one of the candidates, O'Flaherty, against Monahan, then attorney general. According to Mitchel, the bailiffs and agents held the tenants' certificates of registry and accompanied them to the polling booths, where voters had to say aloud the name of the person they were voting for. They also had to swear that they had not been bribed, and one Irish speaker was clearly conflicted between committing perjury and obtaining some money to feed his family:

> He spoke only Gaelic, and the oath was repeated, sentence by sentence, by an interpreter. He affected to be deaf, to be stupid, and made continual mistakes. Ten times at least the interpreter began the oath, and as often failed to have it correctly repeated after him. The unfortunate creature looked round wildly as if he meditated breaking away; but the thought, perhaps, of famishing little ones at home still restrained him. Large drops broke out on his forehead; and it was not stupidity that was in his eye, but mortal horror. Mr Monahan himself happened to be in that booth at the time, and he stood close by his solicitor, still urging him to attempt once more to get the oath out of the voter. Murmurs began to arise, and at last I said to Mr Monahan: 'You cannot, and you dare not, take that man's vote. You know, or your solicitor knows, that the man was bribed. I warn you to give up this vote and turn the man out.' In reply, he shrugged his shoulders, and went out himself. The vote was rejected; and, with a savage whisper, the bailiff who had marshalled him to the poll turned the poor fellow away. I have no doubt that man is long since dead, he and all his children.[40]

Monahan won the election by a mere four votes. Mitchel was not an impartial witness; despite this, his description of the Irish-speaking voter rings true and the very fact that people had to swear they had not been bribed is an indicator that bribery was endemic.

38 *An account of expenses incurred by the returning officer at every election for a county, or city, or borough, in Ireland, during the months of June and July 1841*, HC 1843 (620) l, 235, pp 5, 8, 12, 13.
39 *Cork Examiner*, 5 Apr. 1844.
40 J. Mitchel, *The last conquest of Ireland (perhaps)* (London, 1876), p. 149.

The Ballot Act of 1872, which introduced the secret ballot, makes no mention of interpreters. However, there are some newspaper references to interpreters being required for voters who could not read English. For example, at the general election in 1879, in Rathcormick, Cork, 'Some Irish speaking electors lost their votes as there was no magistrates to be had to take the declarations of an interpreter.'[41] In 1887 the *Connaught Telegraph* reported on a voter attempting to exercise his franchise in Mayo:

> The row, the shout, the scuffle, continued at intervals to enliven the scene until another thorough Irishman presented himself; he was too honest to use the language of the enslaver, and therefore it became evident to all, as soon as the interpreter was called for, that the vote was for the popular candidate, and the obstructors did not fail to do all in their power to confuse and puzzle him, but he was as firm as a rock and could not be driven from his purpose.[42]

At the 1892 election in Baltimore, West Cork, there were two interpreters; Mr Jas. Carey in one booth, and Mr John O'Neill, Sherkin Island, in the other, along with a presiding officer, a poll clerk and a personating agent.[43] The scale of expenses at the first elections of county and rural district councillors under the Local Government (Ireland) Act 1898 provided 'for an interpreter, where necessary, not exceeding £1'.[44] In 1902, the chairman of Mayo county council announced that presiding officers or polling clerks who acted as interpreters would not be allowed the fee payable to interpreters. Councillor Daly suggested that all presiding officers and polling clerks should speak Irish but the chairman responded that if that rule were to be applied to all county councillors 'many of them should disappear from the Chamber'.[45] In 1908, also at Mayo county council, a letter from county councillor Patrick O'Donnell was read out. He said that over 50 per cent of the population were Irish speakers and advocated the employment of Irish-speaking presiding officers at elections 'who could discharge the duties and save the expenses of engaging interpreters'.[46]

In 1914, there were a number of newspaper reports relating to interpreters. At the election of councillors in Clonakilty urban district, a reporter for the *Skibbereen Eagle* commented that 'Mr D Donovan's position as interpreter was a sinecure', presumably meaning that his services were not required.[47] However, the

41 *Cork Examiner*, 15 Feb. 1879.
42 *Connaught Telegraph*, 15 Apr. 1887.
43 *Southern Star*, 23 July 1892.
44 *Annual report of the local government board for Ireland, being the 27th report under the Local Government Board (Ireland) Act 35 & 36 Vic, c. 69* 1899 (C.9480), xxxix, 1.
45 *Mayo News*, 26 July 1902.
46 *Connaught Telegraph*, 7 Mar. 1908.
47 *Skibbereen Eagle*, 24 Jan. 1914.

council allowed election fees of 10*s*. 6*d*. to interpreter Dan Donovan.[48] In the same year, interpreters were provided for the election of county councillors in Cork.[49] In 1914, in Valentia, Kerry, in relation to an election petition, Mr Geoffrey O'Connell stated that there 'was quite a number of persons who could not record their votes for want of English', and an interpreter was made available.[50]

SELECT COMMITTEES AND COMMISSIONS

Interpreters were provided for select committees and commissions set up to investigate various matters. However, the number of witnesses who availed of interpreters was small. There were a number of select committee enquiries concerning elections. In 1853, at the select committee on the Clare election petition, Thomas Studdard was sworn as interpreter.[51] In 1857 the select committee on the Mayo county election petition focused in part on the words allegedly uttered by a priest, Father Conway, curate for Castlebar. One of the witnesses, David Ruttledge, magistrate of the county of Mayo, claimed that although he understood Irish from sitting in court and from dealing with his labourers, and he understood the controversial words of Father Conway, he could not repeat them exactly in Irish, but could provide an explanation in English. Mr Montague Smith objected 'that the words being stated to be important words, must be given in the language in which they were uttered, and then interpreted by some impartial person'. Mr Edwin James compared Ruttledge's situation to that of a sworn interpreter and said that 'he might be cross-examined upon the correctness of his interpretation afterwards'. Ruttledge was allowed give what he called 'the substance of it' and not 'the grammatical translation', which was as follows: 'May my curse as a priest, and of the Church, and of the people, be upon you, if you vote for Colonel Higgins.' He then added that the curse was 'seven times'.[52]

The commissioners appointed to investigate the existence of corrupt practices in elections of members to serve in parliament for the county of the town of Galway interviewed witnesses Martin Walsh and William Conneely in October 1857 and the minutes note in both cases that 'The witness being only able to speak Irish, an interpreter named Martin Naughton was sworn to interpret the questions and answers faithfully', and 'The witness was unable to give his evidence except in Irish, and an interpreter was accordingly sworn.'[53] In 1860 the select committee

48 Ibid., 7 Feb. 1914.

49 *Cork Examiner*, 30 Nov. 1914.

50 *Killarney Echo & South Kerry Chronicle*, 12 Sept. 1914.

51 *Clare election: report from the select committee on the Clare election petition; with the minutes of proceedings*, HC 1853 (587) ix, 535.

52 *Mayo election: minutes of evidence taken before the select committee on the Mayo county election petition; with the proceedings of the committee and index*, HC 1857 (182) vii, 357.

53 *Report of the commissioners appointed to investigate into the existence of corrupt practices in elections of members to serve in parliament for the county of the town of Galway, together with the minutes of evidence*, HC 1857–8 (2291) xxvi, 309.

on the Clare election petition included evidence from Michael O'Dea, who had difficulty understanding English. James O'Dea was sworn in as interpreter and Mr Phinn objected, as he was a witness in the case. On being told that O'Dea was 'only a formal witness', he withdrew the objection but checked as to O'Dea's knowledge of English:

> Mr Phinn (To the witness, James O'Dea) – Do you understand Irish well? – Yes.
> Do you talk in it? – Yes.
> And English too? – Yes.

Michael O'Dea went on to explain that he had voted for Colonel White 'because I got 6*l* for it' from Michael Houlihan in the presence of Pat Lynch. Two other witnesses were also examined through the volunteer interpreter.[54] In 1872, on the trial of the Galway county election petition, assizes interpreter Thomas Joseph Reid was sworn and asked to translate what a boy called Patrick Monaghan alleged that Father Loftus had said, in Irish. A witness called Thomas Hannan was sworn in and said: 'I beg your pardon, I have very bad English, and my master don't understand Irish; I beg you to let me speak a few words of Irish.' The judge was amenable to this request, but Mr Macdonagh said, 'I will try whether you can go on in English' and the rest of the examination was carried out in English.[55] In 1874, Pierce Joyce, a candidate at the previous election, gave evidence at the Galway borough before Mr Justice Lawson:

> Did you hear any of those bailiffs or Mr Morris or his son speaking at all to those men whom you were canvassing? – There were a great many of those men who did not speak English, and I do not speak Irish, and, therefore, he conveyed to them what I said.
>
> So that you had always, in fact, in dealing with men of that sort to require the assistance of an interpreter; did you hear anything said upon any occasion during your canvass about the ballot, about knowing how a man voted? – Well, I do not remember that I did.

Patrick John Gannon was sworn as interpreter for two witnesses.[56]

In 1847–8, according to papers relating to proceedings for relief of distress, and state of unions and workhouses in Ireland, 'many of the witnesses being unable to

54 *Clare election: minutes of evidence taken before the select committee on the Clare election petition; with the proceedings of the committee*, HC 1860 (178, 392) xi, 87, 153.

55 *Copy of the shorthand writers' notes of the judgment of Mr Justice Keogh on the trial of the Galway county election petition*, HC 1872 (241) xlviii, 17, 71.

56 *Galway borough election: copy of the shorthand writer's notes of the evidence given before Mr Justice Lawson on the trial of the borough of Galway petition in May 1874, and of the judgment of the judge in the said petition*, HC 1874 (201) liii, 577.

speak English, Mr Thomas J. Read is sworn Interpreter', and he and George S. Bourns interpreted for a number of witnesses.[57] In 1854, according to the *Report from the select committee of house of lords appointed to consider the consequences of extending the functions of the constabulary in Ireland to the suppression or prevention of illicit distillation*, two witnesses, one from Newport, were sworn and examined through an interpreter.[58] The *Report from the select committee on destitution (Gweedore and Cloughaneely)* in 1857 indicates that a man called Charles Gallagher was examined through an interpreter. W.S. Crawford esq. had visited the areas concerned accompanied by the Revd Mr McFadden as interpreter because 'there were only very few individuals in the district and in the houses that I visited that could speak English', and 'if I had not had the assistance of some person who could speak Irish, I could not have obtained any information at all'.[59]

In 1867 the board of trade ordered an inquiry into the wreck of the *San Francisco* in Clonakilty Bay, County Cork. An unsuccessful attempt was made to examine Cornelius Driscoll in English and Constable Hogan was then employed as interpreter. As the captain of the ship was Italian, an interpreter called Mr Tredesco was needed so he could give instructions about what to do with the boat.[60] In 1887 the minutes of the royal commission on the Land Law (Ireland) Act 1881 and the Purchase of Land (Ireland) Act 1885 refer to two Irish-speaking witnesses from Galway, Mr Thomas Hughes and Mr Mark Lanyon, who were examined through an interpreter.[61] In 1892 at the evicted tenants commission, Fr McFadden acted as interpreter for an Irish-speaking tenant from the Olphert estate.[62]

THE LAND COMMISSION

When the land commission was set up in Scotland, a provision was included in the Crofter Holdings (Scotland) Act 1886 that one of the judges should speak Gaelic. Scottish MP Dr R. McDonald commented that: '[I]t is of the utmost importance that the Commissioners should be able to talk to these people in their own language, and ascertain their grievances from their own mouths, instead of through

57 *Papers relating to proceedings for relief of distress, and state of unions and workhouses in Ireland 1848* [C 919, 955, 999], HC 1847–8, liv, 313; lv, 1; lvi, 1.

58 *Report from the select committee of the house of lords appointed to consider the consequence of extending the functions of the constabulary in Ireland to the suppression or prevention of illicit distillation; and to report thereon to the house; together with the minutes of evidence, and an appendix and index*, HC 1854 (53) x, 1.

59 *Report from the select committee on Destitution (Gweedore and Cloughaneely); together with the proceedings of the committee, minutes of evidence, appendix, and index*, HC 1857–8 (412) xii, 89.

60 *The San Francisco: copies of the report upon the inquiry recently held by order of the board of trade in the case of the wreck of the San Francisco in Clonakilty Bay, County Cork, in January last, and of the minutes of evidence taken at the inquiry*, HC 1867 (265) lxiv.1.

61 *Report of the royal commission on the Land Law (Ireland) Act 1881 and the Purchase of Land (Ireland) Act 1885* [C.5015], HC 1887, xxvi, 1241, 432, 436.

62 *Irish Times*, 22 Dec. 1892.

an interpreter.'[63] There was no such provision in the earlier Land Law (Ireland) Act 1881 and no provision was made for interpreters. The Irish act allowed for the establishment of the land commission as a court of arbitration to fix fair rents between landlords and tenants. As the land commission records have not been made available to researchers, we are dependent here on newspaper reports and on questions raised in the house of commons. The newspaper reports indicate that interpreters were provided in Galway and Kerry but cases in Cork, Donegal and Limerick had to be adjourned so an interpreter could be found and there are instances of court criers, priests, law clerks and valuers acting as interpreters. Interpreters employed at the land commission were paid five shillings per day.[64]

In 1883, in the house of commons, Timothy Healy MP cited a recent case in the land court in Bandon where a witness who was asked about rent said he could only speak Irish. According to Healy, at that point 'there was a howl amongst the barristers, and they insisted that he should give his evidence in English, and he had to do so'. However, when he was asked about rent he said he paid £50 a year and everyone present realized there was a problem. An interpreter was called, and it became apparent that the man had meant to say £30 a year. As Healy said, 'Here, then, was a case where a man's whole life would have been affected by a question of words, for it made all the difference in the world to a tenant whether he was charged a high or low rent.' The confusion of fifty and thirty could have been crucial. However, at the same debate, Mr Tottenham, MP for Leitrim, took a different view. He said he had lived in Ireland for twenty-five years and 'in the whole course of that time he had only known it necessary on one occasion to make use of an interpreter' and that was at a winter assizes in Carrick-on-Shannon where a number of witnesses from Galway did not have 'sufficient fluency' in English.[65]

In 1884, Chief Secretary for Ireland George Trevelyan said that 'with regard to witnesses who do not understand or speak English, the practice in all the Courts of the Land Commission is to employ an interpreter, and this course is also adopted when a witness' knowledge of English is imperfect'. This answer was in response to a question from Timothy Healy about a case involving a tenant called Mary Staunton in Fermoy. Trevelyan replied that 'she deliberately attempted to deceive the Court'. Healy asked if this deception 'related to her having spoken a few words of English after she had stated she could speak only Irish', but no reply was given.[66] Later the same day, Healy returned to the topic and Trevelyan said that 'in the opinion of the Judge of First Instance, the woman was deceitful'. It seems that in this case an assumption was made that Mary Staunton was lying when she said she did not speak English and as a result her only option was to lodge an appeal, something that could take several months. This distrust of witnesses and the belief

63 HC Debates, 19 Apr. 1886, vol. 305, cc 22–143.
64 *Kerry Sentinel*, 21 Sept. 1910.
65 HC Debates, 17 Aug. 1883, vol. 283, cc 1022–81.
66 HC Debates, 7 Mar. 1884, vol. 285, cc 855–6.

that they were deliberately misleading the court if they were heard to speak some English was widespread.

In 1881 in Ballina, in a case under the Land Act, a tenant's evidence about her rent was interpreted 'through the crier, William Kearney, an interpreter'.[67] In 1884 at Lifford land court, a number of cases involving tenants from the Glenties heard in Strabane (Tyrone) at the land commission court of appeal had to be adjourned because the interpreter was not available and only half the tenants turned up when the case was rescheduled.[68] In the house of commons, Mr Trevelyan explained to Arthur O'Connor MP that the interpreter usually employed in court was not there when the cases were called, and it was necessary to send to a considerable distance for him.[69] In 1887 at the Ulster subcommission in the Glenties, the chairman decided to adjourn hearings for a large number of Irish speakers in order to obtain the services of an interpreter. Addressing Cornelius Molloy, he suggested that 'I am sure a man of your appearance can give your evidence in English' whereupon Molloy, no doubt keen to have his case heard, said 'Well, I will do my best.'[70]

Various solutions were applied in County Cork. At Clonakilty subcommission in 1882, a tenant's evidence was interpreted by the Revd Mr O'Leary.[71] Also in 1882, an interpreter was provided for an Irish-speaking witness.[72] At the subcommission in Macroom, some of those present were of the view that a particular tenant spoke English very well. However, he persisted, and was examined through the interpreter.[73] In 1885, an interpreter was provided when Lord Bantry's tenants took a case to do with the payment of rates.[74] However, at Skibbereen land commission in 1890, 450 cases were heard relating to tenants from Cape Clear and their 'able and intelligent valuer', Mr T. O'Donovan, acted as interpreter.[75] In 1896, in Macroom, there were twenty-nine cases relating to fair rents for tenants on the estate of Sir George Colthurst; most of the tenants were exclusively Irish-speaking and the law clerk acted as interpreter.[76] In 1900 at the Southern Land Subcommission in Clonakilty, a tenant told the court that he had very bad English and the chairman said he would not force him to speak English. However, the tenant's own solicitor, Mr P.W. O'Donovan, said, 'His English will do well enough', and the case was heard in English.[77] In 1904 at the land commission in Schull, 'Mr P. Walsh, valuer' acted as interpreter for an Irish-speaking witness who spoke about improvements to his farm.[78]

67 *Irish Times*, 12 Nov. 1881.
68 *Morning News*, 14 and 15 May 1884.
69 HC Debates, 6 June 1884, vol. 288, c. 1687.
70 *Londonderry Sentinel*, 7 June 1887.
71 *Cork Examiner*, 17 Feb. 1882.
72 Ibid., 28 Feb. 1882.
73 Ibid., 11 Mar. 1882.
74 Ibid., 2 Sept. 1885.
75 *Skibbereen Eagle*, 5 Oct. 1890.
76 *Cork Examiner*, 24 Nov. 1896.
77 *Southern Star*, 17 Nov. 1900.
78 Ibid., 21 May 1904.

In 1897, William Bourke, court interpreter at assizes and quarter sessions, acted as interpreter at the Galway sittings of the Land Acts commission, where he interpreted for two tenants from Spiddal.[79] In 1914 at the land judge's court in Galway, almost all the twenty-six tenants on Michael O'Kelly's estate were Irish speakers and an interpreter 'had always to be employed'.[80]

In 1909 in Dingle, in a case involving a large number of Irish-speaking tenants, Maurice Ferriter, described by one newspaper as 'the interpreter of the court', interpreted the evidence on a number of occasions. Assistant Land Commissioner Mr R.J. Kelly

> remarked that in every case where a witness, whether imperfectly or not, could speak English or not, still preferred to give his evidence in Irish, he should be facilitated in doing so in order that he should feel himself under no disability or disadvantage.[81]

This is perhaps evidence of a changing attitude towards Irish speakers, but one that was not emulated in all quarters.

CENSUSES

Censuses were taken every ten years starting in 1821. Enumerators were members of the local community authorized to employ churchwardens, constables, peace officers and sub-constables if necessary,[82] and it is likely that many enumerators either spoke Irish or obtained the aid of Irish speakers to help them collect people's names, addresses and occupations. In 1831 expenses were paid to enumerators, peace and town clerks and others, and the list includes at least four assize interpreters – James O'Brien in Clare, John Anderson in County Kilkenny, Simon Conway in Mayo, and John Carter in County Galway.[83] In 1841 the enumerators were mainly members of the constabulary, supplemented by members of the coast guard and civilians selected by police superintendents.[84] In 1851 enumerators were members of the Dublin Metropolitan Police plus members of the constabulary force and 'such other competent persons as the Lord Lieutenant should appoint'.[85] Mairéad Nic Craith suggests that in 1851 enumerators 'did not necessarily have Irish',[86] but it was in the state's interest to collect information, and provision was made for Irish-speaking enumerators:

79 *Irish Times*, 26 Nov. 1897.
80 Ibid., 11 Nov. 1914.
81 *Freeman's Journal*, 22 Oct. 1909.
82 *Census of Ireland 1821: appendix to abstract of answers and returns* (1824), p. 384.
83 *Detailed account of expenses incurred under Population Act for Ireland, 1831*, HC 1833 (442) xxxix, 45.
84 *Census of Ireland 1841: report of the census commissioners, Ireland* (1843).
85 *Census of Ireland for the year 1851, part VI, general report* [C 2134], HC 1856, xxxi, 1.
86 M. Nic Craith, 'Legacy and loss: the Great Silence and its aftermath' in J. Crowley, W.J. Smyth and M. Murphey (eds), *Atlas of the Great Irish Famine* (Cork, 2012), p. 583.

> In those Districts where the Irish language prevails, or that many persons are to be found who do not speak English, the Enumerators shall be chosen from persons well acquainted with the Irish language, in order to avoid the necessity and expense of employing interpreters.[87]

In 1861, 1871 and 1881, census enumerators were mainly Royal Irish Constabulary officers and 'when necessary they were supplied with maps, boats, and in the Irish-speaking districts, with interpreters'.[88] In 1871 an enumerator wrote to the *Irish Times* to complain that he and others had advanced money out of their own pockets to cover expenses and pay 'for hire of interpreters, boats, cars, &c' and were awaiting reimbursement.[89] For the 1881, 1891, 1901 and 1911 censuses, interpreters could be paid 1*s.* 6*d.* a day where they were 'indispensable', but superintendents were recommended to employ enumerators who spoke Irish 'in order to avoid the necessity of employing interpreters'.[90]

A different approach was taken in Wales, where from 1841, the census form was made available in Welsh and the answers were then translated into English by the enumerators for the returns. In 1851, 'For the use of the poorer native population of Wales a certain number of the Forms was printed in the language of that country.'[91] However, Ireland was the first to introduce a question on language – a question on the use of Irish was introduced in a footnote in 1851. In Scotland, a question on Scots Gaelic first appeared in 1881 and in Wales, a question on Welsh first appeared in 1891.

PENSIONS

The *Cork Examiner* reported in 1909 that the Old Age Pensions Act (1908) led to the employment of supervisors, assistant supervisors and 306 pensions officers in Ireland. An additional 200 officers had to be brought in from England and Scotland to deal with the 261,668 claims made under the act. Ultimately, 43,299 claims were rejected. A Blue Book reported that:

> In Ireland we had some officers well acquainted with Erse who were very useful in the West, and ministers, priests, schoolmasters, and others very willingly assisted as interpreters when necessary. So far as is known, no claimant in any district in the three countries was prejudiced by a want of knowledge of the vernacular by the Pension Officer.[92]

87 *Census of Ireland 1851: appendix to general report page cxxvii: instructions for superintendents* (1856).
88 'Census of Ireland April 1861 – preliminary results', *Journal of the Statistical Society of London*, 24:3 (1861), pp 402–10.
89 *Irish Times*, 14 June 1871.
90 General reports for 1881, 1891, 1901 and 1911 censuses.
91 *Census of Great Britain 1851: population tables 1, vol. I: England and Wales: divisons I–VII* (1852–3), p. xiii.
92 *Cork Examiner*, 28 Sept. 1909.

As official state records for births, marriages and deaths only commenced in 1864, and some people were unsure of their date of birth, parish baptism registrations and census forms were used to verify whether claimants met the requirement of being 70 or over. The pension itself was five shillings a week or seven shillings and six pence for married couples. Anyone earning more than £31 10*s.* a year was not entitled. Some petty sessions cases were taken against Irish-speaking claimants who claimed to be older than they were in order to be entitled to a pension.[93] In 1910, the *Kerryman* reported on a particular pensions officer named S.B. Roche who acted as an interpreter at a pension prosecution in Killorglin and who had advocated the use of Irish as 'the proper thing to do' at an old-age pension committee in Caher.[94] In 1915, the *Liberator* reported on a play – 'The pension officer' by Padraig O'Shea, aka Padraig na Leime[95] – focusing on a pension officer and his interpreter.[96]

CONCLUSION

Where the interests of the state were involved, solutions could be found for the language issue. The authorities were willing to provide interpreters at select committees and commissions in order to ensure that they could access the necessary information to come up with reports and recommendations. Solutions were also found to allow for collection of information for censuses and to establish if people were entitled to old-age pensions. The provision of interpreters at elections was belated and problematic, particularly from 1829, with barriers such as having to submit letters in English to – and appear before – the assistant barrister, and if unsuccessful, having to appeal the decision at assizes, and applicants who appeared in court had to run the gauntlet of allegations that they did in fact speak English. Given that coroners were paid by the grand juries, it is surprising that no remedy was found for inquests where coroners and juries needed to understand what was said by Irish-speaking witnesses. Interpreters were not universally employed in land commission cases.

93 *Kerry Sentinel*, 21 Sept. 1910, *Killarney Echo & South Kerry Chronicle*, 3 Feb. 1912.
94 *Kerryman*, 24 Sept. 1910.
95 Pádraig Ó Séaghdha (1880–1921), ainm.ie.
96 *Liberator*, 15 June 1915.

CHAPTER ELEVEN

Power and language

POWER HAS BEEN a constant theme in the preceding chapters – the power to decide that English would be the language of the courts, the power to legislate for interpreters in certain settings but not in others, the power to decide not to permit salaried interpreters to work in civil cases, the power to select interpreters, the power to reduce or terminate interpreters' salaries. Neal Garnham has suggested that 'the fact that interpreters were provided at all is a clear indication that the legal process was not designed to be exclusive'.[1] The difficulty here is implementation – throughout the period under discussion, access to interpreters was restricted to monolingual Irish speakers. If it was thought that they spoke English, they faced a hostile environment where they could be intimidated, bullied, threatened that they would not be allowed witness expenses, charged with perjury and even imprisoned for contempt of court.

Power lay in the hands of a mostly Protestant elite. The penal laws that discriminated against Catholics began to be eased in the late eighteenth century and from 1793 some Catholic men could vote in parliamentary elections and become members of grand juries but were not permitted to take seats in parliament. Catholics were excluded from posts in the higher reaches of administration such as lord lieutenant, chief secretary, chancellor of the exchequer and attorney general. They could not become judges, king's counsel, sheriffs or sub-sheriffs. In 1828, a mere 39 out of 1,314 posts in the administration of justice were held by Catholics. Of 3,033 other posts paid for out of public funds, 134 were held by Catholics.[2] In 1833, there were no Catholic judges or stipendiary magistrates, just one Catholic high sheriff and a small number of Catholic unpaid magistrates (often landlords) and grand jurors. The five inspectors-general and 32 sub-inspectors of police were Protestant.[3] In 1909, of 17 judges, 3 were Catholic. Of 21 county court judges and recorders, 8 were Catholic. Five out of 37 county inspectors, 62 out of 202 district inspectors of police and 1,805 out of 5,518 justices of the peace and 8 out of 68 privy councillors were Catholic.[4] There was endemic, state-sanctioned discrimination on religious grounds against the majority of the population. The state decided who could work where, who could vote, and who could take part in society.

1 Garnham, *The courts, crime and the criminal law*, pp 112 and 93.

2 S.J. Connolly, 'The Catholic question, 1801–12' in W.E. Vaughan (ed.), *New history of Ireland*, v: *1801–1970*, (Oxford, 1989), p. 26.

3 O'Brien, *Dublin Castle and the Irish people*, p. 60.

4 Ibid., p. 79.

The state decided that English was the language of the courts. The grand juries could decide if a case should go to trial or not; the courts held the power to hear cases; the juries could decide if a defendant was guilty or not guilty; the judge could decide on a prison sentence or even, in the case of murder or treason, the death sentence. Such power is what Bourdieu calls 'symbolic power'. Another area of power held by the courts involved conditions around jury service; between 1833 and 1871, jurors had to be 'between the ages of 21 years and 60 years' and had to 'have property' (this requirement that jurors be property holders was eased somewhat with the passage of the O'Hagan Act in 1871).[5] These conditions were laid down by law, and worked to exclude the not-so-well-off. The Juries Act 1871 led to some monolingual Irish speakers being called to serve on juries. In order to address this issue, in 1873 anyone who could not read and write the English language was exempted from jury duty.[6] Mr C.H. Hemphill of Kerry suggested that jurors who could not understand English should be struck off.[7] In the same year, in Lifford, there were complaints that some jurors did not even understand the English language.[8]

The official language of Ireland and of the courts was English and a climate was created that would ensure 'recognition for a new language of authority'.[9] For Bourdieu, this involves the devaluation of the linguistic capital of the dominated:

> [I]t is the dominated who is obliged to adopt the language of the dominant [...] In this case, the dominated speaks a *broken language,* [...] and his linguistic capital is more or less completely devalued, be it in school, at work, or in social encounters with the dominant.[10]

Bourdieu and Wacquant give the example of a French person talking to an Algerian, or a black American to a WASP; if we substitute an Irish person talking to an Englishman, we can make their point that 'it is not two persons who speak to each other but, through them, the colonial history in its entirety, or the whole history of the economic, political, and cultural subjugation'.[11] This was the case in the nineteenth century, when the two groups were separated socially, geographically and economically. It was even more the case in the courts, where the non-English speaking witness or defendant was separated from the judges and lawyers because they occupied 'asymmetric positions in the distribution of the relevant capital'

5 Vaughan, *Murder trials in Ireland*, p. 127.
6 Juries (Ireland) Amendment Act 1873, 36 & 37 Vict., c. 27.
7 *First, second and special reports from the select committee on Juries (Ireland); together with the proceedings of the committee, minutes of evidence, and appendix*, HC 1873 (283) xv, 2.
8 *Irish Times*, 28 Feb. 1877.
9 P. Bourdieu, *Language and symbolic power*, trans. G. Raymond and M. Adamson (Cambridge, 1991), p. 48.
10 P. Bourdieu and L.J.D. Wacquant, *An invitation to reflexive sociology* (Cambridge, 2007), p. 143.
11 Ibid., p. 144.

and in this situation, even more than in more everyday situations, 'every linguistic exchange contains the *potentiality* of an act of power'.[12] For Bourdieu, language is 'an instrument of power'; over time, English became the 'legitimate language' in Ireland and the Irish language was devalued.[13] 'A language is worth what those who speak it are worth',[14] and it could be argued that monolingual Irish speakers came to be worth less than their English-speaking counterparts. This can be seen in newspaper reports, where Irish speakers, if they are described at all, are often portrayed as old, feeble, poor, poorly dressed and even stupid. Here is a selection of examples:

> Eileen Connelly, a wild-looking half-dressed woman, with a blue cloak hanging from her head loosely over her shoulder, and with a large glibhe, or roll of hair on her forehead, was then examined.[15]

> The first witness produced was Thomas Harnett. He appeared to be a very stupid countryman and could not speak English.[16]

> The witness, a miserable looking creature, her costume not far removed from that scant supply that would leave her very nearly in *puri,* being unable to speak English, had to be examined through the interpreter.[17]

> Mary Walsh, a very old woman, was examined by Mr Curtis, through an interpreter.[18]

> [A] very old man, in a very tattered suit, was produced on the part of the defendant.[19]

> The prosecutor (who was a very feeble man, of nearly 80 years of age, and dressed in the garb of the mendicant) was examined, through an interpreter, in Irish ...[20]

> Manus Gallagher, an old man who could neither understand nor speak English, was called ...[21]

12 Ibid., p. 145.
13 P. Bourdieu, 'The economics of linguistic exchanges', *Social Sciences Information,* 16:6 (1977), pp 645–68 at p. 654.
14 Ibid., p. 652.
15 *Cumberland Pacquet and Ware's Whitehaven Advertiser*, 30 Aug. 1825.
16 *Tralee Mercury*, 19 Aug. 1835.
17 *Kerry Examiner*, 22 Oct. 1841.
18 *Freeman's Journal*, 10 Mar. 1858.
19 *Irish Times*, 11 Aug. 1860.
20 *Saunders's News-Letter*, 21 Mar. 1863.
21 *Irish Times*, 28 Oct. 1889.

> Defendant, an old woman of about eighty years, intervened and delivered a long harangue in Irish ...[22]
>
> An old man named John Lucey was next put into the witness chair by Mr Herley, and immediately proceeded to speak very quickly in Irish.[23]
>
> Jeremiah Dennis, an old Irish-speaking man.[24]

It is of course probably the case that monolingual Irish speakers *were* old, as younger people became proficient in English. Nevertheless, the association of Irish with being old was unlikely to act as an incentive for younger people to use the language. If we transfer Bourdieu's ideas to Ireland, the linguistic market had to be unified and over time English became the dominant language, identified with education, better employment prospects and the option of emigration – or, in short, with profit. English was imposed as 'the sole legitimate competence on the legitimate linguistic markets'.[25] Irish speakers, the dominated class, came to realize that the value accorded to their language was very low. Bourdieu would see Irish as 'threatened capital', a competence that could not be saved 'without saving the market i.e. all the social conditions of the production and reproduction of producers and consumers'.[26]

Bourdieu saw the school system as key to access administrative positions in France and underlined the importance of such posts in rural areas.[27] This was certainly the case in Ireland, where there were few employment possibilities in the mid- to late nineteenth century. Families were large, and after the Great Famine, sons, often the eldest, inherited farms and their siblings had to find alternative employment, marry into land or emigrate. The industries of the time were wool and cotton in the early part of the nineteenth century and subsequently, shipbuilding, brewing, distilling and linen.[28] English was the 'legitimate language' of the national school system and education was the key to prospects.

Power is of course expressed through language as well, with legal language being a specialized domain. Mellinkoff characterizes English legal language as a specialized language containing:

(1) Frequent use of common words with uncommon meanings.
(2) Frequent use of Old English and Middle English words once in common use, but now rare.
(3) Frequent use of Latin words and phrases.

22 *Southern Star*, 27 Oct. 1894.
23 Ibid., 22 Jan. 1898.
24 Ibid., 2 July 1910.
25 Bourdieu, 'The economics of linguistic exchanges', p. 654.
26 Ibid., p. 651.
27 Bourdieu, *Language and symbolic power*, p. 49.
28 Lyons, *Ireland since the Famine*, p. 57.

(4) Use of Old French and Anglo-Norman words which have not been taken into the general vocabulary.
(5) Use of terms of art, i.e. technical words with a specific meaning.
(6) Use of argot or professional language.
(7) Frequent use of formal words.
(8) Deliberate use of words and expressions with flexible meanings.
(9) Attempts at extreme precision of expression.[29]

These features posed additional obstacles to understanding and participating in court proceedings for people who did not have a high degree of proficiency in English and, indeed, for interpreters. John Gibbons writes of the address forms used in court, where judges are addressed as 'Your Honour', 'Your Lordship', or 'Your Worship' depending on their rank, and are not addressed by name. Instead of using the first person, judges can refer to 'the court' or 'the bench'. Lawyers refer to each other as 'my friend' or 'my learned friend' or by function in the court case as 'the crown', 'counsel for the crown' or 'counsel for the defence'. As Gibbons points out, all of these honorifics and ways of addressing legal colleagues link in with a strict social hierarchy.[30] The way people speak is a reflection of their social prestige and can affect how they are perceived in court. William O'Barr found that:

> witnesses who speak in a powerful style, avoid unnaturally formal speech patterns, testify with minimal assistance from the lawyer, and resist efforts by the opposing counsel to cut short their remarks will enhance their credibility because they will make more favorable impressions on the jury.[31]

In the case of witnesses who do not speak the language of the court, there is less chance of being able to fulfil these criteria. Therefore, witnesses whose first language was Irish and who were compelled to use English were at a great disadvantage. Irish speakers had an additional handicap in that many were illiterate and belonged to an oral culture with a very different view of the world from that of educated English speakers. Walter Ong has suggested that literate people 'regard oral peoples, for example, as dishonest in fulfilment of promises or in response to queries'.[32]

PRESSURE TO SPEAK ENGLISH

Patricia Palmer has focused on the 'pattern of Elizabethan linguistic colonization in its paired guises of denigrating Irish and promoting English'.[33] The denigration

29 D. Mellinkoff, *The language of the law* (Eugene, 2004), p. 11.
30 J. Gibbons, *Forensic linguistics: an introduction to language in the justice system* (Oxford, 2003), p. 83.
31 W.M. O'Barr, *Linguistic evidence: language, power and strategy in the courtroom* (San Diego, 1982), p. 114.
32 W. Ong, *Orality and literacy: the technologizing of the world* (Abingdon, 2003), p. 167.
33 Palmer, *Language and conquest in early modern Ireland*, p. 6.

of Irish and promotion of English would continue into the nineteenth century. The 1806 Thresher trials heard by the special commission of oyer and terminer provide a good illustration of the attitudes towards witnesses and their choice of language at the start of the nineteenth century. The question of language arose for three witnesses. The first, Laurence Summerton, took the initiative, and before being sworn in, stated in Irish that he could not speak English, but 'after some expostulation', he did in fact give his evidence in English. He was cross-examined by the attorney general:[34]

> Q. Did you ever hear, that O'Neil swore he could not speak English?
> A. I did.
> Q. And that he spoke good English after – was he not a perjured fellow when he did that?
> A. He was.
> Q. And you took an oath, that you could not speak English?
> A. No, I was not sworn, when I said that.
> Q. You were only near it. Where are Bryan Tighe and his wife?

The attorney general took the opportunity to challenge Summerton, and perhaps to intimidate or rattle him in the hope of obtaining more information about Bryan Tighe.

There is no sense here of a right to an interpreter in a witness' first language. Rather, there is distrust of anyone who attempts to use Irish. Another witness, Martin Sweeny, was allowed give evidence in Irish through an interpreter who was instructed to ask the witness 'upon his oath did he ever speak English to any person?' The question is quite extraordinary – apparently, anyone who spoke even a little English on one occasion could have to manage in court using that language. Sweeny replied, 'when he was drunk, and then he spoke a little gibberish of English' and was granted an interpreter. It was accepted that the third person, Margaret Lavin, did not speak English, and an interpreter was sworn.[35]

In 1825, at Ennis assizes, a rape case focused entirely on complainant and prosecutrix Bridget McNamara and whether or not she could speak English. 'Considerable efforts' were made to establish if she could speak the language but she swore that she could not and was allowed give her evidence through the court interpreter. The cross-examination focused on her credibility and:

> She solemnly swore that she did not know the import of a 'Yes' or 'No' in English; that she had been at school, but could not swear that her primmer

34 In Ireland, the attorney general acted as public prosecutor. D. Greer, 'A security against illegality?' in Norma Dawson (ed.), *Reflections on law and history* (Dublin, 2006), p. 193.

35 W. Ridgeway, *A report of the proceedings under a special commission of oyer and terminer, and gaol delivery, for the counties of Sligo, Mayo, Leitrim, Longford and Cavan in the month of December 1806* (Dublin, 1807).

> [*sic*] was in English or Irish; that she had never known the prisoner before this occurrence; had never agreed to marry him, if he thought proper, and denied in toto any knowledge of his character.

There was clearly a suspicion that Bridget McNamara was hoping for a ruling that the defendant should marry her. However, the focus is on whether she was telling the truth, whether she knew what simple words like 'yes' and 'no' meant, whether she ever went to school, whether she ever learnt to read in English. Amazingly, Bridget McNamara, the complainant in a rape case, was found guilty of perjury.[36]

In *R v. Burke*, Chief Justice James Monahan outlined the usual practice where Irish-speaking witnesses swore to tell the truth and were immediately asked to swear that they did not speak English:

> We are all conversant with this on circuit, that when a witness is produced, and when he tenders himself to be examined in Irish, the counsel on the opposite side says, 'This man can speak English' and he is at once examined on oath to see whether he can give his testimony in English. That is done merely for the purpose of enabling the judge to decide, not whether his evidence shall be received, but for the purpose of deciding whether Irish evidence shall be received. I am satisfied that it has occurred in my own experience, that the judge being satisfied that the witness can speak English, refuses to allow him to answer in Irish, and says, 'If I find you in the progress of the examination under any difficulty, I shall allow you to be examined in Irish.'[37]

Irish speakers were quizzed on whether they had been to school, if they could read, and sometimes a book was produced and they were asked if they could read a word or even identify a letter. Witnesses were produced who swore that they had conversed with them in English, as did other court attendees. Every effort was made to discredit those who wished to use their first language in court. Lawyers too, including those who spoke Irish, could, when it suited them, exert pressure on witnesses to speak English in order to undermine them. For example, in 1829 at the famous Doneraile conspiracy case held at a special commission in Cork, witness Thomas Murphy was examined through an interpreter. Daniel O'Connell commenced his cross-examination by launching an attack on Murphy's ability to speak English:

> Mr O'Connell – Upon your oath can you speak English? A little, sir.
> Mr O'Connell – Did you not swear you could not speak English? I don't know, sir.

36 *Southern Reporter & Cork Commercial Courier*, 26 July 1825.
37 Cox, *Reports of cases*, viii, p. 62.

> Mr O'Connell – How long have you been at school – one year, two, three, five years? I don't know.
> Mr O'Connell – Have you ever been at school? – Oh, yes.
> Mr O'Connell – What did you learn there? My ABC (loud laughter).[38]

For Bourdieu, 'All linguistic practices are measured against the legitimate practices, i.e., the practices of those who are dominant',[39] and linguistic exchanges 'are also relations of symbolic power in which the power relations between speakers or their respective groups are actualized'.[40] This is particularly evident in the Irish courts, where there was collusion from all sides to oblige people to speak the dominant language. Whenever it was suspected, believed or known that a witness spoke English or some English, police constables, court clerks, interpreters, land agents and others could be asked to testify to their use of English. Doubt was often cast on the reliability of evidence given by Irish speakers on the grounds that they had sworn in court that they did not speak English but various people had heard them speak the language. For example, in 1840 at Mayo assizes in a case of assault with intent to do bodily harm, William Bingham esq. gave evidence that the prosecutrix's character 'was such that she ought not to be believed on her oath, she swore to day that she did not speak English and he often heard her speak it'.[41]

There was constant suspicion that Irish speakers were feigning lack of knowledge of English in order to have more time to think about suitable answers or even to create confusion. As Mayo defence solicitor Mr O'Dowd put it, '[W]itnesses spoke Irish for the purpose of baffling cross-examination.'[42] An editorial in the *Cork Examiner* in 1864 commented somewhat sarcastically:

> Every one knows the habit so common amongst the country people, when compelled to appear as witnesses, of refusing to speak English, evidently in the belief that they may be overreached unless they have the privilege of speaking a tongue whose niceties are more thoroughly known to them.[43]

For example, in 1832 at a murder case heard at Ennis assizes, five witnesses attempted to provide an alibi and 'Some of them professed not to understand English, in order to evade the direct and pertinent questions put on cross-examination; and they were examined in Irish through an interpreter.'[44] The views expressed here appear to be those of the reporter, who assumes that the purpose of speaking Irish is evasion. It seems unlikely that witnesses prepared to provide an alibi to a defendant in a

38 *Freeman's Journal*, 29 Oct. 1829.
39 Bourdieu, *Language and symbolic power*, p. 53.
40 Ibid., p. 37.
41 *Connaught Telegraph*, 5 Aug. 1840.
42 *Mayo Constitution*, 15 June 1869
43 *Cork Examiner*, 26 Jan. 1864
44 *Limerick Evening Post*, 2 Mar. 1832.

murder case would wish to evade questions. There seems to be a further implication here that the alibi has been concocted and the men are not to be trusted. The prisoners were found guilty. In 1889 at Carrick-on-Shannon county court, in the Gweedore murder case, there was an example of distrust of Irish speakers and a belief that they could in fact speak English perfectly well. In this case, a witness called Manus Gallagher gave evidence through the interpreter. The attorney general got up to examine the witness, asked the interpreter to leave the box and proceeded to ask Gallagher in English: 'What sort of a day was it?' The witness answered in Irish 'Sunday' and as it was obvious that he did not understand the question, the interpreter immediately resumed his duties.[45] It was clear that while the witness understood the word 'day' he failed to understand the purport of the question.

Pressure to speak English took different forms in different courts. There were consequences for those who were suspected of feigning ignorance of the English language: judges at assizes could refuse to pay witness expenses while magistrates in the petty sessions courts could send people to prison for contempt, try them for perjury or opt for a combination of these options. We have already seen that the year after the *R v. Burke* (1858) case, Judge Christian stated that he 'would not allow expenses to any witness as did not give evidence in English'.[46] Expenses could be paid to witnesses in cases heard at assizes but were probably most important to the poorest people in society. There was regular correspondence with the chief secretary's office in Dublin Castle on this issue.[47] Table 4 outlines the rates payable in 1882 according to people's occupations.

Justice Christian was not the only judge to refuse to pay expenses to Irish-speaking witnesses.[48] In 1843, at the Clonmel assizes record court, a young boy called James Dalton was sworn in as a witness but 'refused' to speak English. Colonel Phibbs, who was also a magistrate, said from the grand jury gallery that he had examined the boy in English 'and he seemed perfectly to understand it'. This information was then taken from Phibbs under oath. The judge allowed the boy to give his evidence through the interpreter but said he was sending him to jail for twenty-four hours and would not allow him expenses because 'Justice must not be trifled with in this way.'[49] The decision to send a young boy to prison because he refused to speak English when possibly he just did not have enough of the language to give evidence or was nervous about doing so seems harsh, particularly when the case was heard in the assizes, where an interpreter was employed.[50]

Sometimes the threat not to pay expenses had the desired effect and people switched to English. In 1875 at the second queen's bench in Dublin, a witness

45 *Irish Times*, 28 Oct. 1889.
46 *Mayo Constitution*, 15 Mar. 1859.
47 Country letter books, NAI.
48 See also: *Clare Journal*, 28 Feb. 1848; *Kerry Evening Post*, 16 July 1864.
49 *Nenagh Guardian*, 26 July 1843.
50 See also: *Clare Journal*, 28 Feb. 1848; *Kerry Evening Post*, 16 July 1864, *Connaught Telegraph*, 20 Jan. 1917.

Table 4 Witness expense rates, 1882[51]

Personal allowance	Minimum per day	Maximum per day	Minimum per night	Maximum per night
1. Labourers	2*s.*	5*s.*	1*s.* 6*d.*	2*s.* 6*d.*
2. Farmers, shopkeepers and their assistants, commercial and law clerks, artisans etc.	5*s.*		5*s.*	
3. Warders and other gaol officials, except governors	5*s.*		5*s.*	
4. Governors of gaols and petty sessions clerks	7*s.* 6*d.*		7*s.* 6*d.*	
5. Merchants, bank officials etc.	5*s.*	10*s.*	5*s.*	10*s.*
6. County surveyors' assistants, land surveyors etc.	4*s.*	10*s.*	4*s.*	5*s.*
7. Resident magistrates, other government officials not classed above	10*s.*		10*s.*	
8. Doctors, solicitors, engineers, and handwriting experts	21*s.*	42*s.*	10*s.*	10*s.*
9. Clergymen, private gentlemen, officers of the navy and army etc.	5*s.*	42*s.*	5*s.*	10*s.*

'dressed in the garb of the peasants of the West of Ireland' stated that he could not speak English and another witness was sworn in to act as interpreter. Judge Barry told the man that if he did not speak English he would not be allowed expenses. According to the newspaper, these words had a magical effect and the man spoke thereafter in excellent English.[52] In 1897, in another example of code-switching, an interpreter was called to Macroom petty sessions for a witness who declared he could not speak English and on being asked the first question, he switched to English. When a second witness started giving his evidence in Irish, saying that he had no English, he was asked in English 'Do you want your expenses?' and replied in English 'Yes, sir, that's what I want.'[53]

The petty sessions courts were particularly severe in their dealings with Irish speakers, who, if perceived as lying, could be sent to prison. For example, in 1876 at Killorglin petty sessions, a complainant in an assault case was sworn in English but switched to Irish. One person swore that the complainant had spoken to him in

51 *Annual report of the local government board for Ireland, being the eleventh report under the Local Government Board (Ireland) Act 35 & 36 Vict., c. 69, with appendices* (1883).

52 *Leinster Express*, 13 Feb. 1875.

53 *Southern Star*, 14 Aug. 1897.

English while another said he would swear that she could not speak the language. The chairman, Edward Rae, who occasionally acted as interpreter, had the woman committed to prison for eight days.[54] The following year, again at Killorglin, a small farmer who swore he could not speak English was sent to jail for contempt of court after Constable Hutchinson informed the court that he did in fact speak the language.[55]

It is impossible to know the extent of miscarriages of justice due to cases being dismissed because Irish speakers did not speak English, or, in the eyes of the court, refused to do so. The newspapers contain some examples. In a particularly unjust case heard at Castlebar petty sessions in 1859, a labourer who was suing for wages without the help of a lawyer and who did not speak English well was told that he 'must make his complaint in the best English he could' but could only provide what the reporter described as a 'blundering narrative'. The case was dismissed and as he left the court he shouted in English, 'I am robbed, sure enough – that's what I am.'[56] In 1866 at a police office hearing in Cork, Margaret Lehane summoned a man for a severe assault; as she could not speak English, her complaint was dismissed, with the newspaper commenting that 'Head Constable O'Neill, and perhaps a dozen other persons might be found in court who could interpret for her.'[57]

A highly controversial case that attracted much newspaper coverage and led to questions in the house of commons took place in 1897. The case itself related to a fatal attack by a dog on a sheep and was heard by Mr William Orr, RM at Dungarvan petty sessions. An interpreter translated what a female witness had to say. The next witness was Patrick Connors, a young man of about 18 years of age, who also spoke in Irish but was told by the chairman, 'I warn you if you can speak English to do so.' Constable Kelleher told the court:

> I am stationed at Ring. I know the witness, Patrick Connors, who lives at Helvick, and has declined to answer questions put to him in the English language by the solicitor for the complainant. About three months ago I had a conversation with him in the English language, with which he was familiar, he knows the language well enough to carry on a conversation in it and give evidence in a court of justice. I believe that he is now shamming ignorance of the language.

Mr Orr asked Connors if he wished to ask Constable Kelleher any questions but there was no response. Orr then requested a warrant and said he would adjourn the case for a week and, 'If in the meantime he recovers his acquaintance with the

54 *Kerry Evening Post*, 13 Sept. 1876.
55 Ibid., 11 July 1877.
56 *Connaught Telegraph*, 19 Oct. 1859.
57 *Southern Reporter & Cork Commercial Courier*, 6 Apr. 1866.

English tongue he can be discharged.' The town clerk and a number of Connors' friends spoke to him in Irish, attempting to persuade him to answer the questions. Orr told him that if he did not answer he would go to Waterford gaol because, 'I cannot allow anyone to defeat the administration of justice in this way.' Connors did eventually say, 'I did not see any sheep or any dog', but Orr was not satisfied with this tardy response. Connors was removed by the police and once in the constabulary barracks, he explained 'that he was afraid he could not speak what he wanted in English', whereupon Orr cancelled the warrant.[58] The *Derry Journal* questioned Constable Kelleher's assertion that Connors could speak English well enough to give evidence in a court of justice and suggested that he could only give 'crippled and confused evidence' in English.[59]

The Gaelic League immediately passed a resolution protesting against 'the injustice of punishing Irish-speaking people who prefer to give their evidence in the language they understand best'.[60] Gaelic League Secretary James Casey wrote to Chief Secretary of Ireland Gerald Balfour making three points: first, there was a large number of Irish speakers in Ring and Dungarvan; second, an interpreter was present in court; and third, a somewhat dubious point from a legal perspective:

> Every person has a perfectly legal right to be examined in the language he knows best, it being held that it would be unfair to submit a man to examination and cross-examination by a hostile advocate in a language with which he was but imperfectly acquainted.

Casey went on to recommend the appointment of Irish speakers to public positions in Irish-speaking districts and that magistrates 'must not take up a position of antagonism to the Irish language in the discharge of their duties'.[61] Michael Cusack, an Irish teacher and founder of the Gaelic Athletic Association, wrote to the *Cork Examiner* that 'No man should be compelled to give his evidence in English. Interpreters should be forthcoming.'[62]

The matter was raised in the house of commons where Mr Power, MP for Waterford East, asked Balfour about this case, and pointed out that over 50 per cent of the population of the barony of Decies without Drum spoke Irish, and 1,000 people spoke Irish only. Balfour replied that Connors 'was detained in custody for a couple of hours only' and that 'solicitors on both sides expressed approval of the intention to compel Connors to give evidence in English, and when he notified his willingness to do so he was at once discharged'. According to Balfour, 'the person who is usually employed to act as interpreter at this Court was not present on the

58 *Cork Examiner*, 11 Jan. 1897.
59 *Derry Journal*, 15 Jan. 1897.
60 *Southern Star*, 23 Jan. 1897.
61 *Freeman's Journal*, 23 Jan. 1897.
62 *Cork Examiner*, 13 Jan. 1897.

occasion, although another person who was competent to interpret was present.'[63] When the case resumed, Connors gave his evidence in English.

Dungarvan town commissioners took the opportunity to pass a resolution calling on the lord chancellor to 'make it a condition that any future Justices of the Peace or Resident Magistrates appointed by him shall know Irish'. According to the *Kerry Sentinel*, the lord chancellor responded in a letter that:

> while unable to concur with the Commissioners in their view as to the necessity of making it a condition of appointment to the Commission of the Peace in Ireland that all Justices should possess a knowledge of the Irish language, he fully recognizes the obligation upon all Magistrates of securing to Irish speaking witnesses the utmost facility for expressing themselves fully and clearly when giving evidence in a Court of Justice, and trusts that Magistrates will satisfy themselves before requiring any such witness to give evidence in English that he is as fully capable of giving evidence in that language as in his own.

This reply was welcomed by the newspaper as 'a direct and well deserved censure on the Removable Magistrates' involved in the Connors case.[64] However, in reality, it did nothing more than restate the status quo.

The notion that it could be an advantage to have an interpreter persisted. In 1899, Judge Dane issued a denial about newspaper reports that he had dismissed a case at Ballinrobe Sessions because a litigant named Michael Connor could not give evidence in English. The story was true but the judge felt justified because the person involved spoke English well. His explanation is interesting:

> I think it only right to add that every Irish-speaking witness has the fullest latitude in this court, which is provided with an official interpreter, sworn to interpret the evidence faithfully, but I am sorry to say that, in many instances, people who are speakers of the Irish language, and also understand English, sometimes avail themselves of that fact to come up here and try to frustrate the ends of justice, because they think that being sworn in Irish they will have time to hear the questions put and to consider what kind of an answer they will give.

He went on to say that he 'should be sorry [...] that it be thought for a moment that the poorest man in the country, if he happens to be an Irish-speaking man, won't get the fullest justice in this court'.[65]

63 HC Debates, 25 Jan. 1897, vol. 45, c. 403.
64 *Kerry Sentinel*, 3 Mar. 1897.
65 *Irish Times*, 27 Oct. 1899.

Journalist Andrew Dunlop provides a sympathetic perspective on Irish speakers with a knowledge of English. He was sent to 'Glencumbkille [*sic*]' in Donegal to report for the *Daily News* in 1882. His report on Irish speakers there is in sharp contrast to the picture presented by Justice O'Brien and others in the courts:

> These poor women, whom Father Gallagher had summoned over-night to be interviewed by me in the morning, could every one of them understand and speak English, but whether from the greater facility with which, naturally, they spoke Irish, or from a feeling that it was more politic to allow their story to filter through the sympathetic mind of their parish priest before it reached me, must be a matter of conjecture, they in fact, although speaking in English when asked to do so, invariably reverted at the first opportunity to the vernacular.[66]

Here, the Irish speakers were not trying to get extra time to process questions and devise their answers; instead, they genuinely preferred to use their first language because they found it easier and more natural. Dunlop's suggestion of a possible preference for speaking though the parish priest as interpreter is improbable. Most people prefer to speak directly to their interlocutor without resorting to an interpreter.

CONCLUSION

It is quite clear from the examples included in this chapter that people who spoke Irish and English could not at any stage decide for themselves which language they wished to use if they appeared in court as a witness, plaintiff or defendant. On the contrary, if it could be shown that they spoke even a few words of English, they risked being humiliated in public, refused their expenses or even sent to prison. People who experienced this treatment, along with their families and community, must have felt that it was not in their interest to speak Irish. In addition, some interpreters may not have been particularly competent or trustworthy, which was another impetus to learn English. The ruling in *R v. Burke* did not improve the situation of this group in any way. They had no right to give evidence in Irish. Rather, the system was designed to discourage and in the long term to eliminate the use of the Irish language and to ensure the dominance of the English language.

66 Dunlop, *Fifty years of Irish journalism*, p. 264.

CHAPTER TWELVE

Irish speakers and interpreter provision in each county

IT IS DIFFICULT to establish a complete picture of the numbers of Irish speakers before the Famine, particularly as the population became more bilingual. A series of statistical surveys were carried out on a county basis for the Royal Society in Dublin; however, they tend to be more impressionistic than statistical, with most researchers emphasizing increased numbers of speakers of English. William Shaw Mason's three-volume *Statistical account or parochial survey* (1814–19) covers seventy-nine Church of Ireland parishes, with information provided by the clergy, who were not without their own prejudices. For example, rector Horatio Townsend referred to the Irish language as a 'barbarous tongue', incompatible with literary attainment:

> The common Irish are naturally shrewd, but very ignorant, and deficient in mental culture, from the barbarous tongue in which they converse, which operates as an effectual bar to any kind of literary attainment; like all of a similar description, they are addicted to pilfering, and have very imperfect notions of moral rectitude.[1]

While the information on the Irish language is useful, Mason's *Statistical account* covers less than 4 per cent of over 2,000 parishes and, in some cases, the information conveyed by different writers is contradictory. Despite this there are some commonalities, with many observing that Irish speakers lived in hilly or mountainous areas, and that old people and, in some cases, women, were more likely to speak the language. Other sources are Dr Whitley Stokes' very short *Observations* pamphlet (1806),[2] in which he outlines the numbers of Irish speakers in each county. Samuel Lewis' two-volume *Topographical directory* (1837) is also useful. Visitors to Ireland such as J.B. Trotter, A.A. Atkinson, Thomas Sheahan and Coquebert de Montbret wrote about their impressions of the country and commented on the use of the Irish language. In 1825 Henry Monck Mason, secretary of the Irish Society, which translated Scriptures into Irish, gave an overview of the situation in Leinster and Ulster:

1 Horatio Townsend in W.S. Mason, *A statistical account or parochial survey of Ireland* (Dublin, 1816), ii, p. 311.
2 W. Stokes, *Observations on the necessity of publishing the Scriptures in the Irish language* (Dublin, 1806).

> Irish is much spoken in the counties of Louth, Meath and Westmeath, in Kilkenny, Carlow and Longford, and somewhat in the south-west of Wexford, in the province of Leinster; in Ulster it is understood I believe by about one half the inhabitants of Tyrone and Donegal, by many in Cavan and Monaghan, and by some in Down and Fermanagh; there are also some few speakers in most of the remaining counties.[3]

He also commented that 'I think the English language is gaining ground on Irish perceptibly', and that while 'the children are more desirous of acquiring English than the Irish', 'adults' hearts are with the Irish as their native language'. He estimated that half a million people were monolingual Irish speakers and that 1.5 million had enough English to buy and sell at a fair but not enough to hold a continued conversation.[4] By contrast, in 1835, William Roche, MP for Limerick and a magistrate, estimated the number of monolingual Irish speakers as half a million and stated that 'whether at Assizes, Quarter Sessions, or Petty Sessions, the aid of an Irish interpreter is now seldom or never required'.[5]

Censuses are potentially less impressionistic and more reliable sources of information on this subject. Overall statistics drawn from the censuses are available online in the form of general reports available at histpop.org. The figures for speakers of Irish and English and speakers of Irish in the 1851 census, the first to include this question, are shown in table 5.

According to these figures, 23.3 per cent of the much-reduced population of 6.5 million spoke Irish. However, as indicated in the general report of the 1851 census,[6] this underestimated the number of Irish speakers, as did the subsequent censuses in 1861 and 1871. Garret FitzGerald points to this issue,[7] originally highlighted by Adams in the 1970s, namely that the question relating to language

Table 5 Irish speakers in 1851 census

Province	Irish and English	Irish only	Total who spoke Irish
Ulster	100,693	35,783	136,476
Munster	669,449	146,336	815,785
Leinster	58,976	200	59,176
Connaught	375,566	137,283	512,849
Total	1,204,684	319,602	1,524,286

3 *First report of the commissioners of education*, HC 1825 (400) xii, 745.
4 Ibid., pp 744–5.
5 HC Debates, 6 Apr. 1835, vol. 27, cc 837–61.
6 *Census of Ireland 1851: part vi, general report* (1856), p. xlvi.
7 FitzGerald, 'Levels of Irish-speaking 1771–1871', p. 118.

spoken in these three censuses was in a footnote and may have been missed by the enumerators who were to fill in 'Irish' or 'Irish and English' in the column on education.

In contrast, in the 1881 census, the question appeared on the form with the instruction to write 'Irish' in the column for any member of the family who spoke the language, and 'Irish and English' for those who spoke both languages. The enumerators confirmed with respondents that the information in this column was filled in correctly.[8] This information helps explain the increase in the number of speakers of Irish and English in 1881. There is another increase in 1901, most likely due to a change in attitude thanks to the Irish language revival. While the census figures relating to the number of Irish speakers are not accurate, they do indicate broad trends in the numbers of speakers of Irish and the overall picture is one of decline.

The information in this chapter has been divided up by province, beginning with Ulster, and then moving on to Munster, Leinster and Connaught. Information from the various statistical surveys and the censuses is compiled for each county and considered in the context of court interpreter provision. The use of interpreters has been described by Gerard O'Brien as 'a barometer of the survival of Irish' and, despite some exceptions, this is, overall, a good description.[9]

ULSTER

According to Dr Whitley Stokes, writing in 1806:

> in Ulster, there is a greater proportion of Irish speakers than is generally supposed; Cavan and Monaghan contain many; Tyrone about half its inhabitants; Donegal more than half; Armagh and Down a few; Antrim a few along the eastern coast; Derry a few in the mountains to the south-west; Fermanagh scarce any.[10]

The information in the 1851 census confirms some of Stokes' estimates – Cavan and Monaghan both have about 7 per cent Irish speakers, as has Armagh, while in Down the number is less than 1 per cent. However, court interpreter provision ended at an early date – in 1807 in Armagh – while it continued until 1850 in Cavan and an unknown date between 1849 and 1858 in Monaghan. The percentages of Irish speakers given for Tyrone are slightly lower (5 per cent) than for these three counties, but interpreter provision continued there for longer (until 1859). Donegal stands out from all the other counties, with at least 28 per cent speaking Irish (see table 6).

8 Ibid., p. 139.
9 O'Brien, 'The strange death of the Irish language', p. 169.
10 Stokes, *Observations*, p. 2.

Table 6 Irish speakers in Ulster (1851 census)

County	Number of Irish speakers	Percent of Irish speakers	Salaried court interpreters
Antrim	3,033	1.2%	No interpreter
Armagh	13,736	7.01%	Interpreter until 1807
Belfast town	295	0.29%	
Carrickfergus	17	0.2%	
Cavan	13,027	7.48%	Interpreter until 1850
Donegal	73,258	28.71%	Interpreter until 1925
Down	1,153	0.36%	No interpreter
Fermanagh	2,704	2.33%	Interpreter until 1807
Londonderry	5,406	2.81%	Interpreter until 1801
Monaghan	10,955	7.72%	Interpreter until 1849–58
Tyrone	12,892	5%	Interpreter until 1859
Total	**136,476**		

Antrim

While Revd John Dubourdieu reported in 1812 that 'All speak English' in Antrim,[11] more nuanced parochial reports published in 1816 reported a mix of English and Irish. For example, in the parish of Ramoan 'The English language is generally spoken; Irish also is very much used.'[12] Similarly, in the parishes of Ardclinis and Laid, both languages were spoken:

> Here (Laid), as well as in Ardclinis, they speak Irish fluently among themselves, and most of them very good English. Irish, in the hills and tops of glens, is the most prevalent language; and there are some old people in remote places who can speak no other language, though they know the meaning of most English phrases; there are also some who cannot speak Irish though they know it in part.[13]

Some years later, according to Lewis, all on Rathlin Island reportedly spoke English, 'but in the western part of the island the Irish language is universal'.[14] Overall, even if underestimated, the census figures would imply that the Irish language had died out in Antrim sometime in the eighteenth century (see table 7).

In 1852, Richard Davison (1796–1869), a solicitor and MP, addressed a meeting at the Wesleyan chapel in Belfast, where he spoke of the effect of new roads on language usage and explained that at the start of his career, presumably in

11 J. Dubourdieu, *Statistical survey of the County of Antrim* (Dublin, 1812), p. 497.
12 Luke Connolly in Mason, *A statistical account or parochial survey of Ireland*, ii, p. 501.
13 Stewart Dobbs in ibid., iii, p. 26.
14 S. Lewis, *A topographical directory of Ireland* (London, 1837), ii, p. 502.

Table 7 Irish speakers in Antrim (census data)

	1851	1861	1871
Irish only	11 people	11	14
Irish and English	3,022 or 1.2%	1,903 or 0.8%	454
Total	3,033 or 1.2%	1,914 or 0.8%	468 or 0.2%

the 1820s, he regularly needed interpreters when dealing with Irish speakers from the Glens of Antrim:

> In that neighbourhood is a district called the Glens, then inhabited by a peculiar people – a settlement of native Irishmen – who wore the old grey frieze of their own manufacture, spoke only the Irish language, professed the religion of the country, intermarried only among one another, and had no intercourse whatever with the rest of the world around them. I am speaking now of what is within my own recollection, within a period of about twenty-five years. The coast road was made, and corresponding means of communication effected from the shore into the interior of the country and the great market towns. What was the result of this intercourse? A most remarkable change took place. The language of the people entirely disappeared. I remember, when I commenced my professional career in this county, I never was able to examine a witness from the neighbourhood of the Glens without being obliged to have recourse to an interpreter.[15]

Despite reports about Irish speakers in more remote areas, there is no evidence in surviving books of presentments that court interpreters were ever paid a salary in Antrim.[16] No grand jury books of presentments for the town of Carrickfergus were located.

Armagh

Charles Coote reported in 1804 that 'The English tongue has long been the general language of the county, and is firmly established',[17] but it cannot have been as firmly established as he implied because Revd Henry Stewart wrote in 1814 about the Creggan that:

> The people all speak the Irish language and some can speak no other, particularly in the county of Louth part of this parish; however the English

15 *Belfast News-Letter*, 16 Apr. 1852.
16 Searches were carried out of Antrim books of presentments for 1727–67 and 1775–84 (PRONI); 1807 (Google Books); and 1828, 1829, 1830, 1836 (RIA).
17 C. Coote, *A statistical survey of the County of Armagh* (Dublin, 1804), p. 282.

Table 8 Irish speakers in Armagh (census data)

	1851	1861	1871	1901	1911
Irish only	148 or 0.08%	249 or 0.1%	21		
Irish and English	13,588 or 6.93%	8,716 or 4.6%	3,903		
Total	13,736 or 7.01%	8,965 or 4.7%	3,924 or 2.2%	3.6%	2.3%

> language is gaining ground upon the other and very few cases occur to me as a magistrate, where I am obliged to have recourse to an interpreter, for I am, myself, totally ignorant of the Irish language.[18]

In 1837 Samuel Lewis reported on Cargins or Carrgans, a small mountainous district where only Irish was spoken by all 355 inhabitants.[19] In 1843, Edward Tickell, assistant barrister for the county of Armagh, acknowledged that 'I am occasionally obliged to swear an interpreter where witnesses or parties come from the Fews.' According to him, the Irish lived in the mountainous districts and, 'I dare say twelve months have not elapsed since I was obliged to swear an interpreter to interpret the evidence of one of the inhabitants of this district who appeared as a witness before me at Ballybot.'[20] The census statistics confirm the existence of a small community or communities of speakers of Irish in the 1850s (see table 8).

The existence of Irish speakers at the end of the eighteenth and start of the nineteenth century is confirmed by the payment of salaries of £5 per half-year to court interpreters from at least 1797 in the earliest surviving book of presentments through to 1807.[21] However, it is surprising that provision ended at that stage when it continued in other counties, namely Cavan and Monaghan, with similar numbers of Irish speakers.

Cavan

Charles Coote reported in 1802 that 'The English language is entirely spoken, indeed very few of the lower order understand the Irish tongue'.[22] Samuel Lewis provided a different perspective in 1837 when he reported that 'The English language is generally spoken, except in the mountain districts towards the north and west, and even there it is spoken by the younger part of the population, but the aged people all speak Irish, particularly in the district of Glan.'[23]

18 Henry Stewart in Mason, *A statistical account or parochial survey of Ireland*, i, p. 208.
19 Lewis, *A topographical directory of Ireland*, i, p. 253.
20 *Report from Her Majesty's commissioners of inquiry into the state of the law and practice in relation to the occupation of land in Ireland* (1845), p. 113.
21 County of Armagh books of presentments, ARM/4/1, PRONI.
22 C. Coote, *Statistical survey of the county of Cavan* (Dublin, 1802), p. 254.
23 Lewis, *A topographical directory of Ireland*, i, p. 318.

Table 9 Irish speakers in Cavan (census data)

	1851	1861	1871	1881	1891	1901	1911
Irish only	54 or 0.03%	202 or 0.1%	58				
Irish and English	12,973 or 7.45%	7,425 or 4.8%	3,800				
Total	13,027 or 7.48%	7,627 or 4.9%	3,858 or 2.4%	5.4%	3%	5.6%	3.3%

While the census figures (see table 9) are broadly similar to those for Armagh, interpreter provision in County Cavan continued until 1851 or 1852; there was some opposition among the grand jury to a presentment for an Irish interpreter in 1850 but the presentment was passed,[24] and in 1853 there was no court interpreter payment.[25]

Donegal

We have seen that Donegal appears to have led the way in introducing a salary for an interpreter at assizes in 1754, followed by a salary for an interpreter at quarter sessions in 1797. Another innovation was emoluments paid to interpreters at the end of the nineteenth century.

In 1802, James McParlan linked the Irish language with poverty, lack of education and the need for children to work on the land:

> In the mountain region the English language is very little known; parents would wish to instruct their children, but are too poor to pay for any education for them, in some instances; in many parts there are no schools, and sometimes where they are, the children cannot be spared from working for the potatoe and barley. In the champain parts the English is quite general.[26]

In 1812, Edward Wakefield wrote:

> On the coast of Donegal, I met with a peasantry who appeared to be native Irish, and who were very different from the people in the inland parts. Most of them speak the original language; many do not know a word of English, which they call Scotch.[27]

In 1814, F.L. Molloy acknowledged widespread use of Irish in one parish but saw a desire to speak English in order to engage in trade:

24 *Anglo-Celt*, 5 July 1850.
25 County of Cavan, abstract of presentments granted, summer assizes, 1853, NLI.
26 J. McParlan, *Statistical survey of the county of Donegal* (Dublin, 1802), p. 101.
27 E. Wakefield, *An account of Ireland statistical and political* (London, 1812), ii, p. 737.

> Parish of Clonmany, Donegal – The vernacular language is what is used by the people in common, although they are acquiring a tolerable knowledge of the English now, since their ideas were whetted by a commercial intercourse in the neighbouring fairs and markets.[28]

In 1856, School Inspector P.J. Keenan found there was a passion among the islanders on Tory, Inisboffin, Gola and Owey for education, which he linked to the desire to learn English. He explained that:

> They see, whenever a stranger visits their islands, that prosperity has its peculiar tongue as well as its fine coat; they see that whilst the traffickers who occasionally approach them to deal in fish, or in kelp, or in food, display the yellow gold, they count it out in English; and if they ever cross over to the mainland for the 'law,' as they call any legal process, they see that the solemn words of judgment have to come second-hand to them through the offices of an interpreter.[29]

Keenan also quoted an English-speaking Tory islander as saying of fellow islanders who only spoke Irish that he 'was ashamed of them; they stood like dumbies; the cattle got on as well as them'. Despite their enthusiasm, the actual success rate in learning English at school on the islands was very low and Keenan recommended that, as in Scotland, pupils be taught in Irish first, and later in English.

The census statistics, clearly considerable underestimates for 1851, 1861 and 1871, show that there were fewer and fewer monolingual Irish speakers, with increased rates of bilingualism from 1881. About a third of the population stated that they spoke both Irish and English on the censuses between 1881 and 1911 (see table 10).

Table 10 Irish speakers in Donegal (census data)

	1851	1861	1871	1881	1891	1901	1911
Irish only	34,882 or 13.67%	22,156 or 9.3%	18,629				
Irish and English	38,376 or 15.04%	49,170 or 20.7%	44,506	71,764	62,037	60,677	59,313
Total	73,258 or 28.71%	71,326 or 30%	63,135 or 28.9%	71,784 or 34.8%	62,037 or 33.4%	60,677 or 34.9%	59,313 or 35.2%

28 F.L. Molloy in Mason, *A statistical account or parochial survey of Ireland*, i, p. 184.
29 *The twenty-third report of the commissioners of national education in Ireland (for the year 1856)* [C 2304–1], HC 1857–8, xx, 143, 213, 573.

In 1917, summons server John Ward, who frequently acted as interpreter at Dungloe petty sessions, resigned. The chief secretary's office queried if it would be possible to find an interpreter from Dungloe or nearby. However, T. Dolan, county inspector, replied that nobody in Dungloe was willing to interpret for one shilling, the amount paid to Ward for intereting at an assault case, *King v. Campbell*.[30]

The chairperson of Donegal county council suggested discontinuing interpreter provision in 1925.[31] Despite this, Daniel Carr, a retired RIC sergeant, was appointed 'official Irish interpreter' to Letterkenny circuit court in 1927.[32] There were no interpreters at Donegal district court as the two judges spoke Irish.[33]

Down

Revd John Dubourdieu reported of the inhabitants of County Down in 1802 that:

> The English language is so general, that every person speaks it; but, notwithstanding, the Irish language is much used in the mountainous parts, which in this, as well as in most other countries, seem to have been the retreat of the ancient inhabitants.[34]

In relation to the parish of Holywood in County Down, Revd William Holmes wrote in 1819 that 'The Irish is unknown except to a few individuals, and these not natives of the parish.'[35] Seamus Ó Casaide quoted three sources in relation to Irish speakers in the nineteenth century in County Down.[36] The first relates to 1843, just before the Great Famine, when Mr and Mrs C. Hall stated that:

> Until about a century ago, an extensive 'Irish-speaking' population existed near Downpatrick; but they have all disappeared; and the only traces of the language are to be found in the mountainous districts, where the people are almost exclusively Irish, or in the neighbourhood of Carlingford Bay at the south.

30 CSO/RP/1917/187, NAI.
31 Chairperson of finance committee of Tirconaill county council, 17 Nov. 1925, Donegal County Archives, Lifford.
32 *Derry Journal*, 6 July 1928.
33 *Irish Times*, 28 Jan. 1928.
34 J. Dubourdieu, *Statistical survey of the county of Down* (Dublin, 1802), p. 260.
35 William Holmes in Mason, *A statistical account or parochial survey of Ireland*, iii, p. 206.
36 S. Ó Casaide, 'The Irish language in Belfast and County Down, 1601–1850', *Down and Connor Historical Society's Journal*, 2 (1930), pp 4–63.

According to their second source, Abraham Hume, writing in 1874:

> So late as 1820, or say half a century ago, the Irish language was spoken, along with English, from Ballynahinch to near Newry and Newcastle, in Down; and from Ballycastle, by Cushendall, to near Glenarm, in Antrim. An intermediate period occurred, and thirty years later nothing but popular Irish expressions were known, while the number who employed them was greatly reduced. To-day, there is little to be found of it beyond single words, and a strongly marked Hibernic pronunciation or 'brogue'.

The third source, W.H. Patterson, wrote in 1880 that:

> I have made enquiry this year, and a correspondent sends me the following note from the mountainous district in the South of Down: – 'There are a good many Irish-speaking people in the neighbourhood of hill-town, but I think nearly all of them can speak English; when, however, they frequent fairs in the upper parts of the Co Armagh, for instance at Newtownhamilton or Crossmaglen, they meet numbers of people who speak English very imperfectly, and with these people the Down men converse altogether in Irish.

Despite this evidence of the existence of Irish speakers, the numbers in the censuses are extremely low (see table 11). No records of payments to interpreters were found among the surviving books of presentments for Down for the years 1778–92 and 1803–7.[37]

Fermanagh

Samuel Lewis found in 1837 that in Fermanagh, 'The English language is universally spoken, and most of the children are educated in the parochial and national schools,'[38] a view supported by the censuses (see table 12). Despite Lewis' findings,

Table 11 Irish speakers in Down (census data)

	1851	1861	1871
Irish only	2	4	2
Irish and English	1,151 or 0.36%	763 or 0.3%	336
Total	1,153 or 0.36%	767 or 0.3%	338 or 0.1%

37 County Down books of presentments, DOW/4/4/1–2, PRONI.
38 S. Lewis, *A topographical directory of Ireland* (2nd ed. London, 1840), ii, p. 622.

Table 12 Irish speakers in Fermanagh (census data)

	1851	1861	1871	1911
Irish only	10 or 0.01%	15	10	
Irish and English	2,694 or 2.32%	1,663 or 1.6%	349	
Total	2,704 or 2.33%	1,678 or 1.6%	359 or 0.4%	2.5%

there is one record of a payment to a court interpreter in 1807.[39] Unfortunately, there is a dearth of records for Fermanagh, with very few surviving books of presentments. There was no interpreter payment in surviving records for summer 1838 and 1841–3.[40]

Londonderry

In 1802, Revd G. Vaughan Sampson, rector of Aghanloo, reported in his *Statistical survey* that Irish was 'little spoken, except in the mountainous and retired parts'.[41] Similarly, in 1819, according to Lawder, in Killelagh, the mostly Catholic peasantry 'do not all of them speak the Irish'.[42] Ashe reported that in Tamlaght 'the Irish was still spoken, though it is much on the decline, being chiefly confined to some of the lower classes'. However, in 1837 Samuel Lewis reported that 'The Irish, shut up within their secluded mountain ravines, retain many of their peculiarities of language, customs, and religion.'[43]

The census figures from 1851 onwards indicate that Irish was not widespread in Londonderry in the second half of the nineteenth century and the situation was not that different to Fermanagh (see table 13). However, interpreters were provided in Londonderry in the late eighteenth century. Searches of books of presentments revealed that interpreter provision was somewhat irregular, with court criers acting as interpreters intermittently until 1793, but with a gap from 1794 until Lent 1798. Provision recommenced in summer 1798 with

39 *Accounts presented to the house of commons of the presentments passed by the grand juries of Ireland* (1808).

40 County of Fermanagh grand jury presentment book, summer 1838, NLI; *Minutes of evidence taken before Her Majesty's commissioners of inquiry into the state of the law and prectice in relation to the occupation of land* (1845).

41 G.V. Sampson, *Statistical survey of the county of Londonderry with observations on the means of improvement; drawn up for the consideration and by order of the Dublin Society* (Dublin, 1802), p. 460

42 Hume Lawder in Mason, *A statistical account or parochial survey of Ireland*, iii, p. 231.

43 S. Lewis, *A topographical directory of Ireland* (London, 1837), ii, p. 296.

Table 13 Irish speakers in Londonderry (census data)

	1851	1861	1871	1911
Irish only	28 or 0.01%	22	65	
Irish and English	5,378 or 2.8%	3,910 or 2.1%	1,819	
Total	5,406 or 2.81%	3,932 or 2.1%	1,884 or 0.8%	2.1%

various court criers cum interpreters and continued until Lent 1801, when it ended.

Monaghan

According to Charles Coote, in the barony of Cremorne in 1801, 'The men all speak the English tongue, but the women seem rather inclined to the Irish language.'[44] Land agent William Trench reported that in the barony of Farney in 1843, 'Irish was the language at that time chiefly spoken by the people.'[45]

The census figures show the usual rise in 1881 and it is likely that the figures from earlier censuses are underestimates, particularly given the fact that salaried court interpreters were employed in the first half of the nineteenth century (see table 14). The last instance of a payment found for an interpreter in Monaghan was in 1849,[46] but there is a gap in the records for 1850–7; by 1858 payments had stopped.[47] Therefore, interpreter provision ended sometime between 1849 and 1858.

Table 14 Irish speakers in Monaghan (census data)

	1851	1861	1871	1881	1891	1901	1911
Irish only	243 or 0.17%	311 or 0.2%	138				
Irish and English	10,712 or 7.55%	7106 or 5.6%	4,964				
Total	10,955 or 7.72%	7,417 or 5.8%	5,102 or 4.4%	6.4%	3.3%	7.1%	7.6%

44 C. Coote, *Statistical survey of the county of Monaghan* (Dublin, 1801), p. 86.
45 W.S. Trench, *Realities of Irish life* (London, 1869), p. 70.
46 County of Monaghan book of presentments, summer 1849, Monaghan Local Studies.
47 A copy of the treasurer's account of payments at summer assizes 1859 and of the discharged and undischarged quaeres, and of the presentments laid on the county of Monaghan at spring assizes 1859, NLI.

Tyrone

John McEvoy reported in his statistical survey in 1802 that:

> Except through the wilds of Munterloney (chiefly in the barony of Strabane) the English language is most prevalent; indeed throughout the county it is gaining ground every day. The Roman Catholics are the only sect, who are fond of speaking the Irish language, and with them too it is wearing off very much.[48]

In 1819 for the parish of Errigall-Keroge, Revd John Groves reported on the increased use of English:

> Here, as in every other place where there has been opportunity for observation, the use of the Irish language is declining. It is now an unusual thing to meet with any one, at a fair or market, who cannot express himself in English. This improvement is of late date. There are few who cannot recollect when groups might be seen, in the markets, who could not speak English. Mutual intercourse is greatly facilitated, and business much more easily transacted, by this dissemination of one language.[49]

As regards interpreter provision, in 1836, grand juror Mr Graham objected to payment of £4 12*s.* 4*d.* to Stephen Nealis on the grounds that 'every person in this County can now speak English'.[50] Despite this, and the views of McEvoy and Groves above, and the relatively low numbers of Irish speakers reported in the census of 1851 (see table 15), Stephen Nealis or Nealius was paid a salary as an interpreter for some thirty-three years, from at least 1826 until his death in October 1859. In 1910 at the revision court in Trillick, an Irish teacher called Philip Waldron from Kilskeery was allowed to answer questions in Irish and

Table 15 Irish speakers in Tyrone (census data)

	1851	1861	1871	1881	1891	1901	1911
Irish only	405 or 0.16%	206 or 0.1%	130				
Irish and English	12,487 or 4.88%	10,654 or 4.4%	6,421				
Total	12,892 or 5.04%	10,860 or 4.5%	6,551 or 3%	5%	3.9%	4.3%	5.3%

48 J. McEvoy, *Statistical survey of Tyrone* (Dublin, 1802), p. 201.
49 John Groves in Mason, *Statistical account or parochial survey of Ireland*, iii, p. 160.
50 *Derry Journal*, 2 Aug. 1836.

the revising barrister, Mr Whittaker, informed the court of his own attempt to learn Irish.[51]

MUNSTER

Munster was a stronghold of the Irish language. Interpreter provision ended first in the cities of Cork, Limerick and Waterford, and later in counties of Limerick and Tipperary, but continued well into the twentieth century in the counties of Clare, Cork, Kerry and Waterford. Dr Whitley Stokes stated in 1806 that 'in all the counties of Munster the Irish language prevails beyond comparison, if we except the large towns, their immediate neighbourhoods, and some of the country along the coast'.[52] In 1826, an 'enlightened and experienced Judge' commented that 'as to Munster; from my experience of what passes in the courts on that circuit – the majority of cases, I should say, proceed without an interpreter; but still he is frequently required'.[53]

The census figures for 1851, despite the issues around capturing information, show that there were very high numbers of Irish speakers in Munster, with high percentages of the population speaking Irish in Waterford, Kerry, Clare and Cork (see table 16).

In 1904, according to the *Irish Times*:

> There are court-houses too, in the South in which the interpreter is still heard at Petty Sessions and Quarter Sessions, but I fear he is a vanishing

Table 16 Irish speakers in Munster (1851 census)

County	Number	Percentage	Interpreter provision
Clare	126,996	59.78%	Interpreter until 1926
City of Cork	10,381	12.11%	Interpreter until at least 1856
Cork	296,034	52.53%	Interpreter until 1928
Kerry	146,498	61.49%	Interpreter until the 1940s
City of Limerick	4,204	7.86%	Interpreter until 1855
Limerick	77,982	37.57%	Last payment in 1884
Tipperary	62,764	18.93%	Last payment in 1899
City of Waterford	4,103	16.22%	Until at least 1875
Waterford	86,823	62.59%	Last payment in 1921
Total	815,785		

51 *Ulster Herald*, 15 Oct. 1910; *Belfast Morning News*, 11 Oct. 1859.
52 Stokes, *Observations on the necessity*, p. 2.
53 'On the utility of the Irish language and the ministry of the established church', *Christian Examiner and Church of Ireland Magazine*, 2:7 (1826), p. 295.

quantity, and not because the lawyers and magistrates are learning Irish, but because Irish itself is not so widely spoken as it was twenty years ago.[54]

Clare

There is agreement on the widespread use of Irish in County Clare. In 1808 Hely Dutton reported that:

> There are very few, except in remote situations, that do not at least understand a little English, but from an apprehension of not speaking correctly they frequently pretend not to understand it; I have often heard them declare in good English, that they could not speak a word of it; almost all the better kind of people speak Irish to the country people, but scarcely one of their sons is able to hold a conversation in this language.[55]

In 1816, in Kilrush and surrounding parishes:

> The Irish language is in general use here, but the English is rapidly gaining ground; most of the rising generation understand it; a sworn interpreter is however still used at the assizes of Ennis and the different quarter sessions, and a country gentleman, ignorant of the Irish language, would be much at a loss how to transact his business at the fairs and markets.[56]

According to Mason, in the parishes of Kilrush, Killard, Kilfieragh, Moyferta and Kilballyhone in 1816 and referring to 'the poorer classes':

> The language generally spoken here, except in the remote parts of the union, is English. Many persons however are still utterly ignorant of the English language; and a great proportion of the inhabitants speak Irish in preference.[57]

Three years later, in 1819, in the parish of Noughaval and Carrune, 'The language used by the people in general is the Irish.'[58] In August 1846, a diary entry by Fr Thomas O'Carroll during an outing to the Cliffs of Moher noted that:

> I was very much amused during the day at the flippancy, the variety of tone and gesture, with which the children spoke Irish. It appeared to be the

54 *Irish Times*, 2 Jan. 1904.
55 Hely Dutton, *Statistical survey of the county of Clare* (Dublin, 1808), p. 302.
56 John Graham in Mason, *A statistical account or parochial survey of Ireland*, ii, p. 462.
57 John Graham in ibid., ii, p. 456.
58 Robert Gabbett in ibid., iii, p. 283.

> favourite vehicle of communication between themselves, though they spoke English very intelligibly when interrogated in that language.[59]

In 1829, according to the Irish Society, the situation in Clare was as follows:

> In courts of justice here the witnesses are constantly examined in Irish; and though a person appearing and anxious to give evidence on behalf of his dearest friend should be pressed to speak English, and threatened if he did not with punishment, or that he would [be] put down without having his evidence taken (it being ascertained that he could speak English, and was heard to do so), he would declare in Irish that he would not trust his soul to any other, and retire without giving his evidence, or submit to punishment sooner than do so.[60]

Scottish Whig Robert Graham, far from an impartial observer, wrote of Kilrush petty sessions in the 1830s:

> [...] I went in and was very much amused with the characteristic traits of the common people. Their improvidence, lying habits, keenness for law questions, and spirit of tribalism were all made manifest in the hour I attended to the cases. It lessened my amusement much, however, that the majority of witnesses declared their ignorance of English and were examined thro' an interpreter.[61]

The numbers in the censuses confirm high numbers of Irish speakers in Clare (see table 17). However, Máire Ní Chiosáin has described the decline of the language in Clare as 'precipitous' and the reasons for the decline as 'somewhat of a mystery.'[62]

Table 17 Irish speakers in Clare (census data)

	1851	1861	1871	1881	1891	1901	1911
Irish only	25,446 or 11.98%	7,126 or 4.3%	4,432				
Irish and English	101,550 or 47.8%	72,074 or 43.3%	53,713	65,085	46,878	43,486	36,704
Total	126,996 or 59.78%	79,200 or 47.6%	58,145 or 39.3%	65,085 or 46%	46,878 or 37.7%	43,486 or 38.7%	36,704 or 35.2%

59 T. O'Carroll, 'The O'Carroll diaries' (unpublished).
60 Irish Society, *Eleventh report: reports of the Irish Society* (Dublin, 1829), p. 14.
61 H. Heaney, *A Scottish Whig in Ireland, 1835–1838: the Irish journals of Robert Graham of Redgorton* (Dublin, 1999), p. 218.
62 Ní Chiosáin, 'The Irish language in Co. Clare in the early twentieth century', p. 503.

1. Judge Day, courtesy of National Library of Ireland.

2. Judge Barry Yelverton, courtesy of National Library of Ireland.

3. John Philpot Curran, courtesy of National Library of Ireland.

4. Peter Burrowes, court of insolve debtors, courtesy of National Libra of Ireland.

5. Judge Jonathan Christian, courtesy of King's Inns Library.

6. Peter O'Brien, courtesy of King's Inns Library.

7. Galway city court, courtesy of National Library of Ireland.

8. Kinsale court house, courtesy of National Library of Ireland.

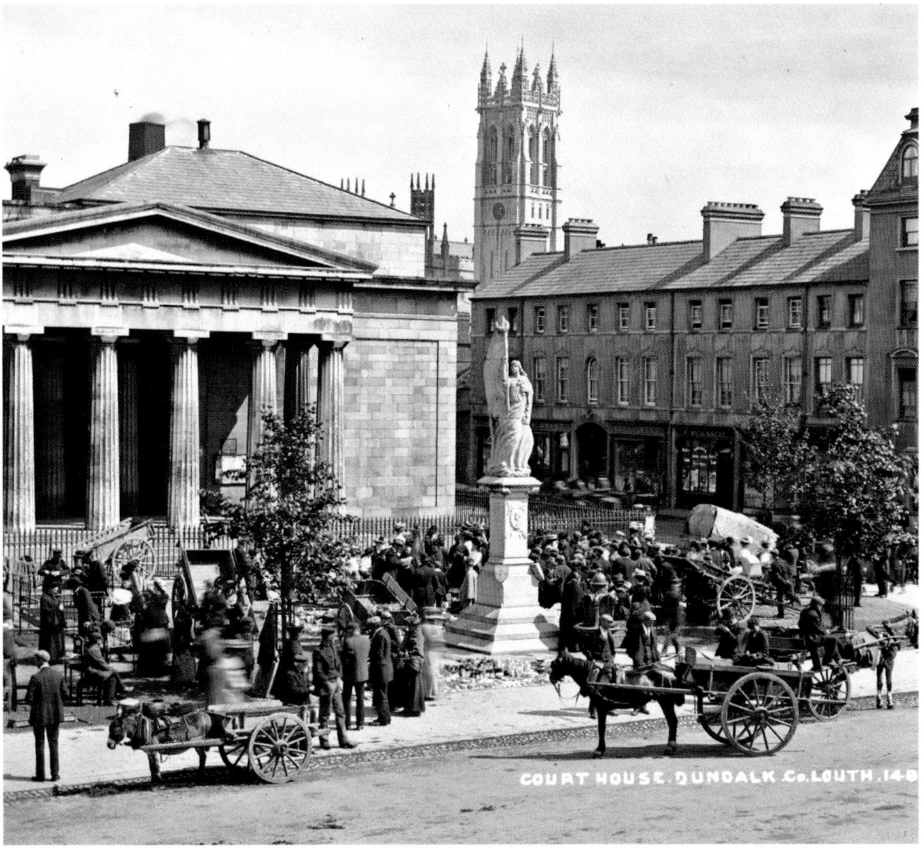

9. Dundalk courthouse, courtesy of National Library of Ireland.

10. Ballyvaughan courthouse, courtesy of National Library of Ireland.

11. Court in session in Ballyragget, Co. Kilkenny, courtesy of National Library of Ireland.

12. The square, Dungarvan, courtesy of National Library of Ireland.

13. George's Street, Limerick city, courtesy of National Library of Ireland.

14. Sligo gaol: governor James Beatty was also Irish interpreter at assizes, courtesy of National Library of Ireland.

15. Swiss Cottage, Cahir, Co. Tipperary, where interpreter Thomas Heffernan lived for a number of years, courtesy of Office of Public Works.

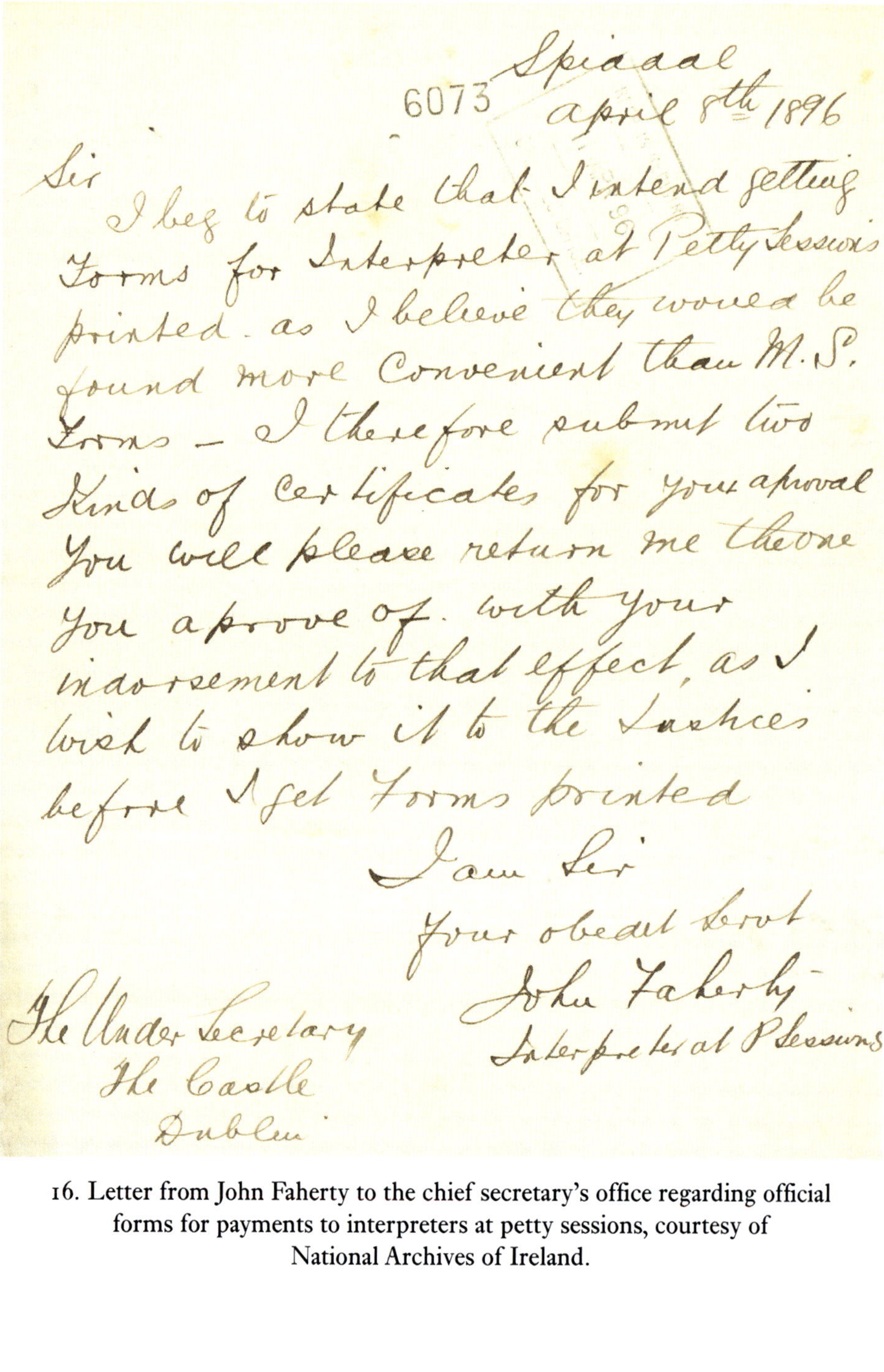

6073

Spiddal
April 8th 1896

Sir
I beg to state that I intend getting Forms for Interpreter at Petty Sessions printed. as I believe they would be found more Convenient than M.S. Forms — I therefore submit two Kinds of Certificates for your aproval You will please return me the one You aprove of. with your indorsement to that effect, as I wish to show it to the Justices before I get Forms printed

I am Sir
Your obedt Servt
John Faherty
Interpreter at P Sessions

The Under Secretary
The Castle
Dublin

16. Letter from John Faherty to the chief secretary's office regarding official forms for payments to interpreters at petty sessions, courtesy of National Archives of Ireland.

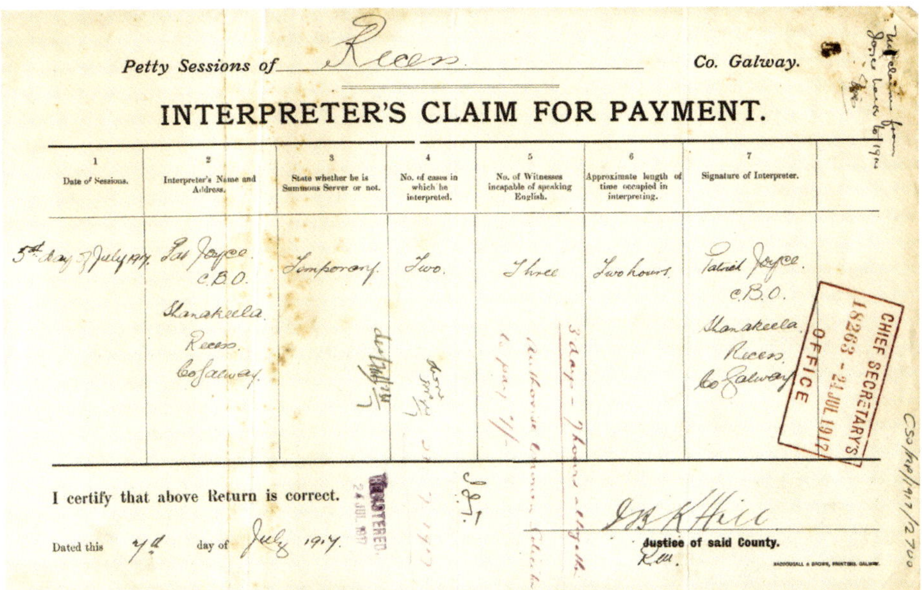

Petty Sessions of *Recess* Co. Galway.

INTERPRETER'S CLAIM FOR PAYMENT.

1 Date of Sessions.	2 Interpreter's Name and Address.	3 State whether he is Summons Server or not.	4 No. of cases in which he interpreted.	5 No. of Witnesses incapable of speaking English.	6 Approximate length of time occupied in interpreting.	7 Signature of Interpreter.
5th day of July 1917.	Pat Joyce. C.B.O. Shanakeela. Recess. Co Galway.	Temporary.	Two.	Three	Two hours.	Patrick Joyce. C.B.O. Shanakeela. Recess. Co Galway.

CHIEF SECRETARY'S OFFICE 18263 - 21 JUL 1917

I certify that above Return is correct.

Dated this 7th day of July 1917.

REGISTERED. 24 JUL 1917

J B K Hill

Justice of said County.

Recess.

CSO/RP/1917/2700

17. The form adopted in Galway for petty sessions interpreters by 1917, courtesy of National Archives of Ireland.

18. The last Donegal grand jury, 1899, courtesy of Donegal County Archives.

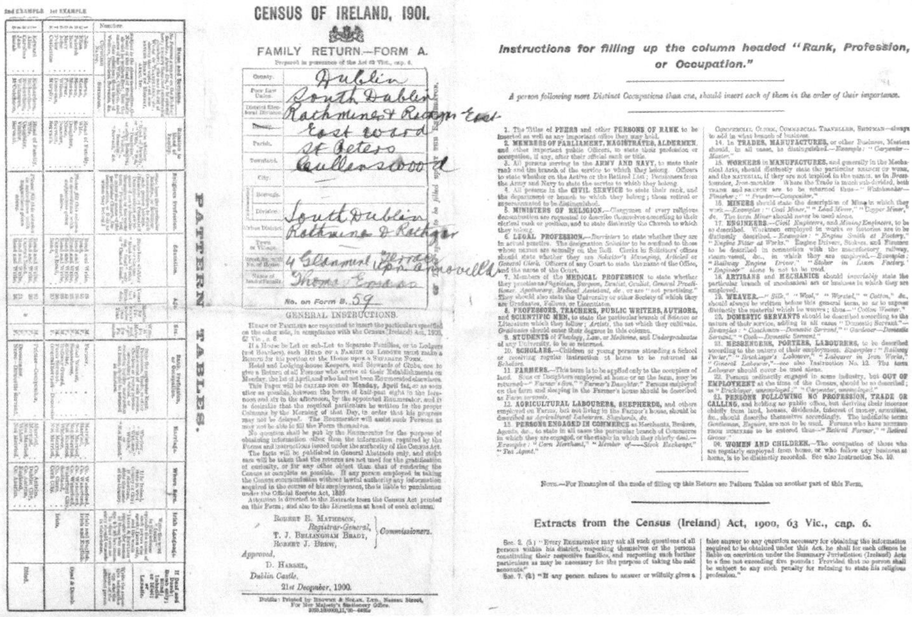

CENSUS OF IRELAND, 1901.

FAMILY RETURN.—FORM A.

Prepared in pursuance of the Act 63 Vict., cap. 6.

County.	Dublin
Poor Law Union.	South Dublin
District Electoral Division.	Rathmines & Rathgar East
~~Barony~~	East ward
Parish.	St Peters
Townland.	Cullenswood
City.	—
Borough.	
Division.	South Dublin
Urban District.	Rathmines & Rathgar
Town or Village.	—
Street, &c., with No. of House.	4 Glenmount Terrace Upr Annaville
Name of Head of Family.	Thomas Evans

No. on Form B. 59

GENERAL INSTRUCTIONS.

Heads of Families are requested to insert the particulars specified on the other side, in compliance with the Census (Ireland) Act, 1900, 63 Vic., c. 6.

If a House be Let or sub-Let to Separate Families, or to Lodgers (not Boarders), each Head of a Family or Lodger must make a Return for his portion of the House upon a Separate Form.

Hotel and Lodging-house Keepers, and Stewards of Clubs, are to give a Return of all Persons who arrive at their Establishments on Monday, the 1st of April, and who had not been Enumerated elsewhere.

This Paper will be called for on Monday, April 1st, or as soon after as possible, between the hours of half-past eight in the forenoon and six in the afternoon, by the appointed Enumerator, and it is desirable that the required particulars be written in the proper Columns by the Morning of that Day, in order that his progress may not be delayed. The Enumerator will assist such Persons as may not be able to fill the Form themselves.

No question shall be put by the Enumerator for the purpose of obtaining information other than the information required by the Forms and instructions issued under the authority of the Census Act.

The facts will be published in General Abstracts only, and strict care will be taken that the returns are not used for the gratification of curiosity, or for any other object than that of rendering the Census as complete as possible. If any person employed in taking the Census communicates without lawful authority any information acquired in the course of his employment, he is liable to punishment under the Official Secrets Act, 1889.

Attention is directed to the Extracts from the Census Act printed on this Form; and also to the Directions at head of each column.

Robert E. Matheson, Registrar-General,
T. J. Bellingham Brady,
Robert J. Brew,
Commissioners.

Approved,
D. Harrel,
Dublin Castle,
21st December, 1900.

Dublin: Printed by Brown & Nolan, Ltd., Nassau Street, For Her Majesty's Stationery Office.

PATTERN TABLES.

Instructions for filling up the column headed "Rank, Profession, or Occupation."

A person following more Distinct Occupations than one, should insert each of them in the order of their importance.

Note.—For Examples of the mode of filling up this Return see Pattern Tables on another part of this Form.

Extracts from the Census (Ireland) Act, 1900, 63 Vic., cap. 6.

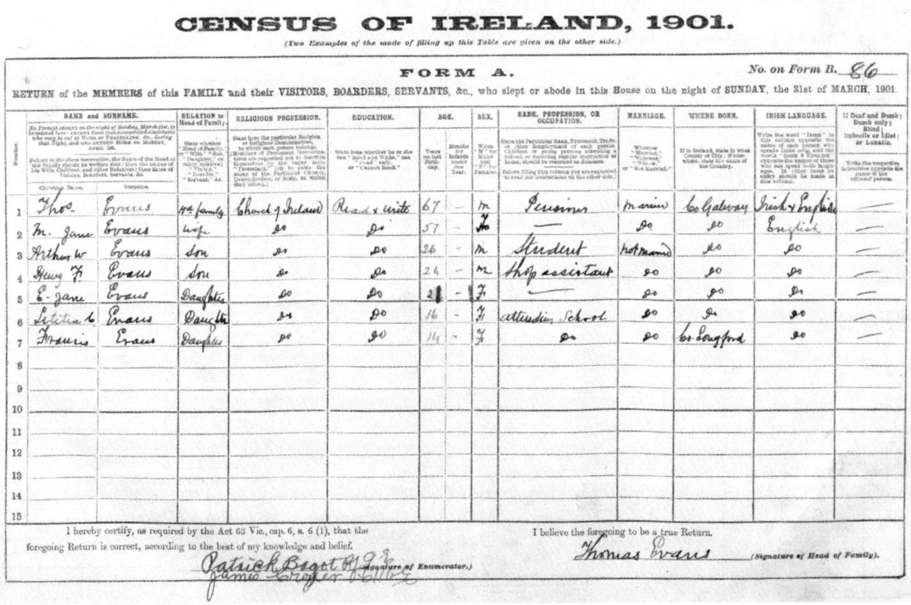

CENSUS OF IRELAND, 1901.

(Two Examples of the mode of filling up this Table are given on the other side.)

FORM A. No. on Form B. 86

RETURN of the MEMBERS of this FAMILY and their VISITORS, BOARDERS, SERVANTS, &c., who slept or abode in this House on the night of SUNDAY, the 31st of MARCH, 1901.

Number	Christian Name	Surname	Relation to Head of Family	Religious Profession	Education	Age: Years on last Birthday	Age: Months for Infants under one Year	Sex	Rank, Profession, or Occupation	Marriage	Where Born	Irish Language	If Deaf and Dumb; Dumb only; Blind; Imbecile or Idiot; or Lunatic
1	Thos.	Evans	Head of family	Church of Ireland	Read & write	67	–	M	Pensioner	married	Co Galway	Irish & English	—
2	M. Jane	Evans	Wife	do	do	57	–	F	—	do	do	English	—
3	Arthur W	Evans	Son	do	do	26	–	M	Student	not married	do	do	—
4	Henry F.	Evans	Son	do	do	24	–	M	Shop assistant	do	do	do	—
5	E. Jane	Evans	Daughter	do	do	21	–	F	—	do	do	do	—
6	Letitia L.	Evans	Daughter	do	do	16	–	F	attending School	do	do	do	—
7	Francis	Evans	Daughter	do	do	14	–	F	do	do	Co. Longford	do	—
8													
9													
10													
11													
12													
13													
14													
15													

I hereby certify, as required by the Act 63 Vic., cap. 6, s. 6 (1), that the foregoing Return is correct, according to the best of my knowledge and belief.

Patrick Bogot RIC, James Crozier RIC (Signature of Enumerator.)

I believe the foregoing to be a true Return.

Thomas Evans (Signature of Head of Family).

19 and 20. The 1901 census form for Thomas Evans, RIC interpreter at the Maamtrasna murder trials, courtesy of National Archives of Ireland.

21. Chief secretary's office, Dublin Castle, courtesy of National Library of Ireland, with thanks to William Derham, Office of Public Works.

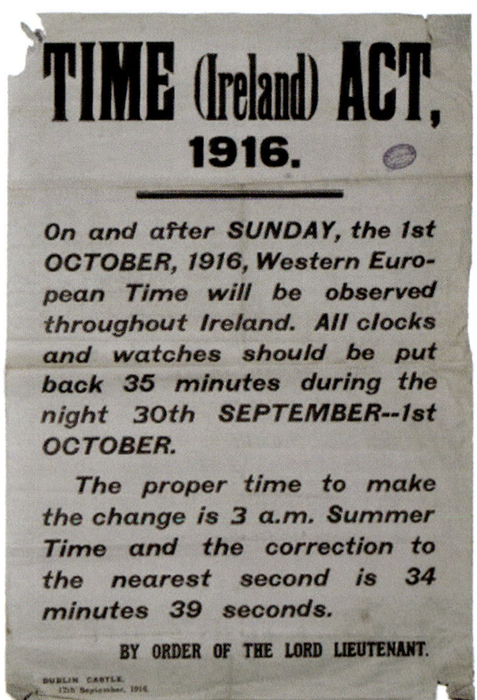

TIME (Ireland) ACT,
1916.

On and after SUNDAY, the 1st OCTOBER, 1916, Western European Time will be observed throughout Ireland. All clocks and watches should be put back 35 minutes during the night 30th SEPTEMBER--1st OCTOBER.

The proper time to make the change is 3 a.m. Summer Time and the correction to the nearest second is 34 minutes 39 seconds.

BY ORDER OF THE LORD LIEUTENANT.

DUBLIN CASTLE,
12th September, 1916.

22. Time (Ireland) Act 1916, courtesy of Dublin City Library & Archive.

In 1887 Michael Lynch requested payment from Dublin Castle for work carried out at Carrigaholt petty sessions and was told that only the clerk of petty sessions could apply for same.[63] He was paid five shillings for interpreting in 1890, on three occasions in 1892 and in 1893 and once in 1895.[64] William Blood, also a civil bill officer, was paid five shillings for interpreting at Ballyvaughan petty sessions on a number of occasions between 1892 and 1905.[65] In 1889, the *Cork Examiner* described Michael Keane as 'a retired policeman, and Irish interpreter at the court of Petty Sessions of Corofin'.[66] A salaried interpreter was employed at assizes and quarter sessions in Clare until at least 1926.[67]

Cork city

In 1812 Edward Wakefield reported that:

> The Irish language is so much spoken among the common people, in the city of Cork and its neighbourhood, that an Englishman is apt to forget where he is, and to consider himself in a foreign city.[68]

According to Revd John Quarry, in the parish of St Mary, Shandon, in 1819:

> The language used by the people in general is English; the lower orders in their dealings with one another frequently speak the Irish language, but this last is falling a good deal into disuse amongst them; the tradespeople transacting their business in English for the most part, so that the poor Irishman now finds it to his advantage to know that language for more easy communication in his dealings.[69]

Table 18 Irish speakers in Cork city (census data)

	1851	1861	1871	1901[70]	1911[71]
Irish only	123 or 0.14%	126 or 0.2%	96		
Irish and English	10,258 or 11.97%	6,476 or 8.3%	5,294		
Total	10,381 or 12.11%	6,602 or 8.5%	5,390 or 6.9%	10.2%	8.7%

63 CSO/LB/52, p. 123, NAI.
64 CSO/LB/57, p. 754; CSO/LB/64, p. 752; CSO/LB/65, p. 751; CSO/LB/66, pp 469, 653; CSO/LB/68, pp 115, 484; CSO/LB/73, p. 866, NAI.
65 CSO/LB/64, pp 752, 935; CSO/LB/68, p. 199, CSO/LB/75, p. 938; CSO/RP/18179/05, NAI.
66 *Cork Examiner*, 16 Sept. 1889.
67 *Limerick Leader*, 5 July 1926.
68 Wakefield, *An account of Ireland statistical and political*, ii, p. 766.
69 John Quarry in Mason, *A statistical account or parochial survey of Ireland*, iii, p. 375.
70 County borough.
71 County borough.

Census statistics indicate that there was a small but significant proportion of Irish speakers (see table 18).

An interpreter was paid £3 8*s.* 3*d.* in the city of Cork in 1807.[72] The same uneven amount is recorded for the years 1808, 1811 and 1815.[73] In 1826, the interpreter was 'in hourly demand' at Cork assizes.[74] We have already seen that the interpreter in the city of Cork was paid £3 per half-year in 1841–3. Newspaper reports provide supplementary information. In 1840, an application was made to the court to appoint an interpreter for the city sessions court which 'was absolutely necessary in consequence of the great extent of the jurisdiction of the court'. However, there was some doubt about whether such courts were covered under the act.[75] This doubt was reiterated in 1843 when application was made for payment to the court interpreter. It was felt that an interpreter was necessary because 'the Irish language was the only one spoken by the majority of the country witnesses'.[76] A few days later Mr Justice Jackson told the court that he 'could not find a clause' in the act giving the grand jury the power to make a presentment to pay an interpreter.[77] However, newspaper reports from the 1840s indicate that interpreter Bartholomew Neenan continued to be paid £3 per half-year until at least 1856.[78]

County Cork

There is quite a lot of information available on the situation regarding the preferred language of the inhabitants of Cork. Horatio Townsend reported in 1810 that 'Except in towns, they seldom use any language but Irish, and even in some of the best cultivated districts most of the people can speak no other'. In Abbeymahon, 'the far greater number of the common people speak only Irish'.[79] In 1812 Wakefield commented on the widespread use of Irish by 'the common people' in Youghal.[80]

Mason's *Statistical account* provides additional information at parish level. Revd Horatio Townsend reported that in 1816 in Kilgeriff, 'The language of the common Roman Catholic peasantry is Irish; Protestants of the lower order speak

72 *Accounts presented to the house of commons of the presentments passed by the grand juries of Ireland* (1808).
73 *Statement of assessement at the summer assizes 1808: published by order of the then grand jury of the county of the city of Cork*; *Statement of assessement at the summer assizes 1811: published by oder of the then grand jury of the county of the city of Cork*; *Statement of assessement at the summer assizes 1815: published by oder of the then grand jury of the county of the city of Cork*, all NLI (digitized).
74 *Cork Constitution*, 8 Apr. 1826.
75 *Limerick Reporter*, 4 Aug. 1840.
76 *Cork Examiner*, 31 Mar. 1843.
77 Ibid., 3 Apr. 1843.
78 *Southern Reporter & Cork Commercial Courier*, 4 Mar. 1856.
79 H. Townsend, *Statistical survey of the county of Cork* (Dublin, 1810), p. 75.
80 Wakefield, *An account of Ireland statistical and political*, ii, p. 766.

both English and Irish; in town [Cloghnakilty] English is frequently spoken by both.'[81] Also in 1816, according to Revd Thomas Newenham, Carrigaline, 'with very few exceptions, they understand and speak the English language, but conversations among themselves are most frequently held in Irish'.[82] In 1819 Revd Philip Townsend reported that in Kilcorney, 'Irish is invariably used, but they can all speak English.'[83] According to Revd William Alleyn Evanson, in the Union of Tracton Abbey, 'The English language is, however, gaining ground, in consequence of it being taught in the schools, and of the frequent intercourse of the inhabitants with the towns of Kinsale and Cork.'[84] In the parish of Ballyvoorney, according to Revd Basil Orpen, 'Irish is the language most generally spoken; very few speak English.'[85] Revd John Macbeth reported that in the parish of Ardagh, 'The language generally used is Irish; yet the great majority of the parishioners can speak English tolerably.'[86] Of the parish of Middleton Revd Robert Austen stated that 'The English language is generally understood and spoken; the lower class commonly speak Irish.'[87]

Thomas Sheahan wrote of his travels around Bandon in 1825:

> An Englishman travelling through certain parts of Ireland, labours under a great disadvantage, in not being acquainted with the Irish tongue. To be sure, there is scarcely a district, in which he may not find several persons capable of conversing in English, but if he do not chance to fall in with such, he must depend altogether upon his eye, for the state of the country. Such, in a great measure was my case this day. – Seven tenths of those I interrogated, knew none other than their native tongue.[88]

In 1837, according to Samuel Lewis, 'The peasantry … generally, except in the mountain districts, speak the English language.'[89] However, he had this to say of the more isolated Cape Clear:

> It is separated from the mainland by the sound of Gaskenane, in which is always a strong tide, and in high winds a very heavy sea; and having, consequently, less intercourse with it than the islands nearer the coast, the

81 Horatio Townsend in Mason, *A statistical account or parochial survey of Ireland*, ii, p. 311.
82 Thomas Newenham in ibid., ii, p. 132.
83 Philip Townsend in ibid., iii, p. 222.
84 W.A. Evanson in ibid., iii, p. 472.
85 Basil Orpen in ibid., iii, p. 116.
86 John Macbeth in ibid., iii, p. 26.
87 Robert Austen in ibid., iii, p. 271.
88 T. Sheahan, *Excursions from Bandon, in the south of Ireland, by a plain Englishman* (London, 1825), p. 34.
89 Lewis, *A topographical directory of Ireland* (2nd ed.), i, p. 407.

Table 19 Irish speakers in County Cork (census data)

	1851	1861	1871	1881	1891	1901	1911
Irish only	ER: 13,088 WR: 33,398 Total: 46,486 or 8.25%	ER: 4,561 WR: 11,917	11,532				
Irish and English	ER: 145,760 WR: 103,788 Total: 249,548 or 44.28%	ER: 96,327 or 34.2% WR: 82,652 or 46.4%	135,437	162,356	119,720	97,979	77,205
Total	ER: 158,848 WR: 137,186 Total: 296,034 or 52.53%	ER: 100,888 or 35.8% WR: 94,569 or 53.1% Total: 195,457	146,969 or 33.5%	162,356 or 39.1%	119,720 or 27.3%	97,979 or 29.8%	77,205 or 23.8%

> native inhabitants have retained more of their original manners, language, and customs.[90]

The 1851 and 1861 censuses divided up information from the east and west ridings, with greater numbers of Irish speakers in the west riding (see table 19).

In 1870, an unnamed correspondent reported on increased bilingualism in Cork for the *Pall Mall Gazette*:

> The Irish language has been long since doomed, but its decline has been remarkable of late. It was no uncommon thing thirty years back to find well-to-do peasant farmers unable to speak a word of English. Ten years since the southern county courts had interpreters constantly at work to repeat the evidence of witnesses in the Saxon tongue, and attorneys were obliged to have a special clerk in their offices to hold converse in their native dialect with the country people. The other day I was snipe shooting in a district where, in 1864, without understanding Irish it was impossible to get any information from the peasantry. Even for the bird of the air and the fishes of the stream they had their own terms. I now observe that the peasantry in this quarter speak English, after an odd fashion, to be sure; and in no case on my last visit did I discover a man or a woman unable to use English. The vernacular of the area is still, however, Irish – that is, the people constantly converse with each other in that tongue, and on Sundays the discourse addressed to them by the priests is in Irish too. The place I refer to is crossed by a railway, and is within easy reach of Cork.[91]

90 Ibid., p. 249.
91 *Cork Examiner*, 31 Jan. 1870 (from the *Pall Mall Gazette*).

There are some interesting nuggets of information in this account, according to which interpreters were 'constantly at work' in 1860 in the southern county courts, presumably Cork, Kerry and Waterford. It is also very interesting that attorneys employed Irish-speaking clerks to enable communication with country people. For some people bilingualism was advantageous.

Cork was divided into east and west ridings in 1823; separate interpreters were appointed in each riding from at least 1845, possibly earlier. In the county of Cork, there was a salaried interpreter until at least 1928.[92]

Kerry

In 1850 Irish was the only language of most of the 3,500 former tenants of Lord Lansdowne's estate in Kenmare whose passages to America were organized by land agent William Trench.[93] In 1873 Mr C.H. Hemphill gave evidence to a select committee that:

> I am sorry to say that there are many instances of apparently very respectable men in Kerry, who, when they come to be examined as witnesses, cannot either speak or understand English even now, strange as it might appear. At my quarter sessions I am obliged to have an interpreter in the outlying districts to take the evidence. [...] In Dingle, in the county of Kerry, which is one of my quarter sessions' towns, and at Cahirciveen, almost every second case requires the intervention of an interpreter.[94]

The experiences of Trench and Hemphill are confirmed by the high numbers of Irish speakers in the censuses, particularly those who spoke Irish only (probably an underestimate) in 1851 and 1861 (see table 20).

Table 20 Irish speakers in Kerry (census data)

	1851	1861	1871	1881	1891	1901	1911
Irish only	44,455 or 18.66%	24,971	12,009				
Irish and English	102,043 or 42.83%	90,130	69,959	99,338	74,182	71,671	60,719
Total	146,498 or 61.49%	115,101 or 57%	81,968 or 41.7%	99,338 or 49.4%	74,182 or 41.4%	71,671 or 43.2%	60,719 or 38%

92 *Southern Star*, 8 Dec. 1928.
93 Trench, *Realities of Irish life*, p. 125.
94 *First, second and special reports from the select committee on juries (Ireland) 1873: minutes of evidence*, p. 2.

Interpreters were employed in Kerry from at least 1807 and continuously through the nineteenth and early twentieth century. In 1859, Mr Copinger, chairman of Killarney quarter sessions, expressed the view that the interpreter's annual salary of £30 'was inadequate to the expenses consequent on travelling over the county'.[95] In 1867 two interpreters were appointed,[96] one to work in north Kerry and the other in south Kerry. In 1898, questions were raised in the house of commons about Patrick O'Sullivan's remuneration. It was asserted that he 'has to spend £140 each year … while he only received 4s 3d per day, and has to pay his own railway and hotel expenses'. It was claimed that O'Sullivan had the support of the grand jury for an increase in salary. However, Gerald Balfour stated that the lord chancellor had no power in the matter and that 'even if he had the power, he does not consider that a case has been made out which would justify him in entertaining O'Sullivan's application for an increase in salary'.[97] In 1902 it was reported that the interpreter was not present at Tralee courthouse because 'the rule in Tralee is that notice should be given if his services were required'[98] – an indication that witnesses were using English in court. Kerry county council continued to pay John Sugrue, who had started working as an interpreter at quarter sessions in 1917, a quarterly amount, probably a retainer, of £1 17*s.* 6*d.* as official interpreter to the circuit court into the 1940s.[99]

In 1907, Michael Dowd, quarter sessions interpreter, was also the Dingle petty sessions interpreter.[100] After his death in 1917, requests to provide a replacement at petty sessions were sent to the chief secretary's office and there was some unsuccessful canvassing for James Curran, who submitted claims for interpreting.[101] There was also correspondence about the adjournment of some cases in Dingle 'for want of Irish interpreter'.[102]

In 1892, the arrival of a 27-year-old monolingual Irish speaker called John Kearney or Carney at Ellis Island prompted two short newspaper articles on the tenacity of the Irish language in certain areas. An interpreter had to be found for Kearney,[103] who was 6 feet 9 inches tall, and from the Blasket Islands. He was planning to join his two brothers and sister in Connecticut. The authorities called a Father Callaghan and by chance a Miss Maggie McGillicuddy was available and 'proved unexpectedly equal to the emergency'.[104]

95 *Kerry Evening Post*, 2 July 1859.
96 *Tralee Chronicle & Killarney Echo*, 12 Feb. 1867.
97 HC Debates, 4 Mar. 1898, vol. 54, cc 603–4.
98 *Killarney Echo & South Kerry Chronicle*, 8 Nov. 1902.
99 Kerry county council financial statements – expenditure, Kerry County Archives, Tralee.
100 *Kerryman*, 30 Nov. 1907.
101 CSO/RP/13282/18 and 17015/18, NAI.
102 CSO/RP/2649/18, NAI.
103 *Anglo-Celt*, 25 June 1892.
104 *Connaught Telegraph*, 11 June 1892.

Limerick city

Records dating from 1807 show that salaried interpreters were employed at the city of Limerick. However, in 1844, the judge objected to a presentment for £5 for an interpreter because 'his services were not required' and then went on to relent and sanction the payment.[105] In 1850, Mr Vereker's proposal that the interpreter's salary be halved from £5 to £2 10*s.* was passed unanimously by the city grand jury.[106] In 1851 'one of the Borough Club' also objected and the interpreter John Roberts was asked if he was 'well acquainted with the Irish language' and could he ask for his presentment in Irish. According to the *Limerick Reporter*:

> The interpreter was for a moment puzzled [...] Scratching his head, however, and looking with wistful eye on the bench, he said: 'Thouraigh me PRESENTMENT, ma she dhe he la (laughter) – (give me my **present-ment, if you please). The presentment was accordingly passed.[107]

In 1854, there were questions about whether Roberts (also a court keeper) could even speak Irish,[108] one member of the grand jury suggesting 'not a word'. Another, however, suggested that Roberts was very old and should be paid. The mayor was unsympathetic, saying that if Roberts could not act as interpreter, then he should not be paid. It was suggested that an interpreter had not been needed for twenty years. After this discussion, 'The presentment for £2 10s, for an Irish interpreter was disallowed, and the office done away with.'[109] However, in 1854 a payment of £2 10*s.* seems to have been made.[110] In 1860, John Roberts applied to be reappointed but this was not allowed.[111] Despite this, he was paid £1 for interpreting in July 1868.[112] Census figures indicate that there were fewer speakers of Irish in the city of Limerick (County borough from 1901) than in the city of Cork (see table 21).

Table 21 Irish speakers in Limerick city (census data)

	1851	1861	1871	1901[113]	1911[114]
Irish only	313 or 0.58%	80 or 0.2%	13		
Irish and English	3,891 or 7.28%	2,404 or 5.6%	1,655		
Total	4,204 or 7.86%	2,484 or 5.8%	1,668 or 4.2%	4.5%	6.8%

105 *Limerick Reporter*, 16 July 1844.
106 Ibid., 5 Mar. 1850.
107 Ibid., 6 May 1851.
108 Ibid., 7 Feb. 1854.
109 *Limerick & Clare Examiner*, 8 Feb. 1854.
110 *Waterford News*, 25 May 1855.
111 Ní Mhunghaile, 'The legal system in Ireland and the Irish language', p. 333.
112 *Tipperary Vindicator*, 17 July 1868.
113 County borough.
114 County borough.

County Limerick

In a letter to a friend about his travels around Kilmallock and Limerick in September 1817, J.B. Trotter wrote that he took shelter in some cottages, 'where Irish was almost entirely their language'.[115] Significant numbers of Irish speakers in County Limerick were reported in 1851, but the numbers seem to have diminished rapidly in the succeeding decades (see table 22).

According to county court Judge Mr Purcell, during his ten years on the bench from 1875 to 1885 'he had never required the services of the interpreter'.[116] However, the last payment to an interpreter in County Limerick was in 1884 to Roger Green, who was paid the full rate of £5 at assizes plus £15 at quarter sessions.[117] It is unusual that there was no reduction in salary commensurate with the alleged reduction in work. At Limerick assizes in 1910 a witness acted as interpreter for an Irish-speaking witness in a case involving the discharge of firearms.[118]

Tipperary

In 1816, the language situation in the parishes of Carrick, Kilmurry and Kilsheelan was described by the Revd Standish Grady as follows:

> The English language is but little used in the hilly parts, but is universally understood by the inhabitants of the low-lands; Irish, however, is the language which even there is commonly used; and it is only when they perceive they are not understood in that tongue, that they speak the other, which they always do with evident reluctance.[119]

Table 22 Irish speakers in County Limerick (census data)

	1851	1861	1871	1881	1891	1901	1911
Irish only	6,800 or 3.26%	2,111 or 1.2%	1,389				
Irish and English	71,182 or 34.11%	45,556 or 26.4%	21,708	29,404			
Total	77,982 or 37.37%	47,667 or 27.6%	23,097 or 16.1%	29,404 or 20.8%	10.7%	11.4%	10.4%

115 J.G. Trotter, *Walks throughout Ireland in the years 1812, 1814 and 1817* (London, 1819), p. 302.
116 *Limerick Chronicle*, 5 Mar. 1885.
117 County of Limerick presentments and undischarged quaeres at summer assizes 1884, Limerick Local Studies.
118 *Limerick Leader*, 5 Dec. 1910.
119 Standish Grady in Mason, *A statistical account or parochial survey of Ireland*, ii, p. 113.

Table 23 Irish speakers in Tipperary (census data)

	1851	1861	1871	1881	1891	1901	1911
Irish only	728 or 0.22%	NR: 126 or 0.1% SR: 554 or 0.4%	675				
Irish and English	62,036 or 18.71%	NR: 3,684 or 3.4% SR: 33,547 or 24.1%	21,245				
Total	62,764 or 18.93%	NR: 3,810 or 3.5% SR: 34,101 or 24.5%	21,920 or 10.1%	11.9%	7.1%	6.1%	6.6%

Tipperary was divided into north and south ridings in 1838 and the statistics from the 1851 census reflect this division, with greater numbers of Irish speakers in the south riding, the part of the county nearest to Waterford, and far fewer Irish speakers in the northern part of the county (see table 23).

In 1849 at the spring assizes, Mr Gason questioned the need for an interpreter at assizes but Mr Sadlier responded that 'if the interpreter were removed, you would find very many unable to speak anything but Irish'.[120] In 1899, North Tipperary county council agreed to pay the interpreter Michael Nugent as he was 85 years of age and had no other source of income.[121] This is the last payment to an interpreter in Tipperary.

Waterford city

The censuses show that there was a small number, but a relatively large proportion, of Irish speakers in the city of Waterford (see table 24).

The situation regarding interpreter provision in the city of Waterford is unusual because interpreters were provided there in 1807, but not in 1841–3; we have already seen Thackeray's description of a court clerk or usher acting as interpreter at the assizes in 1842. It seems that the post was left vacant for some years. However

Table 24 Irish speakers in Waterford city (census data)

	1851	1861	1871	1901	1911[122]
Irish only	140 or 0.55%	253	121		
Irish and English	3,963 or 15.67%	3,074	1,857		
Total	4,103 or 16.22%	3,327 or 14.3%	1,978 or 8.5%	8%	7.7%

120 *Tipperary Vindicator*, 24 Mar. 1849.
121 *Nenagh News*, 5 Aug. 1899.
122 County borough.

there are newspaper records of a payment of £2 10*s*. to an unnamed interpreter in 1854.[123] At the 1860 assizes interpreter Denis Hackett applied for payment of £10 but members of the grand jury 'expressed an opinion that no such officer was warranted in the city'[124] and suggested that he be paid one shilling for each sessions.[125] However, another newspaper reported that a presentment for £2 had been passed.[126] In 1862, the interpreter (probably Patrick Hackett) wrote to the grand jury requesting an increase in salary because 'his present salary barely defrayed his expenses from Dungarvan, as he had to attend four times each year, besides the Assizes, at the quarter sessions'. An unnamed barrister had apparently stated that the interpreter 'was already receiving enough for his services', while Mr Power 'said he never knew of such a thing as an Irish interpreter in the city court. They might as well have a Greek interpreter.'[127] The last record located is for a payment of £1 to an interpreter in March 1865.[128] However, in 1875 the *Munster Express* reported that the Irish interpreter could not be found for an Irish speaker at the city court and 'his Lordship said he wished he had the fiating of the interpreter's presentment', which would suggest that there was still a salaried interpreter at that late stage.[129]

County Waterford

Revd John Devereux reported of the parish of Stradbally in 1819 that 'the language mostly used is the Irish'.[130] The censuses show high percentages of Irish speakers throughout the nineteenth century (see table 25).

Table 25 Irish speakers in County Waterford (census data)

	1851	1861	1871	1881	1891	1901	1911
Irish only	21,845 or 15.75%	10,214	3,700				
Irish and English	64,978 or 46.84%	47,568	41,659	49,115	37,479	29,460	21,692
Total	86,823 or 62.59%	57,782 or 52.1%	45,359 or 45.4%	49,115 or 54.4%	37,479 or 38.1%	29,460 or 48.8%	21,692 or 38.4%

123 *Waterford News*, 21 July 1854.
124 *Waterford Mail*, 16 July 1860.
125 *Waterford Chronicle*, 21 July 1860.
126 *Waterford News*, 20 July 1860.
127 *Waterford Mail*, 16 July 1862.
128 *Waterford News*, 3 Mar. 1865.
129 *Munster Express*, 31 July 1875.
130 John Devereux in Mason, *A statistical account or parochial survey of Ireland*, iii, p. 383.

While there was extensive and extended interpreter provision in County Waterford, the remuneration at quarter sessions never exceeded £5 per half-year even though there was provision by law for a payment of £15. In July 1861 in the county court, the services of the interpreter 'were repeatedly called in to requisition'.[131] By 1888 the amount paid at both assizes and quarter sessions had been reduced to £3 per half-year. In 1898 the County Waterford grand jury decided against making a permanent appointment at assizes, preferring to ask the Dungarvan quarter sessions interpreter to attend 'if an occasion should arise'.[132] Salaried interpreters continued to be employed until 1921.[133]

LEINSTER

In 1806, Dr Whitley Stokes wrote that:

> To begin then with the province of Leinster: in Louth, Meath and Westmeath, Irish is mostly spoken; in Dublin, Kildare and Wicklow, scarcely any; in the King's and Queen's counties, very few speak Irish; in the south-west part of Carlow, a considerable portion speak Irish; in Kilkenny, the language prevails greatly; in Wexford, it is very little used in the south-east part of the county, but is pretty general in the north-west.[134]

In 1815 Atkinson noted the presence of Irish speakers during his travels in Waterford and Kilkenny:

> From Ballyhale, one of the villages on the public road between Kilkenny and Waterford, the traveller proceeds over a chain of lofty ground, called the Welch mountains – several of the inhabitants of this wild tract of country, occupy much ground in the dairy department, and are famous also for extensive breeding of pigs, a description of stock for which they have a very good market at Waterford. It is a little singular, however, that some of these extensive pig breeders and dairy men, cannot speak a single sentence of plain English.
>
> This class of the population of the county, or rather of the southern district, (by which we principally mean, the country lying between Waterford and Kilkenny) appear, in a considerable proportion, in a state of rude nature, similar to those of the same class in most parts of Connaught – A person speaking to them in the English language, will often find it difficult to make

131 *Tipperary Vindicator*, 9 July 1861.
132 *Freeman's Journal*, 19 July 1898.
133 Waterford County Archives, Dungarvan.
134 Stokes, *Observations on the necessity of publishing the Scriptures in the Irish language*, p. 2.

Table 26 Irish speakers in Leinster (1851 census)

County	Number	Percentage	Interpreter provision
Carlow	243	0.36%	Only in 1812 and 1814
City of Dublin	3,426	1.33%	No record of interpreters
County of Dublin	1,281	0.87%	No record of interpreters
Kildare	514	0.54%	No record of interpreters
City of Kilkenny	590	2.96%	On one occasion, in 1824
Kilkenny	20,830	15.01%	Last payment in 1854
King's (Offaly)	403	0.36%	No record of interpreters
Longford	1,465	1.78%	One record in 1777
Louth	18,762	20.66%	In 1810 and 1820 but not from 1822 onwards
Town of Drogheda	599	3.57%	No record of interpreters
Meath	8,963	6.37%	Last payment in 1826
Queen's (Laois)	244	0.22%	No payments from 1805 onwards
Westmeath	921	0.83%	Last payment in 1827
Wexford	800	0.44%	One record for 1807
Wicklow	135	0.14%	One record for 1807
Total	59,176		

himself understood; my patience in this respect, when enquiring about the roads or other ordinary objects of the country, was often put to a severe trial.[135]

The numbers of Irish speakers in Leinster, with the exceptions of Kilkenny and Louth, were very low (see table 26). Interpreter provision in Louth ended surprisingly early, possibly around 1820, while in County Kilkenny it continued until 1854. There were salaried court interpreters in Meath and Westmeath until 1826 and 1827 respectively, which casts doubt on the very low numbers of Irish speakers reported in the 1851 census for Westmeath.

Carlow

In Carlow there were no payments to interpreters in surviving books of presentments for 1800, 1802, 1805, 1807 or 1809, but there were payments in 1812[136] and

135 A.A. Atkinson, *The Irish tourist* (Dublin, 1815), pp 471–2.
136 County of Carlow spring assizes, 24 March 1812, NLI.

Table 27 Irish speakers in Carlow (census data)

	1851	1861	1871	1901
Irish only	0	0	3	
Irish and English	243 or 0.36%	124 or 0.2%	127	
Total	243 or 0.36%	124 or 0.2%	130 or 0.3%	>1%

1814;[137] the schedule for spring assizes 1812 provides '£5 for Sub-Sheriff for providing stationary [*sic*] and £11 7s 6d, also to the Sub-Sheriff, for two interpretors [*sic*] at this Assizes'. Similarly, in 1814, Dudley Smith, late sub-sheriff, was paid the same amount, £11 *7s. 6d.*, for two interpreters.

City of Dublin

The county and city of Dublin had a different court system from the rest of the country. There were no assizes there, and criminal cases were heard at the court of king's or queen's bench, which was 'the most senior of the criminal courts in Ireland',[138] but cases were usually heard at the Dublin commission in Green Street.[139] In the city of Dublin itself, there was a quarter sessions presided over by the city justices alongside the lord mayor and the city recorder. A tholsel or civil court in the city was held four times a year and presided over by the Recorder.[140] The census supports the view that there were very few Irish speakers in Dublin city (see table 28).

A search of the county of the city of Dublin grand jury presentments for 1849–50, 1861–70 and 1877 yielded no results for interpreters. One report from 1823 was found where a Kerry woman called Martha Mansergh was charged at

Table 28 Irish speakers in Dublin city (census data)

	1851	1861	1871	1901	1911[141]
Irish only	27 or 0.01%	1	3		
Irish and English	3,399 or 1.32%	2,780 or 1.1%	1,085		
Total	3,426 or 1.33%	2,781 or 1.1%	1,088 or 0.4%	3.3%	3.9%

137 *Report from the select committee on grand jury presentments of Ireland, 1814–15*, HC 1815 (283) vi, 1661.

138 Garnham, *The courts, crime and the criminal law*, p. 81.

139 Vaughan, *Murder trials in Ireland*, pp 4–5.

140 Ibid.

141 Dublin city borough.

the recorder's court with stealing children's clothes and 'the celebrated Lewy O'Halloran' was the interpreter.[142]

County Dublin

In 1801 Joseph Archer reported of Dublin that:

> The English language is the general one spoken in this county; very few are in the habit of speaking Irish, nor do many understand it, except those that have removed here from remoter counties.[143]

Quarter sessions were held at Kilmainham for the county of Dublin and could try 'all manner of felonies', but only if committed outside the limits of the city of Dublin.[144] Earlier provisions for salaried court interpreters did not apply to Dublin; to remedy this, the County Dublin Grand Jury Act 1844 set the rate for interpreters at quarter sessions in the county:

> It shall be lawful for the grand jury of the said county to present, without any previous application at sessions, to be levied off such county at large, [...] and any sum not exceeding ten pounds, at each presenting term, for an interpreter, if such payment shall be recommended by the court.

The introduction of this law would suggest that there was a need for an Irish interpreter. However, despite the existence of this law, and the influx of Famine victims in the late 1840s,[145] no records of payments to interpreters were found in the county of Dublin grand jury abstracts of presentment from 1845 to 1898.[146] The census figures support the view that there were extremely few Irish speakers in County Dublin (see table 29).

Table 29 Irish speakers in County Dublin (census data)

	1851	1861	1871	1901	1911
Irish only	5	2	5		
Irish and English	1,276 or 0.87%	1,062 or 0.7%	553		
Total	1,281 or 0.87%	1,064 or 0.7%	558 or 0.4%	2.2%	3.4%

142 *Connaught Journal*, 2 Oct. 1823.
143 Archer, *Statistical survey of the county of Dublin* (Dublin, 1801), p. 221.
144 Garnham, *The courts, crime and the criminal law*, p. 82.
145 C. Ó Gráda, *Black '47 and beyond* (Princeton, 1999), p. 94.
146 Fingal County Council Archives, Swords.

Table 30 Irish speakers in Kildare (census data)

	1851	1861	1871
Irish only	1	0	0
Irish and English	513 or 0.54%	554 or 0.6%	260
Total	514 or 0.54%	554 or 0.6%	260 or 0.3%

Kildare

In 1807 Rawson reported of Kildare that 'From its vicinity to the capital, the English language is very general and the Irish seldom used.'[147] In 1837 Lewis commented that 'The English language is everywhere spoken.'[148] These findings are confirmed by the very low numbers of Irish speakers in the county – less than 1 per cent in 1851 (see table 30) and the apparent total absence of interpreters – searches of grand jury books of presentments for County Kildare from 1791 to 1811 yielded no results. One instance, in 1853, was found of an interpreter being required at County Kildare quarter sessions. The complainant in a case of robbery was staying in a lodging house after working at harvesting in England and did not understand English 'sufficiently well to be examined'.[149]

Kilkenny city

In the city of Kilkenny, one payment, of £2 10*s*., to John Anderson esq. who also worked as an interpreter for the county of Kilkenny, was located for 1824, but there are no payments for 1803–23 or for 1837–40. The census figures for Irish speakers here are much lower than in other cities such as Cork, Limerick and Waterford (see table 31).

Table 31 Irish speakers in Kilkenny city (census data)

	1851	1861	1871
Irish only	5 or 0.03%	4	0
Irish and English	585 or 2.93%	483 or 3.5%	82
Total	590 or 2.96%	487 or 3.5%	82 or 0.6%

147 T.J. Rawson, *Statistical survey of the county of Kildare* (Dublin, 1807), p. 95.
148 S. Lewis, *A topographical directory of Ireland* (London, 1837), i, p. 84.
149 *Leinster Express*, 29 Oct. 1853.

County of Kilkenny

In 1802 William Tighe in his *Statistical observations* found that Irish was widely spoken in south Kilkenny:

> English being taught at all the schools, it is understood by most of the younger part of the lower classes; but there are many persons, and particularly women, in the hilly districts, who cannot speak a word of English; in the hills of Idagh, Irish is said to be tolerably well spoken. The common people seldom speak any other language among themselves; but Irish is more prevalent about Kilkenny and near Munster, than near the county of Carlow. The priests often preach alternatively in Irish and English; but always in Irish, if they are desirous to be well understood.[150]

In 1816 Revd William Latta reported that in the parish of Kilmacahill, 'Their language is for the most part English, which they all speak fluently; this was not the case some years ago. The Irish language is understood by all, and occasionally used; it is however on the decline'.[151] In 1819 Revd James A. Ker wrote of the parish of Listerling that 'The languages used are English and Irish; many of the people, particularly those advanced in years, know no other language than the latter'[152] and Revd Robert Shaw in the same volume wrote of Tullaroan that:

> Both the English and Irish languages are spoken in the parish – the latter is greatly on the decrease, and must continue to decrease rapidly both here, and in every part of the nation, from two principal causes: first the hedge schools, where English alone is taught, and secondly the necessity imposed upon the country people of speaking English in all their trafficking; they are fond of bargaining both in buying and selling, and as very few of the corn and pig dealers and town shop-keepers can speak Irish, they feel the want of English a serious inconvenience, and they cannot bear to traffic through an interpreter. Our paper circulation likewise makes it necessary for them to read English, especially as they have suffered so severely by the failure of country banks; in consequence of which, a country fellow will often walk about a fair, with notes in his hand, asking every person the amount and the bank, &c. and is scarcely satisfied with the answers. Through this the English language rapidly advances, for so anxious are the people to speak it in the country, that the mountain farmers who cannot speak English, and who send their children to hedge schools, will scarcely allow them to speak Irish when at home.[153]

150 W. Tighe, *Statistical observations relative to the county of Kilkenny* (Dublin, 1802), p. 515.
151 William Latta in Mason, *A statistical account or parochial survey of Ireland*, ii, p. 339.
152 James A. Ker in ibid., iii, p. 244.
153 Robert Shaw in ibid., iii, pp 624–5.

Table 32 Irish speakers in County Kilkenny (census data)

	1851	1861	1871	1881	1891	1901	1911
Irish only	99 or 0.07%	194 or 0.2%	316				
Irish and English	20,731 or 14.94%	13,522 or 12.2%	6,342				
Total	20,830 or 15.01%	13,716 or 12.4%	6,658 or 6.9%	10.1%	4.5%	4.5%	4.4%

By 1837 Lewis found that in Kilkenny 'the English language is very generally spoken'.[154] However, the census figures indicate that bilingualism was not unusual (see table 32).

John Anderson esq. worked as an interpreter in County Kilkenny from at least 1817 to 1839 when he was replaced by Richard Hickey at assizes and John Ryan at sessions. In 1840 at the county assizes, Captain Bryan objected to the interpreter at quarter sessions being paid £5 on the grounds that he was paid 'a considerable sum', in reality £5, as crier. Bryan opined that criers and interpreters were the assistant barrister's 'servants'. Mr Flood disagreed, suggesting that the interpreter's duties were 'sometimes very onerous'. However, it was agreed to reduce the interpreter's salary to £2.[155] The salaries were capped at £3 for assizes and £2 for sessions until the last payment in 1854. A decade later, Constable Murphy, Freshford, acted as interpreter at quarter sessions for a prosecutor from Galway.[156]

King's County (Offaly)

In 1801 Charles Coote, in his *Statistical survey*, provided information on the use of English and Irish in the different baronies. In Clonlisk, he found that 'The English language is spoken by all sorts; but the peasants, when conversing together, speak in their native tongue only.'[157] In Balliboy, 'They all speak the English and Irish languages with equal fluency.' In the barony of Eglish, or Fircal, 'The poor speak the English and Irish tongues with equal fluency.'[158] In the barony of Coolestown, 'English is almost entirely spoken.'[159] In the barony of Geshill, 'The English language almost entirely spoken, and few can converse in Irish.'[160] In the barony of Philipstown, 'English language generally spoken,

154 Lewis, *A topographical directory of Ireland*, ii, p. 108.
155 *Kilkenny Journal*, 14 Mar. 1840.
156 *Kilkenny Journal & Leinster Commercial and Literary Advertiser*, 19 Oct. 1864.
157 C. Coote, *Statistical survey of King's County* (Dublin, 1801), p. 64.
158 Ibid., p. 98.
159 Ibid., p. 141.
160 Ibid.

Table 33 Irish speakers in King's County (census data)

	1851	1861	1871	1901
Irish only	0	0	1	
Irish and English	403 or 0.36%	396 or 0.4%	245	
Total	403 or 0.36%	396 or 0.4%	246 or 0.3%	<1%

and the Irish tongue evidently decreasing.'[161] In the barony of Kilcoursey, 'The English and Irish tongues are spoken here, but the latter declining as manufacture gains ground.'[162] In 1816, Revd Patrick Fitzgerald wrote of the parishioners of Clonmacnois that 'Their general language is English, though they sometimes speak Irish to one another.'[163] Drawing on Garret FitzGerald's work, Nicholas Willams finds that in Garrycastle 10–19 per cent of the population born in 1771–81 was made up of Irish speakers, with a lower proportion of 9–12 per cent born in 1821–31.[164] The information compiled by these sources would imply that there were speakers of Irish in King's County, possibly more than are recorded in the censuses (see table 33). However, no records of payments to interpreters were found for King's County.

Longford

In 1819 Revd James Farrell found that in the parish of Rathcline, 'The English language is universally spoken and the Irish rather on the decline; at least it is not so much in use as the English.'[165] Meanwhile, in the parish of Shruel, 'English is universally spoken here, although the great body of the people understand Irish, and many of them prefer using it.'[166] By 1837, Lewis reported that 'The Irish language is scarcely ever heard, except in the mountainous districts among the old people; adults and children everywhere speak English.'[167] These findings are confirmed by the very low figures for Irish speakers in the censuses from 1851 onwards (see table 34).

Longford is a bit of a mystery when it comes to interpreter provision. At Longford County Archives, there is a manuscript book of presentments for

161 Ibid., p. 152.
162 Ibid., p. 166.
163 Patrick Fitzgerald in Mason, *A statistical account or parochial survey of Ireland*, p. 146.
164 N. Williams, 'The Irish language in County Offaly' in William Nolan and Timothy P. O'Neill (eds), *Offaly: history and society* (Dublin, 1998), p. 543.
165 James Farrell in Mason, *A statistical account or parochial survey of Ireland*, p. 291.
166 Ibid., p. 346.
167 Lewis, *A topographical directory of Ireland*, ii, p. 310.

Table 34 Irish speakers in Longford (census data)

	1851	1861	1871	1901
Irish only	3	34	0	
Irish and English	1,462 or 1.78%	774	246	
Total	1,465 or 1.78%	777 or 1.1%	246 or 0.4%	<1%

1759–78 which contains just one payment to an interpreter, Wm Bignall, in 1777. Later printed books of presentments from 1817 to 1845 do not include payments to interpreters.

Louth

According to Dr D.A. Beaufort's notes from 1808 on the level of English at baronial level in County Louth, in Baronstown, 'English increasing of late but Irish still used among themselves.' In Carlingford 'English generally spoken and increasing.' In Dundalk, 'the English language established – Habits of industry and English much increasing'. In Castlebellingham, 'English language is commonly spoken.' In Louth – Fortescue, 'English in general well spoken by men, not so by women.' In Charlestown, English was 'Very tolerably established'. In Ardee, 'Lower orders [...] little disposed to habits of industry or to acquire English language.' In Kildemock, 'English becoming very general' and in Tallanstown 'Increasing'. In Port (including Rathdrumming), 'English language well established and increasing'. In Terfeckin, there were differing opinions: 'All speak English' (D.A. Beaufort) and 'Habits of industry are well established, the English but slowly' (P. Brabazon). In Clonmore, 'English language general, daily increasing', and in Drumiskin 'English general'.[168] In 1816, Revd Gervais Tinley found that most of the poorer classes 'can speak English tolerably well; but their common language with each other is Irish'.[169] Elias Thackeray wrote in the statistical survey of Ballymascanlon parish in 1816 that 'it is gratifying to a person attached to British policy, to have it in his power to say, that the English language is gaining ground fast; and that it is very generally spoken and taught'.[170]

Given the relatively high numbers of Irish speakers in the 1851 census (see table 35), it is very surprising that there was not more extensive interpreter provision

168 D.A. Beaufort and C.C. Ellison, 'Materials for the Dublin Society Agricultural Survey of County Louth', *Journal of the County Louth Archaeological and Historical Society*, 18:2 (1974), pp 121–31.

169 Gervais Tinley in Mason, *A statistical account or parochial survey*, ii, p. 210.

170 Quoted in T. Dooley, *The murders at Wildgoose Lodge: agrarian crime and punishment in pre-Famine Ireland* (Dublin, 2007), p. 59.

Table 35 Irish speakers in Louth (census data)

	1851	1861	1871	1901	1911
Irish only	50 or 0.06%	0	3		
Irish and English	18,712 or 20.60%	9,007 or 11.9%	4,076		
Total	18,762 or 20.66%	9,007 or 11.9%	4,079 or 5.8%	4.9%	5.9%

in Louth. An exceptionally early manuscript of presentments has survived for County Louth for the years 1713–32[171] and although it contains payments to other court officials, it does not contain any interpreter payments. While Louth was not included in the 1807 figures, one record was located for 1810 – Charles Connor, Cryer, for acting as interpreter £2 5*s.* 6*d.* – and in 1820 there was a payment of £5 to the clerk of the peace for providing an interpreter. However, there were no payments to interpreters in 1815, or 1823–40.[172]

Newspaper reports suggest that, in the absence of a salaried interpreter, local solutions were found. For example, in 1829, despite having spoken to a police sergeant in English, Owen Hamill was allocated an interpreter at Louth assizes. Hamill alleged he had been assaulted and robbed of £9. He 'disavowed any knowledge of the English language' and 'lent a deaf ear' to 'many sly interrogatories … directed to him by the Bar'.[173] Similarly, in 1837 at Dundalk assizes, two Irish-speaking witnesses 'were, of course, examined through the medium of a sworn interpreter'.[174] Dundalk petty sessions was more problematic. In 1880, the *Dundalk Democrat* reported on an assault case between brothers where Mrs Mathews, the litigants' mother, spoke Irish and her daughter proved a somewhat problematic interpreter:

> The mother of the litigants – an ancient dame, apparently more than an octogenarian – was put forward as a witness for the defence, but not being able to express herself in the English tongue, her daughter – a Mrs Conlon – acted as interpreter. While transferring the oath in Gaelic to the Dowager Mathews, the interpreter, who, it seemed, calculated that the language was common to themselves only in court, took advantage of the situation to caution her mother, that while she was to tell the whole truth, &c, she should also 'hold her tongue'. This significant interlarding of the adjuration was quickly noticed by Mr Supple, S.I. [Sub-Inspector], who, to the interpreter's surprise, detected the surreptitious warning (he

171 MS 11,949, NLI.
172 Louth County Archives, Dundalk.
173 *Drogheda Journal*, 5 Aug. 1829.
174 *Drogheda Argus & Leinster Journal*, 11 Mar. 1837.

> having some knowledge of the Irish language) and gave it out in court. – The circumstances created much merriment. – However, the examination of the old woman was proceeded with, and whether the verbosity of the answers as given by the interpreter in comparison with their conciseness when leaving the old woman in the vernacular was to be attributed to the comprehensiveness of the Gaelic language or to a pretty liberal sandwiching they received *en route* to their worships, the reporter is unable to say.[175]

Later that year Mrs Mathews returned to court for another case to do with the larceny of a trap and mare and an attempt was made to cross-examine her in English:

> Mr Moynagh – Do you and defendant live in the same house? *Tha* (great laughter).
> Chairman – That means 'Yes.'
> Mr Moynagh – Oh, then, your worship will translate for me.

However, the chairman did not 'display any more extensive acquaintance with the vernacular than the interpretation of the word "Tha" so the court was at a loss for an interpreter'. The court rejected Mrs Mathews' daughter as interpreter this time, on the grounds that she had previously 'put her own construction on the answers given by her mother'. The head constable was asked if any police officers could be of help, but he did not think so. The chairman suggested an Irish speaker could be asked to attend court but in the end the court decided not to proceed with questioning Mrs Mathews.[176]

Town of Drogheda

The numbers of Irish speakers in the town of Drogheda were very low. No grand jury records were located for the town.

Table 36 Irish speakers in town of Drogheda (census data)

	1851	1861	1871
Irish only	1 or 0.01%	0	0
Irish and English	598 or 3.56%	344 or 2.3%	30 or 0.2%
Total	599 or 3.57%	344 or 2.3%	30 or 0.2%

175 *Dundalk Democrat*, 14 Feb. 1880.
176 Ibid., 4 Sept. 1880.

Meath

According to Revd John Brady, diocesan historian, in 1797 a Frenchman found it difficult to find an English-speaking person in Slane. In 1802, Robert Thompson described a society that was becoming more bilingual:

> The English language is pretty generally in use throughout the county, and we very seldom meet with any person, who is not capable of speaking it with some degree of fluency; yet, when together, the peasants all converse, and if they have a story to tell, or a complaint to make, they still wish it to be heard in Irish; understanding the idioms of that language better than they possibly can those of the English, their story can be conveyed more expressively, and, of course, work more upon the feelings of their auditors; indeed there is no language more copiously supplied with pathetic expressions, or more calculated to touch the feelings, than that of the Irish; so much so, that it has become a proverbial expression, 'Plead for your life in Irish.'[177]

John Carr, who travelled around Ireland in 1805, provided a slightly different picture: 'In the county of Meath, which borders upon the metropolis, it has been said that a justice of the peace must understand Irish, or keep an interpreter.'[178] According to Revd Brabazon Disney, by 1819 in the union of Syddon, 'The language used by the people in addressing each other is Irish, but there are very few who do not speak English well',[179] and by 1837, according to Lewis, 'The English language is spoken throughout every part of the county.'[180] The last payment to an interpreter in Meath was made in 1826.[181]

Queen's County (Laois)

Charles Coote reported in 1801 that:

> The English language is most generally spoken, except towards the mountains; but, indeed, throughout, they can all converse in both tongues, with equal fluency, but 'till proper schools are established, they must remain in the same barbarous ignorance, that still prevails.[182]

177 *Meath Chronicle,* 30 Mar. 1946. R. Thompson, *Statistical survey of the county of Meath* (Dublin, 1802), p. 95.
178 J. Carr, *The stranger in Ireland* (Philadelphia, 1805), p. 197.
179 Brabazon Disney in Mason, *A statistical account or parochial survey*, p. 391.
180 Lewis, *A topographical directory of Ireland*, i, p. 364.
181 J. Brady, 'Irish interpreters at Meath assizes', *Ríocht na Midhe*, 2 (1959), pp 62–4.
182 C. Coote, *General view of the agriculture and manufacture of the Queen's County* (Dublin, 1801), p. 88.

Table 37 Irish speakers in Meath (census data)

	1851	1861	1871	1901	1911
Irish only	7 or 0.01%	2	37		
Irish and English	8,956 or 6.36%	5,414 or 4.9%	2,165		
Total	8,963 or 6.7%	5,416 or 4.9%	2,202 or 2.3%	2%	3.8%

In the parish of Aghaboe in 1814, according to Revd Edward Ledwith, the parishioners 'all speak English, few of them Irish; many do not understand a word of the latter'.[183] In 1819, in the union of Rosenallis or Oregan, the Revd John Baldwin reported that 'They all speak English, and the use of the Irish language has much declined; even among the peasants it is not so much used now as the English.'[184] Surviving books of presentments for Queen's County from 1805 to 1823 do not include any payments to interpreters.

Westmeath

According to Revd Fred. Aug. Potter, in the parish of Rathconrath in 1801, 'The language in general used is the English; but the Irish is also spoken, particularly in their intercourse among themselves.'[185] By 1837, Lewis reported that 'The English language is everywhere spoken, except by some of the old people, and that only in ordinary conversation among themselves.'[186]

The census figures for Westmeath indicate that there were very few Irish speakers in Westmeath (see table 39). However, this information is contradicted by payments to the high sheriff and later the sub-sheriff for providing interpreters in 1807, 1814, 1815, 1816, 1826 and 1827 (although not in 1804, 1805, 1810, 1812,

Table 38 Irish speakers in Queen's County (census data)

	1851	1861	1871	1901
Irish only	0	0	0	
Irish and English	244 or 0.22%	103 or 0.1%	89	
Total	244 or 0.22%	103 or 0.1%	89 or 0.1%	<1%

183 Edward Ledwith in Mason, *A statistical account or parochial survey*, p. 48.
184 John Baldwin in Mason, *A statistical account or parochial survey*, p. 323.
185 F.A. Potter in ibid., iii, p. 303.
186 Lewis, *A topographical directory of Ireland* (2nd ed.), p. 698.

Table 39 Irish speakers in Westmeath (census data)

	1851	1861	1871	1911
Irish only	1	0	0	
Irish and English	920 or 0.83%	483 or 0.5%	276	
Total	921 or 0.83%	483 or 0.5%	276 or 0.1%	3.5%

1813),[187] which would indicate that the Irish language was still alive in the first quarter of the nineteenth century.

Wexford

While Wakefield noted that 'the language every where spoken is the English',[188] J.B. Trotter expressed surprise at the amount of Irish he heard during his travels in Wexford. He walked from New Ross to Dunbroady in June 1812 and observed that 'The Irish language is almost universally spoken' and of Newtown Barry he wrote that:

> In the morning a fair enlivened the town (Newtown Barry); woollens, crockery-ware, and cattle, were the chief objects of sale. The Irish language is spoken almost generally in the county of Wexford; we heard it every where in the fair. Is it not surprising, that in the very part where the English first settled, this language should to this hour remain and flourish?[189]

However, the census figures indicate that the Irish language had died out in Wexford by 1851 (see table 40). Very few books of presentments for Wexford have

Table 40 Irish speakers in Wexford (census data)

	1851	1861	1871
Irish only	1	1	1
Irish and English	799 or 0.44%	240 or 0.2%	209
Total	800 or 0.44%	241 or 0.2%	210 or 0.2%

187 *Accounts presented to the house of commons of the presentments passed by the grand juries of Ireland* (1808); County of Westmeath, abstract of presentments, 1805, 1810, 1812, 1813, 1814, 1815, 1816, RIA; County of Westmeath, abstract of presentments granted at assizes, 1826, 1827, 1828, NLI.
188 Wakefield, *An account of Ireland statistical and political*, ii, p. 582.
189 Trotter, *Walks through Ireland*, p. 39.

survived and a mere two records of payments to an interpreter in Wexford were found, both relating to 1807.[190]

Wicklow

In June 1790 Coquebert de Montbret visited Glenmalure where everybody could speak English but some older people also knew Irish.[191] Robert Fraser and Samuel Lewis (1801) agreed that Irish was not spoken at all in Wicklow in the early nineteenth century. According to Fraser:

> It is very remarkable, that although the Irish language is common in all the counties around, in the county of Wicklow, the Irish language is unknown. Nor did I find any of the natives of this county, even in the most remote vales in the midst of the mountains, accustomed to speak the Irish language.[192]

Samuel Lewis wrote in 1837 that:

> with regard to their language, it is remarkable that while the Irish is often spoken in the contiguous counties, it is never heard here, and scarcely a peasant even of the wildest districts understands it.[193]

These observations are supported by the extremely low census figures for speakers of Irish (see table 41). Despite this evidence, payments were made to an interpreter in spring and summer 1807. There was no payment in spring 1818, the earliest subsequent surviving record.[194] The 1807 payments would suggest that there was a need for a court interpreter.

Table 41 Irish speakers in Wicklow (census data)

	1851	1861	1871
Irish only	0	0	5
Irish and English	135 or 0.14%	182 or 0.2%	89
Total	135 or 0.14%	182 or 0.2%	94 or 0.1%

190 *Accounts presented at the house of commons of the presentment passed by the grand juries of Ireland* (1808).
191 S. Kennedy, 'Coquebert de Montbret in search of the hidden Ireland', *Journal of the Royal Society of Antiquaries of Ireland*, 82:1 (1952), pp 62–7.
192 R. Fraser, *General view of the agriculture and mineralogy, present state and circumstances, of the county Wicklow* (Dublin, 1801), p. 274.
193 Lewis, *A topographical directory of Ireland*, ii, p. 721.
194 County of Wicklow abstract of presentments, spring assizes 1818, Wicklow County Archives.

CONNAUGHT

In 1806 Dr Whitley Stokes wrote that 'The native language is more prevalent in Connaught than in the rest of Ireland. In this province the gentlemen often find it convenient to acquire the language, in order to deal with the peasantry without an interpreter.'[195] An 'enlightened and experienced Judge' commented about the situation in Connaught that:

> I can have no hesitation in saying, that in my own judgment, according to the experience I have on this circuit, the Irish language is the vulgar tongue in Connaught. I feel confident that I am not in error when I state, that in the majority of cases in which many witnesses were examined, we were obliged to have recourse to an interpreter.[196]

There were high numbers of Irish speakers in Connaught, in Galway county and town and in Mayo in particular. Sligo came next, followed by Roscommon and finally Leitrim. Interpreter provision ended in Roscommon twenty-three years before it ended in Leitrim, which is surprising given that there were many more Irish speakers in the former than the latter. School attendance was lower in Connaught than in other provinces; according to the 1851 census only 20 per cent of children aged between 5 and 15 attended school while in 1861 the figure had increased only slightly to 23 per cent.

Table 42 Irish speakers in Connaught (1851 census)

County	Number	Percentage	Interpreter provision
Town of Galway	14,595	61.35%	Until 1898 when town was subsumed into county
County Galway	207,649	69.7%	Discontinued in Oughterard and Kinvara in 1930
Leitrim	15,003	13.41%	Last payment in 1888
Mayo	180,078	65.6%	Until at least 1922
Roscommon	46,296	26.69%	Last payment in 1865
Sligo	49,228	38.3%	Mention of John Downes, court interpreter, in 1919[197]
Total	512,849		

195 Stokes, *Observations*, p. 2.
196 'On the utility of the Irish language to the ministry of the established church', *Christian Examiner and Church of Ireland Magazine*, 2 (1826), p. 295.
197 *Sligo Champion*, 12 Apr. 1919.

Town of Galway

In a letter dated 17 September 1818, J.B. Trotter captures the atmosphere in the town of Galway:

> Galway appeared, in this walk, to great advantage, and crowned the scene. We heard no language but Irish; and as our eyes met the bright red colours of the women's and children's dress (a crimson or coquelicot), we had, for a moment, the idea of a foreign city.[198]

In 1824 Hely Dutton commented that: 'It is somewhat curious that near Galway, and particularly in the town (at the Claddagh), many do not speak English, but a harsh Irish, not very well understood in general.'[199] An 'enlightened and experienced Judge' commented in 1826 about the situation in the town of Galway that:

> it is well known that in the very capital of this country, which is a maritime town, Irish is almost exclusively the language of the people. One of your Sub-Committee, who has been lately there, has ascertained, that it is in general use even by the tradesmen behind the counters of the best of the shops; and that many of the gentry employ it colloquially, and of necessity.[200]

These comments are confirmed by the figures for Irish speakers in the censuses (see table 43).

Interpreters were a regular feature at the assizes and sessions in the town of Galway. However, a mere two books of presentments for the town of Galway have survived.[201] In 1828, John Murphy was paid £4 12*s.* 3½*d.* for interpreting. The

Table 43 Irish speakers in town of Galway (census data)

	1851	1861	1871
Irish only	3,511 or 14.75%	891 or 5.2%	2,434
Irish and English	11,084 or 46.6%	7,581 or 44.7%%	6,929
Total	14,595 or 61.35%	8,472 or 49.9%	9,363 or 47.2%

198 Trotter, *Walks through Ireland*, p. 409.
199 Hely Dutton, *Statistical survey of the county of Galway*, p. 464.
200 'On the utility of the Irish language to the ministry of the established church', *Christian Examiner and Church of Ireland Magazine*, 2 (1826), p. 295.
201 County of the town of Galway presentment books summer assizes 1828 and 1829, County Library Headquarters, Galway.

following year, the same amount was paid to W. Hanburry, who was also appointed high constable that year. In 1863 the chief secretary's office registered papers include the entry 'Write to O'Farrell (C. Sol) to enquire whether an interpreter is absolutely necessary at Galway Assizes.'[202] The motivation for the letter may have been the fact that there were no longer salaried interpreters in other towns and cities. Unfortunately, the file has been lost; it would be very interesting to read the correspondence. The record is an indicator of attitudes in Dublin Castle towards the Irish language.

Interpreter provision in the town of Galway continued until 1900 when under the Local Government Act 1898 the town was subsumed into the county and the post abolished. In 1902, Timothy Healy asked a question about this change in the house of commons. He pointed out that the previous salary of £25 a year for interpreting in the town of Galway was no longer being paid, which meant that the work was still being carried out, but without any payment. The reply from Mr Wyndham was to the effect that the interpreter, Anthony O'Donnell, was not an existing officer under the act because he was appointed in March 1901 and therefore was not entitled to any payment. This decision was discussed in the *New Irish Jurist* which commented:

> Of course this strict view of the law is right, and the gentleman is not entitled to any compensation as an 'existing' officer; but if it is a fact, as it appears to be, that he is doing the work in the Galway county court for which former interpreters got £25 yearly more than he is receiving, and if that result has been brought about by reason of the abolition of Galway as a county of a city by the Local Government Act, 1898, it would appear equitable and proper that his claim should be recognized by the Executive to some extent. The Local Government Board and other administrative bodies are very keen in watching the interests of officials in the employment and pay of the county and district councils. We hope that the executive authorities in the present instance will not show the local councils a bad example.[203]

This advice seems to have been ignored and the county council wrote to the chief secretary's office in 1908 requesting that the salary be reinstated.[204] Questions were raised again in the house of commons about the issue in 1911 to no avail.[205] Anthony O'Donnell applied to Galway county council for a war bonus in 1920, and the Council agreed to pay him £25.

202 CSO/RP/5191/63, NAI.

203 'Local government notes', *New Irish Jurist and Local Government Review*, 2:4 (1902), p. 345.

204 Galway county council minutes of quarterly meeting of the proposal committee, 4 Aug. 1908, www.galway.ie/digitalarchives.

205 HC Debates, 31 July 1911, vol. 20, c. 160W.

County Galway

Hely Dutton reported in 1824 that 'The use of the English language is increasing rapidly all through the county, but in no part more than in Cunnamara, and generally with a good accent', and went on to observe that:

> Many understand English, who, from an apprehension they do not speak correctly, deny their knowledge of it. A witness at an assizes at Galway was proceeding to swear, *in good English,* that he could not speak a word of it, he meant that he did not speak English sufficiently well to give his testimony in that language. English is always spoken in the country schools, as the parents are anxious their children should speak it. I may therefore safely assert that the English language is gaining ground fast. In the next generation there will not probably be a gentleman that will be able to speak Irish.[206]

In 1837, according to Lewis, 'the use of the English language is daily increasing in all parts' and on Arranmore:

> The Irish language is commonly spoken, and being replete with primitive words, varies from the dialect of the natives of the mainland, but not so as to be unintelligible; a great portion of the inhabitants, however, speak good English.[207]

In 1850 Edward Butler, head inspector of national schools, visited Galway county prison and reported on eleven children, most of whom were aged between 10 and 16. Aided by an interpreter, 'as numbers spoke no English', he found that 'not one of these could read, scarcely one of them had ever been within a school; not one of them knew the elements of religious knowledge, and several stated they were "glad to be transported" although they had no idea of where they were going; five of them stole sheep, one a cow, one meal, one clothes, one money, and two were pick-pockets'.[208]

In 1907 questions about the post of interpreter were raised in the house of commons; it was pointed out that the post in Loughrea had been vacant for five months, 'owing to the fact that the salary of £10 is insufficient even to defray the necessary expenses of attendance at the quarter sessions in four towns', and because expenses could not be claimed. Chief Secretary Mr Birrell responded that the salary of £30 per annum was divided into three portions of £10 for Galway,

206 Hely Dutton, *Statistical survey of the county of Galway*, pp 463–4.
207 Lewis, *A topographical directory of Ireland*, i, p. 78.
208 *The seventeenth report of the commissioners of national education in Ireland (for the year 1850)* [C 1405–11], HC 1851, xxiv, 152.

Table 44 Irish speakers in County Galway (census data)

	1851	1861	1871	1881	1891	1901	1911
Irish only	72,075 or 24.19%	40,621 or 16%	27,805				
Irish and English	135,574 or 45.51%	117,311 or 46.1%	102,535	144,591	125,565	108,870	98,523
Total	207,649 or 69.7%	157,932 or 62.1%	130,340 or 57%	144,591 or 64.9%	125,565 or 58.5%	108,870 56.5%	98,523 or 54.1%

Clifden and Loughrea.[209] In 1913 a judge commented that Mr McDonnell, the Irish interpreter, 'was a most charming man whom he had not seen for five years, and who seemed to be thoroughly acquainted with the witnesses, whose evidence he interpreted so well'.[210]

Given the high numbers of Irish speakers reported in the census (see table 44), it is no surprise that interpreter provision in the county of Galway continued until 1930 when the two remaining interpreters, onc in Oughterard and one in Kinvara, were replaced by district court clerks.[211]

Leitrim

In 1802, James McParlan reported that:

> The use of the English language is quite general in this county; very few of the old people, who don't speak it; the children are all sent to school; any of them addressed in Irish will always answer in English.[212]

In 1809, however, Edward Wakefield observed that 'Irish is the common language of the district'.[213] In 1837, Samuel Lewis made similar observations to McParlan:

> the English language is everywhere spoken by adults and children, and mostly by elderly people, except in the remote mountain districts, and even there it rarely occurs that a person is met who cannot speak it.[214]

209 HC Debates, 27 Mar. 1907, vol. 171, cc 1776–1777.
210 *Connacht Tribune*, 22 Mar. 1913.
211 *Connaught Telegraph*, 8 Feb. 1930.
212 J. McParlan, *Statistical survey of the county of Leitrim* (Dublin, 1802), p. 85.
213 Wakefield, *An account of Ireland statistical and political*, ii, p. 751.
214 Lewis, *A topographical directory of Ireland*, ii, p. 256.

Table 45 Irish speakers in Leitrim (census data)

	1851	1861	1871	1881	1891	1901	1911
Irish only	144 or 0.13%	82 or 0.1%	341				
Irish and English	14,859 or 13.28%	13,745 or 13.1%	6,514				
Total	15,003 or 13.41%	13,827 or 13.2%	6,855 or 7.2%	10.6%	7.2%	5.8%	6.2%

Wakefield's view is supported by census data indicating that levels of bilingualism were perhaps greater than realized by the other two writers (see table 45). The interpreter in Leitrim was paid £10 per half-year in 1841–3.[215] The earliest book of presentments located for Leitrim was for spring 1875 when Myles Bartley was paid £7 10*s.* 0*d.* for his work at quarter sessions. The next record is for summer 1887 when his salary had been halved to £3 15*s.* 0*d.* His last payment was in summer 1888. Interpreter provision in Leitrim lasted many years longer than in other counties where there were more speakers of Irish.

Mayo

Information on interpreting is particularly rich for Mayo, thanks to a combination of sources: a memorial from assizes interpreter Simon Conway in 1822 to the chief secretary's office, the *R v. Burke* case, which began at Mayo assizes in Castlebar, a file containing applications for the post of court interpreter in 1893 in the National Archives and detailed coverage of court cases in the *Connaught Telegraph* and the *Ballinrobe Chronicle*.

McParlan reported in his *Statistical survey* in 1802 that:

> The use of the English language through this county is rather general, though still in a defective state. Most of the old people speak a little but bad English; the children, being mostly sent to school, speak in general some English.[216]

In Erris, he reported that use of the English language 'is rather general, and in some state of improvement, but still very defective; many can't speak a word of it'.[217] Wakefield described the Irish language as 'universally spoken' in Mayo in 1812.[218] J.B. Trotter travelled around Ireland in 1812, 1814 and 1817 and wrote

215 *Appendix to the minutes of evidence taken before Her Majesty's commissioners of inquiry into the state of the law and practice in relation to the occupation of land in Ireland* (1845).
216 J. McParlan, *Statistical survey of the county of Mayo* (Dublin, 1802), p. 127.
217 Ibid., p. 168.
218 E. Wakefield, *An account of Ireland statistical and political* (London, 1812), i, p. 271.

that in Erris, 'almost all the people speak English and Irish, and both well',[219] and in Achill, 'The language is universally Irish, but the majority speak English very well.'[220] By 1837, Samuel Lewis reported that Irish was becoming the language of the older generation:

> The Irish language is generally spoken by the old inhabitants, but young people almost everywhere speak English, and many of the children, even in the mountainous districts and along the sea shore, are unacquainted with the Irish language.[221]

Nevertheless, in 1845 Baron Richards told a crowded court in Mayo that the Irish language was stronger than in any other county:

> He could not but also regret the great difficulty he felt in arriving at the facts of the cases, or at the truth, owing to the unfortunate want of education among the peasantry of the country. There was scarcely a case in which he was not obliged to examine the witnesses through the medium of an interpreter. He did not find this to anything like the same extent in other counties in Ireland. The interpreter here [Simon Conway] was quite competent to discharge his duty, was a good Irish scholar, and well able to interpret the language, yet from the ignorance of the people he (the learned judge) felt it almost impossible to understand the cases or get at the truth. That was a misfortune which he hoped would some day or other cease, and that the people in this county would be as well able to communicate their ideas in English as the people of other counties. It would be for their own benefit to learn the English language and receive education, for when they left the country, went to England and elsewhere they would find themselves in great difficulty from their not knowing that language, and from not being able to transact their business in it.[222]

However, Cormac Ó Gráda has found that the population of Mayo fell by 29 per cent between 1841 and 1851 and that almost 100,000 people died of famine-related causes while the extent of emigration cannot be quantified.[223]

In 1869 Fr Lavelle told the court of queen's bench that 3,000 people in Partry parish located between Castlebar and Ballinrobe spoke Irish and only two or three really understood English.[224] From 1865 the Mayo grand jury decided that the

219 Trotter, *Walks through Ireland*, p. 491.
220 Ibid., p. 467.
221 Lewis, *A topographical directory of Ireland*, ii, p. 358.
222 *Connaught Telegraph*, 19 Mar. 1845.
223 Ó Gráda, *Black '47 and beyond*, p. 28.
224 *Irish Times*, 22 June 1869.

Table 46 Irish speakers in Mayo (census data)

	1851	1861	1871	1881	1891	1901	1911
Irish only	49,643 or 18.08%	32,228 or 12.7%	16,509				
Irish and English	130,435 or 47.52%	124,148 or 48.7%	122,452	147,738	110,365	99,764	
Total	180,078 or 65.6%	156,376 or 61.4%	138,961 or 56.5%	147,738 or 60.2%	110,365 or 50.4%	99,764 or 50.1%	88,601 or 46.1%

interpreter at assizes should provide assistant interpreters when needed at his own expense.[225] All interpreter presentments thereafter until 1899 mention that the salary was for interpreting 'and for providing an assistant interpreter when required'. Presumably this meant that if the interpreter could not attend court for any reason, he would pay a substitute. There was a salaried interpreter, Peter O' Toole or Toole, in Mayo until at least 1922.[226]

Roscommon

In 1816 Revd William Digby wrote of the parish of Killuken:

> Hitherto the Irish language has been much spoken here by the aboriginal inhabitants, but it is now much declining, chiefly owing to the rising generation, learning as they are so generally, to read English at the little country schools, which are becoming very common.[227]

In the same year, his colleague Revd William Thompson wrote of the parish of Kilmore: 'English is the language spoken by the people in general; they all indeed understand Irish, but it is not so much used among them as formerly.'[228] In 1819 Revd Annesley Strean wrote of the parish of St Peter's in Athlone, County Roscommon, that:

> Most of the natives of this parish speak English; there are only a very few, and these the oldest grandmothers, who speak nothing but Irish; another generation will probably not find an individual ignorant of the English language, for all the children speak it, and many of them cannot speak Irish;

225 *Connaught Telegraph*, 19 July 1865.
226 *Western People*, 2 Dec. 1922.
227 William Digby in Mason, *A statistical account or parochial survey of Ireland*, ii, p. 325.
228 William Thompson in Mason, *A statistical account or parochial survey of Ireland*, ii, p. 404.

Table 47 Irish speakers in Roscommon (census data)

	1851	1861	1871	1881	1891	1901	1911
Irish only	1,326 or 0.76%	530 or 0.3%	739				
Irish and English	44,970 or 25.93%	32,616 or 20.9%	17,364				
Total	46,296 or 26.69%	33,146 or 21.2%	18,103 or 12.9%	16.3%	13%	15.1%	10.8%

> but in the more western parts this is not the case, though even in these the native language is on the decline.[229]

The figures for Irish speakers in the 1851 census are quite healthy with just under 27 per cent of the population speaking the language (see table 47). The comparative health of the language is corroborated by the fact that interpreter provision ended in Roscommon in 1864,[230] when the last payment was made to John Eaton who had been employed since at least 1849.

Sligo

In 1802, the use of the English language, according to James McParlan, was as follows:

> The greatest part of the common people speak bad English. Common schoolmasters and their schools are to be found dispersed every where throughout the county. It may be said the English language is in a progressive, though slow and bad state of improvement.

In 1816, Revd James Nelligan reported that in the parish of Kilmactige, Sligo, 'The Irish language is universally spoken, and but few of them can speak English.'[231] In 1837 Lewis reported that 'The English language is generally spoken through every part of the county, but elderly people in the mountainous districts still speak Irish.' In Innismurray, 'the inhabitants, consisting of about 18 families, and occupying about the same number of dwellings, form a community, generally intermarrying with each other, and speaking their original language'.[232]

229 Annesley Strean in ibid., iii, pp 71–2.
230 County of Roscommon abstract of the discharged and undischarged presentments, summer 1864, Roscommon County Library.
231 James Nelligan in Mason, *A statistical account or parochial survey of Ireland*, ii, p. 363.
232 Lewis, *A topographical directory of Ireland*, ii, p. 24.

The last official record for Sligo located relates to 1899, when two interpreters were employed – John Downes was interpreter at assizes and at quarter sessions Ballymote Division, while Pat Boland was interpreter at quarter sessions Sligo Division.[233] However, newspaper records suggest that John Downs continued working as interpreter until at least 1919.[234]

Table 48 Irish speakers in Sligo (census data)

	1851	1861	1871	1881	1891	1901	1911
Irish only	10,584 or 8.23%	3,466 or 2.8%	2,326				
Irish and English	38,644 or 30.07%	36,263 or 29%	24,263	31,930	21,336		15,927
Total	49,228 or 38.3%	39,729 or 31.8%	26,589 or 23%	31,930 or 28.6%	21,336 or 21.8%	17,570 or 20.9%	15,927 or 20.1%

233 Sligo County Library, County Sligo grand jury presentments, spring 1899, LGOV782.
234 *Sligo Champion*, 12 Apr. 1919.

CHAPTER THIRTEEN

Conclusion

THE GRAND JURIES have often been criticized because they were composed of well-off land owners who were more concerned about catering for their own interests than about promoting the common good. However, if the grand juries had not taken the initiative in creating a new post for salaried interpreters, the state would not have stepped in. We need only look to the example of Wales for confirmation of this. While nineteenth-century advocates for the Irish language frequently referred to Wales as an example of good practice,[1] in the mistaken belief that speakers of Welsh could choose to speak either Welsh or English and that judges and juries all spoke Welsh, in reality the law was the same in both jurisdictions. There was no right to speak Welsh until the Welsh Language Act 1967.[2] In fact, the situation in the Welsh courts could be considered inferior to that in Ireland, as there was never a system of salaried interpreters there.[3] Instead, interpreter provision in all courts in Wales bore greatest resemblance to the Irish petty sessions, with their dependence on volunteers, court officials and policemen as interpreters.

In Ireland, there was a pattern of local initiatives at grand jury level, followed many years later by an official response at state level. The county of Donegal grand jury appears to have been the first to pay a salary to an interpreter at assizes in 1754. The post was no doubt introduced out of expediency and purely on practical grounds as the grand jury had to deal with Irish speakers when deciding if cases should go to trial. Furthermore, the assizes could not function effectively without a suitable person who would be available to attend all court cases. Other grand juries followed Donegal's example. The Irish parliament has also been the subject of criticism, but fortunately it was in place in 1773–4 and in a position to pass a law to make payment of a salary to interpreters at assizes official, capping the amount at £5 per half-year. This law would prove useful because it set an important precedent, to pay a salary to court interpreters. However, the same pattern of official neglect was evident a century later in 1882, when winter assizes were introduced; the earliest record located of a payment by

1 *Nation*, 12 Oct. 1844. Also, after the Maamtrasna trials, George Sigerson, using the pseudonym 'An tEirionnach' (The Irishman), suggested that the situation was very different (in a positive sense) in Wales (*Nation*, 28 Apr. 1888). Judges in Irish-speaking areas should speak Irish, *Pilot*, 28 Nov. 1845. Courts should use Irish and do without interpreters, *Morning News*, 3 Sept. 1885.

2 D.L. Jones, 'The Welsh Language Act 1967: the first 50 years' (Cardiff, 2017), p. 3.

3 See HC Debates, e.g. HC Debates, 8 Mar. 1875, vol. 22, cc 1394–8; HC Debates, 9 Apr. 1886, vol. 304, c. 1171; HC Debates, 19 Feb. 1892, vol. 1, cc 811–63.

the chief secretary's office to a salaried interpreter for the extra work involved was in 1894.[4]

As the same need for interpreters existed at quarter sessions, once again Donegal apparently led the way in 1797 and introduced a salary for interpreters who worked in those courts. Legal provision followed forty years later in 1837, providing for a payment capped at £15 per half-year to interpreters at quarter sessions. Responsibility for appointments rested with assistant barristers, who favoured process servicers for these new posts. The state tolerated the system because the amount involved was small and the money was raised through local taxes, meaning that it had no impact on the exchequer and those counties with more Irish speakers had to bear the cost. Also, grand juries in counties with fewer Irish speakers had the option of abolishing the post.

If the petty sessions courts had been established even a decade earlier, perhaps the grand juries would have created posts for interpreters there as well. However, by the 1820s they had lost their earlier autonomy and were limited to 'imperative presentments', spending that was agreed by law. As there was never any legislation to provide for salaries to interpreters at petty sessions, the grand juries were powerless. Instead, a common expedient solution found was for summons servers to act as petty sessions interpreters, a most unsatisfactory solution. Even here, there is a pattern of delay with the chief secretary's office eventually agreeing in the late 1880s to pay summons servers a small sum of money for acting as interpreters.

There is an enormous contrast between interpreter provision in Ireland and in the Austrian and Austro-Hungarian empires under the Hapsburg monarchy,[5] where in the same time period a dozen languages were spoken. Michaela Wolf's research shows that there were other possible, more enlightened solutions to language issues than those found in Ireland and Wales. She quotes a court decree from 1835 that stated:

> Every appellate court shall, after consulting the land laws subject to it and the higher collegiate courts, establish the number of such interpreters; have them proposed by the lowest level courts, which is where they shall be appointed, and seek to ascertain to its fullest possible conviction the knowledge and good moral conduct of the interpreters proposed.[6]

The knowledge of interpreters, presumably their knowledge of languages, was seen as important, as was their 'good moral conduct'. In 1849 provision was made for a university language examination that could be taken by interpreters.[7] From this time onwards, work was carried out on legal terminology, hugely important for

4 CSO/RP/915.94, NAI.
5 Austrian empire, 1804–67 and Austro-Hungarian empire, 1867–1918.
6 M. Wolf, *The Habsburg monarchy's many-languaged soul* (Amsterdam, 2015), p. 73.
7 Ibid., p. 73.

the languages included in this initiative.[8] The 1853 Code of Criminal Procedure provided that both questions and answers were to be recorded in the language of the witness and the language of the court and this could be done by the interpreter. This would slow down interpreters' work but would be of use if there was any suggestion of incorrect interpretation. Wolf quotes article 19 of the 1867 constitution, which she describes as controversial due to the 'vagueness of its formulation':

> All the state's ethnic groups are equal, and each has an inviolable right to preserve and cultivate its nationality and language.
>
> The state recognizes the equality of all languages current in a region within schools, administration and public life.
>
> In those lands which are home to various ethnic groups, the institutions of public education shall be organized in such a way that each of these groups receives the means to be educated in its own language, without being forced to learn a second regional language.[9]

In comparison to the situation in Ireland at the time, these provisions seem quite amazing. In fact, mentions of words like 'right' and 'equality' in the context of language are quite startling. However, Wolf goes on to state that there was an 'assumption of German speakers' cultural superiority',[10] and as a result German was given priority. Nevertheless, article 19 did contribute to improving the situation. For example, laws had to be 'intelligible to all the state's citizens',[11] meaning that they had to be translated. This was very different from Ireland where all laws and proclamations were in English. Wolf goes on to say that the selection process for some civil service posts included language tests and in 1887 existing civil servants were obliged to take these tests.[12] Sworn translators had more professional profiles than most interpreters in Ireland; they were consuls, editors, general civil servants, high school teachers, judges, lawyers, legal advisors, notaries and private scholars.[13]

While the Hapsburg monarchy made arrangements for a professional level of interpreting in twelve languages, the British in Ireland just had to accommodate one language, Irish. It would have been relatively straightforward to introduce a system for recruiting and testing Irish interpreters. Work could have been carried out on legal terminology, something that would have been extremely useful. However, we have to conclude that the British had no interest in accommodating Irish speakers. The Administration of Justice (Language) Act (Ireland) 1737 provided that all court proceedings had to be in English but made no provision

8 Ibid., p. 83.
9 Ibid., p. 42.
10 Ibid., p. 42.
11 Ibid., p. 63.
12 Ibid., p. 64.
13 Ibid., p. 78.

for interpreters for the large numbers of Irish speakers. State involvement only happened due to pressure from judges and lawyers and was restricted to eventually following the lead of the grand juries and introducing legislation decades after it was needed and to ensuring that interpreters' salaries would be capped. There was no effort to control matters centrally, to consider ethical issues, to examine applicants, to encourage work on legal terminology, to ensure that all parties, including the courts, were provided with a good service. No select committee or commission was ever established to examine the needs of Irish speakers. No statutory provision was made for payment to interpreters who worked at newly established courts or at the land commission. Volunteers had to be found to interpret at inquests. Irish speakers involved in civil cases had to pay interpreters out of their own pocket. The system was hugely discriminatory against Irish speakers. However, when it came to state matters such as censuses, state commissions and enquiries, and applications for the old age pension, interpreters could be paid centrally. The overall policy was monolingualism and as J.J. Lee suggests, 'the whole state apparatus was an agency of anglicization'.[14]

Just as court interpreters were provided to foreigners who did not speak English, and to deaf people, so too were they provided to Irish speakers, who were treated, in effect, as foreigners in their own country. However, newspaper reports suggest that judges and lawyers were a lot more sympathetic to foreigners, rarely questioning their need for an interpreter, than to indigenous Irish speakers, whom they regarded with distrust and suspicion. In general, there was little or no official awareness of or interest in possible degrees of bilingualism. Instead, many judges, magistrates and lawyers held a very black-and-white view – either people spoke English or they did not, there was no middle ground.

Brian Ó Cuív has written of the 'disregard for Irish' manifested in Irish speakers being 'denied justice in the courts because of their inability to understand evidence given against them'.[15] We will never know how many Irish speakers gave up on seeking justice because they knew that they might not be allocated an interpreter or that once they had been sworn in they could be challenged about their knowledge of English. We will never know how many cases fell because witnesses could not explain themselves in English or left the witness box when they were not allocated an interpreter. We will never know how many defendants stood in court like Myles Joyce without understanding a word of what was said by English-speaking witnesses, lawyers and judges. We will never know how many Irish-speaking men were excluded from voting before 1817 when provision was finally made for interpreters at elections. We will never know how many Irish-speaking freeholders from 1829 onwards did not or could not write a letter of application in English. Of those that did submit such a letter, we will never know how many decided not to appear before the assistant barrister and risk possible public humiliation.

14 Lee, *Ireland, 1912–1985*, p. 666.
15 B. Ó Cuív, 'Irish language and literature, 1845–1921' in Vaughan (ed.), *A new history of Ireland*, vi, p. 392.

Negative attitudes to Irish speakers have been downplayed by many and indeed the Irish language scarcely merits a mention in many histories of Ireland. But when the population of a country actually stops using a language that it has used for centuries despite a nationalist movement and a struggle for independence, and subsequently opts for the language of the colonizer rather than reverting back to the original language or choosing bilingualism, something very unusual is happening. One of the reasons was the repression of the language, the way the authorities looked down on it and denigrated it. There was general acceptance of the status quo with all parties, including interpreters themselves, internalizing the idea that English should be spoken, English versions of names and surnames should be provided, everyone could and should speak English. In this context, it is surprising that in recent years, the ruling in *R v. Burke* has been misinterpreted as giving bilingual people the right to choose to speak either Irish or English, whichever they preferred, in court.

While the situation in Ireland was perhaps better than in Wales in that salaried interpreters were provided in the assizes and quarter sessions courts, their presence demonstrated to all that English was the important, dominant language while Irish was unimportant and insignificant. In addition, the fact that there was no centralized appointment system and testing of interpreters along with the cynical use of summons servers, process servers and civil bill officers all acted as huge disincentives for Irish speakers. Richard McMahon finds that in pre-Famine Galway the 'language … of ordinary people did not present insuperable difficulties',[16] and to an extent this is true – interpreters of one kind or another were found – but the system meant that Irish speakers were treated as second-class citizens, dependent on the sometimes dubious abilities of salaried interpreters at assizes and quarter sessions and of volunteers elsewhere. All of these pressures operated as incentives to learn English. The court was a hostile environment for Irish speakers who in many cases were warned that if they did not speak English they would be put in the dock, would not receive their expenses or would be sent to jail. These were not just threats: we have seen examples of people being refused expenses and being sent to jail because of their 'refusal to speak English'. These circumstances made the prospect of speaking English, and thereby being able to have some control over one's own destiny, an attractive one.

There are some unanswered questions. One is why the County Dublin Grand Jury Act 1844 was passed to provide a salaried interpreter at quarter sessions. No instance of any such payment has been located. Another is why interpreters were provided at elections from 1817. As more files are catalogued in the National Archives, perhaps supplementary information will come to light on some of these issues and indeed on other matters covered in this book.

16 R. McMahon, 'The court of petty sessions and society in pre-Famine Galway' in R. Gillespie (ed.), *The remaking of modern Ireland, 1750–1950* (Dublin, 2004), p. 129.

PAST AND PRESENT

Historical attitudes to the Irish language are evident in modern times, particularly in Northern Ireland. In Ireland, there was a strong belief that the best solution to the language issue would be to follow what was believed to be the Welsh model and to have Irish-speaking judges, thus bypassing the need for interpreters. For example, in 1906, the Tralee branch of the Gaelic League passed a resolution proposing that 'the time has come when one or two Magistrates having a knowledge of the Irish language should be appointed for each Petty Sessions district in this Irish-speaking County'.[17] After independence, interpreters were associated with British rule. Article 4 of the 1922 constitution of the Irish Free State provided that 'The National language of the Irish Free State (Saorstát Éireann) is the Irish language, but the English language shall be equally recognized as an official language.' The new government was keen to bring in measures to support the Irish language.

The Courts of Justice Act 1924 included two provisions designed to abolish the post of interpreter in Irish-speaking districts. The first was article 44, which provided that:

> So far as may be practicable having regard to all relevant circumstances, the Circuit Judge assigned to any Circuit which includes a district where the Irish language is in general use shall possess such a knowledge of the Irish language as would enable him to dispense with the assistance of an interpreter when evidence is given in that language.

The second was article 71, which contained similar wording, but applied to the new district courts, which replaced the petty sessions. The wording 'So far as may be practicable' indicates some awareness of potential difficulties in sourcing judges with a good knowledge of the Irish language. An advantage of this innovation was that Irish-speaking lawyers, if available, could examine witnesses in Irish without the need for an interpreter. Further measures were brought in. From 1928, district court clerks in Gaeltacht areas had to speak Irish. In 1935, under the Gaeltacht Order, members of an Garda Síochána in scheduled areas had to speak Irish in court. While well-intentioned, these changes created new problems, largely because there was an ongoing need for interpreters for monolingual English-speaking witnesses, prosecutors, defendants and lawyers. Issues also arose outside Gaeltacht areas when people opted to use Irish, with the courts resorting to whatever solution they could find and judges themselves, lawyers, court clerks, court registrars and policemen acting as interpreters.

The 1937 constitution prioritized Irish, making it the 'first official language', with English as the second official language. However, Irish speakers have had to continually fight for their right to use the first official language. For example,

17 *Kerryman*, 21 July 1906

the right to sign a hotel register in Irish;[18] refusal to pay rates because demand notes were in English;[19] and refusal to pay for television licences due to the small number of programmes in Irish.[20] A number of cases reached the supreme court. For example, the Ó Monacháin cases on the right to have a case heard in Irish without any interpreter input;[21] the MacCárthaigh cases about Irish-speaking juries,[22] and access to simultaneous rather than consecutive interpreting;[23] the Ó Maicín cases about the right to a bilingual jury from a specially designated area of Connemara. In his supreme court judgment, in the Ó Maicín case, Hardiman dissented and described the state's efforts to promote the Irish language as 'uniformly minimalist and grudging' and stated that he did not believe there is any other country in the world 'in which a citizen would not be entitled to conduct his business before a court in the national and first official language, and to be understood directly by such court in that language'.[24] Previously, in *Ó Beoláin v. Fahy*, Hardiman had commented that 'only a person of unusual independence of mind and pertinacity will attempt to conduct his or her legal business through the medium of Irish'.[25]

The attitudes to the Irish language and to Irish speakers detailed in this book echo down through the centuries and reverberate strongly in Northern Ireland, where attitudes to the language have become increasingly complex and politicized in recent years. The Good Friday Agreement recognized the Irish language, Ulster-Scots and 'the languages of the various ethnic communities' and provided that the British government would do the following in relation to Irish:

- take resolute action to promote the language;
- facilitate and encourage the use of the language in speech and writing in public and private life where there is appropriate demand;
- seek to remove, where possible, restrictions which would discourage or work against the maintenance or development of the language;
- make provision for liaising with the Irish language community, representing their views to public authorities and investigating complaints;
- place a statutory duty on the Department of Education to encourage and facilitate Irish medium education in line with current provision for integrated education ...[26]

18 *Irish Independent*, 17 Sept. 1930.
19 *Irish Times*, 2 Dec. 1965.
20 *Irish Press*, 11 Jan. 1994.
21 *Irish Press*, 20 Jan. 1976.
22 *Irish Independent*, 15 Sept. 1994.
23 *Irish Times*, 7 Mar. 2008.
24 *Irish Times*, 27 Feb. 2014.
25 *Ó Beoláin v. Fahy*, 2 IR 279 (4 Apr. 2001)
26 Good Friday Agreement, https://www.dfa.ie/media/dfa/alldfawebsitemedia/ourrolesandpolicies/northernireland/good-friday-agreement.pdf, accessed 5 Apr. 2019.

The United Kingdom signed and ratified the Charter for Regional or Minority Languages in 2000 and 2001 and it came into force in July of that year. Under the St Andrews Agreement (2006), the British government agreed to introduce an Irish Language Act 'reflecting on the experience of Wales and Ireland' and to work with the incoming Executive to enhance and protect the development of the Irish language. The government also stated that it firmly believed 'in the need to enhance and develop the Ulster Scots language, heritage and culture'.[27] While Sinn Féin supports an Irish Language Act that, among other things, would facilitate the use of Irish in court and with all state bodies including the police, the Democratic Unionist Party is opposed. In 2007 Minister Edwin Poots (DUP) told the Northern Ireland Assembly that the projected cost of simultaneous interpreting for Irish in the courts would be almost £200,000 a year.[28]

No progress had been made on these matters at the time of writing and the Administration of Justice (Language) Act (Ireland) (1737) was still in force in Northern Ireland; as a result, Irish speakers are not permitted to use the language in court and documents in languages other than English are not accepted. When Caoimhín Mac Giolla Catháin's Irish-language application for an occasional drinks licence for a concert was turned down, he challenged the decision in 2009, arguing that it was discriminatory, contravened his human rights, and breached the European Convention on Regional and Minority Languages. The court found against him, and in 2010 he appealed the verdict, claiming that the law was discriminatory, and breached the European Convention on Human Rights, and that the equivalent act applying to Scotland and Wales had been repealed. However, the court of appeal upheld the ban. Lord Justice Girvan found that there had been no breach of the convention and stated that:

> In a jurisdiction where English is the language of the overwhelming majority of the population the requirement that court documents initiating proceedings be in English as the working language of the court is a practical necessity in the interests of fairness.[29]

In 2014, Gregory Campbell, a DUP member of the Northern Ireland Assembly, parodied the phrase 'Go raibh maith agat a Cheann comhairle', a phrase frequently used by members of Sinn Féin and the SDLP at the assembly and meaning 'Thank you speaker', as 'Curry my yogurt can coca coalyer'.[30] In 2016, funding for an Irish-language bursary was withdrawn by a DUP minister, something that contributed

27 St Andrews Agreement, https://assets.publishing.service.gov.uk/government/uploads/system/uploads/attachment_data/file/136651/st_andrews_agreement-2.pdf, accessed 5 Apr. 2019.

28 16 Oct. 2007, https://www.theyworkforyou.com/ni/?id=2007-10-16.1.1&s=%22irish+language+act%22+2006-01-01..2017-01-19+section%3Ani#g1.59.

29 'Belfast Court upholds ban on Irish', *Irish Times*, 2 June 2010.

30 BBC News, '"Curry my yoghurt": Gregory Campbell, DUP, barred from speaking for day', 4 Nov. 2014. https://www.bbc.com/news/uk-northern-ireland-29895593, accessed 15 May 2019.

to Martin McGuinness' resignation as deputy first minister in 2017. Negotiations to restore the Northern Assembly foundered with one of the factors being Sinn Féin's support for – and the DUP's opposition to – an Irish Language Act. Irish speakers in Northern Ireland seek the right to use Irish in court through an interpreter, something that they are not legally entitled to do because they speak English. Their situation has remained unaltered since 1737. Irish speakers in Ireland are allowed to use Irish in court, but only through an interpreter, which means that there has been very little improvement compared to the nineteenth century. Historically, Irish speakers looked to the Welsh courts as an example of good practice. While we have seen that this view was mistaken, perhaps Ireland, both north and south, could look to changes introduced in Wales in recent years. The Welsh Language Act 1993 provides that Welsh and English 'be treated on the basis of equality' and there is a right to speak Welsh in court through an interpreter. This shows that it is possible for one part of the United Kingdom to accommodate people who choose to use a language other than English in court, even though they speak English. An interesting aspect is that court interpreting is provided simultaneously by Welsh-English interpreters who have been tested by the Association of Welsh Translators and Interpreters, ensuring that they can provide a quality service and reducing delays associated with consecutive interpreting. A similar initiative would be very welcome in Ireland where simultaneous interpreting has only ever been provided on one occasion (*MacCárthaigh v. Éire* 2008) and where there is no testing system in place to ensure that Irish-language court interpreters meet standards.

APPENDIX A

Interpreters and the 1901 and 1911 censuses

THE IRISH CENSUSES for 1901 and 1911 give an erroneous impression of the extent of interpreter provision. In 1901 only nine people, all male, listed their occupation as 'interpreter', five for Irish and four for other languages. In fact, according to county council accounts, correspondence with the chief secretary's office, and newspaper reports, at least seventeen interpreters were employed in eight counties in 1901. In addition, there was a separate unnamed interpreter for Cork's east riding until at least 1899.[1] Some interpreters could not be located in the census. In some cases, this was because they had very common names and it was impossible to locate the correct person.

Table 49 Interpreters and the 1901 census

County	Name	Address	Age	Occupation in census
Clare	Patrick Curtis	Corofin	68[2]	
Cork	Humphrey Kelleher	Barrack Road, Bantry	74	Civil bill officer and interpreter, west riding
Cork	Patrick Stanton (Pádraig Stúndún)	Evergreen Road, Cork Urban no. 5	67	Irish interpreter
Donegal	Daniel Boyce	Drumany, Greenfort	76	Farmer
Donegal	John Boyce	Arryheernabin, Fanad North (visitor)	40	Farmer and deputy county court interpreter
Donegal	Condy Boyle	Dungloe	82	Farmer
Galway	Antony O'Donnell	Fairhill road, Galway	45	Clerk, 'commercial'
Galway: Clifden	John McDonagh			

1 County of Cork, schedule of the approved applications to obtain presentments, spring assizes, 1899, NLI Ir 94145 C13.
2 According to his death certificate, Patrick Curtis, 'Gaelic interpreter to courts for Clare', died aged 75 on 11 Mar. 1908.

County	Name	Address	Age	Occupation in census
Galway: Loughrea	Patrick Smith			
Kerry	James Clifford	Mountluke, Castlequin	40	Civil bill officer
Kerry	Richard P. Conway	Cloon, Emlagh	36	Civil bill officer and interpreter Irish for Cahirciveen court
Kerry	William C. Dineen	Ballycullane, Rathmore	66	Farmer
Kerry	Michael Dowd[3]	Knockeen, Dingle	49	Farmer
Mayo	John Keane (John Kane)	Ballywalter, Newbrook	30	Interpreter
Sligo	Patrick Boland	Tullylin, Castleconor East	40	Farmer and civil bill officer
Sligo	John Downs	Riverstown		
Waterford	Patrick Keane	Shears street, Dungarvan	82	Civil bill officer

Ten years later, in the 1911 census, just two Irish-language interpreters – Edward Collins and John Boyce – are listed (plus two for foreign languages). Anthony O'Donnell and Thomas Veale completed the census form in the Irish language but gave their main occupations as clerk and Irish teacher rather than interpreter. At least fourteen interpreters were still employed at this stage in eight counties.

Table 50 Interpreters and the 1911 census

Clare	Michael McNamara	Abbey Street, Ennis	55	Practising 'Bachelor of Law'
Cork	Edward Collins	Mountmassy Road, Macroom	59	Irish interpreter
Cork	Patrick Staunton			
Donegal	John Boyce	Drumany, Greenfort	51	Irish interpreter
Donegal	Patrick Kennedy	Glenties	59	Solicitor's clerk
Galway	Antoine Ó Domhnaill (Antony O'Donnell)	Fairhill Road, Galway	47	Cleireach (clerk)
Galway: Clifden	John McDonagh			

3 According to the *Kerry Weekly Reporter*, 17 Nov. 1900, Michael Dowd was process server for Knockeen, Dingle.

Galway: Loughrea	Thomas Connolly	Shessanagirba, Kinvarra	41	Herd and labourer
Kerry	Richard P. Conway	Cloon, Emlagh	47	Farmer etc.
Kerry	Michael Dowd	Knockeen, Glin	62	Farmer
Kerry	Timothy D Sullivan[4]			
Mayo	Peter Toole	Glebe street, Ballinrobe	68	No occupation listed
Sligo	John Downs	Riverstown		
Waterford	Tomás de Bhial (Thomas Veale)	Ballymacart, Waterford	26	Oide na Gaedhilge (Irish teacher)

4 Timothy Sullivan and Timothy O'Sullivan were very common names in Kerry in 1911.

APPENDIX B

Interpreter micro-histories

THESE MICRO-HISTORIES CONSIST of biographical information on some ninety interpreters, many of whom worked in the courts for decades. The information has been compiled from books of presentments, county council accounts, newspaper reports, census records, correspondence with the chief secretary's office, civil birth, marriage and civil death records (irishgenealogy.ie), the ancestry.com website and the censuses. As interpreting was often just one source of income, the micro-histories are organized in sections based on the interpreters' other main sources of income.

COURT OFFICIALS

Michael Canny

In 1807 the grand jury presentments for Clare provide details of payments to Michael Canny, who fulfilled a number of functions. He was deputy clerk of the crown at the assizes court and in addition, he was interpreter in the crown and record courts. He earned £40 for the year as clerk and £30 as interpreter in the two courts. At the summer assizes, Canny was paid £10 'for supplying an interpreter in the Record Court'.[1] We do not know if that £10 was paid in full to the interpreter or if Canny paid himself a percentage.

John Carter

According to grand jury presentment books,[2] in 1813 John Carter was court crier in Galway quarter sessions. By 1818 he was interpreter at quarter sesssions and he continued in this role until at least 1835, by which time he was also deputy to the clerk of the peace.[3]

Simon Conway (1792–1859)

Mayo interpreter Simon Conway was exceptional in terms of his personal contacts and the variety of posts he held. In 1822, he sent a petition to the lord lieutenant,[4]

1 *Accounts presented to the house of commons of the presentments passed by the grand juries of Ireland* (1808).
2 County of Galway books of presentments, NAI, and Galway County Library Headquarters.
3 Pettigrew and Outlon, *Dublin almanac and general register of Ireland* (Dublin, 1835), p. 194.
4 CSO/RP/1822/68, NAI.

Richard Wellesley, about salary reductions. He had been working as a sworn interpreter since 1813 and his annual pay amounted to £60, a considerable sum at the time, and more than was being earned by any of his contemporaries. However, in summer 1821, the grand jury had changed the payment to £5 per assizes in line with 13 & 14 Geo. 3, c. 32, s. 22, which of course dated back almost half a century, to 1773–4. The change had been made, not because the amount being paid to Conway was 'excessive or unreasonable', but because the grand jury did not have the legal right to pay more than £5 per half-year.

According to Conway, £10 was the equivalent of about half the expenses involved in travelling some 314 miles to eight sessions, two assizes and two insolvent courts in Clare, Ballinrobe, Castlebar, Westport and Ballina over the course of sixty or seventy days. He stated that there had been 'an immense increase in population' and suggested that a salary of £70 a year would be adequate and sought 'reasonable remuneration' for the last half-year. He made the case that 'he is the only Public Officer attending said Several Courts who does not receive a salary adequate to his trouble' and that, unlike other court officials, he was not entitled to any presentment for prisoners convicted or acquitted. Here, Conway was referring to fees paid to the clerk of the peace, the sub-sheriff, the crier and the deputy clerk of the crown.

Conway wrote that he enclosed certificates from members of parliament, members of the grand jury, the high sheriff, the clerk of the peace, the assistant barrister for Mayo, three 'respectable attorneys' and the chief justice of the king's bench, all of whom testified that he performed his interpreting work satisfactorily. According to a handwritten note on the back of the memorial, Conway was 'a very deserving public officer'. All of this information would indicate that Conway had substantial social capital; he was part of a network and had the support of influential people.

Conway reported that he was 'no sooner disengaged in the one Court than required in the other' and that 'The lower Classes of people in the County don't speak the English language'. His work included administering the oath of allegiance to 'the peasantry'. He made the point that the civil bill court and the insolvent court did not exist when 13 & 14 Geo. 3, c. 32, s. 22 was passed in 1773–4. The Act for the Relief of Insolvent Debtors in Ireland (1 & 2 Geo. 4, c. 59) became law in 1821 and established a new court for the relief of insolvent debtors, with two commissioners in Dublin who were also expected to hear cases in the assize courts around the country up to three times a year. The difficulty was that the new laws made no provision for interpreters, which meant that Conway was not entitled to any payment if he worked there.

Undersecretary William H. Gregory forwarded Simon Conway's memorial to Peter Burrowes and John Parsons, the commissioners for the relief of insolvent debtors, explaining that Conway had received no remuneration in the insolvent court and asking if payments could be authorized. Burrowes replied that Conway was 'inadequately compensated by the law as it now stands' and suggested that the 'proper remedy' was 'a legislative enactment extending the limit within which

Grand Juries may present for all the services performed by interpreters in all the Courts in the several Counties'. He said that no demand for compensation had been made by any interpreters and that if the commission were to pay one, 'it would lead to a claim from the interpreters of every county, whether his services were required or not'.[5] The other commissioner, Parsons, also replied to Gregory, to the effect that Conway had acted as interpreter on a recent circuit in Castlebar, but had not requested any compensation. Parsons wrote that if Conway had requested payment, he would have been paid 'at the expense of the Circuit but his trouble was so small that I thought he did not mean to broker any charge for it'. Parsons also wrote that 'that part of the population who can not speak English is diminishing'.[6]

The information supplied by Simon Conway on his earnings is very different from the surviving records on payment for other court interpreters.[7] In Mayo, between 1792 and 1795, the grand jury presentments detail payments of a half-year's salary of £5 to interpreters Mathew Waters and Thomas Bennis. Four years after writing his memorial, Simon Conway was still working as a court interpreter. He was paid £23 in summer 1826 for interpreting at assizes and sessions or a possible £46 for the full year. In spring 1827, he was paid a half-year's salary of £13 16*s.* 11*d.*, which would mean that his annual salary was the uneven amount of £27 13*s.* 10*d.* This was less than half of his previous salary of £60, but a lot more than the mooted £10. It is worth comparing Simon Conway's pay to that of John Kirwan in the county of Galway around the same time. At the Lent assizes in 1822, Kirwan was paid £16 and in summer 1823, £15. His pay for the year was around £31, or slightly more than Conway's.[8] In 1830 a committee suggested reforms to the grand jury laws and recommended reductions in 'enormous allowances', including a reduction of the interpreter's salary from £50 to £30.[9] Despite this, in 1834, Conway's salary had increased again to £25 per half-year; once again this payment was questioned, this time by the foreman of the grand jury, who had looked over the acts and found there was only power to grant £5 at assizes. In response, Conway stated:

> I must say I attend Assizes and four Quarter Sessions, and the duties are extremely severe, and I believe every gentleman who hears me will testify that I am not wanting in attention, and have been Interpreter in this County for the last 22 years.

All the other members of the grand jury, apart from the foreman, supported the £25 payment to Conway,[10] who informed them that his brother shared the

5 CSO/RP/1822/21, NAI.
6 CSO/RP/1822/1979, NAI.
7 County of Mayo books of presentments, NLI.
8 County of Galway books of presentments, NAI.
9 *Connaught Telegraph*, 27 Oct. 1830.
10 Ibid., 30 July 1834.

interpreting work with him. The grand jury engaged in some creative accounting by 'considering the sessions as assizes' and paying him £5 for each quarter sessions.[11] The following year, a man called Richard Stanton offered to take Conway's place for £10 per half-year. Stanton produced certificates from the assistant barrister and magistrates as to his qualifications, but the grand jury did not take up his offer.[12]

How did Conway's salary increase from £10 per annum to £60 and why was it not reduced to £10? The explanation may well lie in his social capital and connections. In addition to his well-remunerated interpreting work, Simon Conway had an amazing array of sources of revenue. He was a freeholder, entitled to vote at elections from at least 1830.[13] He was also:

- agent to James Browne;[14]
- provider to the sessions courts at Claremorris of £5 worth of lights, fuel and stationery in 1833;[15]
- master extraordinary of the high court of chancery from 1833 – to receive affidavits and take special bail for certain courts;[16]
- perpetual commissioner from 1834 for taking the acknowledgment deeds, to be executed by married women under the act passed for the abolition of fines and recoveries;[17]
- Claremorris petty sessions clerk from at least 1835 (over a three-year period from 1842 onwards Simon Conway was paid a total of £131 5*s*. 0*d*. in fees);[18]
- replevinger from 1836 – a replevin was a legal action whereby people could recover seized items of personal property.

As land agent Simon Conway would most likely have been expected to draw up agreements with tenants, collect rent, and superintend improvements to the land. Land agents were generally paid a commission of 5 per cent on rents collected.[19] Questions were raised in the *Connaught Telegraph* about a possible conflict of interest between Conway's role as land agent for absentee landlord James Browne and that of replevinger. If a tenant was unable to pay rent, personal property could be seized by a land agent.[20] If Simon Conway in his function of land agent seized property, a tenant could have to apply to him to recover their items. His knowledge

11 *Mayo Constitution*, 24 July 1834.
12 *Connaught Telegraph*, 25 Mar. 1835.
13 Ibid., 15 June 1831.
14 Ibid., 16 Nov. 1836.
15 Ibid., 25 Sept. 1833.
16 Ibid., 5 June 1833.
17 Ibid., 31 Dec. 1834.
18 Ibid., 11 June 1845.
19 S.M. Hussey, *Reminiscences of an Irish land agent* (London, 1904), p. 39.
20 *Connaught Telegraph*, 16 Nov. 1836.

of Irish probably facilitated his various functions. Simon Conway is buried in the Carmelite Abbey of St Mary Ballinasmalla in the parish of Kilcolman outside Claremorris.[21]

William Lavelle

William Lavelle had commenced as interpreter at Mayo quarter sessions by 1841,[22] and his brother Pat was interpreter at crown court by 1849.[23] Both men were paid the full rate: £5 per half-year at assizes and £15 per half-year at quarter sessions. William was also deputy clerk of the peace for the county of Mayo,[24] replevinger[25] and master extraordinary and commissioner for receiving affidavits in the court of chancery, queen's bench and other courts.[26] However, in 1853, he lost all these posts, including that of interpreter, when a case was taken against him at the court of chancery in Dublin on the grounds that he had signed his name to an affidavit without administering the oath. The court accepted that he had no improper motive but, for the sake of the administration of justice, he was dismissed by the lord chancellor and ordered to pay costs.[27]

Stephen Nealis or Nealus (1798–1859)

Stephen Nealis or Nealus was appointed interpreter at the Tyrone summer assizes in or before 1826. In Lent 1830, he was paid for 'transmitting prisoners' and continued doing this until 1833, when he reverted to solely carrying out his interpreter duties.[28] In 1837 his name appeared on a list of bailiffs appointed to execute the decrees and orders of the civil bill court.[29] By 1859 he was also court crier when he had a fit of apoplexy in the main street in Omagh while talking to the sub-sheriff. His death was described as a 'public loss, as the sheriffs of Omagh will not easily supply his place'.[30]

Thomas J. Reid/Read (1817–77)

Like Simon Conway, Thomas J. Reid held a number of posts. Interpreter at Galway crown, record and insolvents courts from 1833, he was also clerk at

21 Thanks to Paul Conway for this information.
22 County of Mayo book of presentments, spring 1841, Mayo County Library.
23 *Connaught Telegraph*, 21 Mar. 1849.
24 *Dublin Evening Packet*, 25 Jan. 1853.
25 *Connaught Telegraph*, 11 Feb. 1852.
26 *Catholic Telegraph*, 12 Mar. 1853.
27 *Saunders's News-Letter*, 7 Feb. 1853.
28 County of Tyrone books of presentments, TYR/4/1/36–42, PRONI.
29 *Strabane Morning Post*, 7 Feb. 1837.
30 *Belfast Morning News*, 11 Oct. 1859.

Galway petty sessions, honorary secretary[31] and later chairperson of Petty Sessions' Clerks of Ireland. In addition, he was high constable/baronial collector from 1844 until 1848,[32] clerk of the Galway union,[33] clerk to the conservators of salmon and inland fisheries[34] and inspector of fisheries for the district of Galway.[35] He was also inspector of weights and measures,[36] registrar of the county of Galway infirmary and in 1847 was appointed assistant clerk to the board of guardians on a salary of £40 a year.[37] His roles as inspector of fisheries and inspector of weights and measures involved taking prosecutions. He retired from all his posts in 1877 due to illness and the *Galway Vindicator* reported that his salary as first-class clerk of petty sessions was £300 a year and his pension was £200.[38]

John Ryan

John Ryan, court crier at Kilkenny quarter sessions, was appointed interpreter in 1840. However, Captain Bryan, a member of the grand jury, objected to a proposal to pay him £5 per half-year on the grounds that he was already being paid as crier. A Mr Flood commented that 'the duties of the interpreter were sometimes very onerous'.[39] As a result of Bryan's intervention, according to the presentments, Ryan was paid £2 per half-year for the decade of his service as interpreter.[40]

LAWYERS

Patrick Curtin

Pat Curtin was interpreter at Clare quarter sessions and occasionally at crown court from 1817 until 1836.[41] He was also a notary public and a commissioner for taking affidavits.[42]

31 *Limerick & Clare Examiner*, 29 Jan. 1851.
32 *Thom's Irish Almanac*, 1844, 1845, 1946, 1848.
33 *Galway Vindicator*, 4 Mar. 1848.
34 *Galway Mercury*, 4 Feb. 1860.
35 *Tuam Herald*, 16 May 1863.
36 *Galway Mercury*, 23 Oct. 1852.
37 Ibid., 20 Nov. 1847.
38 *Galway Vindicator*, 27 June 1877.
39 *Kilkenny Journal*, 14 Mar. 1840.
40 County of Kilkenny books of presentments, Kilkenny County Library.
41 County of Clare books of presentments, 1817, 1820, 1824, 1825 (NAI), 1829 (NLI), 1829 (Clare County Archives), 1836 (NAI).
42 *The Treble Almanac*, 1822, p. 130.

W. Green, Benj. Green and Michael Cullinan

There are three instances of attorneys acting as interpreters in Clare. In 1815, W. Green was paid £5 for interpreting at Clare assizes. Similarly, in 1825, Benj Green, also an attorney,[43] and possibly his son, was paid £5 for interpreting in the record court, while Michael Cullinan was paid £5 for interpreting in the crown court.[44]

John Kirwan

Solicitor John Kirwan was interpreter in County Galway between 1813 and 1832. According to Oliver J. Bourke, he was 'a most respectable gentleman and member of one of the oldest families in the county of Galway'. He was also described as 'the wittiest man in the province' and 'eccentric'.[45] Bourke recounts an anecdote featuring Kirwan as interpreter. When the witness saw Judge Fletcher he said in Irish 'Dar mo chianseois, is an fear is granach dha chonnairch me ariamh.' The judge asked Kirwan to interpret what had just been said, but he replied, 'Oh, my lord, I could not tell your lordship.' When the judge threatened to send Kirwan to jail for a month, presumably for contempt of court, he agreed to interpret the sentence and said 'that, upon my conscience, you are the ugliest man that ever I saw', a sentence that was greeted by 'shouts of laughter'. Anyone in the court who was bilingual had probably expected Kirwan to invent a more palatable version and the reaction was one of surprise that he would actually interpret the sentence accurately.[46] A very similar story was told about Baron Dowse (1824–90) and repeated again and again over the decades in different newspapers from 1895 to 1962:

> Baron Dowse once was judge where the accused could understand only Irish, and an interpreter was accordingly sworn. The prisoner said something to the interpreter, and the latter replied.
>
> 'What does he say?' demanded the judge.
>
> 'Nothing, my lord.'
>
> 'How dare you say that, when we all heard him? Come, sir, what was it?'
>
> 'My lord', said the interpreter, beginning to tremble, 'it had nothing to do with the case.'
>
> 'If you don't answer I'll commit you sir. Now what did he say?'
>
> 'Well, my Lord, you'll excuse me, but he said 'Who's that ould woman with the red bed curtain round her, sitting up there?'
>
> At which the court roared.

43 *Pigot & Co City of Dublin and Hibernian Provincial Directory* (1824).
44 Ibid.
45 O.J. Burke, 'History of the Connaught circuit', *Dublin University Magazine*, 85 (1875), pp 690–702 at p. 697.
46 O.J. Burke, *Anecdotes of the Connaught circuit from its foundation in 1604 to close upon the present time* (Dublin, 1885), pp 186–7.

> 'And what did you say?' asked the baron, looking a little uncomfortable.
> 'I said, 'Whist, ye spalpeen! That's the old boy that's going to hang yes!'[47]

An abridged version of the story was:

> It has been stated that a Mayo prisoner in the dock once said to an interpreter: 'Oh, mavrone, will you tell me who is the ould woman above rolled up in the ould blankets?' 'Hould your whist', said the interpreter, 'That's the judge, and the same chap would hang you while you'd be saying Jack Robinson'[48]

In this version, the dilemma of the interpreter, who has to decide whether or not to interpret what has been said, is lost.

Michael McNamara (1856–1927)

Michael McNamara was described by A.M. Sullivan as 'an expert counsellor, card-player, farmer, land valuer, County Court interpreter, and matchmaker'.[49] Maurice Healy described him as 'not alone a barrister, he was also a mapper; he was parish match-maker to the parish of Kilshanny; but it is believed that his principal source of income was his skill at the game of "Forty Five". He was also the court interpreter in Irish'.[50]

A barrister, he was appointed interpreter in 1909 by county court Judge Bodkin on a salary of £30 per year, paid by Clare county council. Perhaps McNamara found that he was being expected to interpret for his clients who used Irish and decided he might as well be paid as interpreter if he was doing the work anyway. His interpreting work would have meant a small extra income each year. At the time, appointments could be made by the county court judge, or later the circuit court judge, for 'so long as was necessary'.

Sullivan makes a cryptic reference to McNamara 'holding on to his farm and facing danger courageously until a local patriot got him shot'.[51] It seems that in January 1913, as a result of a dispute over a field he had bought the previous year, he was shot in the arm with a shotgun. McNamara fired back with his revolver but missed.[52]

A story is told by Sullivan (1928) and McArdle (1995) about the way in which McNamara administered the oath on one occasion. He believed that the defendant intended to lie and he wanted to ensure a fair and just resolution to the case.

47 *Southern Star*, 16 Nov. 1895.
48 *Nenagh News*, 23 Nov. 1907.
49 A.M. Sullivan, *Old Ireland: reminiscences of an Irish K.C.* (London, 1928), p. 125.
50 Healy, *The old Munster circuit*, p. 151.
51 Sullivan, *Old Ireland*, p. 125.
52 *Irish Times*, 22 July 1913.

According to Healy, a Kerry alibi would involve swearing as to what happened on Tuesday 4th October which was in fact a Wednesday and a Tipperary alibi involved proving that the crown witnesses were elsewhere. The bishop of Kerry made perjury a 'reserved sin', meaning that only he could grant absolution to anyone guilty of the offence.[53] McNamara was both lawyer for the plaintiff and court interpreter. He administered the oath in the usual way to the plaintiff, but when it came to the defendant's turn, he invented his own version of the oath:

> Interpreter: Take the book in your right hand and listen to your oath – repeat after me: If I do not tell the truth in this case.
> Defendant: If I do not tell the truth in this case
> Interpreter: May all my sheep be clifted.
> Defendant: My God, Counsellor, I never heard an oath like that.
> Interpreter: I shall tell His Honour that you refuse to be sworn if you do not repeat –
> Defendant: May all my sheep – but Counsellor, I have three hundred sheep.
> Interpreter: Are you going to repeat the oath?
> Defendant: May all my sheep – may all – may all – may all my sheep be clifted – God help the poor sheep.
> Interpreter (sternly): May all my cattle die of the murrain.
> Defendant: Oh Counsellor, I have only three little beasts.
> Interpreter: Very well, you will be decreed.
> Defendant: But this is dreadful altogether. May all – may all – may all my cattle die of the murrain – I'm a ruined man.
> Interpreter: And may all my potatoes be blighted, and rot in the ground.
> Defendant: What?!!
> Interpreter: Go on, Sir, and repeat your oath.
> Defendant (laying down the Bible): Oh, Counsellor, I'll admit the debt, I'm only asking for time.[54]

Healy adds that McNamara argued that he had done the right thing because an oath is 'a calling on God to punish you if you don't tell the truth'.[55] As a barrister, and probably a court character, McNamara could take a risk and get away with it because he was part of the field of law. If another interpreter had administered the oath in this fashion, there would have been a different reaction. Cronin suggests that the humour of the anecdote derives from the roots of the 'ritual curse' in oral culture, which contrasts with the formal, legal setting where it is uttered.[56]

53 Healy, *The old Munster circuit*, p. 168.
54 Sullivan, *Old Ireland*, pp 125–6.
55 Healy, *The old Munster circuit*, p. 153.
56 M. Cronin, *Translation and identity* (London, 2006), p. 92.

The humour also derives from the defendant, who, instead of simply repeating the words of the oath as instructed, introduces his own comments.

In 1863 in *Robert Holmes v. the Revd Patrick Lavelle* at Ballinrobe petty sessions, Fr Lavelle took a similar approach with a witness:

> Revd Mr Lavelle (to witness): To the best of your belief – and for the wealth of the world do not tell a lie – which did Holmes or I appear on that occasion the more violent?
> Mr Griffin objected.
> Revd Mr Lavelle (to the interpreter): Impose it on him, as he hopes for heaven.[57]

In 1925, McNamara sued Clare county council for three years' salary, a total of £90. He told the court that he had interpreted in nine or ten cases but had not worked at all for six or seven years. The judge described his role as a 'cushy job'.[58] Apparently, the county council had dismissed him by resolution in November 1924 but only the judge had the power to dismiss an interpreter. McNamara was awarded £60 for the years 1922 and 1923.[59] He was in the news again in 1926 as court interpreter at the circuit court in Ennis for a case of serious assault on 'Sergeant William Mc Gill of the Civic Guards', which he interpreted, to laughter, as 'Liam MacGill, a sargint of the peelers'. After the case, he was asked why he had chosen to 'translate' in this manner and replied, 'Because it is the only correct way of translating it, in my opinion. Garda Siothcana is not proper Irish, and does not convey the correct idea to a man who presumably does not understand English. "Peeler" in my view, is the correct way of translating Civic Guard – it conveys the proper idea of a genuine Irish speaker, and that is my duty as interpreter.'[60]

GAOLERS AND BRIDEWELL KEEPERS

James Beatty

James Beatty was Sligo gaoler from at least Lent 1811, when he was paid £20 in that function, plus £3 10*s.* for transmitting prisoners, £5 for whipping William Black, £7 6*s.* 8*d.* for assizes fees and £2 for fees on prisoners at quarter sessions. In spring 1816, he was paid £7 for 'providing an executioner to execute two & whip one convicted at last Assizes'. Over a twelve-year period, from 1814–26, he was the Sligo crown court interpreter.[61] In 1837 Sir William Parke, then high sheriff, removed Beatty as governor of the gaol. However, it seems that the grand jury did

57 *Dublin Evening Mail*, 3 Apr. 1863.
58 *Irish Times*, 28 Apr. 1925.
59 *Irish Independent*, 28 Apr. 1925.
60 *Limerick Leader*, 5 July 1926.
61 County of Sligo books of presentments, LGOV780, Sligo County Library.

not agree with this decision; they voted to make the governor's residence a house of correction and to appoint Beatty as its governor. In this way, he managed to remain *in situ* for an extra year.[62]

James Kennedy (1742–1831)

James Kennedy, Croom, County Limerick, wrote to the lord lieutenant in 1828 to say that Baron Pennefather had refused payment for his work at quarter sessions in Rathkeale and Limerick. Kennedy claimed that he was 81 years of age and had been working as an interpreter for forty-five years, as bridewell keeper for twenty years, and also instructed gentlemen's children. In 1821, he was robbed of £109 18*s.* 4*d.* in gold and Bank of Ireland notes. In a second letter, he requested a pension.[63] In spring 1832, James Kennedy was replaced by Michael McNamara as interpreter and Rathkeal courthouse keeper.

Michael McNamara (–1848)

Michael McNamara, who had formerly been a linen manufacturer in the North Liberties barony of Limerick,[64] was appointed interpreter at County Limerick assizes and quarter sessions in December 1831. Grand jury presentment records show that he was paid for his work as interpreter, as keeper of the courthouse in Rathkeal and as bridewell keeper from 1832 to 1848. He was also paid for providing fuel and stationery to the court and for 'subsistence for prisoners'.

SUMMONS SERVERS, PROCESS SERVERS AND CIVIL BILL OFFICERS

Pat Boland (1860–1935)

Pat Boland was interpreter at the quarter sessions court, Sligo division, from at least 1896 until at least 1899. In the 1901 census he is a 40-year-old farmer and civil bill officer living in Castleconor East.

Daniel Boyce (1825–1915)

Daniel Boyce of Drumany was civil bill officer for the Fannet district from 1865 until his resignation in 1876 because 'his other duties precluded his discharging those of process server satisfactorily'.[65] His other duties were as court crier,[66] as interpreter at quarter sessions for the division of Lifford and as interpreter at

62 *Sligo Champion*, 5 May 1838.
63 CSO/RP/1828/878, NAI.
64 *Limerick Chronicle*, 15 Mar. 1848.
65 *Londonderry Sentinel*, 15 July 1876.
66 Ibid., 14 July 1887.

assizes in Donegal from spring 1876 until 1904, when he was replaced by his son John Boyce. In the 1901 census his occupation is farmer.

Condy Boyle (1819–1909)

In 1851, Condy Boyle from Dungloe, Donegal, combined a number of roles: he was a process server for the division of Donegal,[67] quarter sessions interpreter, court crier and also bailiff to the marquis of Conyngham. For some years he was also a poor law guardian in the Glenties.[68] He claimed payments for work carried out at Dungloe petty sessions in 1894 and 1895. In 1904 Judge Cooke asked solicitors to give early notice if they needed an interpreter so that Condy Boyle, who was 86 years of age, could be requested to attend. According to a somewhat exaggerated account in the *Irish Independent*, when he died in 1909 he was close to 100 years old and had been crier and interpreter for over 75 years.[69] His death record suggests that he was 90 years of age, while the presentment records indicate that he worked at quarter sessions for the division of Donegal from spring 1876 until at least 1898.

Thomas, William and Michael Brew

Thomas Brew acted as interpreter at Clare quarter sessions in 1854 and 1855 and was replaced in 1855 by William Brew, Knock, also a process server.[70] William was immediately replaced by Michael Brew (1808–77) who continued in the role until 1877. It seems likely that the three were related.

John Clancy (1813–96)

The bridewell in Oughterard, Galway, was inspected in 1872 and the inspector general recorded that the unnamed bridewell keeper was paid £24 12*s.* and was also employed as court keeper and interpreter at quarter sessions. At the time of the inspection of the bridewell, there were no prisoners in custody, but there was a cow in the exercise yard, which, according to the Inspector-General, was 'clearly illegal. See 10th rule of 109th section of Prisons Act'. However, the keeper/interpreter pleaded he had no scythe to cut the grass, and the cow 'was brought in to eat it'.[71] This man is John Clancy, who, according to *Thom's Directory*,[72] was the Oughterard bridewell keeper and whose name appears as interpreter at quarter sessions for the division of Clifden in 1868.

67 *Ballyshannon Herald*, 31 Jan. 1851.
68 *Donegal Independent*, 6 Apr. 1889.
69 *Irish Independent*, 22 Jan. 1909.
70 *Clare Journal & Ennis Advertiser*, 23 Feb. 1860.
71 *Fiftieth report of the inspectors-general on the general state of the prisons of Ireland 1871, with appendix* [C 535], HC 1872, xxxii, 381.
72 *Thom's Irish Almanac and Official Directory for the Year 1872*, findmypast.ie.

John Clancy was process server and interpreter at Clifden quarter sessions, Galway, from at least 1868 until 1896. The Outerard petty sessions clerk applied to the chief secretary's office for a payment of 15 shillings in 1894 and for two payments of 10 shillings for Clancy in 1895.[73] According to his death certificate, he was also a court keeper.

James Clifford (1860–1943)

James Clifford, Castlequin, Kerry, was a sheriff's bailiff from at least 1891[74] and summons server from 1889.[75] He seems to have begun interpreting at petty sessions level.[76] He worked as interpreter at quarter sessions from 1898–1900 and intermittently thereafter at assizes, in 1903 and 1907–9. He may have continued as assizes interpreter until 1925 – it is difficult to be sure because the assizes interpreter is not named for the years 1910–24. In the 1901 census his occupation is civil bill officer and in 1911 he is a farmer.

Edward Collins (1855–1928)

Edward Collins was appointed quarter sessions interpreter for Cork's west riding in about 1880 and was a civil bill officer from at least 1888.[77] In 1907 Collins refused to get involved in an action to recover £72 in rent and wrote to the judge at king's bench division as follows:

> Sir – Owing to the disturbed state of the country, I could not serve writs for rents. I am sorry that I can't do it, but my life would be in danger, as the people are mad in that part of the county. I shall be happy to attend to any other business at any time. Your obedient servant Edward Collins CBO[78]

The Courts of Justice Act 1924 abolished the division of the county into two ridings, and this created problems for Collins, as his interpreter salary, previously paid without question, was not paid in 1926.[79] The case of Edward Collins, civil bill officer for Macroom, occupation 'interpreter' in the 1911 census, was raised in the Dáil in 1927. At that stage, he was 77 years of age and had worked as a summons server for fifty-eight years and as a civil bill officer for fifty-seven years. He was discharged from his job without any form of compensation or pension. The posts

73 CSO/LB/71, pp 647, 861, NAI.
74 *Kerry Weekly Reporter*, 14 Feb. 1891.
75 Ibid., 3 Mar. 1889.
76 CSO/LB/46, p. 607, NAI.
77 *Cork Examiner*, 6 Apr. 1888.
78 Ibid., 17 Apr. 1907.
79 Ibid., 23 Jan. 1926.

of summons server and civil bill officer were combined into one post, that of summons server, under the Court Officers Act 1926.[80]

Michael Collins (1820–87)

Michael Collins got tangled up in a scandal where it was alleged that he had paid £30 to Kerry assistant barrister William McDermott in order to procure an appointment as interpreter.[81] Collins, who worked at Kerry assizes from 1856, was appointed interpreter at quarter sessions along with Patrick O'Sullivan in 1867 and the *Tralee Chronicle* noted that Collins was 'well qualified for the office'.[82] In addition, he was a civil bill officer in Tralee and served legal papers 'for many respectable firms'. He was a bailiff until 1867, when he resigned and commented that 'for a £100 a year I would not be mixed up with such a set'.[83] Shortly before his death he was appointed court keeper.[84] According to a brief newspaper obituary, Collins had also worked as sheriff's officer and as court crier. The writer commented that 'for a man in such a peculiarly insidious position he always managed to retain his popularity'.[85]

Richard P. Conway (1864–1917)

Richard P. Conway worked as a process server for the barony of Iveragh and the division of Killarney from at least 1896.[86] He went on to be appointed interpreter[87] and civil bill officer at Caherciveen quarter sessions in March 1900.[88] As secretary of Cahirciveen school attendance committee on a salary of £15 a year, he was required to attend petty sessions prosecutions of parents who did not send their children to school. However, there was an issue about payment and Conway informed the committee that if he was not paid for this work, 'I will not be long there.'[89]

Michael Curreen

In 1871, Michael Curreen replaced disgraced Michael Hackett as county of Waterford quarter sessions interpreter, a post he held until 1884.[90] He was also process server for Lismore, Waterford.[91]

80 Dáil Éireann, vol. 19, 26 Apr. 1927.
81 *Kerry Evening Post*, 19 June 1858.
82 *Tralee Chronicle & Killarney Echo*, 12 Feb. 1867.
83 *Kerry Evening Post*, 10 Dec. 1870.
84 *Kerry Sentinel*, 28 May 1887.
85 *Kerry Weekly Reporter*, 19 Nov. 1887.
86 *Kerry Sentinel*, 6 May 1896.
87 Kerry county council, 1900 financial statement – expenditure (Kerry Local History & Archives, Tralee).
88 *Kerry Evening Post*, 5 Dec. 1900.
89 *Kerry Sentinel*, 21 Sept. 1910.
90 County of Waterford books of presentments, Waterford County Archives.
91 *Waterford Standard*, 16 Apr. 1884.

William Dineen (1835–1922)

William Dineen, Rathmore, Killarney, was appointed interpreter at quarter sessions in Kerry in 1899[92] and worked there until 1910.[93] He was also a process server from at least 1900.[94]

Michael Dowd (1848–1917)

Michael Dowd was employed originally as a civil bill officer from at least 1895,[95] then as an interpreter at quarter sessions in Kerry from 1899 until 1917.[96] In addition, he was special bailiff from 1892,[97] and process server from 1900.[98] He was also a regular interpreter at Dingle petty sessions.[99]

John Eaton

John Eaton, Lanesborough, was assizes interpreter, court crier and bugler in Roscommon from at least 1849 until 1864. In addition, he was a process server.[100] As sheriff's bailiff he was once threatened with a pitchfork and forced out of a man's house when he attempted to execute a decree.[101]

Bernard Farrell

Bernard Farrell, Ballintobber, was appointed civil bill officer in 1832.[102] Grand jury books of presentments indicate that he was quarter sessions and assizes interpreter in Roscommon in 1837.[103] After that date, names of interpreters are not included in subsequent books until John Eaton appears in 1849.[104]

92 County of Kerry, spring 1899 forms and receipts, NAI.
93 Kerry county council, financial statement – expenditure, March 1910, Kerry Local History & Archives, Tralee.
94 *Kerry Weekly Reporter*, 17 Nov. 1900.
95 *Kerry Sentinel*, 27 July 1895.
96 Kerry county council, 1899 financial statement – expenditure, Kerry Local History & Archives, Tralee.
97 *Kerry Weekly Reporter*, 27 Feb. 1892.
98 Ibid., 23 Nov. 1901.
99 *Kerryman*, 30 Nov. 1907.
100 *Roscommon Journal*, 18 Jan. 1845.
101 Ibid., 23 Feb. 1839.
102 *Roscommon & Leitrim Gazette*, 7 Apr. 1832.
103 County of Roscommon summer assizes 1837, NLI.
104 County of Roscommon books of presentments, Roscommon County Library.

George Fenton

George Fenton's name appears once in the grand jury presentments for Sligo in summer 1826 when he was listed as crown court interpreter.[105] He was also a process server for Easky.[106]

Michael Hackett (1829–)

Michael Hackett, who had been in India for twelve years serving his 'Queen and country', was appointed interpreter and civil bill officer for Dungarvan district in June 1868.[107] In December 1869 he was summoned to petty sessions to explain why he broke the door of a house when serving a process but the case was dismissed.[108] In 1871, he was still an interpreter at quarter sessions, but by now 'late process server' and was charged at petty sessions with receiving 4*s.* 1*d.* to serve two processes that he neither served nor handed over to a process server. He was sent to trial at quarter sessions,[109] sentenced to three calendar months in jail[110] and a new interpreter was appointed in his place.

Patrick Hackett

Patrick Hackett was interpreter at Waterford quarter sessions and process server from 1861. He was also a gamekeeper, an occupation that was far from highly regarded. According to folklore sources: 'They weren't popular. They'd prosecute any man they found crossing the land whether he had a dog or no dog with him. If you crossed it without anything at all, you were summoned.'[111] In 1864, while serving a summons, he was struck and cut. However, when the case was heard at petty sessions, Hackett told the court that he did not want the man, who frequently appeared in court, to be severely punished.

Philip Harrington (1798–1865)

Philip Harrington is listed as a publican in *Slater's Directory* in 1846.[112] He was interpreter at Cork's west riding quarter sessions from at least 1845 and process server for Bantry from at least 1852[113] until 1865, when an advertisement appeared

105 Sligo book of presentments summer 1826, Sligo County Library.
106 *Sligo Journal*, 24 Dec. 1830.
107 *Waterford Mail*, 24 June 1868.
108 Ibid., 22 Dec. 1869.
109 *Waterford News*, 7 Apr. 1871.
110 Irish prison registers, County and City of Waterford Gaol, criminal register and description book 1871, p. 44, NAI.
111 Irish Folklore Commission, vol. 1196, p. 255.
112 Slater National Commercial Directory of Ireland, 1846, p. 196.
113 *Cork Examiner*, 2 Aug. 1852, 6 June 1855.

in the *Cork Examiner* for a replacement interpreter.[114] In 1852 at Cork spring assizes he gave evidence concerning the sentence of seven years' transportation passed against Cornelius Healy four years previously. Healy had been sentenced but when he fell ill with fever he was confined in a fever shed, recovered and escaped from custody. In 1863 at Cork county court, Harrington was examined and gave a good character to a prisoner charged with stealing two lambs.[115]

William Hegarty

William Hegarty was appointed process server for Cork's east riding in 1843.[116] By 1845 he was also interpreter at east riding quarter sessions and continued to hold the two posts until at least 1864.

Patrick Keane (1831–1902)

Patrick Keane was a civil bill officer and interpreter at Waterford quarter sessions from 1885 until 1902. He also interpreted regularly at Dungarvan petty sessions. In 1902 the clerk of the crown and peace wrote to the council to inform them that Keane 'was old and incapable of performing the duties of the position'. The councillors agreed to ask Keane to resign unless he was competent.[117] In the 1901 census, Keane is an 82-year-old civil bill officer in Dungarvan. However, according to his death certificate in 1902 he was 71 years of age.

Humphrey Kelleher (1825–1902)

Humphrey Kelleher was a process server in Bantry from at least 1865[118] and may have been appointed interpreter for Cork's west riding quarter sessions that year.

In 1901, in a case taken by a man and his son against a woman for beating their cattle and using abusive language, then former county interpreter Humphrey Kelleher was present at Bantry petty sessions when an interpreter was required but refused to take on the role unless he was paid five shillings. The defendant's husband offered two and six, which Kelleher 'indignantly refused' and the bench said they would not allow Kelleher to accept payment from him and instead said they would send a certificate to the crown solicitor and 'he should be satisfied with what he would get'. Apparently, Kelleher had previously been paid one shilling for similar work, so he then said he would accept two and six. The bench again refused permission and Kelleher eventually agreed to await payment from the crown solicitor.[119]

114 Ibid., 8 Jan. 1865.
115 Ibid., 24 July 1863.
116 Ibid., 3 Nov. 1843.
117 *Waterford Standard*, 15 Feb. 1902.
118 *Skibbereen & West Carbery Eagle*, 18 Nov. 1865
119 *Southern Star*, 24 Aug. 1901

In 1902 solicitor James Flynn of Bantry wrote to Cork county council to request that Kelleher be granted superannuation. The chairman refused the request stating that Kelleher had been appointed by the county court judge. Flynn replied that Kelleher did not know where to look for superannuation.[120] In September the same year, the interpreter took his own life. Apparently, he had been in an accident some time previously and was unable to work and 'the bad state of his health and the absence of means to support him appear to have unhinged his reason and driven him to the desperate deed which launched him into eternity'.[121]

Patrick Kildea or Kilday (1802–88)

Process server Patrick Kildea of Brockagh was replaced in this role on his appointment as interpreter, after an examination as to his fitness, at Donegal quarter sessions in 1853.[122] He was employed as Irish interpreter at quarter sessions and assizes on full salary of £40 a year until 1874. Unusually, he appears to have resigned from his post, and even more unusually, in 1878 the Donegal grand jury paid him a once-off half-year's superannuation of £20.[123]

Francis Mannion

Francis Mannion from Claregalway, a 'respectable solicitor's clerk', applied for and was appointed to the post of summons server in 1867 with the support of three attorneys 'on the grounds that he could act as interpreter'.[124] In 1868 he was paid £5 for interpreting at assizes in Galway. He was also a process server.[125]

James McGrath

James McGrath, Quin, was interpreter at Clare assizes from summer 1855 until 1874. He was also a process server.[126]

William Morris (1826–80)

William Morris was process server for Kinvarra in the division of Loughrea, County Galway. In addition, he was interpreter at quarter sessions for the division of Loughrea from at least 1868.

120 Ibid., 5 July 1902.
121 Ibid., 27 Sept. 1902.
122 *Ballyshannon Herald*, 9 Dec. 1853.
123 County of Donegal, grand jury presentments, 1878, Donegal County Archives.
124 *Galway Vindicator*, 23 Jan. 1867.
125 Ibid., 14 Nov. 1866.
126 *Clare Journal & Ennis Advertiser*, 23 Feb. 1860.

Richard Phelan (1831–94)

Richard Phelan was a summons server at Half-way House, Waterford[127]and process server in Passage, district of Waterford.[128] He was appointed interpreter at assizes in County of Waterford in 1868 and employed there until 1894.[129]

Edward Walsh (1839–97)

Interpreter at Waterford assizes for two years from 1895,[130] according to his death certificate. Edward Walsh was also a civil bill officer.

PETTY SESSIONS INTERPRETERS

William Blood (1846–1909)

William Blood acted on occasion as Irish interpreter at Ballyvaughan petty sessions in Clare. In *Guy's Cork Almanac 1891*, he is listed as a civil bill officer,[131] which is also his occupation in the 1901 census.

Michael Connor (1858–1928)

Michael Connor was a process server,[132] civil bill officer[133] and interpreter at Ballinrobe petty sessions from at least 1887. The following year he was appointed bailiff to assist the under-sheriff for Mayo.[134] However, he had a chequered history. In 1892, he was charged at Ballinrobe petty sessions with assaulting and using vilifying language towards a woman and sentenced to one month with hard labour in Castlebar jail.[135] Later that year he was again sentenced to one month in jail for being drunk and disorderly.[136] In April 1893 he appeared in court charged with assaulting his wife, promised to take the pledge to abstain from drink and was bound over to keep the peace.[137] The following month he was prosecuted for assaulting a man and for being drunk and fined 10*s.* and £1 respectively.[138] In September 1893 he

127 *Guy's Cork Almanac*, 1891.
128 *Waterford Standard*, 5 Dec. 1877.
129 County of Waterford, books of presentments, Waterford County Archives, Dungarvan.
130 Ibid.
131 *Guy's Cork Almanac*, 1891.
132 *Ballinrobe Chronicle*, 12 Nov. 1887.
133 Ibid., 3 Dec. 1887.
134 Ibid., 8 Dec. 1888.
135 Ibid., 26 Mar. 1892.
136 Ibid., 29 Oct. 1892.
137 Ibid., 22 Apr. 1893.
138 Ibid., 6 May 1893.

was charged with assaulting the police and sentenced to three months' imprisonment with hard labour and fined 40 shillings for being drunk and disorderly or in default one month's imprisonment.[139] In January 1898 he was an inmate at the workhouse, charged with insubordination for leaving the premises without permission on Christmas Day,[140] and in July he was charged with forcibly entering the workhouse grounds.[141] In September 1899 he unsuccessfully requested permission to leave the workhouse without his wife.[142]

However, he seems to have reinvented himself because he was still *in situ* as summons server and interpreter in 1909 and 1915 when there were confrontations about who should act as interpreter – the summons server who also acted as interpreter, or the salaried interpreter. In 1909 in an assault case there were a number of Irish-speaking witnesses; Connor acted as interpreter for the first witness, but Peter O'Toole, interpreter of the county court, had been recruited for the other witnesses. Mr Bell said Connor was an official of the petty sessions court (i.e. a summons server), and had not been employed by either side and the court agreed that he should continue interpreting.[143] A similar standoff occurred in 1915 in an assault case: Connor objected to O'Toole acting as interpreter for a defendant, stating that 'he [Connor] was appointed by the magistrates to be interpreter in this court' and was paid one shilling each time he carried out this work. The defendant's solicitor argued that there was no official interpreter in the court and the witnesses could nominate whoever they liked provided he was approved by the court. The chairman suggested that the two toss up for the work but by that stage O'Toole had left the courtroom.[144]

John Faherty

In 1895 Resident Magistrate Gardiner wrote to the undersecretary at Dublin Castle on two occasions about the claim of John Faherty, interpreter, for acting as interpreter at Spiddal petty sessions. These letters were followed by three letters from John Faherty himself and payment was duly authorized. However, Faherty must have been frustrated with the lack of a system for payment, and long delays involved in obtaining payment. On 8 April 1896 he wrote again, this time to say he intended 'getting Forms for Interpreter at Petty Sessions printed as I believe they would be more convenient than MS forms' and enclosed two prototypes (figs 7 and 8) with a request for 'indorsement [*sic*]' of one which he could show 'to the Justices'.

139 Ibid., 2 Sept. 1893.
140 Ibid., 29 Jan. 1898.
141 Ibid., 9 July 1898.
142 *Western People*, 16 Sept. 1899.
143 *Mayo News*, 15 May 1909.
144 *Western People*, 10 July 1915.

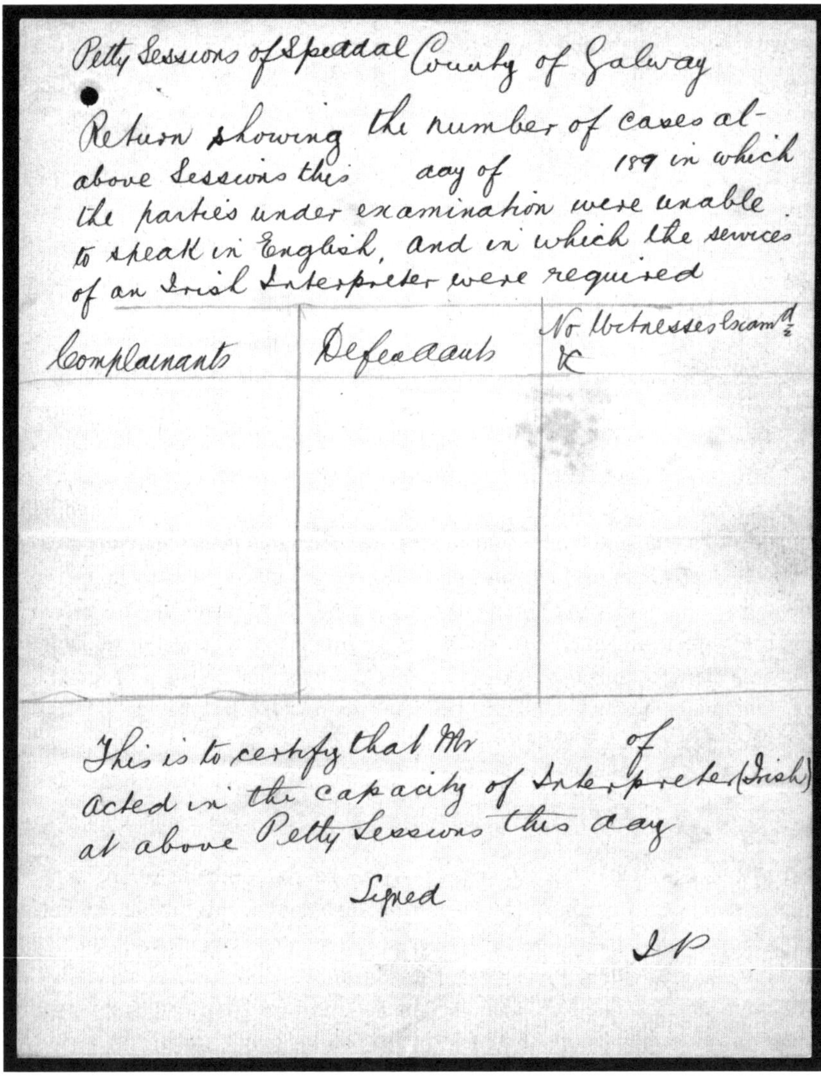

Petty Sessions of Speddal County of Galway

Return showing the number of cases at above Sessions this day of 189 in which the parties under examination were unable to speak in English, and in which the services of an Irish Interpreter were required

Complainants	Defendants	No Witnesses Examd &c

This is to certify that Mr of acted in the capacity of Interpreter (Irish) at above Petty Sessions this day

Signed

JP

Figure 7 One of John Faherty's prototype forms for interepreters at petty sessions, courtesy of the National Archives of Ireland.

However, Faherty's suggestion was not welcomed. Instead of corresponding directly with him, a letter was sent to the inspector general of the Royal Irish Constabulary in Galway to say:

> Please have it explained to this man by one of your local officers that his proposal to have forms printed for use in Petty Sessions is not one that can

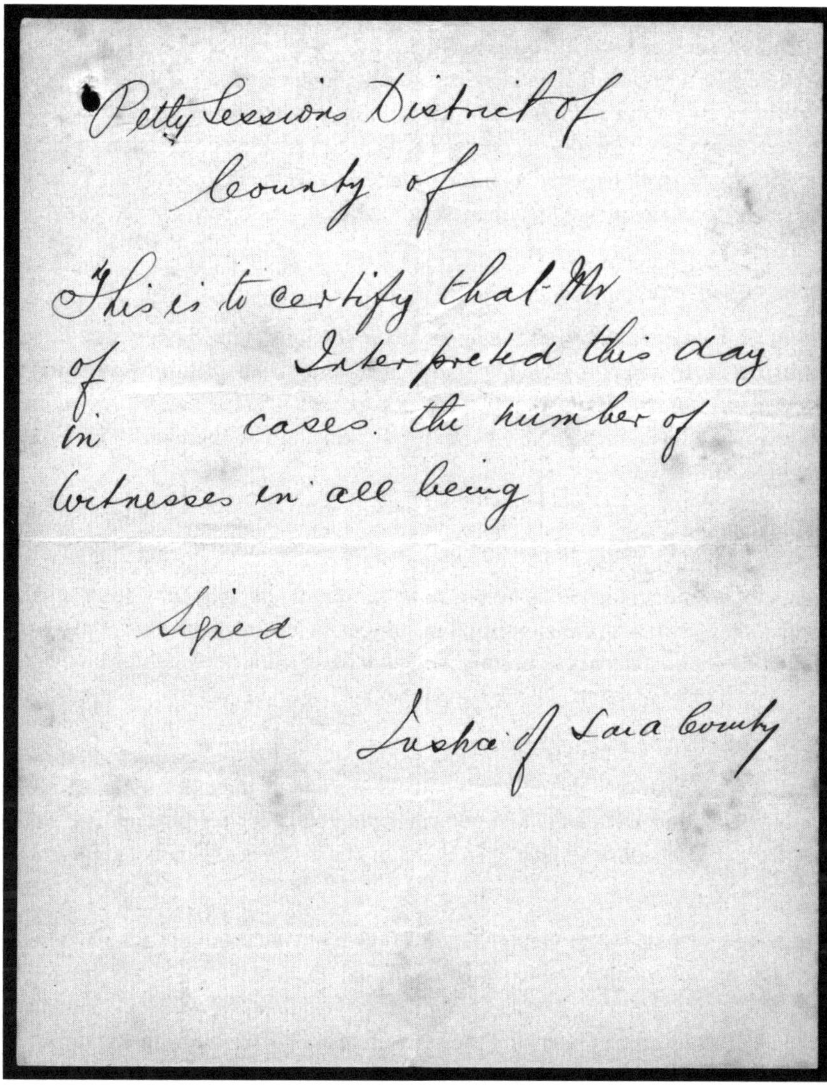

Petty Sessions District of
County of
This is to certify that Mr
of Interpreted this day
in cases. the number of
witnesses in all being

Signed

Justice of Said County

Figure 8 One of John Faherty's prototype forms for interepreters at petty sessions, courtesy of the National Archives of Ireland.

> be sanctioned, and that he is quite unauthorized to sign himself 'Interpreter at Petty Sessions'.[145]

As the post of interpreter at petty sessions did not exist, John Faherty was not entitled to use this title, even though it is possible that he worked there regularly. A

145 CSO/RP/6073/96, NAI.

visit from an RIC officer would put a stop to any ideas above his station. However, by 1917, a form had been introduced for payments to intepreters at petty sessions. Interpreters had to state if they were summons servers and give details of the number of times, cases and witnesses and the amount of time involved.[146]

Faherty was also a process server for Knock Spiddal in the division of Clifden, Galway.[147] In 1895–8, he acted as interpreter on at least eight occasions at Spiddal petty sessions and requested payment from the chief secretary's office.[148]

William Gillespie (1800–51)

William Gillespie was clerk of Newport petty sessions[149] in Mayo where he acted as interpreter. In 1847, together with his wife and seven children, he emigrated to New York. On the ship's manifest his occupation is listed as land agent. In the 1850 census he was living in New York and working as a bookkeeper.[150] He died the following year.[151]

Roger McGuinness (1867–1937)

Roger McGuinness is listed as a summons server in the 1901 and 1911 censuses. Between 1886 and 1888 he submitted a number of claims to the chief secretary's office at Dublin Castle for interpreting work at Crossmolina petty sessions in Mayo.[152]

Edward Tighe (1824–1910)

Edward Tighe, Gladree, Belmullet, was in contact with the chief secretary's office at Dublin Castle in 1885 and 1886 about remuneration for his interpreting work at Belmullet petty sessions in Mayo.[153] In the 1901 census he is a 74-year-old postmaster.

RELIEVING OFFICER AND SANITARY OFFICER

Owen Dunne (1802–78)

In 1862 Owen Dunne applied for the post of assizes interpreter in Mayo but was unsuccessful.[154] In 1869 he was appointed summons server and in 1870 he was

146 CSO/RP/1917/2109 and CSO/RP/1917/2700, NAI.
147 *Galway Vindicator*, 30 July 1887.
148 CSO/RP/19549/95, CSO/RP/20185/95, CSO/RP/20830/95, CSO/RP/22366/95, CSO/RP/654/96, CSO/RP/2097/96, CSO/RP/3828/96, CSO/RP/15599/98, NAI.
149 *Mayo Constitution*, 22 Nov. 1836.
150 US census, 1850, Wm Gillespie, New York city, ward 7, district 2, roll M432-540, p. 252b, image 139, Ancestry.com.
151 *Mayo Constitution*, 15 Apr. 1851.
152 CSO/RP/13390/87, CSO/RP/2392/88 and CSO/RP/3008/88, NAI.
153 CSO/RP/24399/85, CSO/RP/141/86, CSO/RP/692/86, NAI.
154 *Connaught Telegraph*, 12 Mar. 1862.

a sanitary officer.[155] In 1877 he interpreted at Castlebar petty sessions and was described as 'our well-known local interpreter',[156] suggesting that he was active as an interpreter in other settings as well. He was probably one of many such interpreters whose role was undocumented.

Henry Roach

By March 1862, Henry Roach had been appointed interpreter at quarter sessions in Mayo, 'an appointment which has given general satisfaction'.[157] He immediately applied to be appointed at assizes and his application was supported by a barrister called Mr O'Malley and a solicitor, Mr Gibbons. Another applicant, Owen Dunne, who had 'excellent recommendations' from the rector and parish priest and several other 'respectable gentlemen', had the support of solicitor Mr O'Dowd, who objected to Roach on the grounds that he was a relieving officer, but was overruled by the grand jury foreman. O'Dowd's objection was legitimate: relieving officers, who were paid between £35 and £70 a year, were supposed to devote themselves to the performance of their duties, without following any other trade or profession.[158] Roach's supporters argued that it made more sense to have the same interpreter for both assizes and quarter sessions courts.[159]

However, the combined roles of relieving officer and court interpreter led to problems. In July 1862, Rev. Mr Gibbons wrote to the commissioners for the relief of the poor in Ireland complaining, among other things, that Henry Roach was so busy as an interpreter at assizes, quarter sessions and petty sessions, that he had no time to fulfil his duties as relieving officer. According to this letter, Roach was also a poor rate collector.[160] In 1865, the Castlebar board of guardians read a letter of dismissal for Roach on the grounds of alleged neglect of duty. In September 1865, Roach was appointed sanitary inspector on a salary of £2 a month on the condition that he live in Castlebar. That October, Roach's letter of resignation as relieving officer was accepted.[161] In 1871, the grand jury was informed that Roach had 'quit the country'.[162]

HIGH CONSTABLES AND CONSERVATORS

High constables and conservators were appointed by the grand juries. The former were baronial collectors of grand jury tax, usually appointed for a one-year

155 Ibid., 13 July 1870.
156 Ibid., 3 Mar. 1877.
157 *Dublin Weekly Nation*, 1 Mar. 1862.
158 First annual report of the commissioners for administering the laws for relief of the poor in Ireland (1848), p. 84.
159 *Connaught Telegraph*, 5 and 12 Mar. 1862.
160 Ibid., 23 July 1862.
161 *Connaught Telegraph*, 11 Oct. 1865.
162 *Ballinrobe Chronicle*, 29 July 1871.

period,[163] while the latter were deputed to oversee public roads and were described by the *Southern Reporter* as persons 'appointed to prevent nuisances'.[164]

John Anderson

In County Kilkenny, high constables were 'respectable gentlemen farmers' and could be appointed for longer than one year. As high constable for Gowran barony John Anderson was paid £56 0*s.* 8*d.* in spring 1826 plus £7 7*s.* 2¼*d.* on arrears, and in 1827 he was paid a commission of £62 12*s.* 7*d.* at spring assizes. Anderson interpreted regularly at County Kilkenny assizes from 1817 until 1839 and on one occasion at the city of Kilkenny assizes in 1824. Unusually, his name is followed by 'esq.' or 'esquire', suggesting that he owned property. Apparently, he had studied Latin; the *Kilkenny Journal* suggested that he would be an appropriate person to interpret Baron Smith's Latin phrases for the grand jury.[165]

George James Drinan

In 1815 George Drinan was paid £3 8*s.* 3*d.* as interpreter of the Irish language at city of Cork assizes.[166] As presentment records for a number of years are missing, the duration of his service is unknown. Drinan was also a conservator.[167]

William Hanburry/Hanbury

In 1829, William Hanburry was paid £4 12*s.* 3½*d.* for interpreting at the town of Galway assizes and appointed high constable on a salary of £10. In spring 1834, he was paid £13 16*s.* 10½*d.* for his work as interpreter in the crown court, insolvent court and record court.[168]

AUCTIONEER

Thomas Heffernan (1794–1866)

Interpreter provision was coming under attack at grand jury level in Tipperary's north riding in 1848. Mr John Bayly asked 'if the interpreter for this part of the County was in attendance, or had he attended at Assizes and Quarter Sessions'. Mr Going replied, 'He always does. I heard him called upon several times at the

163 7 Geo. 2, c. 12, s. 3.
164 *Southern Reporter*, 19 Oct. 1833.
165 *Kilkenny Journal*, 30 March 1833
166 County of city of Cork, statement of assessment spring, 1815, NLI.
167 *Pigot & Co City of Dublin and Hibernian Provincial Directory*, 1824, p. 244.
168 Town of Galway books of presentment summer assizes 1828 and 1829, Galway County Library Headquarters.

assizes' and the half-year's salary was passed.[169] The interpreter at the time was Thomas Heffernan, interpreter for Tipperary's north riding and south riding, who was also an auctioneer.[170]

It seems that Thomas Heffernan almost lost his job in 1850 when 'The presentment of Mr Thomas Heffernan, Interpreter of Crown Court &c., which was disallowed by the Grand Jury, was fiated by the Judge, and he was retained in his office.'[171] The report does not explain why the grand jury disallowed this presentment, although there was probably less demand for an interpreter in the north riding than in the more Irish-speaking south riding. Between 1852 and 1860, Heffernan was paid two-fifths of the salary, that is £2, for interpreting at assizes and £6 for interpreting at quarter sessions in Tipperary's north riding. From 1855–62, in Tipperary's south riding, he was paid three-fifths of the salary, or £3 for assizes work and £9 for quarter sessions. In 1860, the *Nenagh Guardian* reported that:

> [T]he several county officers' salaries passed without remark, except the presentment of Mr Thomas Heffernan, £2, his half-year's salary, due this assizes, on the reading of which Mr Lanigan asked if the situation was necessary, as he hadn't known an instance for several years of the interpreter's being required?[172]

Another grand juror, a Mr Dwyer, commented to laughter that 'We can't say when he may be required in Tipperary, as only the other day an interpreter had to be taken before a committee of the House of Commons in the case of the Clare election petition.' The presentment was passed.

In 1861, after giving evidence in a case against a father and son called Connell, Heffernan was called 'an old sinner, who had sworn falsely against the Connells' at the trial in Clonmel by a shopkeeper and farmer called Lonergan. Heffernan took a slander case against Lonergan and was awarded sixpence[173] damages and sixpence costs.[174] Two months later, Heffernan appeared at the Court of bankruptcy and insolvency in Cashel.[175] In July 1861, in a bid to return to solvency, he inserted an advertisement in the *Tipperary Vindicator* (fig. 9).

The *Waterford News* published a pen portrait of Heffernan in 1868:

> Tom Heffernan was for several years the Tipperary interpreter at assizes and quarter sessions, and was, no doubt, considered 'a good Irishian', speaking

169 *Nenagh Guardian*, 18 Mar. 1848.
170 *Freeman's Journal*, 14 Mar. 1861.
171 *Nenagh Guardian*, 23 Mar. 1850.
172 Ibid., 17 Mar. 1860.
173 *Freeman's Journal*, 14 Mar. 1861.
174 *Dublin Evening Mail*, 14 Mar. 1861.
175 Ibid., 18 May 1861.

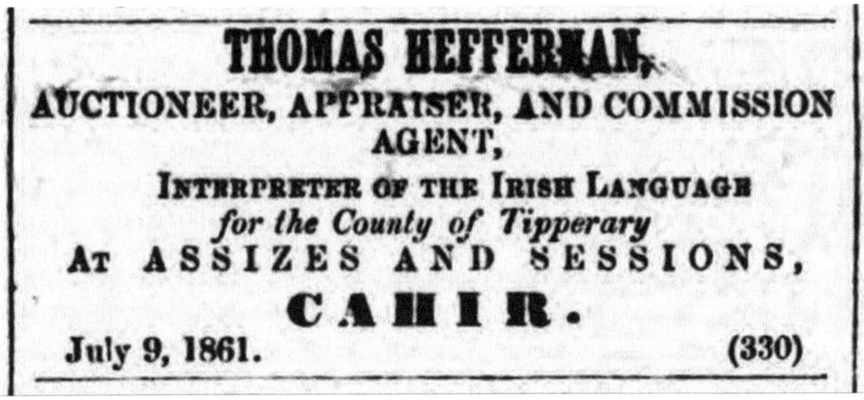

Figure 9 Thomas Heffernan's advertisement, courtesy of British Newspaper Archive.

> like 'one to the manor born'. He was well known wherever he went, with his bright red face – as red as can well be imagined. He was up to all the gossip of the countay, resided at a handsome cottage near the town of Cahir, called the Swiss Cottage, and was on familiar terms with the whole county. In addition to his accomplishments as a 'linguist', he became an auctioneer and broker, but was not equally successful in that capacity. Tom claimed a certain degree of relationship with some of the gentry of his native county of Waterford. How far the claim went I am not in a position to acquaint the reader; and though he loved the Temperance movement, and almost adored Father Mathew, it was at that respectful distance which forbade him to accept the pledge, or enrol himself under the sacred banner of the apostle of the good cause. Tom, in fact, had an eye to the glass, to which his rubicund physiognomy bore ample testimony, and which reflected the sparkle of the 'mountain dew' for which no place was more famous than Cahir. He usually looked well; but it must be confessed that the livery which he was obliged to wear sometimes, in compliance with the wish of the sheriff, did not suit a man of his pretentions, and I am not aware that the 'interpreter' as a rule, is asked to wear it. Tom left the stage for a successor who resides in the same town, and who is very well up to his business too. But I think that the days of interpreters in general are wearing away, and that, like other of our native institutions, they are destined to live only in reminiscences for the time to come.[176]

It would be interesting to know what 'livery' Heffernan was obliged to wear when interpreting in court. From at least 1844, Heffernan lived at Swiss Cottage, a beautiful 'cottage orné' situated outside Cahir, which was built in 1810, restored in the

176 *Waterford News*, 11 Sept. 1868.

1980s and is open to the public. He either rented it or he was a caretaker and/or a water bailiff.[177]

CLERKS

Patrick Flynn (–1862)

Patrick Flynn was appointed interpreter at Galway quarter sessions in 1853, when his selection was described as 'judicious and impartial' by the *Tuam Herald*.[178] As well as being employed as the county interpreter until his death in 1862, he was a law clerk and was described by the *Mayo Constitution* as 'a man of rare intelligence', who knew a lot about local history and genealogy.[179] Law clerks worked in solicitors' offices. In 1869 an advertisement specified: 'writes a good hand; engrosses deeds well, and whose character will bear strict inquiry' and 'a married man preferred'.[180]

Patrick Kennedy (1852–1934)

Patrick Kennedy, Glenties, listed his occupation as 'solicitor's managing clerk' in the 1901 census and 'solicitor's clerk' in the 1911 census. Kennedy was quarter sessions interpreter for the division of Donegal, possibly from 1904. In 1920, he wrote twice to the chief secretary's office, first to apply for an increase in salary[181] and then in relation to the refusal of Donegal county council to pay his salary. In order to resolve the second issue, the decision was that the sheriff would pay.[182] After the formation of the Irish Free State, it was mooted that interpreters were no longer needed in that particular circuit court because the judge spoke Irish.[183] However, there appears to have been a change of heart on the issue and interpreters continued to be employed in 1928.[184]

Antony O'Donnell or McDonnell (1860–1920)

In the 1901 census Antony O'Donnell, Fairhill Road, Galway, is a 45-year-old commercial clerk. In 1911, he completed the census form in Irish. He was court interpreter in Galway from 1901–20. In 1902, Galway county council voted in

177 Personal communication from Patricia Hassett, Office of Public Works, Swiss Cottage.
178 *Tuam Herald*, 5 Mar. 1853.
179 *Mayo Constitution*, 14 Jan. 1862.
180 *Cork Constitution*, 17 Aug. 1869.
181 CSO/RP/3276/1920, NAI.
182 CSO/RP/22726/1920, NAI.
183 Minutes of a meeting of the finance committee of Tirconaill county council was held 18 Aug. 1925, Donegal County Archives, Lifford.
184 *Irish Times*, 28 Jan. 1928.

favour of increasing his salary from £20 to £30 a year.[185] He made a number of applications to the chief secretary's office at Dublin Castle for payment for his work at the winter assizes and at Galway petty sessions. In 1913 a judge commented somewhat sardonically that McDonnell was 'a most charming man whom he had not seen for five years, and who seemed to be thoroughly acquainted with the witnesses, whose evidence he interpreted so well'.[186] O'Donnell was paid a war bonus of £25 in 1920 in addition to his salary of £30.[187]

Peter Rip(p)ingham or Repingham (1828–93)

On the death of Michael Rush, who had been interpreter for a mere three months from April to July 1871, Peter Rippingham, formerly a law clerk with Mr Griffin,[188] was appointed interpreter for Mayo crown court and quarter sessions where he worked until his death in 1893.

Patrick Staunton

Patrick Staunton was appointed Irish interpreter at Cork assizes in 1909. Five years later he was charged with and pleaded guilty to embezzlement. Apparently, he had been working as secretary to a company called Carew Ltd in Tipperary since leaving school but was keen to set up a motor garage and repair shop with some friends in Cork. The managing director of the company took a very lenient view and stated that the accused was 'a brilliant young man – a good French and German correspondent and Irish interpreter to the courts in Cork'. Staunton was let out on bail and reportedly was contemplating going to America.[189]

FARMERS

John Boyce (1861–1931)

In the 1901 census, John Boyce's occupation is farmer and deputy county court interpreter to his father Daniel Boyce. According to the *Donegal Independent*, in 1904, 'on the motion of Mr Hanna, seconded by Mr McArthur, John Boyce, Drumany, was unanimously appointed to the position of Irish interpreter at the assizes at a salary of ten pounds a year'.[190] Boyce was also an auctioneer.[191] He

185 Minutes of proceedings of the Galway county council quarterly meeting held 19 Aug. 1902, galway.ie/digitalarchives.
186 *Connacht Tribune*, 22 Mar. 1913.
187 Ibid., 7 Feb. 1920.
188 *Mayo Constitution*, 1 Jan. 1861.
189 *Limerick Leader*, 13 July 1914.
190 *Donegal Independent*, 25 Nov. 1904.
191 CSO/RP/24346/1910, NAI.

submitted claims to the chief secretary's office for payments as Irish interpreter at winter assizes in 1910 and 1911.[192]

Charles Byrne (1751–)

Very few records from the 1821 census have survived and for just one interpreter, Charles Byrne in Ardbraccan, Meath, a 70-year-old 'farmer, weaver and Irish interpreter Co Meath'. He was paid £5 in Lent 1812,[193] most likely for his work as interpreter at assizes.

John Kane or Keane (1870–1944)

John Kane was appointed interpreter for Mayo in 1893. His letters of application used the surname 'Kane' but 'Keane' is used in newspaper articles and is the name he used in the 1901 and 1911 censuses. He became embroiled in controversy in 1899 when acting as interpreter in an action taken by a man called Michael Connor to recover £10 damages for assault before Judge Dane at Ballinrobe quarter sessions. According to the *Ballinrobe Chronicle*, when Connor stated in Irish that he could not speak English, the defendant's solicitor stated that he 'understood and could speak English if he choose'. At this stage, Kane stated that he had conversed with Connor in English that morning and the previous day and 'the witness was competent to be examined in English'.[194] Connor, who did not understand what was being said, persisted in speaking Irish and 'was roughly dragged from the chair by two constables'.[195] Two days later Judge Dane explained in open court that:

> A litigant came up before me, and noisily insisted upon the interpreter of the court swearing him in in Irish, and the interpreter, who is a paid official of the court, a paid sworn official, proved to my satisfaction that not only was this man not ignorant of English, but that he thoroughly understood English, and that he spoke it, and had been speaking it to him on that very day and the day before.

Judge Dane went on to say that Irish speakers who understand English 'sometimes avail themselves of that fact to come up here and try to frustrate the ends of justice, because they think that being sworn in Irish they will have time to hear the questions put and to consider what kind of an answer they will give'. He also said that he would not like anyone to think that 'the poorest man in the

192 CSO/RP/24346/10, CSO/RP/1087/11, CSO/RP/1810/11, CSO/RP/1947/11, CSO/RP/2785/11, NAI.
193 County of Meath, Lent 1812, RIA HT/Box 381/6 Pamph., RIA.
194 *Ballinrobe Chronicle*, 28 Oct. 1899.
195 *Mayo News*, 28 Oct. 1899.

country, if he happens to be an Irish-speaking man, won't get the fullest justice in this court'.[196]

Ballinrobe district council discussed the issue at their meeting, where the interpreter was allocated some of the blame. Mr Regan stated that 'A good deal of it was due to the interpreter' and 'there is not a merchant in Ballinrobe that won't make a declaration that the man [Connor] cannot speak English'. Regan proposed that the council make a resolution condemning Judge Dane's action and compared the giving of evidence in Irish in Ireland with doing so in Welsh in Wales, suggesting that judges should have a knowledge of Irish. Kane was described by Regan as 'a very poor interpreter' who led Judge Dane 'entirely astray'. Mr Costello told the council that he had served as juror in Castlebar, where he observed that Kane 'was not putting the questions of Counsel at all, neither was he interpreting her answers'. He had informed the judge of this issue but the interpreter being an officer of the court, nothing could be done. Mr Costello went on to assert that Kane had 'admitted to him that he could not interpret properly'.[197]

At a meeting in Castlebar around the same time Douglas Hyde said, 'It was a great mistake on the part of Judge Dane, as a witness should be allowed to speak in any language he wished.'[198] In a letter to the *Freeman's Journal*, Dr Edward Maguire wrote that he had attended the case and that 'O'Connor did not speak a word of English when on the table. I know him for years, and I tended to him during his late illness. He never spoke a word of English to me', and suggested that the case 'be investigated on oath'.[199] It is worth noting that Maguire's son had been unsuccessful in his application for the post of interpreter.

The case was appealed to Castlebar assizes in March 1900, with John Kane acting as interpreter. While Michael Connor was being questioned, Kane 'stated that the witness was not giving proper answers'. Connor's sister gave evidence in Irish 'at a rapid rate to the evident dissatisfaction of the judge, and was stated to evade the questions of the interpreter'. Mr Taylor, solicitor, commented that he knew what she was saying – 'She says this interpreter is not translating her evidence fairly.'[200] Keane resigned in 1901.[201]

Patrick O'Sullivan (1835–99)

Patrick O'Sullivan was appointed interpreter at Kerry quarter sessions in 1867[202] and at assizes in 1887.[203] He continued to work there until his death in 1899. From

196 *Irish Times*, 27 Oct. 1899.
197 *Mayo News*, 4 Nov. 1899.
198 *Freeman's Journal*, 1 Nov. 1899.
199 *Freeman's Journal*, 30 Oct. 1899.
200 *Western People*, 24 Mar. 1900.
201 Ibid., 21 Sept. 1901.
202 *Tralee Chronicle & Killarney Echo*, 12 Feb. 1867.
203 County of Kerry presentments, Kerry Local History & Archives.

Brookhill, Killorglin, County Kerry, in addition to being a court interpreter, he was a large farmer and agent.[204]

OTHER

Thomas Bennis

According to manuscript presentment books, Thomas Bennis was working as an interpreter at the crown and civil bill courts in Clare between 1787 and at least 1791, possibly longer. Bennis was also working in Galway in 1794, the earliest surviving record for the county, and in 1795. And in 1793–5, Bennis was in Mayo. At the time, all three counties formed part of the Connaught circuit,[205] so perhaps Bennis followed the judges on circuit. He signed the books when he was paid. For example, the County Mayo at-large spring assizes 1794 presentment manuscript has this entry on a left-hand page: '£5 be levied of said Barony and paid to Mr Bennis for interpretor [*sic*] to the courts'. And Thomas Bennis' signature appears on the right-hand page. In the summer assizes book for 1794, Bennis writes, 'Recd the opposite presentment in full from Dodwell Brown Esqre 2nd April 1795'. His signature appears on presentment books for all three counties; the similarity of the signatures leads to the inevitable conclusion that the same person was working at assizes in three counties, possibly simultaneously.

Patrick Blake

In 1831, Patrick Blake, Blakemount, Clare, wrote to the lord lieutenant requesting compensation due to the assizes and commission being adjourned, which resulted in his incurring 'heavy expense' for lodging because his home was situated fourteen miles from Ennis. The official response pencilled on the memorial was 'no fund'.[206] Blake continued to work as interpreter at assizes until at least 1845.

Thomas Hogan (1814–90)

Thomas Hogan, Salmon Weir, Galway, wrote to the chief secretary's office in March 1881 applying for payment for his services as Irish interpreter at the court of recorder's sessions for the county of the town of Galway. He was asked to provide the date when he was last paid £3 15*s.* and by whom. In a second letter, Hogan was asked to provide information on whether or not the cheque was drawn upon the county treasury.[207] Hogan is listed as 'Interpreter at Assizes and Recorder's Sessions' in *Thom's Irish Almanac Borough Directory* for the years 1882–8.

204 *Kerry Sentinel*, 18 Mar. 1899.
205 W. Wenman Seward, *Topographia Hibernica* (Dublin, 1797).
206 CSP/RP/1831/2336, NAI.
207 CSO/LB/44, pp 233, 248, NAI.

John Malone (–1847)

John Malone was an interpreter in Kerry. Along with a number of other Listowel quarter sessions court officials, including assistant barrister William McDermott, crown solicitor T.W. Murphy and a turnkey, Malone contracted 'famine fever'. While the others recovered, Malone died a few days later.[208]

Owen McConigal or McConigall

Owen McConigal was the earliest recorded interpreter to be paid a salary by a grand jury. Donegal grand jury paid him £2 a year from 1754 until 1767. In 1759 an extra payment of £1 per year was introduced for sweeping and taking care of the county house and jury room.

Owen McGouldrick or McGoolrick or Goldrick

Owen McGouldrick was appointed interpreter at Sligo crown court in 1827. In 1837, before the new act allowing for payments at quarter sessions, he applied to the grand jury for a payment of £5 for interpreting at quarter sessions but this was refused.[209] In 1839 he and another interpreter called John McElroy were each paid two payments of £15 for interpreting at quarter sessions. In 1848, he was described by the *Sligo Champion* as 'a clever and accurate man in his native language'.[210] As the Sligo grand jury presentments books stopped naming interpreters in summer 1847, it was not possible to determine when his interpreting career ended.

Hugh O Freel or O'Friel

In Tyrone, Hugh O Freel or Friel started off providing fire and candles to the grand jury from 1799–1801, became a doorkeeper briefly in 1800, and by 1802 was paid £3 8*s.* 3*d.* for providing fire and candles, £1 2*s.* 9*d.* for 'attending the grand jury' and £10 as 'Interpreter and for attending sessions'. He continued working as an interpreter until at least 1814.

Michael Rush (1831–71)

In 1863 in a case of assault heard at Ballinrobe petty sessions, *Robert Holmes v. the Revd Patrick Lavelle*, Mr Rush acted as interpreter 'at the pressing request of the litigants and the court'.[211] Rush turned up again in 1869 when he initially declined a

208 *Kerry Examiner*, 20 July 1847.
209 *Sligo Champion*, 18 Mar. 1837.
210 *Sligo Journal*, 10 Mar. 1848.
211 *Ballinrobe Chronicle*, 9 May 1868.

request to act as interpreter because 'he had been materially injured in business' after previously taking on this role. However, he ultimately acquiesced when it was agreed that he would be paid half a sovereign. In 1871 Rush was appointed interpreter at Mayo quarter sessions but died a few months later.

Kerry Tidmarsh (–1836)

Kerry Tidmarsh, Kerry court interpreter from 1831,[212] was returning home on horseback when a pig ran across the road, knocking him off his horse and causing severe injuries resulting in his death a few days later. The fact that the accident was mentioned in the newspaper would suggest that he was a man of property.[213]

PUBLICANS

William Evans (1817–85)

William Evans, a publican based in Cahir,[214] was paid £3 for interpreting at Tipperary's south riding assizes and £9 at quarter sessions in 1872. In 1878, his salary had been reduced to £2 at assizes and £6 at quarter sessions in Tipperary's north riding. As some books of presentments are missing, it is impossible to establish how long he worked as an interpreter.

Roger Green or Greene (1802–84)

Roger Green ran a public house on Main Street, Rathkeale, County Limerick.[215] In 1846 he was appointed inspector of the assistant barrister's courts for County Limerick and acted in that capacity at quarter sessions in Newcastle, Rathkeale, Bruff and Limerick.[216] He began working as an interpreter at quarter sessions in 1848 and at assizes in 1851. In 1856, just before the grand jury meeting, Green wrote to the chief secretary's office saying that he was 'a man with a very large family' and asking the authorities to intervene because his name and payment had been omitted the previous year. The response was that 'his Excellency cannot interfere in the matter referred to'.[217] The grand jury foreman questioned Green's salary of £5 at assizes and £15 at quarter sessions, saying, 'Why give him a double salary?' Mr C. Powell commented, 'His services are but seldom in requisition', but the presentments were passed.[218] Roger Green continued to

212 *Tralee Mercury*, 24 Aug. 1831.
213 *Southern Reporter & Cork Commercial Courier*, 12 Apr. 1836.
214 *Slater's Royal National Commercial Directory of Ireland*, 1881, p. 16.
215 Ibid., 1846, p. 306 and *Henry & Coughlan's General Directory of Cork and Munster*, 1867, p. 371.
216 *Tipperary Vindicator*, 26 Apr. 1846.
217 CSO/LB/42, p. 137, 27 Feb. 1856 ref. 12603, NAI.
218 *Limerick Reporter*, 26 Feb. 1856.

be employed as an interpreter on full salary of £40 a year until his death in 1884.[219]

Peter O'Toole or Toole (1843–1929)

In her memoir, O'Toole's granddaughter recalled that he had a drink problem and, as a result, the family lost their businesses consisting of a grocery, hardware, drapery and pub.[220] In the 1901 census, Peter Toole is a general labourer and his wife is a publican. His economic circumstances probably explain why he applied for the post of court interpreter. At the end of 1901, the *Ballinrobe Chronicle* announced his appointment, stating that his recommendations were 'particularly good', and he enjoyed 'thorough proficiency in the Irish language'.[221]

O'Toole's issues with drink may explain why he was the object of fun in two cases involving deaf people where there was no sign language interpreter in court. In the first report, the solicitor asks, 'O'Toole, will you be able to interpret her evidence?', and the interpreter replies to laughter, 'I will, sir', but when he realizes the issue he says, 'I could not do it in that case.' The judge jokingly says 'he is supposed to interpret all languages' and the solicitors take up the joke:

> Mr Verdon – Even Chinese (laughter).
> His Honor – Now, O'Toole, you had better make yourself up in all these languages before the next Sessions, and if you don't you must take serious notice of it (laughter). You will require French, German, Italian, Greek, Latin, and, of course, Arabic (laughter).
> Mr Verdon – Also Esperanto and Marconigrams (laughter).

In 1915, in another case involving a deaf person, Mr Kennedy, solicitor, suggested, again to laughter, that 'Toole, the interpreter, is here and will interpret their evidence.'[222]

In 1909 O'Toole was fined £5 for not attending at Belmullet quarter sessions. The registrar explained to the court that the interpreter had stopped for the night in Ballina, with the intention of travelling on to Belmullet by the 4 a.m. mail car the next morning, but the people of the house did not wake him. A solicitor joked that 'the car left by English time, but Mr O'Toole, as became his position, awakened at Irish time, when he found he was late'.[223] Before 1916, Dublin Mean Time was based on the time of sunrise and sunset in Ireland and was 25 minutes behind the time in England.

219 *Freeman's Journal*, 28 July 1884.
220 K. O'Toole O'Connell, *Green are the hills far away* (Melkbosstrand, South Afria, 2010).
221 *Ballinrobe Chronicle*, 26 Dec. 1901.
222 *Connaught Telegraph*, 5 June 1909.
223 *Freeman's Journal*, 19 Oct. 1909.

In 1912, at Mayo summer assizes, a witness was being examined through O'Toole but 'evidently being dissatisfied with the way Mr O'Toole, the interpreter was translating his story, he broke into English, to the great amusement of the Bench, Bar and the entire Court'.[224]

The Irish phrase 'cuisde bower' appeared in a deposition being read by county court Judge Morphy, who queried the meaning at the Mayo criminal sessions in the crown court, Castlebar. The solicitor translated it as 'a fairy coach' and the court interpreter, Peter O'Toole, said the literal meaning was 'a silent coach', which meant, in other words, 'a coach without horses'. It is curious that the Irish words were included in the deposition.[225]

In 1916 and again in 1922, O'Toole applied to Mayo county council for an increase in salary. His request was conveyed to the finance committee but no further information was located on whether or not his request was granted.[226] When he died in 1929, the local newspaper reported that 'he owned a public-house and was market manager for Col. Knox'.[227] Colonel Knox had sold his estate including Creagh House to the congested districts board in 1913–14.

TEACHERS

Kean Mahony (–1841)

The name Kean Mahony appears in the books of presentments for County Cork in 1834 and 1838. He may well have been appointed before 1834; at the very least he worked as assizes and record court interpreter between 1834 and his death in 1841. He was also a teacher at the Cork deaf and 'dumb' school.[228]

Daniel O'Leary (1848–1919)

After retiring from his job as a national school teacher, Daniel O'Leary appears to have replaced Patrick Staunton as Cork assizes interpreter in 1914.

GAELIC LEAGUE MEMBERS AND IRISH SCHOLARS

John Downs or Downes

John Downs was secretary to the Riverstown Creamery, had been a school teacher and was generally acknowledged as an Irish scholar.[229] He was involved in the

224 *Connaught Telegraph*, 20 July 1912.
225 Ibid., 28 Oct. 1905.
226 Ibid., 25 Nov. 1916 and *Western People*, 2 Dec. 1922.
227 *Connaught Telegraph*, 12 Jan. 1929.
228 *Cork Examiner*, 29 Dec. 1841.
229 *Sligo Champion*, 13 Mar. 1897.

Society for the Preservation of the Irish Language and spoke at the Irish Teachers' Congress in 1894.[230] In 1895, he was recommended for the post of interpreter by the county court judge and examined by Archdeacon Townsend.[231] Described as 'a most competent Irish scholar', he set up an Irish language class in Riverstown, Sligo.[232] In 1900 he applied for an increase in salary from £15 to £25. He was supported by the county council chairman, who described him as 'a most erudite, gifted, and intelligible interpreter', and the councillors agreed to increase his salary to £20.[233] He was described as 'the worthy and most intelligent court interpreter' in the *Sligo Champion* in 1919.[234]

Patrick Stanton/ Pádraig Stúndún (1834–1908)

Patrick Stanton is listed as 'Irish Interpreter' in the 1901 census and made a number of applications to the chief secretary's office for payments for interpreting at Cork winter assizes between 1895 and 1907. He was a member of the Gaelic League and contributed to the *Gaelic Journal*. He transcribed some manuscripts – a sermon in Irish on St Patrick, and a life of St Finbarr – and compiled an English-Irish dictionary 'with a separate alphabet of names of animals and birds'.[235] An obituary in the *Cork Examiner* stated that 'Nobody had a better command of Irish than he.'[236] A short biography is available on the Irish-language website ainm.ie.[237]

Thomas Veale/ Tomás de Bhial (1884–1954)

In 1902, Thomas Veale was recommended for the post of Irish interpreter at Dungarvan quarter sessions in a letter from the local branch of the Irish League and in a telegram from the general secretary of the Gaelic League.[238] According to ainm.ie, he was a native speaker of Irish who taught Irish in Dungarvan and during the summers in Ring Irish college. He also translated a number of books from English to Irish for the government-established agency An Gúm.[239] Veale was employed as court unterpreter until at least 1922.

230 Ibid., 15 June 1895.
231 Ibid., 15 June 1895.
232 Ibid., 12 Oct. 1895.
233 Ibid., 18 Aug. 1900.
234 Ibid., 12 Apr. 1919.
235 An English-Irish dictionary, with a separate alphabet of names of animals and birds, 1894, MS G.1117, NLI; Life of St Barra of Cork, 1897, MS T.xlvii–ix, UCC Library; Life of St Patrick in Irish, 1895, MS 24C.52 (1182), RIA.
236 *Cork Examiner*, 2 Dec. 1908.
237 'Stúndún, Pádraig (*c.*1820–1908)', ainm.ie.
238 *Cork Examiner*, 26 Nov. 1902.
239 'De Bhial, Tomás (1884–1954)', ainm.ie. *Irish Independent*, 8 Mar. 1954.

SERVING AND RETIRED MEMBERS OF THE ROYAL IRISH CONSTABULARY

William Burke (1829–1901)

Sergeant William Burke retired from the RIC in 1877 and his pension of £69 was paid in Galway,[240] where he was appointed interpreter at assizes and recorder's sessions, possibly in 1890 to replace Thomas Hogan. In 1899 Burke requested an increase in salary due to extra work caused by the addition of two additional courts of quarter sessions in Tuam from the year 1894. There was a proposal at Galway county council that his salary be increased by £2 a year, but the motion seems to have been unsuccessful.[241]

Bryan Collins (1847–99)

Bryan Collins was one of the interpreters involved in the investigation stage of the Lough Mask murders. He was born in Dublin, but grew up in Galway's east riding. His registered number in the RIC was 36,927.[242] Collins worked as a constable in Mayo until his early retirement in 1894 on a pension of £42 per annum, payable in Claremorris.[243]

Thomas Evans (1835–1909)

Born in County Galway, Thomas Evans was 20 years of age when he joined the RIC in 1855, and his registered number was 18813.[244] On 26 December 1873, he married Mary Jane Colvin from Sligo at Spiddale church in the parish of Killannin (Moycullen), in the diocese of Tuam. According to the marriage certificate, the wedding took place at the church of St Joseph, United Church of England and Ireland. Constable Evans worked in Galway and acted as court interpreter at the Maamtrasna, Letterfrack and Lough Mask trials in 1882. He was promoted to head constable and transferred to Longford in 1884. In June 1888, he retired at the age of 55 on a pension of £88 per annum,[245] and in November of that year he acted as interpreter at the Parnell commission in London. His daughters' marriage certificates dating from 1911 and 1913 list his occupation as 'clerk at the Castle, Dublin', and as 'petty sessions clerk DC'.

Patrick Kelly (1838–92)

Patrick Kelly from Roscommon joined the RIC in 1856 and his registered number was 20,753. He worked first in Galway's west riding before being moved to

240 RIC register of deceased pensioners.
241 Minutes of proceedings Galway county council, 12 June 1899, galway.ie/digitalarchives.
242 RIC service records, 1816–1922.
243 RIC pensions, 1873–1925.
244 RIC general register, index vol. 1.
245 RIC pensions, 1873–1925.

Mayo in 1874 and back to Galway's west riding in 1887.[246] He was involved in the Maamtrasna case, acting as interpreter for the taking of depositions and attending to Irish-speaking witnesses during their stay in Ballybough, Dublin, and he was the interpreter at the arraignment at Green Street courthouse. After the trial he was promoted from sub-constable to constable and received a first-class favourable record .[247] Kelly retired in 1886 on a pension of £72, paid in Galway.

Cornelius Leahy (1855–1932)

Born in Kerry, Cornelius Leahy 40675 was assigned to Waterford from 1875, Cork's west riding from 1883 and Cork's east riding from 1885.[248] In 1901, Constable Leahy acted as interpreter in an assault case taken by an Irish-speaking 'respectable elderly farmer' against 'a man apparently of the tramp class'. According to a letter to the *Cork Examiner*, the constable 'appeared to have a perfect knowledge of the language' and was complimented by the judge 'on his quickness and smartness in translation'.[249] Leahy retired to Youghal in 1903.[250]

William Lerhinan (1854 1940)

From Clare, William Lerhinan joined the RIC in 1875 and his registered number was 41,292. He worked first in Waterford city, then as a reserve from 1879, during which time he interpreted at an early stage of the Maamtrasna case between Michael Joyce and Constable John Johnston. He was transferred to Longford in 1883, and in 1891 to Galway's east riding and his final posting was in King's County in 1894.[251] He retired in 1900 and his pension was paid in Kilrush, Clare until at least 1924.[252] He married Julia Anderton in 1883 and she bore eleven children, of whom seven were still alive in 1911. The spelling of the family surname caused much confusion, with their children's surnames recorded in the civil records as Larnon, Learnan, Learman and Learhinan. In the 1901 and 1911 censuses Lerhinan is a farmer in Cloonwhite South, Creegh, County Clare.

Peter Mullins (1852–1926)

Born in Galway's west riding, Peter Mullins joined the RIC in 1871, registered number 38,189, and was stationed first in Cork city then in Limerick from 1887

246 RIC service records, 1816–1922.
247 *Flag of Ireland*, 16 Aug. 1884.
248 RIC service records, 1816–1922.
249 *Cork Examiner*, 18 Oct. 1901.
250 RIC pensions, 1873–1925.
251 RIC service records, 1816–1922.
252 RIC pensions, 1873–1925.

and in Kerry from 1890.[253] He retired from the force in 1900,[254] when he moved to Fairhill Road in Galway city.

In 1921 at Galway assizes, in a murder case, Mullins was present in court as interpreter for defendant Coleman Conneely, who on indictment was asked to plead guilty or not guilty. Mullins told the court that the accused admitted that he did not kill the man with a stone. This was not a satisfactory answer and when Mullins repeated the question, the response was 'he tells me he would not like to say he did not kill the man when he did kill him'. At this stage District Inspector Sugrue, Oughterard, stepped in and volunteered to act as interpreter.[255]

Mullins wrote to the new ministry of finance in 1923 complaining that the state solicitor had refused to pay him a salary of £5 12*s.* 6*d.* for his work at quarter sessions. Internal correspondence includes an allegation by state solicitor Risteard Ó Ceallaigh (aka Richard Jasper Kelly) that Mullins had been recently reprimanded and replaced by the recorder of Galway for incompetency in a serious criminal case.[256]

253 RIC service records, 1816–1922.
254 RIC pensions, 1873–1925.
255 *Connacht Tribune*, 10 Dec. 1921.
256 FIN/1/3713, NAI.

Bibliography

PRIMARY SOURCES

Archives

County archives

Cavan Archives, county of Cavan grand jury books of presentments, 1794–1856
Clare Library Local Studies and Clare County Archives, county of Clare grand jury books of presentments, 1786–1898
Clare Library Local Studies and Clare County Archives, county of Clare lists of county and rural districts with their presentments for six months, 1900–20
Cork City and County Archives, county of Cork grand jury books of presentments, 1834–98
Donegal County Council Archives Service, county of Donegal grand jury books of presentments, 1753–1898
Donegal County Council Archives Service, minutes – meetings of the finance committee of Tirconaill County Council, 1925–7
Donegal County Council Archives Service, county of Donegal abstracts of accounts, 1930–2
Dublin City Archives, city of Dublin grand jury books of presentments, 1849–50, 1861–70 and 1877
Fingal County Council Archives, county of Dublin books of presentments, 1845–98
Galway County Library Headquarters, county of Galway grand jury books of presentments, 1812, 1827, 1828, 1835, 1837, 1840, 1842, 1843, 1868, 1899
Galway County Library Headquarters, minutes of proceedings of the Galway County Council quarterly meeting, 1901–24 [digitised]
Galway County Library Headquarters, county of Galway abstract of accounts of receipts and secretary's statements, 1929–42
Kerry Local History & Archives, county of Kerry grand jury books of presentments, 1873–98
Kerry Local History & Archives, Kerry County Council financial statements, 1899–1945
Kilkenny Local Studies, county of Kilkenny grand jury books of presentments, 1840–65
Leitrim County Library, county of Leitrim grand jury books of presentments, 1887–91
Limerick Studies Archives, county of Limerick grand jury books of presentments, 1807–90
Longford County Archives, county of Longford grand jury books of presentments, 1759–1845
Louth Archives, county of Louth grand jury books of presentments, 1810, 1815, 1823–43
Monaghan Local Studies, county of Monaghan grand jury books of presentments, 1822–34, 1837, 1838, 1849, 1859
Roscommon County Library, county of Roscommon grand jury books of presentments, 1819–70
Sligo County Library, county of Sligo grand jury books of presentments, 1809, 1811, 1813–89
Tipperary Studies, county of Tipperary South Riding grand jury books of presentments, 1855–9, 1862, 1872, 1891, 1897, 1898
Waterford County Archives, county of Waterford grand jury books of presentments, 1854–98
Waterford County Archives, county of Waterford salaries and contracts, 1903–23
Wicklow County Archives, grand jury books of presentments, 1819–47

National Archives of Ireland (NAI)

1C-78-51
County of Clare grand jury books of presentments, 1806, 1809, 1817, 1820, 1824, 1825, 1836, 1838, 1840, 1845, 1854, 1855, 1856, 1858, 1860, 1861, 1862, 1864–78, 1898
County of Dublin grand jury books of presentments, 1841, 1849
County of Galway grand jury books of presentments, 1808, 1809, 1813, 1814, 1816, 1818–26, 1829–32, 1834–41, 1896
County of Kerry grand jury books of presentments, 1893–9
County of Mayo grand jury books of presentments, 1888–99
County of Meath grand jury books of presentments, 1761–76, 1800–2
County of Sligo grand jury books of presentments, 1888–92
CRF/1902/J13/10/9
CRF/1902/J13/25/36
CRF/1902/J13/25/38
CRF/1902/J13/29
CSO/LB/42
CSO/LB/44
CSO/LB/46
CSO/LB/50
CSO/LB/52
CSO/LB/57
CSO/LB/64
CSO/LB/65
CSO/LB/66
CSO/LB/68
CSO/LB/70
CSO/LB/71
CSO/LB/73
CSO/LB/75
CSO/LB/79
CSO/RP/3/045/23
CSO/RP/141/86
CSO/RP/482/15
CSO/RP/654/96
CSO/RP/692/86
CSO/RP/915/94
CSO/RP/1087/11
CSO/RP/1280/15
CSO/RP/1810/11
CSO/RP/1822/21
CSO/RP/1822/68
CSO/RP/1822/1979
CSO/RP/1828/520
CSO/RP/1828/878
CSO/RP/1829/137/3
CSO/RP/1831/2336

CSO/RP/1947/11
CSO/RP/1917/187
CSO/RP/1917/2109
CSO/RP/1917/2700
CSO/RP/2097/96
CSO/RP/2392/88
CSO/RP/2517/02
CSO/RP/2649/18
CSO/RP/2737/02
CSO/RP/2785/11
CSO/RP/3103/02
CSO/RP/4630/02
CSO/RP/6073/96
CSO/RP/13282/18
CSO/RP/13390/87
CSO/RP/15599/98
CSO/RP/17015/18
CSO/RP/18179/05
CSO/RP/20185/95
CSO/RP/20830/95
CSO/RP/21873/14
CSO/RP/22366/95
CSO/RP/23779/04
CSO/RP/24346/10
CSO/RP/24399/85
CSO/RP/24430/03
CSO/RP/25086/05
CSO/RP/3008/88
CSO/RP/3276/1920
CSO/RP/3828/96
CSO/RP/5191/63
CSO/RP/19549/95
CSO/RP/22726/1920
FIN/1/3713
Tipperary North Riding grand jury books of presentments, 1878–99
Tipperary South Riding grand jury books of presentments, 1888, 1896

National Folklore Collection, University College Dublin

Irish Folklore Commission, vol. 1196

National Library of Ireland (NLI)

County of city of Cork statement of assessment, spring 1815 [digitised]
County of Cork schedule of the approved applications to obtain presentments, spring assizes 1899

County of Galway grand jury payments book, 1794–6, 1799, MS 19,803.
County of Louth grand jury book of presentments, 1713–32, MS 11,949p
County Mayo grand jury presentments, 1792–4, MS 10,654.
County of Tipperary grand jury books of presentments, 1817–27, 1828, 1829, 1834
County of Waterford grand jury books of presentments, 1841, 1846
County of Westmeath grand jury books of presentments, 1826–8
County of Wexford grand jury books of presentments 1815, 1883
Day, R.A., *A charge delivered to the grand jury of the county of Dublin at the quarter sessions of the peace held at Kilmainham* (Dublin, 1795)
Day, R.A., *A charge delivered to the grand jury of the county of Dublin at the quarter sessions of the peace held at Kilmainham* (Dublin, 1798)
Presentments laid on the county of Fermanagh at summer assizes 1838
Queen's County grand jury books of presentments, 1805–16, 1823
Statement of assessment at summer assizes, 1808: published by order of the then grand jury of the county of the city of Cork [digitised]
Statement of assessment at summer assizes, 1811: published by order of the then grand jury of the county of the city of Cork [digitised]
Statement of assessment at summer assizes, 1815: published by order of the then grand jury of the county of the city of Cork [digitised]
Statement of the accounts of the treasurer of the county of Waterford spring assizes, 1841 [digitised]
Tipperary North Riding grand jury books of presentments, 1852–5, 1857–60
Tipperary South Riding grand jury book of presentments, 1839

Public Record Office of Northern Ireland (PRONI)

Antrim grand jury books of presentments, 1727–67, 1775–84
Armagh grand jury books of presentments, 1797–9, 1801–3, 1805–7, 1810–12, 1815, 1821–4, 1826–7
Down grand jury books of presentments, 1778–92, 1803–7
Fermanagh grand jury books of presentments, 1792–1819
Londonderry grand jury books of presentments, 1788–1860
Tyrone grand jury books of presentments, 1799–1860
T2929/8/6, letter from Richard Westenra [digitised]

Royal Irish Academy (RIA)

County of Antrim grand jury books of presentments, 1828, 1829, 1830, 1836
County of Carlow grand jury book of presentments, 1836
County of Cavan grand jury book of presentments, 1840
County of city of Dublin grand jury books of presentments, 1844–6
County of Meath grand jury books of presentments, 1804, 1812, 1822, 1826
County of Westmeath grand jury books of presentments, 1804, 1805, 1810, 1812–16
County of Wicklow special sessions, January 1826
King's County grand jury book of presentments, 1830

Directories and almanacs

Guy's Cork Almanac, 1891
Henry & Coughlan's General Directory of Cork and Munster, 1867
Pettigrew and Oulton, *Dublin Almanac and General Register of Ireland*, 1835
Pigot & Co., *City of Dublin and Hibernian Provincial Directory*, 1824
Slater's National Commercial Directory of Ireland, 1846
Slater's Royal National Commercial Directory of Ireland, 1881
Thom's Irish Almanac, 1844, 1845, 1846, 1848
Thom's Irish Almanac: Galway Borough Directory, 1848
Thom's Irish Almanac and Official Directory for the Year 1872, 1872
Treble Almanac, 1822

Government documents

Accounts presented to the house of commons, of the presentments passed by the grand juries of Ireland, at the spring and summer assizes, in the year 1807, HC 1808 (205) xiii, 67.
Parliamentary debates from the year 1803 to the present time, published under the superintendence of T. C. Hansard (London, 1812–20), vol. xxv.
Reports from the commissioners of the board of education in Ireland, 1809–1812, HC 1812 (47) v, 1.
Report from the select committee on grand jury presentments of Ireland, 1814–15, HC 1815 (283) vi, 1661.
Report from the select committee appointed to enquire into the expenses of sheriffs and other returning officers at elections in Ireland; and also into the laws for regulating elections in Ireland, HC 1820 (226) iii, 269.
Sheriffs charges and expenses at elections, 1818 and 1820: returns to an address of the house of commons, of 13th June 1820: for an account of all sums of money paid to sheriffs or undersheriffs, at the general election in 1818, and at the last general election, (1820) for writs and precepts, for either counties, cities, or boroughs, in Ireland; likewise, a return of all fees and expenses paid to sheriffs or undersheriffs, by the candidates, at the several elections in Ireland, in 1818 and in 1820; and likewise, an account of all expenses incurred by sheriffs and undersheriffs, at elections in Ireland, in 1820, HC 1820 (291) ix, 361.
Census of Ireland, abstract of answers and returns, pursuant to act 55 George III, for taking an account of the population of Ireland in 1821, HC 1824 (577) xxii, 411.
First report of the commissioners of education, HC 1825 (400) xii, 1.
Detailed account of expenses incurred under Population Act for Ireland, 1831, HC 1833 (442) xxxix, 45.
Petty sessions, Ireland: a return of the courts of petty sessions in the several counties of Ireland; the periods and places where held, and the magistrates presiding, with the total amount of all costs and charges received, and fines imposed, for the year ending 31 December 1835, HC 1836 (415) xlii, 463.
Report of the commissioners appointed to revise the several laws under or by virtue of which monies are now raised by grand jury presentments in Ireland [C 386] HC 1842, xxiv, 1.
Census of Ireland, 1841: report of the census commissioners appointed to take the census of Ireland for the year 1841 [C 504] HC 1843, xxiv, 1.
Election expenses (Ireland): An account of expenses incurred by the returning officer at every election for a county, or city, or borough, in Ireland, during the months of June and July 1841, HC 1843 (620) l, 235.

Appendix to the minutes of evidence taken before Her Majesty's commissioners of inquiry into the state of the law and practice in relation to the occupation of land in Ireland, part I [C 605–6] HC 1845, xix, 1, 57.

Royal commission of inquiry into state of law and practice in respect to occupation of land in Ireland, appendix to minutes of evidence, part IV, statement of county cess [C 672–3] HC 1845, xxii, 1, 225.

Report from Her Majesty's commissioners of inquiry into the state of the law and practice in relation to the occupation of land in Ireland [C 605–6] HC 1845, xix, 1, 57.

First annual report of the commission for administering the laws for relief of the poor in Ireland [C 963] HC 1848, xxxiii, 377.

Papers relating to proceedings for relief of distress, and state of unions and workhouses in Ireland 1848 [C 919, 955, 999] HC 1847–8, liv, 313; lv, 1; lvi, 1.

Medical charities, Ireland: first annual report of the commissioners for administering the laws for relief of the poor in Ireland, under the Medical Charities Act, 14 & 15 Vict, cap 68 [C 1609] HC 1848, l, 325.

Petty sessions clerks (Ireland): a return, showing the number of petty sessions, the number of clerks, and the amount of fees received by them in each county of Ireland in the year 1848, HC 1850 (304) li, 527.

The seventeenth report of the commissioners of national education in Ireland (for the year 1850) [C 1405–11] HC 1851, xxiv, 101, 641.

Census of Great Britain, 1851 population tables 1, vol. I [C 1631] HC 1852–3, lxxxv, 1.

Clare election: report from the select committee on the Clare election petition; with the minutes of proceedings, HC 1853 (587) ix, 535.

Report from the select committee of the house of lords appointed to consider the consequence of extending the functions of the constabulary in Ireland to the suppression or prevention of illicit distillation; and to report thereon to the House; together with the minutes of evidence, and an appendix and index, HC 1854 (53) x, 1.

Census of Ireland for the year 1851, part VI, general report [C 2134] HC 1856, xxxi, 1.

Mayo election: minutes of evidence taken before the select committee on the Mayo county election petition; with the proceedings of the committee, and index, HC 1857 s. 2 (182) vii, 357.

Report from the select committee on destitution (Gweedore and Cloughaneely); together with the proceedings of the committee, minutes of evidence, appendix, and index, HC 1857–8 (412) xii, 89.

The twenty-third report of the commissioners of national education in Ireland (for the year 1856) [C 2304–1] HC 1857–8, xx, 213, 573.

Report of the commissioners appointed to investigate into the existence of corrupt practices in elections of members to serve in Parliament for the county of the town of Galway, together with the minutes of evidence [C 2291] HC 1857–8, xxvi, 309.

Clare election: minutes of evidence of taken before the select committee on the Clare election petition; with the proceedings of the committee, HC 1860 (178, 392) xi, 87, 153.

Skibbereen and Castletown board of guardians: copies or extracts of correspondence with the Skibbereen and Castletown boards of guardians and the poor law inspectors, with the poor law board, since November 1861, HC 1862 (424) xli, 1, 667.

The census of Ireland for the year 1861, part V, general report [C 3204–IV] HC 1863, lxi, 1.

The San Francisco: copies of the report upon the inquiry recently held by order of the board of trade in the case of the wreck of the San Francisco in Clonakilty Bay, County Cork, in January last, and of the minutes of evidence taken at the inquiry, HC 1867 (265) lxiv, 1.

County and city of Waterford gaol criminal register and description book 1871, Waterford Prison General Register, 1870–6, book 1139/12.

Copy of the shorthand writers' notes of the judgment of Mr Justice Keogh on the trial of the Galway County election petition, HC 1872 (241), xlviii, 17, 71.

Fiftieth report of the inspectors-general on the general state of the prisons of Ireland 1871, with appendix [C 535] HC 1872, xxxii, 1.

First, second and special reports from the select committee on Juries (Ireland); together with the proceedings of the committee, minutes of evidence, and appendix, HC 1873 (283) xv, 389.

Galway borough election: copy of the shorthand writer's notes of the evidence given before Mr Justice Lawson on the trial of the borough of Galway petition in May 1874, and of the judgment of the judge in the said petition, HC 1874 (201) liii, 577.

Census of Ireland 1871, part III, general report, with illustrative maps and diagrams, summary tables, and appendix (C 1377) HC 1876, lxxxi, 1.

Census of Ireland 1881, part II, general report, with illustrative maps and diagrams, tables and appendix [C.3365] HC 1882, lxxvi, 385.

Annual report of the local government board for Ireland, being the 11th report under the Local Government Board (Ireland) Act 35 and 36 Vict. c. 69, with appendices [C 3581] HC 1883, xxix, 1.

Report of the royal commission on the Land Law (Ireland) Act 1881 and the Purchase of Land (Ireland) Act 1885 [C 5015] HC 1887, xxvi, 1241.

Census of Ireland 1891, part II, general report, with illustrative maps and diagrams, tables and appendix [C 6780] HC 1892, xc, 1.

Petty sessions order book CSPS 1/4503 for 30 May 1893

Grand jury officers (Ireland) return to an order of the honorable the house of commons, dated 24th March 1898; for return of officers in the service of the grand jury in each county in Ireland, HC 1898 (237) lxxiv, 47.

Annual report of the local government board for Ireland, being the 27th report under the Local Government Board (Ireland) Act 35 & 36 Vict. c. 69 [C.9480] HC 1899, xxxix, 1.

Local government (Ireland) officials: return to an order of the honourable the house of commons, dated 14th March 1901, for 'a return showing the names, dates of appointments, and emoluments, of all officials transferred by virtue of the provisions of the Local Government (Ireland) Act, 1898, to county, district councils, or boards of guardians, with the salaries of every such official as fixed by those bodies, or as determined by the local government board; the increases in the poundage rates consequent upon the operation of these provisions of the act where the salaries were increased, the amount proposed to be paid by these bodies to any such official by way of compensation or retiring allowance and the amount determined by the treasury on appeal to be payable', HC 1901 (331) lxiv, 673.

Census of Ireland 1901, part II, general report with illustrative maps and diagrams, tables and appendix [C 1190] HC 1902, cxxix, 1.

Census of Ireland 1911, general report, with tables and appendix [C 6663] HC 1912–13, cxviii, 1.

Dáil Éireann, vol. 19, 26 April 1927

Good Friday Agreement (1998), https://www.dfa.ie/media/dfa/alldfawebsitemedia/ ourrolesandpolicies/northernireland/good-friday-agreement.pdf, accessed 5 Apr. 2019.

St Andrew's Agreement (2006), https://assets.publishing.service.gov.uk/government/uploads/system/uploads/attachment_data/file/136651/st_andrews_agreement-2.pdf, accessed 5 Apr. 2019.

Newspapers

Anglo-Celt
Ballinrobe Chronicle
Ballymena Observer
Ballyshannon Herald
Belfast Morning News
Belfast Newsletter
Catholic Telegraph
Clare Journal & Ennis Advertiser
Connacht Tribune
Connaught Journal
Connaught Telegraph
Cork Constitution
Cork Examiner
Derry Journal
Donegal Independent
Donegal News
Drogheda Argus & Leinster Journal
Drogheda Journal
Dublin Evening Mail
Dublin Evening Packet and Correspondent
Dublin Evening Post
Dublin Weekly Nation
Dundalk Democrat
Enniskillen Chronicle & Erne Packet
Finn's Leinster Journal
Flag of Ireland
Freeman's Journal
Galway Mercury
Galway Vindicator and Connaught Advertiser
Irish Independent
Irish Times
Irishman
Kerry Evening Post
Kerry Examiner
Kerry Sentinel
Kerry Weekly Reporter
Kerryman
Kilkenny Journal & Leinster Commercial & Literary Advertiser
Killarney Echo and South Kerry Chronicle
Leinster Express
Liberator
Limerick & Clare Examiner
Limerick Chronicle
Limerick Evening Post
Limerick Leader
Limerick Reporter
Londonderry Sentinel
Mayo Constitution
Mayo Examiner
Mayo News
Meath Chronicle
Morning News
Morning Post
Munster Express
Nation
Nenagh Guardian
Nenagh News
Northern Star
Pilot
Roscommon and Leitrim Gazette
Roscommon Journal
Saunders's News-letter
Skibbereen & West Carbery Eagle
Skibbereen Eagle
Sligo Champion
Sligo Journal
Southern Reporter & Cork Commercial Courier
Southern Star
Strabane Morning Post
Times
Tipperary Free Press
Tipperary Vindicator
Tralee Chronicle
Tralee Chronicle & Killarney Echo
Tralee Mercury
Tuam Herald
Ulster Herald
Waterford Chronicle
Waterford Mail
Waterford News
Waterford Standard
Weekly Irish Times
Western People

Online resources

Ainm.ie
Ancestry.com
Archive.org
Books.google.ie
British Newspaper Archive, britishnewspaperarchive.co.uk
Calendar of Wills and Administrations, willcalendars.nationalarchives.ie/search/cwa/home.jsp
Censuses for 1821, 1901 and 1911, census.nationalarchives.ie
davidalton.net
Dictionary of Irish Biography, dib.cambridge.org
Enhanced Parliamentary Papers, dippam.ac.uk/eppi
Findmypast.ie
Histpop.org
Irishgenealogy.ie
Irish Newspaper Archive, irishnewsarchive.com
Irish Times Digital Archive, irishtimes.com
Newspapers.com
Theyworkforyou.com
Traditionalmusic.co.uk

SECONDARY SOURCES

Addison, H.R., *Recollections of an Irish police magistrate* (London, 1862).

Archer, Joseph, *Statistical survey of the county of Dublin* (Dublin, 1801).

Ashe, Isaac, 'Parish of Tamlaght' in W.S. Mason, *A statistical account parochial survey of Ireland* (Dublin, 1819).

Atkinson, A.A., *The Irish tourist* (Dublin, 1815).

Bairéad, Colm, *Murdair Mhám Trasna* TG4 (2018).

BBC News, '"Curry my yoghurt": Gregory Campbell DUP barred from speaking for day', 4 Nov. 2014, https://www.bbc.com/news/uk-northern-ireland-29895593, accessed 5 Apr. 2019.

Beaufort, D.A. and Ellison, C.C., 'Materials for the Dublin Society agricultural survey of County Louth', *Journal of the County Louth Archaeological and Historical Society*, 18:2 (1974) 121–31.

Beckett J.C., *A short history of Ireland* (London, 1958).

Bodkin, McDonnell M., *Recollections of an Irish judge: press, bar and parliament* (London, 1914).

Bourdieu, Pierre, 'The economics of linguistic exchanges', *Social Sciences Information*, 16:6 (1977), 645–68.

Bourdieu, Pierre, *Language and symbolic power* trans. Gino Raymond and Matthew Adamson (Cambridge, 1991).

Bourdieu, Pierre and Wacquant, L.J.D., *An invitation to reflexive sociology* (Cambridge, 2007).

Brady, John, 'Irish Interpreters at Meath assizes', *Ríocht na Midhe*, 2, (1959), 62–4.

Broeker, Galen, *Rural disorder and police reform in Ireland, 1812–1836* (London, 1970).

Burke, Oliver J., 'History of the Connaught circuit', *Dublin University Magazine*, 85 (1875), 690–702.

Burke, Oliver J., *Anecdotes of the Connaught circuit from its foundation in 1604 to close upon the present time* (Dublin, 1885).

Carr, J., *The stranger in Ireland* (Philadelphia, 1806).

'Census of Ireland April 1861 – preliminary results', *Journal of the Statistical Society of London*, 24:3 (1861), pp 402–10.

Clancy, J.J., *A handbook of local government in Ireland* (Dublin, 1899).

Clother, H., 'Law and disorders – covering the courts' in R. Keeble, *The newspapers handbook* (London, 1999).

Connolly, S.J., 'The Catholic question, 1801–12' in W.E. Vaughan (ed.), *New History of Ireland*, v: *1801–1970* (Oxford, 1989)

Connolly, S.J. (ed), *Oxford companion to Irish history* (Oxford, 2002).

Coote, Charles, *Statistical survey of the county of Monaghan* (Dublin, 1801).

Coote, Charles, *Statistical survey of King's County* (Dublin, 1801).

Coote, Charles, *General view of the agriculture and manufacture of the Queen's County* (Dublin, 1801).

Coote, Charles, *Statistical survey of the county of Cavan* (Dublin, 1802).

Coote, Charles, *A statistical survey of the county of Armagh* (Dublin, 1804).

Crane C.P., *Memoirs of a resident magistrate 1880–1920* (Edinburgh, 1938).

Cronin, Michael, *Translation and identity* (London, 2006).

Cronin, Michael, 'Interpreting Ireland: literary and historical perspectives on the role of interpreters in Ireland' in Tymoczko, M. and Ireland, C. (eds), *Language and tradition in Ireland: continuities and displacements* (Amherst, 2003).

Crowley, Tony, *Wars of words* (Oxford, 2005).

Cullen, L.M., *The emergence of modern Ireland, 1600–1900* (London, 1981).

Curran, W.H., *The life of the Right Honourable John Philpot Curran, late master of the rolls in Ireland* (London, 1819).

Curran J., *Reminiscences of John Adye Curran KC* (London, 1915).

Day, Ella B., *Mr Justice Day, 1745–1841* (Exeter, 1938).

Divall, Colin, *Cultural histories of sociabilities, spaces and mobilities* (Abingdon, 2015).

Doak, Jonathan, McGourlay, Claire and Thomas, Mark, *Evidence in context* (Abingdon, 2012).

Dodd, William H., 'Prize essay on the differences in the organization of local courts in Ireland, Scotland and England, for the discharge of duties of judges and officers, suggesting such changes as would be expedient in case of an assimilation of jurisdiction in the local courts of the three kingdoms', *Journal of the Statistical and Social Inquiry Society of Ireland*, 7:52 (1877–8), pp 189–201.

Donnelly, J.S., 'Mortality and emigration' in Vaughan W.E. (ed.), *A new history of Ireland*, v: *Ireland under the union, 1801–1870* (Oxford, 2010).

Dooley, Terence, *The murders at Wildgoose Lodge: agrarian crime and punishment in pre-Famine Ireland* (Dublin, 2007).

Dorian, Hugh, *The outer edge of Ulster: a memoir of social life in the nineteenth century*, ed. B. Mac Suibhne and D. Dickson (Dublin, 2000).

Dubourdieu, John, *Statistical survey of the county of Down* (Dublin, 1802).

Dubourdieu, John, *Statistical survey of the county of Antrim* (Dublin, 1812).

Dunbar, Ciaran, 'Northern Ireland Assembly divided by Irish language', 28 June 2017, https://www.bbc.com/news/uk-northern-ireland-38601181, accessed 5 Apr. 2019.

Dungan, Myles, *Conspiracy: Irish political trials* (Dublin, 2009).

Dunlop, Andrew, *Fifty years of Irish journalism* (Dublin, 1911).

Durston, Gregory, *Evidence: text and materials* (Oxford, 2008).

Dutton, Hely, *Statistical survey of the county of Clare* (Dublin, 1808).

Dutton, Hely, *Statistical survey of the county of Galway* (Dublin, 1824).

Finnelly, W., *The law and practice of elections in England, Scotland, and Ireland and of the trial of controverted elections* (London, 1830).

FitzGerald, Garret, 'Estimates for baronies of minimum level of Irish-speaking amongst successive decennial cohorts: 1771–1781 to 1861–1871', *Proceedings of the Royal Irish Academy*, 84:3 (1984), pp 117–55.

Fleming, John, 'Correspondence', *Gaelic Journal*, 6:1 (April 1883).

Fraser, Robert, *General view of the agriculture and mineralogy, present state and circumstances, of the County Wicklow* (Dublin, 1801).

Furlong, John Smith and La Touche, Digues, *The law of landlord and tenant, as administered in Ireland* (Dublin, 1869), ii.

Garnham, Neal, *The courts, crime and the criminal law in Ireland, 1692–1760* (Dublin, 1996).

Giambruno, Cynthia, 'The role of the interpreter of sixteenth- and seventeenth-century Spanish colonies in the "New World"' in Carmen Valero Garcés and Anne Martin (eds), *Crossing borders in community interpreting* (Amsterdam, 2008).

Gibbons, John, *Forensic linguistics: an introduction to language in the justice system* (Oxford, 2003).

Greer, D.S., 'The development of civil bill procedure in Ireland' in John McEldowney and Paul O'Higgins (eds), *The common law tradition* (Dublin, 1990).

Greer, Desmond, 'A security against illegality?' in Norma Dawson (ed.), *Reflections on law and history* (Dublin, 2006).

Griffin, Brian, 'Prevention and detection of crime in nineteenth-century Ireland' in Norma Dawson (ed.), *Reflections on law and history* (Dublin, 2006).

Hancock, W.N., 'Local government and taxation in Ireland' in Probyn, J.W. (ed.), *Local government and taxation* (London, 1875).

Hanly, Conor, 'The Maamtrasna murders: the trial of Myles Joyce' in David Nash and Anne-Marie Kilday (eds), *Fair and unfair trials in the age of the early mass media* (London, 2019).

Hardiman, Adrian, *Joyce in court* (London, 2017).

Hardiman, James, *Tracts relating to Ireland* (Dublin, 1843).

Harrington, Timothy, *The Maamtrasna massacre: impeachment of the trials* (Dublin, 1884).

Harrington, Timothy, *Diary of coercion, part III, being a list of the cases tried under the Criminal Law and Procedure Act from September 1888 to 1st January 1890* (Dublin, 1890).

Harris, G. and Spark, D., *Practical newspaper reporting* (Oxford, 2001).

Head, Francis, *A fortnight in Ireland* (London, 1852).

Healy, T.M., *The old Munster circuit* (Dublin, 1939).

Heaney, Henry, *A Scottish Whig in Ireland 1835–1838: the Irish journals of Robert Graham of Redgorton* (Dublin, 1999).

Higginbottom, F., *The vivid life: a journalist's career* (London, 1934).

Hogan, Daire, *The legal profession in Ireland, 1789–1922* (Dublin, 1986).

Howell, T.B., *A complete collection of state trials, 1700–1708*, vol. 14 (London, 1812).

Howlin, Niamh, 'Report on the trial of Myles Joyce, November 1882' (Dublin, 2017), http://www.justice.ie/en/JELR/Report_by_Dr_Niamh_Howlin_Maamtrasna_Murders.pdf/Files/Report_by_Dr_Niamh_Howlin_Maamtrasna_Murders.pdf.

Humphreys, H., *The justice of the peace for Ireland* (Dublin, 1867).

Hurley, J.W., *Shillelagh: the Irish fighting stick* (Pipersville, PA, 2007).

Hussey, S.M., *Reminiscences of an Irish land agent* (London, 1904).

Irish Society, *Eleventh report: reports of the Irish Society* (Dublin, 1829).

Jackson, Claire, 'Irish political opposition to the passage of criminal evidence reform at Westminster, 1883–98' in John McEldowney and Paul O'Higgins (eds), *The common law tradition* (Dublin, 1990).

Jones, David Lloyd, 'The Welsh Language Act 1967: the first 50 years' (Cardiff, 2017), http://www.comisiynyddygymraeg.cymru/English/Publications%20List/20170614%20DG%20S%20Sir%20David%20Lloyd%20Jones%27s%20Address.pdf.

Joyce, James, 'Ireland at the bar' in Ellsworth Mason and Richard Ellmann (eds), *The critical writings of James Joyce* (Ithaca, 1989).

Kelleher, Margaret, *The Maamtrasna murders: language, life and death in nineteenth-century Ireland* (Dublin, 2018).

Kennedy, Sheila, 'Coquebert de Montbret in search of the hidden Ireland', *Journal of the Royal Society of Antiquaries of Ireland*, 82 (1952), 62–7.

Larkin, Felix M., 'Double helix: two elites in politics and journalism in Ireland, 1870–1918' in Ciaran O'Neill (ed.), *Irish elites in the nineteenth century* (Dublin, 2013).

Lee, J., *The modernisation of Irish society, 1848–1918* (Dublin, 1973).

Lee, J.J., *Ireland, 1912–1985: politics and society* (Cambridge, 1989).

Levinge, E.R., *The justice of the peace in Ireland* (Dublin, 1862).

Lewis, Samuel, *A topographical directory of Ireland*, vol. 1 (London, 1837).

Lewis, Samuel, *A topographical directory of Ireland*, vol. 1 (2nd ed., London, 1840).

Lewis, Samuel, *A topographical directory of Ireland*, vol. 2 (London, 1837).

Lewis, Samuel, *A topographical directory of Ireland*, vol. 2 (2nd ed., London, 1840).

'Local government notes', *New Irish Jurist and Local Government Review*, 2:40 (15 Aug. 1902).

Lyons, F.S.L., *Ireland since the Famine* (London, 1985).

Lyons, John Charles, *The grand juries of the County Westmeath* (Ledestown, 1853).

Macdonald, John, *Diary of the Parnell commission revised from the Daily News* (London, 1890).

Mac Giolla Chríost, Diarmait, *The Irish language in Ireland from Goidel to globalisation* (Abingdon, 2005).

McArdle, J., *Irish Legal anecdotes* (Dublin, 1995).

McAree, Noel, *Murderous justice* (Limerick, 1990).

McCabe, Desmond, 'Magistrates, peasants, and the petty sessions courts: Mayo 1823–50', *Cathair na Mart*, 5:1 (1985), pp 45–53.

D. McCabe, 'Law, conflict and social order: County Mayo, 1820–45' (PhD, UCD, 1991) cited in Richard McMahon, 'The court of petty sessions and society in pre-Famine Galway' in Raymond Gillespie (ed.), *The remaking of modern Ireland, 1750–1950* (Dublin, 2004).

McCavitt, John, 'Good planets in their several spheares', *Irish Jurist*, 24: 2 (1989), pp 248–78.

McDowell, 'The Irish courts of law, 1801–1914', *Irish Historical Studies*, 10:40 (1957), pp 363–91.

McEvoy, John, *Statistical survey of Tyrone* (Dublin, 1802).

McMahon, Richard, 'The court of petty sessions and society in pre-Famine Galway' in Raymond Gillespie (ed.), *The remaking of modern Ireland, 1750–1950* (Dublin, 2004).

McParlan, James, *Statistical survey of the county of Donegal* (Dublin, 1802).

McParlan, James, *Statistical survey of the county of Leitrim* (Dublin, 1802).

McParlan, James, *Statistical survey of the county of Mayo* (Dublin, 1802).

McParlan, James, *Statistical survey of the county of Sligo* (Dublin, 1802).

Mellinkoff, D., *The language of the law* (Eugene, 2004).

Mitchel, John, *The last conquest of Ireland (perhaps)* (London, 1876).

Murphy, G., 'The Gaelic background' in M. Tierney (ed.), *Daniel O'Connell: nine centenary essays* (Dublin, 1948).

Ní Chiosáin, Máire, 'The Irish language in Co. Clare in the early twentieth century: a census-based perspective' in Matthew Lynch and Patrick Nugent (eds), *Clare history and society* (Dublin, 2008).

Ní Chonaill, Síghle, *Maum*, peformed at An Taidhbhearc Theatre, Galway (2015).

Nic Craith, Mairéad, 'Legacy and loss: the Great Silence and its aftermath' in John Crowley, William J. Smyth and Mike Murphy (eds), *Atlas of the Great Irish Famine* (Cork, 2012).

Ní Dhonnchadha, Máire, 'Irish language interpreting in the courts since the 1850s' (MA, DCU, 2000).

Ní Mhunghaile, Lesa, 'The legal system in Ireland and the Irish language, 1700–*c.*1843' in Michael Brown and Seán Patrick Donlan (eds), *The laws and other legalities in Ireland, 1689–1850* (Burlington, 2011).

Nun, R. and Walsh, J.E., *The powers and duties of the justices of the peace in Ireland, and of constables as connected therewith; with an appendix of statutes and forms* (Dublin, 1841).

O'Barr, W.M., *Linguistic evidence: language, power and strategy in the courtroom* (San Diego, 1982).

O'Brien, G., 'The strange death of the Irish language, 1780–1800', in Gerard O'Brien (ed.), *Parliament, politics and people: essays in eighteenth-century Irish history* (Dublin, 1989).

O'Brien, Georgina (ed.), *The reminiscences of Lord O'Brien (of Kilfenora), lord chief justice of Ireland* (London, 1916).

O'Brien, Mark, 'Evolution of a discipline' in Kevin Rafter (ed.), *Irish journalism before independence* (Manchester, 2011).

O'Brien, R.B., *Dublin Castle and the Irish people* (London, 1909).

O'Carroll, Thomas, 'The O'Carroll diaries' (unpublished).

Ó Casaide, Séamus, 'The Irish language in Belfast and County Down, 1601–1850', *Down and Connor Historical Society's Journal*, 2 (1930).

Ó Ciosáin, Niall, 'Gaelic culture and language shift' in Laurence M. Geary and Margaret Kelleher (eds), *Nineteenth-century Ireland: a guide to recent research* (Dublin, 2005).

Ó Cuirreáin, Seán, *Éagóir* (Dublin, 2016).

Ó Cuív, B., *Irish dialects and Irish-speaking districts* (Dublin, 1980).

Ó Cuív, B., 'Irish language and literature, 1845–1921' in W.E. Vaughan (ed.), *A new history of Ireland, 1801–1870*, vol. 6 (Oxford, 1989).

Ó Faoláin, Seán, *King of the Beggars* (Dublin, 1980).

O'Flanagan, Roderick, *The Irish bar: comprising anecdotes, bon-mots, and biographical sketches of the bench and bar of Ireland* (London, 1879).

Ó Gráda, Cormac, *Black '47 and beyond* (Princeton, 1999).

O'M, J., 'Irish interpreters', *New Irish Jurist and Local Government Review*, 2:7 (27 Dec. 1901).

'On the utility of the Irish language and the ministry of the established church', *Christian Examiner and Church of Ireland Magazine*, 2:7 (1826).

Ong, Walter, *Orality and literacy: the technologizing of the world* (Abingdon, 2003).

O'Reilly, E., *Sanas Gaoidhilge Sagsbeurla: an English-Irish dictionary* (Dublin, 1817).

O'Toole O'Connell, Kathleen, *Green are the hills far away* (Melkbosstrand, 2010).

Ó Tuathaigh, Gearóid, *Ireland before the Famine, 1798–1848* (Dublin, 1982).

Palmer, Patricia, *Language and conquest in early modern Ireland* (Cambridge, 2009).

Palmer, Stanley H., *Police and protest in England and Ireland, 1750–1850* (Cambridge, 1988).

'Parishioners of Timoleague, County Cork, appellants, the Revd Charles Ferguson, prebendary and vicar, respondents', *Irish Law Recorder*, 22 Dec. 1827.

Pender, Séanus, *A census of Ireland Circa* 1659 (Dublin, 1939).

Raithby, John, *The statutes of the United Kingdom of Great Britain and Ireland*, vol. 8 (London, 1822).

Ravenstein, E.G., 'On the Celtic languages in the British Isles: a statistical survey', *Journal of the Statistical Society of London*, 42:3 (1879), pp 579–636.

Rawson, Thomas Joseph, *Statistical survey of the county of Kildare* (Dublin, 1807).

Report of the trials of the Caravats and Shanavests at a special commission for the several counties of Tipperary, Waterford and Kilkenny, taken in short-hand by Randall Kernan esq. (Dublin, 1811).

Ridgeway, W., *A report of the proceedings under a special commission of oyer and terminer, and gaol delivery, for the counties of Sligo, Mayo, Leitrim, Longford and Cavan in the month of December 1806* (Dublin, 1807).

Routledge evidence lawcards (Abingdon, 2012).

Sampson, G.V., *Statistical survey of the county of Londonderry with observations on the means of improvement; drawn up for the consideration and by order of the Dublin Society* (Dublin, 1802).

Sheahan, Thomas, *Excursions from Bandon, in the south of Ireland, by a plain Englishman* (London, 1825).

Stokes, Whitley, *Observations on the necessity of publishing the Scriptures in the Irish language* (Dublin, 1806).

Sullivan, A.M., *Old Ireland: reminiscences of an Irish KC* (London, 1928).

Sullivan, Joseph Matthew, 'Irish police gleanings', *J. Am. Inst. Crim. L. & Criminology*, 4:876 (May 1913 to March 1914).

Thackeray, W.M., *The Irish sketch book: and notes on a journey from Cornhill to grand Cairo* (London, 1845).

TheyWorkForYou.com, 'Outcome of the proposed Irish-language legislation consultation process', ministerial statement in the Northern Assembly, 16 Oct. 2007, https://www.theyworkforyou.com/ni/?id=2007-10-16.1.1&s=%22irish+language+act%22+2006-01-01..2017-01-19+section%3Ani#g1.59, accessed 8 Apr. 2019.

Thompson, Robert, *Statistical survey of the county of Meath* (Dublin, 1802).

Tighe, William, *Statistical observations relative to the county of Kilkenny* (Dublin, 1802).

Todd, Alpheus, *On parliamentary government in England*, vol. 2 (London, 1869).

Townsend, Horatio, *Statistical survey of the county of Cork* (Dublin, 1810).

Trench, W.S., *Realities of Irish life* (London, 1869).

Trotter, J.B., *Walks throughout Ireland in the years 1812, 1814 and 1817* (London, 1819).

Uí Chollatáin, Regina, 'Newspapers, journals and the Irish revival' in Kevin Rafter (ed.), *Irish journalism before independence* (Manchester, 2011).

Vaughan, W.E., *Murder trials in Ireland, 1836–1914* (Oxford, 2009).

Wakefield, Edward, *An account of Ireland, statistical and political*, vol. 1 (London, 1812).

Wakefield, Edward, *An account of Ireland, statistical and political*, vol. 2 (London, 1812).

Waldron, Jarlath, *Maamtrasna: the murders and the mystery* (Dublin, 2004).

Wenman Seward, William, *Topographia Hibernica* (Dublin, 1797).

Williams, Nicholas, 'The Irish language in County Offaly' in William Nolan and Timothy P. O'Neill, *Offaly: history and society* (Dublin, 1998), pp 543–68.

Williams, Thomas Walter, *An accurate abstract of the public general statutes passed in X Geo IV Anno 1829* (London, 1829).

Wolf, Michaela, *The Habsburg monarchy's many-languaged soul* (Amsterdam, 2015).

Wolf, Nicholas, *An Irish-speaking island* (Madison, 2014).

Wolf, Nicholas, 'When Irish was still the greatest little language in the world', *Irish Times,* 29 Jan. 2015.

Table of legislation

Table of cases

Index

Compiled by Julitta Clancy

Note: '(t)' following a page reference denotes material occurring in tables, and italicized page references refer to images

Irish Legal History Society

Established in 1988 to encourage the study and advance the knowledge of the history of Irish law, especially by the publication of original documents and of works relating to the history of Irish law, including its institutions, doctrines and personalities, and reprinting or editing of works of sufficient rarity or importance.